Register Your Book

at ibmpressbooks.com/ibmregister

Upon registration, we will send you electronic sample chapters from two of our popular IBM Press books. In addition, you will be automatically entered into a monthly drawing for a free IBM Press book.

Registration also entitles you to:

- Notices and reminders about author appearances, conferences, and online chats with special guests
- Access to supplemental material that may be available
- Advance notice of forthcoming editions
- Related book recommendations
- Information about special contests and promotions throughout the year
- Chapter excerpts and supplements of forthcoming books

Contact us

If you are interested in writing a book or reviewing manuscripts prior to publication, please write to us at:

Editorial Director, IBM Press
c/o Pearson Education
800 East 96th Street
Indianapolis, IN 46240

e-mail: IBMPress@pearsoned.com

Visit us on the Web: ibmpressbooks.com

Persistence in the Enterprise

A Guide to Persistence Technologies

IBM Press

The developerWorks® Series

The IBM Press developerWorks Series represents a unique undertaking in which print books and the Web are mutually supportive. The publications in this series are complemented by their association with resources available at the developerWorks Web site on ibm.com. These resources include articles, tutorials, forums, software, and much more.

Through the use of icons, readers will be able to immediately identify a resource on developerWorks which relates to that point of the text. A summary of links appears at the end of each chapter. Additionally, you will be able to access an electronic guide of the developerWorks links and resources through ibm.com/developerworks/dwbooks that reference developerWorks Series publications, deepening the reader's experiences.

A developerWorks book offers readers the ability to quickly extend their information base beyond the book by using the deep resources of developerWorks and at the same time enables developerWorks readers to deepen their technical knowledge and skills.

For a full listing of developerWorks Series publications, please visit: **ibmpressbooks.com/dwseries**.

IBM Press

Information Management

An Introduction to IMS™
Meltz, Long, Harrington, Hain, and Nicholls ■ ISBN 0131856715

DB2® 9 for Linux®, UNIX®, and Windows®
Baklarz and Zikopoulos ■ ISBN 013185514X

Understanding DB2® 9 Security
Bond, See, Wong, and Chan ■ ISBN 0131345907

Understanding DB2®, Second Edition
Chong, Wang, Dang, and Snow ■ ISBN 0131580183

Computing

Implementing ITIL Configuration Management
Klosterboer ■ ISBN 0132425939

Inescapable Data
Stakutis and Webster ■ ISBN 0131852159

Mainframe Basics for Security Professionals
Pomerantz, Vander Weele, Nelson, and Hahn ■ ISBN 0131738569

On Demand Computing
Fellenstein ■ ISBN 0131440241

A Practical Guide to Trusted Computing
Challener, Yoder, Catherman, Safford, and Van Doorn ■ ISBN 0132398427

RFID Sourcebook
Lahiri ■ ISBN 0131851373

Service-Oriented Architecture (SOA) Compass
Bieberstein, Bose, Fiammante, Jones, and Shah ■ ISBN 0131870025

Business Strategy & Management

Can Two Rights Make a Wrong? Insights from IBM's Tangible Culture Approach
Moulton Reger ■ ISBN 0131732943

Developing Quality Technical Information, Second Edition
Hargis, Carey, Hernandez, Hughes, Longo, Rouiller, and Wilde
ISBN 0131477498

Do It Wrong Quickly: How the Web Changes the Old Marketing Rules
Moran ■ ISBN 0132255960

Irresistible! Markets, Models, and Meta-Value in Consumer Electronics
Bailey and Wenzek ■ ISBN 0131987585

Mining the Talk: Unlocking the Business Value in Unstructured Information
Spangler and Kreulen ■ ISBN 0132339536

Reaching the Goal: How Managers Improve a Services Business Using Goldratt's Theory of Constraints
Ricketts ■ ISBN 0132333120

Search Engine Marketing, Inc.
Moran and Hunt ■ ISBN 0131852922

The New Language of Business: SOA & Web 2.0
Carter ■ ISBN 013195654X

Rational and Software Development

IBM Rational® ClearCase®, Ant, and CruiseControl
Lee ■ ISBN 0321356993

IBM® Rational Unified Process® Reference and Certification Guide
Shuja and Krebs ■ ISBN 0131562924

Implementing IBM® Rational® ClearQuest®
Buckley, Pulsipher, and Scott ■ ISBN 0321334868

Implementing the IBM® Rational Unified Process® and Solutions
Barnes ■ ISBN 0321369459

Outside-in Software Development
Kessler and Sweitzer ■ ISBN 0131575511

Project Management with the IBM® Rational Unified Process®
Gibbs ■ ISBN 0321336399

Requirements Management Using IBM® Rational® RequisitePro®
Zielczynski ■ ISBN 0321383001

Software Configuration Management Strategies and IBM® Rational® ClearCase®, Second Edition
Bellagio and Milligan ■ ISBN 0321200195

Visual Modeling with IBM® Rational® Software Architect and UML™
Quatrani and Palistrant ■ ISBN 0321238087

WebSphere

Enterprise Java™ Programming with IBM® WebSphere®, Second Edition
Brown, Craig, Hester, Pitt, Stinehour, Weitzel, Amsden, Jakab, and Berg
ISBN 032118579X

Enterprise Messaging Using JMS and IBM® WebSphere®
Yusuf ■ ISBN 0131468634

IBM® WebSphere®
Barcia, Hines, Alcott, and Botzum ■ ISBN 0131468626

IBM® WebSphere® System Administration
Williamson, Chan, Cundiff, Lauzon, and Mitchell ■ ISBN 0131446045

WebSphere® Business Integration Primer
Iyengar, Jessani, and Chilanti ■ ISBN 013224831X

Lotus

IBM® WebSphere® and Lotus®
Lamb, Laskey, and Indurkhya ■ ISBN 0131443305

Lotus® Notes® Developer's Toolbox
Elliott ■ ISBN 0132214482

Open Source

Apache Derby—Off to the Races
Zikopoulos, Baklarz, and Scott ■ ISBN 0131855255

Building Applications with the Linux® Standard Base
Linux Standard Base Team ■ ISBN 0131456954

Performance Tuning for Linux® Servers
Johnson, Huizenga, and Pulavarty ■ ISBN 013144753X

Persistence in the Enterprise

A Guide to Persistence Technologies

developerWorks® Series

Roland Barcia, Geoffrey Hambrick, Kyle Brown, Robert Peterson, Kulvir Singh Bhogal

IBM Press
Pearson plc
Upper Saddle River, NJ • Boston • Indianapolis • San Francisco
New York • Toronto • Montreal • London • Munich • Paris • Madrid
Capetown • Sydney • Tokyo • Singapore • Mexico City
ibmpressbooks.com

IBM Press Program Managers: Tara Woodman, Ellice Uffer

Cover design: IBM Corporation
Associate Publisher: Greg Wiegand
Marketing Manager: Kourtnaye Sturgeon
Publicist: Heather Fox
Acquisitions Editor: Katherine Bull
Development Editor: Kevin Howard
Managing Editor: Gina Kanouse
Designer: Alan Clements
Senior Project Editor: Lori Lyons
Copy Editor: Cheri Clark
Indexer: Erika Millen
Senior Compositor: Gloria Schurick
Proofreader: Lori Lyons
Manufacturing Buyer: Dan Uhrig
Published by Pearson plc
Publishing as IBM Press

IBM Press offers excellent discounts on this book when ordered in quantity for bulk purchases or special sales, which may include electronic versions and/or custom covers and content particular to your business, training goals, marketing focus, and branding interests. For more information, please contact:

U. S. Corporate and Government Sales
1-800-382-3419
corpsales@pearsontechgroup.com

For sales outside the U. S., please contact:

International Sales
international@pearsoned.com.

Library of Congress Cataloging-in-Publication Data

Persistence in the enterprise : a guide to persistence technologies / Roland Barcia ... [et al.].
p. cm.
ISBN 0-13-158756-0 (pbk. : alk. paper) 1. Object-oriented databases. 2. Java (Computer program language) I. Barcia, Roland.
QA76.9.D3P494 2008
005.75'7—dc22

2008001531

Pearson Education, Inc
Rights and Contracts Department
501 Boylston Street, Suite 900
Boston, MA 02116
Fax (617) 671 3447

ISBN-13: 978-0-13-158756-4
ISBN-10: 0-13-158756-0

Text printed in the United States on recycled paper at Courier Westford in Westford, Massachusetts.
First printing May 2008

Contents

Acknowledgments

The Author Team:

Behind any technical book are the reviewers who greatly increase its quality. This book is no exception. We would like to thank Eberhard Wolff, Jens Coldewey, Scott Ambler, Keys Botzum, and Brandon Smith, who reviewed one or more chapters. In addition, we would like to thank several others who helped provide details or answers to specific questions about the technologies that we evaluated. We would like to give a huge thank-you to these people: Kevin Sutter, Tom Alcott, Steve Brodsky, Timo Salo, Jim Knutson, Randy Schnier, Daniel Lee, Jack Woodson, Gang Chen, Billy Newport, Steve Ims, the Hibernate Development Team, and again, Keys Botzum, Brandon Smith, Scott Ambler, and Eberhard Woolf. Finally, we would like to give a special thanks to the IBM Press and Pearson Staff who had great patience with our busy schedules and often late submissions. Specifically, we would like to thank Kevin Howard, Katherine Bull, Lori Lyons, Cheri Clark, and Gloria Schurick for all the work they did in finally bringing this book to press.

Roland Barcia:

All Praise, Glory, and Honor goes to God the Father and my Lord Jesus Christ! I would like to thank my wife and best friend, Blanca, whom I love with all my heart and soul. Writing books takes too much time away from my family, and she often bears the burden of our day-to-day life because of it. Thank you to Savannah, Alyssa, Joseph, and Amadeus for being wonderful children. Thank you to my father and my mother, Rolando and Maria Barcia, for raising me and loving me. I would like to thank my mother-in-law and friend Nery Leon, especially for watching the kids many times during this book project. I would like to thank my coauthors for writing this book with me. Thank you Kyle and Geoff for mentoring me and helping me achieve many career goals. Thanks Robert for being the best protégé a mentor could have, and thanks to Kulvir for taking me to "Baby Acapulcos" to eat fajitas and for being my friend. Thank you to several of my managers and leaders who have helped me along the way, especially Albert Scardino, Hicham Badawi, Peter Bahrs, Rachel Reinitz, and Tom Kristek. Finally, I would like to thank many other friends and family for praying for me, supporting me, and being my friends: Pastor Gary Stefanski, Michael Kenna, Alain Ratsimbazafy, Gang Chen, Avelino Barcia (Tio Cabezon), Nancy Quevedo (Tia), Javier and Maria Leon, Amelia Jorge (Mami), my brothers and sisters at Fairview Gospel Church, and my sister, Adriana Cantelmo, whom I forgot to mention in my last book, and who, to this day, does not let me forget about it.

Geoffrey Hambrick:

I'd like to thank my wife, Cindy; two sons, Austin and Alex; daughter, Lesli, and her husband, Tod; and my two grandkids, Ella and Clara. They have given up family time with me for years while I have been working on one writing project or another. Hopefully now that I have "the book project" out of my system, that will be that. I'd like to thank my Dad and Mom, James O. and Elizabeth A Hambrick, who did a great job raising six kids, and finding a way to make this "fourth of six" feel special and capable of doing anything that I put my mind to. I'd also like to acknowledge Robert Peterson, who had the idea to turn our internal whitepaper comparing persistence mechanisms into a book—I will forgive him someday (just kidding!). I'd like to thank Roland Barcia, who really carried the baton on this project until the end. Finally, I'd especially like to thank Tom Kristek, who has been a friend and mentor for more than 15 years—his straightforward approach and keen ability to focus on the essential details of a problem have truly made me who I am professionally today. WATFT!

Kyle Brown:

I would like to thank my wonderful wife Ann and my son Nathaniel for the support and love that they gave me through this project. I'd also like to thank the people who I learned about the ins and outs of object persistence from and with: Ken Auer and Sam Adams, Bruce Whitenack, Wayne Beaton, Justin Hill, Timo Salo, Art Jolin, Mark Weitzel, Rachel Reinitz, Martin Fowler, and especially Scott Rich, who besides being a fantastic collaborator in the early days of EJB was a great help and source of stories about the early days of VisualAge® Persistence for this book. Thanks also to the members of the IBM Software Group Architecture Board for carefully reviewing an earlier version of this document and hosting some lively discussions on the findings. Finally, I'd like to thank our wonderful reviewers, especially Scott Ambler and Eberhard Wolff, and anyone else we've forgotten who we've asked for information, help, or assistance during the writing of this book.

Robert Peterson:

I'd like to thank my father, who patiently taught me how to read and write in English during those trying childhood years in Mexico, and my mother for her loving support and reassurance. I'd like to thank my coauthors, particularly Roland, my mentor, to whom I credit any of my success—including this book. A special thanks to my manager, Mike Morin, who fully supported the countless hours I spent with my coauthors gradually and exhaustively molding this project into fruition.

Kulvir Singh Bhogal:

I'd like to thank God for all the grace He has shed upon me. Without Him, I am nothing. I thank my beloved wife, Meeti, whose smile always turns my frowns upside down. I'd also like to thank my parents, Kirpal and Manjit, who brought me into this world and patiently taught me how to walk on it. I also thank my sister Pummi and niece Sajal for their love and support. It goes without saying, but Roland, Robert, Kyle, and Geoff, thanks for being patient with my hectic consulting schedule and giving me the opportunity to work with you guys in putting this book together. Finally, I'd like to thank Andy Sweet for being a great, supportive manager and good friend.

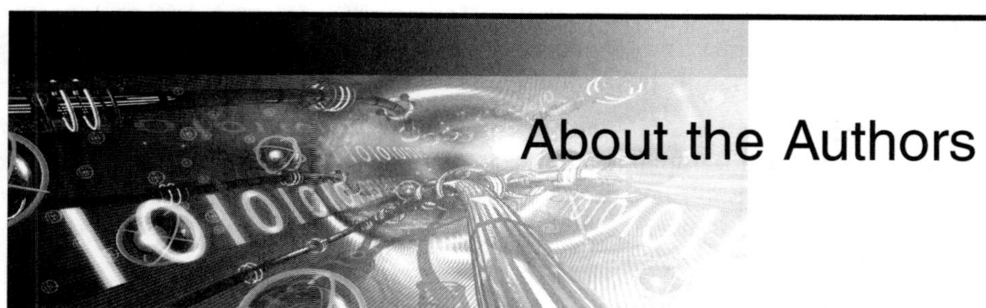

About the Authors

Roland Barcia is a Senior Technical Staff Member (STSM) and Lead Web 2.0 Architect within IBM Software Services for WebSphere®. He is the coauthor of the book *IBM WebSphere: Deployment and Advanced Configuration*. He has published more than 40 articles and papers on topics such as Java™ Persistence, Ajax, REST, JavaServer Faces, and Messaging Technologies. He frequently presents at conferences and customers on various technologies. He has spent the past 10 years implementing middleware systems on various platforms, including Sockets, CORBA, Java EE, SOA, and most recently the Web 2.0–based platform called Project Zero. He has a Masters Degree in Computer Science from the New Jersey Institute of Technology. Roland maintains a blog called "Web 2.0 and Middleware" (http://www.ibm.com/developerworks/blogs/page/barcia).

Geoffrey M. Hambrick is a Distinguished Engineer in the IBM Software Services for WebSphere Enablement Team, whose mission is to help develop and disseminate best practices for using IBM WebSphere runtimes, tools, and technologies. Geoff has long been a pioneer in the area of Distributed Object Technology, and was involved in the development of various standards, such as the Object Management Group CORBA Object Services and the Enterprise JavaBeans specifications. Geoff has engaged with numerous clients and is often asked to present at conferences throughout the world. Geoff is the author of the *IBM developerWorks®* column "The EJB Advocate," which describes various best practices patterns for using EJB technologies, especially entity bean components. Geoff's current focus is in pattern authoring tools that can be used to automate application of best practices. He and Chris Gerken invented the Design Pattern Toolkit, which extended the Eclipse Java Emitter Templates standard and has helped make Pattern Based Engineering a practical reality.

Kyle Brown is a Distinguished Engineer with IBM Software Services and Support. He is a coauthor or contributor to several books, including *Enterprise Java Programming with IBM WebSphere* and *Enterprise Integration Patterns*. He is a well-known authority on patterns, and has been a past chair of the PLoP (Pattern Languages of Programs) Conference. Kyle was one of the coauthors of one of the first papers on patterns of object-relational mapping, "Crossing Chasms," which was published in Pattern Languages of Program Design 2. In his day job, Kyle helps IBM customers adopt emerging technologies, and teaches best practices for using the IBM WebSphere family of products.

Robert R. Peterson is a Senior Managing Consultant for IBM Software Services for WebSphere. He travels the world implementing strategic proof of concept projects for future IBM software systems. He has published numerous technical books and papers, is a frequent conference speaker, and has filed several U.S. Patents for enterprise systems. You can visit his website at http://juzzam.org/PersonalSite/.

Kulvir Singh Bhogal works as a Senior Managing Consultant with IBM Software Services for WebSphere, devising and implementing WebSphere-centric, SOA solutions at customer sites across the nation. He has more than a hundred patents filed in a myriad of technology areas. Kulvir has written for numerous publications, including *JavaPro Magazine, IBM developerWorks, O'Reilly Media, Java Developer's Journal, DevX, InformIT*, and *WebSphere Advisor Magazine*. He is also a frequent presenter at numerous technology conferences.

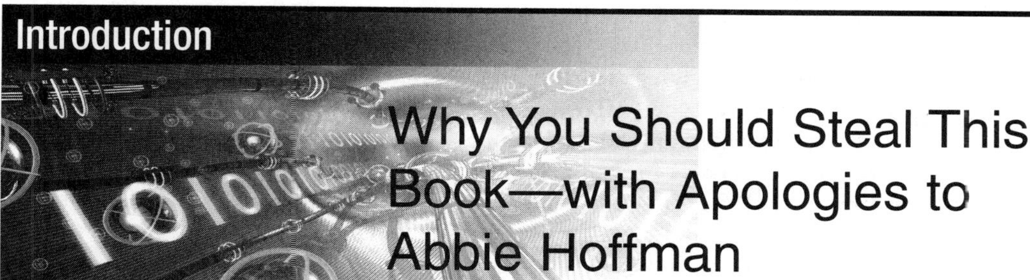

Introduction

Why You Should Steal This Book—with Apologies to Abbie Hoffman

Wise men often say that the first step to wisdom is learning that we know nothing—not even the right questions to ask. The implication is that we must listen to those with experience and contemplate the deeper meaning of their questions and answers. And in the end, a new experience may undo much of what everyone thought to be true.

This observation applies not only to sages on a mountaintop contemplating esoteric subjects such as philosophy, but also to those of us needing to know about a highly technical subject like providing persistent data within enterprise Java applications.

Imagine you were asked to choose the persistence mechanism for new Java applications within your company, and then review your architectural decision with various stakeholders in the company. Right at the start of the review, you would have to be prepared to answer some questions of general interest:

- Which persistence mechanisms were evaluated and why?
- Of those evaluated, which ones were chosen for use and why?

Then, depending on the exact role of the stakeholders invited to the review, you would have to be prepared to drill down and answer specific questions about the details of the proposed architecture that are relevant to each reviewer and the job each must do. For example:

- **Manager and Executive** roles evaluate the costs associated with making the transition to a new technology in terms of time, money, and other resources. They are interested in answers to questions about such topics as which vendors market a particular technology, the kinds of licensing agreements involved (and the restrictions those bring), the availability of skills, and references of successful applications using a given mechanism.

- **Analyst and Architect** roles need to assess whether a given mechanism can support the business and IT requirements of applications expected by the **End Users and Operators** for whom they serve as advocates. They are interested in questions about functionality, such as whether the mechanism supports relationships, a wide variety of attribute types, triggers, and constraints. They are also interested in whether the mechanism can scale up to response time, throughput, and other "nonfunctional" goals of the application.
- **Developer and Tester** roles are most impacted by the complexity of the framework and API in terms of the code they must write when implementing the services as objects mapped to a relational database layer. They are curious about how to handle specific coding tasks like creating connections, and reading/updating data in the context of the detailed database design for representative use cases.

The reality is that architecture of any type is more of an art than a science—which is what makes it such a challenging job to do well. It requires not just deep knowledge about methods and best practices that have worked in the past, but also a good sense of intuition about when to try something innovative.

A search of the Web for "Java and relational databases" returns a number of useful links to articles and books, but most are specific to a given mechanism—such as Java Database Connectivity (JDBC), Enterprise JavaBeans (EJB), Hibernate, or the new Java Persistence API (JPA). Some of these references go into detail on how to design the databases. Others are mainly guides on how to use the APIs to build a sample application. None of these references takes an end-to-end application architecture view that helps you understand the issues involved with choosing a persistence mechanism for relational data stores, and then helps you make a choice.

The reason that this end-to-end view is important is that, as noted above, good architects know the answers to the kinds of questions that will be asked by various stakeholder roles during a review. The better ones anticipate the questions and use those questions to drive their approach to design in the first place. But the best architects document these questions and answers in a cookbook form such that they guide every phase of an application development project, including analysis, design, construction, test, deployment, operations, and maintenance. Having the answers to these questions documented in a reusable form not only increases the quality of the applications, but also accelerates the development process—because the amount of time the team spends "reinventing the wheel" through trial and error is drastically reduced.

That end-to-end view is what makes this book different. We are all consultants with the IBM Software Services for WebSphere (ISSW) team. Our job is to help clients fully exploit our products, such as IBM WebSphere Application Server, WebSphere Portal Server, WebSphere Commerce Server, and WebSphere Process Server. We are often involved in proof of technology and head-to-head bake-offs that pair us with a client's architects who are making build-versus-buy decisions or vendor and technology selections; so we are experts at taking this broader application-centric view and finding answers to tough questions.

This book looks at persistence frameworks, mostly Java based, in the same way so that you can propose a solution that satisfies all the stakeholders—from your CTO to your fellow architects, to the developers, testers, and operations team. And if you play one of these specific roles and find yourself in a review, this book will help you ask the right kinds of questions and be able to interpret the answers.

Another thing that makes this book different is that we endeavor to capture our unique on-the-job mentoring-based consulting approach. In a nutshell, we like to both "give you a fish" and "teach you how to catch it" at the same time. The ideal result of an ISSW engagement is that you have an early success with our products yet become self-sufficient for the future.

Although a book will never fully substitute for a live consultant directly engaging with you on a project, we make an attempt by informally dividing this book into two parts:

- **Part I, "A Question of Persistence,"** teaches you about fishing so that you can "eat for a lifetime." Specifically, it helps you understand what the issues and trade-offs are in choosing a Java persistence mechanism for relational data stores. These issues are organized into chapters based on the questions asked by the various stakeholder roles described previously. Specifically, there are three chapters that cover the following topics: Chapter 1 provides a brief history of relevant persistence mechanisms; Chapter 2 covers business drivers and associated IT requirements; and Chapter 3 discusses implementation issues associated with object-relational mapping. We end this part of the book with Chapter 4, which extracts a questionnaire from the issues and trade-offs discussed in the first three chapters so that each mechanism can be evaluated with a consistent "yardstick" and best-practice-based approach.
- **Part II, "Comparing Apples to Apples,"** gives you some fish so that you can "eat for today." Each chapter gathers the data for five popular mechanisms using the approach and questionnaire found in Chapter 4. In this section we explore Java Database Connectivity, iBATIS, Hibernate, Java Persistence API, and pureQuery as representative examples of the various approaches to Java persistence outlined in Chapter 1. We wrap up this part and the book itself with a summary in Chapter 10 that compares the mechanisms side by side and enumerates some scenarios in which one or the other best applies.

It has been said that "the more things change, the more they stay the same." But they still change. The questionnaire developed in Chapter 4, "Evaluating Your Options," is crucial to the longevity of this book because it is relatively easy to apply the same yardstick to new persistence frameworks and APIs as they become available. So to further enhance the value of the book, we include a reference to a download site for the questionnaire and code examples associated with the evaluations that you can use as is or customize for use within your own company as you evaluate these or other mechanisms.

Because this is a developerWorks book, we make use of some special references called "Links to developerWorks" that appear with a special icon in the margin and in their own section at the end the chapter. These references can be linked to the IBM developerWorks site at www.ibm.com/developerWorks/. We have found this feature to be a very exciting one because you can follow along on the site while you are reading the book and get instant access to those and other related articles and online books. The net effect is to extend this book into the World Wide Web, further enhancing its longevity.

We've also included a "References" section at the end of the chapters, which lists additional resources cited throughout the chapter. These resources are cited by [Author] within the chapter text.

We hope you agree that this book is worth stealing; but please take it to the nearest check-out counter or click the Add to Cart button now. If this happens to be a friend's copy, please put it back on your friend's desk or bookshelf and buy your own—it is available for purchase at online retail web sites and traditional brick-and-mortar stores that sell technical books about Java or database technologies.

PART I

A Question of Persistence

Chapter 1

A Brief History of Object-Relational Mapping

Imagine that you are an IT architect at a leading retailer that has been in business for over 150 years. From the beginning your company innovated by augmenting their in-store sales with mail-order catalog sales to serve those customers living on the frontier. Later, when telephones became commonplace, they were one of the first retailers to institute call centers to decrease the turnaround time on orders and increase customer satisfaction. In the 1990s, when the World Wide Web became ubiquitous, they were one of the first retailers to develop applications to enable customers to enter orders and check on their status wherever they could connect to the Internet.

Unfortunately, your company's innovations in customer service have not been matched in their IT infrastructure. The majority of the mission-critical business logic is encapsulated in batch applications and legacy terminal-based applications written in COBOL. Newer web applications are C programs invoked from the web server through CGI connecting to these back-end functions through a gateway. These applications have proven to be extremely difficult to modify, slowing down the improvements in customer service.

Your newly hired CTO has decided that now is the right time to modernize the legacy systems—so that she can start a legacy of her own, we suppose. She chose Service Oriented Architecture (SOA) and Java-based applications on top of existing and new relational databases as the best way to provide for maximum flexibility in the new systems. SOA will facilitate declarative assembly of new applications from a set of reusable services. Java will provide write-once-run-anywhere service implementations that will provide more options for deployment. And you are charged with making the decision about which persistence mechanism to use within your Java-based services.

You may be wondering why we are telling you all of this background. One reason is that just as we work with our clients in the context of concrete scenarios to ensure that we focus on the issues necessary to be successful, we want to scope this book to a particular point of view (an architect), style of Java application (object-oriented in general, and SOA in particular), and underlying database (relational). Another reason we start with this background is related to this adage:

Those who do not study history are doomed to repeat it.

Even worse, in our opinion, is that those who do not study history may not be able to repeat the successes of the past. They usually only stumble onto an enterprise-quality solution through a long period of trial and error. The result is that most simply reinvent the wheel, at great expense.

Therefore, the purpose of this chapter is to bring you up to the present moment with a brief (and admittedly incomplete) history lesson of relational database persistence mechanisms associated with object-oriented languages.

The Object-Relational Impedance Mismatch

Since the invention of object-oriented programming, developers have faced a problem. Although they can build elegant and complex object models in their development environments, the data that corresponds to those object models is often locked away in relational databases. There are good reasons for this: Relational databases are the most common in the world; the relational model is mathematically based and sound; and relational database products, from industry leaders such as IBM, Oracle, and Microsoft®, as well as open-source products like MySQL, are mature and well-known.

But when a developer first sits down and considers how to connect this relational data to his objects, he begins to understand what has been termed the "object-relational impedance mismatch." In short, this refers to the problem of the world of tables, rows, and SQL not being the same as the world of objects, classes, and Java. Anytime a developer looks at bridging this gap, there will always be little things to overcome, such as

- How can inheritance be represented in a relational database?
- How do types map from a relational database to the different type system of Java?
- How can it be handled when an object model structure looks nothing like the relational model that its data is stored in?

A Pre-Java History Lesson

As the German Philosopher Friedrich Hegel once said, *"The only thing we learn from history is that we learn nothing from history."* Unfortunately, this is true in many aspects of life. To understand the best ways to deal with this impedance mismatch and what a modern application developer should do to take advantage of the right patterns and tools for handling the common issues, we need to take a brief look back at how this problem has been handled in different languages and toolkits over time. By studying the evolution of the solutions, it's possible to better understand and compare the current solutions.

There was a time not too long ago when the developer landscape was fractured among a number of competing object-oriented (OO) languages. Although the introduction of Java changed the language landscape, it didn't alter the basic patterns and approaches to handling object-relational (OR) persistence. In fact, in a moment of history repeating itself, it's possible to see the same lessons learned in Smalltalk and other languages learned again in Java.

Although this history lesson will be very brief and not altogether complete, it should at least give you a sense of how the problems in object-relational mapping (ORM) were originally discovered, when they were discovered, and what the proposed solutions have been.

Delphi

In the early days of the OO language wars, it was unclear which languages would survive and become the dominant players among OO developers. One of the early leaders, which did not gain the wide adoption of some other languages like C++ and Java, was Borland's Delphi. Delphi was based on Object Pascal, and first released in 1995. By 1996, Delphi featured a set of database programming tools that encouraged more of a *Transaction Script* approach than a true object-relational mapping. Programmers would query for and manipulate Row objects that represented the rows in a relational table. Delphi featured forms-based programming and nonvisual relational database management system (RDBMS) components that would plug into its visual form builder tooling.

Rogue Wave DBTools.h++

Because C++ had wide adoption, many libraries attempted to address the relational mismatch. Rogue Wave is still one of the most popular C++ library providers around. Their DBTools libraries attempted to address the object relational problem by overloading the stream inputs and outputs to accept SQL. SQL queries could then be projected onto objects and vice versa. Although programmers would write their own SQL, it allowed one to think about object representation of their domain. Today, many developers still feel comfortable writing SQL, and modern frameworks like iBATIS take advantage of this fact.

NeXT DbKit

In 1992 the developers at NeXT (founded by Steve Jobs) released their first stab at addressing the issue of connecting objects written in Objective-C, the primary programming language of the NeXT and NeXTStep, to relational databases. This effort resulted in the DbKit, which was an abstraction layer that allowed access to different relational databases without the need to write database-specific code. This approach presaged many later efforts such as JDBC and similar frameworks. In time (and after at least one complete rewrite), the NeXTStep developers released the Enterprise Object Framework (EOF), which eventually became a complete object-relational mapping framework.

TopLink for Smalltalk

Our story really begins in 1995, however, with the release of the initial version of the TopLink object-relational mapping tool by The Object People, a small Canadian Smalltalk consulting company [Smith]. At the time, an advanced object-oriented development community of professors and students had formed at Carleton University, resulting in the creation of a number of small but important companies in the history of OO development. TopLink wasn't the first OR mapping tool for Smalltalk (for instance, the ParcPlace ObjectLens toolset, which was included as part of the ParcPlace VisualWorks development environment for Smalltalk, was released in 1993), but it differed from some of the earlier tools for Smalltalk in that it contained nearly all the features now expected in an ORM tool. For instance, TopLink 1.0 contained the following:

- The capability to map database fields to object attributes, and to perform type conversions between the two.
- The capability to represent 1-1, 1-N, and N-M relationships in the object model as relations between database tables.
- The capability to map a single row in the database table to multiple objects.
- An implementation of the Proxy pattern, by which a proxy object "stands in" for an instance of another class that has not yet been fetched from the database.
- Object caching to reduce the number of repetitive database queries.
- Support for multiple database vendors.

This toolset was the standard by which other Smalltalk relational database tools were judged, and it implemented many of the patterns that are now standard practice in Java object-relational mappers as well.

IBM ObjectExtender

But TopLink wasn't the only game in town, even in Smalltalk. IBM had begun supporting the Smalltalk language with the purchase of Object Technology International, another small Canadian company founded by students and professors from Carleton University. OTI developed Smalltalk technology—which became the basis of IBM's VisualAge® for Smalltalk product. Seeing the need to provide relational database connectivity to its Enterprise customers, IBM developed its own object-relational mapping tool for VisualAge for Smalltalk, which was internally used with several customers before it was released as part of VisualAge (called the ObjectExtender) in 1998. Even though IBM was a late entry into the Smalltalk persistence game, their experience is important to the story, as discussed later. The ObjectExtender contained many of the same types of features as TopLink:

- Full support of mapping Smalltalk fields to relational database columns
- Full support of 1-1 and 1-N relationships
- Transactions support
- "Lite" (proxy) collections

First-Generation Java Solutions

But for the purposes of this book, the release of TopLink for Smalltalk wasn't the most interesting thing that happened in 1995. In May 1995, Sun announced the Java programming language, and in January 1996 Sun released the first public version of the Java Development Kit (JDK). Java didn't catch on immediately for enterprise development because it was initially targeted as an Internet programming language, so many of the initial libraries were specifically designed to work within a browser. In fact, connecting to a relational database was one of the things that applets could not easily do, because the Java security sandbox limited outgoing connections to the same machine that the applet was downloaded from.

People began really becoming interested in database access through Java with the release of JDK 1.1, in February 1997, which included the JDBC 1.0 classes (which allowed access to relational databases, although they didn't provide object-relational mapping). This toolkit began to open developers' eyes to the possibility of Java in the enterprise, and set the stage for the development of more complex frameworks, and the eventual creation of Java 2 Enterprise Edition (J2EE).

JDBC 1.0 and 2.0

Using the Java Database Connectivity API (JDBC) is often a person's first exposure to manipulating a database with Java. JDBC 1.0 introduced most of the ideas that are still found even in the most recent JDBC 4.0 specification. Note that these are not new concepts first introduced in JDBC; JDBC is itself based off of Microsoft's ODBC API, which was in turn based on the X/Open SQL CLI (Call Level Interface). In short, there are three major concepts:

- The basic object for manipulating a database is a *Connection*. A Connection represents a link to a relational database process running somewhere (either on the same machine as the JVM or on a different machine).
- Connections are used to obtain *Statements*. Statements are the Java representations of SQL code. You can either provide a SQL string to a Statement immediately prior to execution (using the `Statement` class) or provide the SQL string at the creation of the Statement (using the `PreparedStatement` class). The `PreparedStatement` is unique in that the SQL string can be parameterized; that is, it can contain macros whose values can be replaced at statement execution time.
- Statements that represent SQL queries, when executed, return a *ResultSet*. A ResultSet is a Java object that represents the set of rows that are returned from the SQL query to be processed one row at a time. You can access the data from a ResultSet either through the name of a column or through its position in the row currently active.

In JDBC 1.0 you could only move forward through a ResultSet. JDBC 2.0 (released with JDK 1.2 in December 1998) expanded this to allow backward movement through a ResultSet, and also allowed changes to the values of the ResultSet (which result in implicit SQL `UPDATE` statements). Simultaneous with the release of JDBC 2.0 was the release of the first JDBC Standard Extension, which introduced concepts such as database pooling, accessing named pools through the Java Naming and Directory Interface API (JNDI), and support for two-phase commit transactions through the use of the Java Transaction API (JTA) or Enterprise Java Bean components (EJBs).

TopLink for Java

Given their experience with TopLink for Smalltalk, in 1996 the TopLink team began work on a version of TopLink for Java. The product officially came available in 1997. The TopLink ORM for Java contained all the same types of features as TopLink for Smalltalk, and over the years it would also come to support multiple application server vendors as well as working standalone. TopLink was acquired by WebGain in 1999 and became part of Oracle in 2002.

EJB 1.0

In late 1997 and 1998, engineers from Sun, IBM, and many other companies began working together and releasing early versions of what would become the first Enterprise Java Bean (EJB) specification. The EJB specification was an ambitious project to redefine the way in which distributed applications were built. The EJB specification attempted to build from the foundation laid by the CORBA specifications and the lessons learned from the Java RMI specification to result in a framework for building enterprise applications that would combine distribution, persistence, and two-phase commit cross-datasource transactions.

From a persistence point of view, the EJB 1.0 specification introduced the idea of an entity bean, which was an EJB component that exposed information contained in external datasources as first-class Java objects. There were two flavors of entity beans described in the first EJB specification: those with "bean-managed" persistence (BMP), and those with container-managed persistence (CMP). In a BMP, logic implementing persistence would be explicitly coded by the developer, using facilities like JDBC, within the methods of the entity EJB. A CMP made the logic associated with persistence implicit, with the promise that vendors would provide tools and frameworks to provide object-relational mapping.

VisualAge Persistence Builder

The initial EJB specification left a lot of implementation details open to interpretation for the vendors to fill in. Somewhat representative of the very early EJB persistence implementations was the VisualAge Persistence Builder (or VAP), released in 1998. This product was the first IBM toolkit for creating persistent Java objects similar to EJB components. It was developed by the same team that developed the ObjectExtender framework, and shared a number of the same design principles and goals.

VAP occupied an interesting niche that differentiated it from some other early EJB 1.0 implementations; it wasn't part of a full EJB container, but instead was a standalone EJB runtime environment designed to be upward-compatible with the architecture of IBM's EJB server environments. Like several other persistence solutions that followed, it was a server environment that could be plugged into a Servlet or EJB container to provide persistence.

The way in which VAP achieved this "amibidextrous" nature is by beginning with a set of tools built in the VisualAge for Java Enterprise Edition environment that were capable of generating objects (that were, in fact, Plain Old Java Objects or POJOs). These POJOs implemented the entity bean interfaces, together with other objects that implemented the EJB Home interfaces, and the other parts of its persistence implementation. VAP code would be packaged into a JAR file that would then run on top of the VAP runtime framework, which, as noted earlier, could run inside a Servlet or EJB 1.0 container, or could also run within a Java application.

VAP supported almost all the standard ORM features, such as these:

- Caching support
- Transaction isolation policies and concurrent and nested transaction support
- Full support for database relational integrity (RI), including statement ordering
- Full relationship support for 1:1, 1:N, and M:N relationships
- Full support of inheritance with single-table, parent-child, and separate-table inheritance
- Prefetching of rows in 1:N relationships (joins)

However, the very strength of VAP (its relationship support) hid a number of issues that developers soon discovered with the EJB 1.0 specification. For example, the specification did not include details of how relationships were to be described for CMP entity components. As a result, each vendor's approach to capturing this important information in a "deployment descriptor" was different. Another issue that people soon ran into with the EJB 1.0 specification was that EJBs were always considered remote objects. This made it possible, for instance, to access the individual attributes of an entity EJB (which represented a single database table row) one-at-a-time across the network, something that was neither efficient nor scalable. These drawbacks, among others, led to the EJB specification being significantly revised in EJB 2.0.

EJB 2.0

EJB 2.0 [EJB 2] was finally released in 2001 (after a long revision process that included two separate final drafts that differed significantly from one another). Although EJB 2.0 introduced a number of new features such as Message Driven Beans that do not concern this story, a major portion of the revised sections of the specification dealt with persistence. In short, EJB 2.0 attempted to improve the poor portability situation of EJB 1.0 by describing relationship support directly within the specification. EJB 2.0 accomplished its relationship support by substantially enlarging the role of the XML deployment descriptor that had been introduced as a class in the EJB 1.0 specification, and then changed into an XML file in the EJB 1.1 specification (1999).

At the heart of this was the simple idea that a substantial portion of the description of how the Container-Managed Persistence Entity bean is implemented can be described in an XML file. EJB 1.1 had introduced the idea that the persistent fields of an Entity bean can be described in the `EJB-JAR.xml` deployment descriptor using the `<cmp-field>` element. EJB 2.0 extended this idea by giving the responsibility for generating the actual concrete classes that implemented those persistent fields to the EJB container, which used the field-level information in the deployment descriptor (plus the information in the EJB Entity abstract class) to build the persistence layer. It was in representing links between Entity classes that the EJB 2.0 spec took a step forward. By introducing the `<ejb-relation>` element and `<ejb-relationship-role>` element, the EJB 2.0 spec allowed the definition of relationships with varying multiplicity (1:1, 1:N, or M:N) between entity classes.

The second major element added in the EJB 2.0 specification that was applicable to persistence was the introduction of the Local EJB interface. As noted previously, in EJB 1.0 and 1.1 all EJBs were remote—a feature that makes sense for large-grained Session beans, but not for fine-grained Entity beans. By introducing Local EJB interfaces, EJB 2.0 allowed the developer to declare his Entities to be local only—and thus accessible only within a transaction controlled by an external Session bean. This approach made explicit some of the best practices and patterns that had been developed for EJB 1.0 and 1.1—most notably how *Distributed Façade* in Fowler [Fowler] was applied to EJB components and known as Session Façade by Deepak Alur [Alur] and Kyle Brown [Brown] in their books on J2EE design patterns.

Open Source and the Next Generation

However, the EJB 2.0 specification stopped short of a number of features that many developers had been asking for. For one, it left the problem of mapping of Entity attributes to relational database tables to the vendors. Also, it left the issue of how to transfer data out of an Entity bean into application contexts beyond the EJB container to the realm of best practices and patterns (specifically the Value Object pattern—again see [Alur]). But finally, there was something about the EJB specification as a whole that began to rub many developers in the wrong way. A substantial and vocal minority of Java developers began to complain in conferences, on blogs, and on forums like TheServerSide that the EJB specification was too heavyweight to be of use to the average business developer. They expressed a desire for a simpler persistence solution, one that would be based entirely on POJOs and that would not require an EJB container at runtime to complicate the architecture. In looking for a solution to their perceived problems, many practitioners began to turn to second-generation Java solutions such as Hibernate and iBATIS.

Hibernate

The Hibernate story begins in November 2001 when Gavin King started a SourceForge project to build an open-source object-relational database mapping system for Java. Given the dissatisfaction with the EJB 2.0 specification at the time, and the paucity of other cheap object-relational mapping solutions, the Hibernate project began attracting a significant amount of interest. By mid-2002 the project was well-established enough to announce a 1.0 version with considerable fanfare on sites like TheServerSide. Almost a year later, in June 2003, Hibernate 2.0 was released, which was a fully featured, robust system that was on par with commercial ORM offerings and that also featured tooling available on several open-source frameworks such as NetBeans and Eclipse. In October 2003, Hibernate "hit the big time" when the lead Hibernate developers were hired by JBoss.

Several simple principles underlie the success of Hibernate and its influence on later ORM specifications and frameworks. Chief among them is the fact that Hibernate is extremely lightweight, and that the programming model is very simple—Hibernate is based on a POJO model, and you do not have to implement special interfaces or extend special classes to render your classes persistent.

Some of its design principles we have already seen in the development of the EJB 2.0 specification—for every persistent class in Hibernate, there are corresponding entries in an XML mapping document that (for instance) lists the names and types of the persistent attributes of that class. Likewise, to represent collections (a 1:N relationship), you would simply add an element in the mapping document that declares a set, list, or other collection. However, one unique part of the Hibernate mapping file is that it contains all the information necessary to determine the mapping to a relational database. Table and column names are defined along with class and attribute names. This "all in one" approach made it possible to implement persistent objects quickly and easily. Another key aspect is that Hibernate can run inside or outside of an EJB container. Because of this, Hibernate is less restrictive and more complete in mapping object-oriented concepts to relational databases.

Perhaps the most important contributor to Hibernate's success was its price—free. Because it was an open-source project, Hibernate was easy and cost-effective for developers to try first and then decide they liked both it and the idea of object-relational mapping. Although the EJB spec did much to make object-relational mapping acceptable to the Java development community, it was Hibernate that popularized it among developers.

iBATIS

The iBATIS framework took a different route than Hibernate. Rather than hiding SQL, iBATIS created a persistence framework much like Rogue Wave's DBTools, in which SQL statements were projected to and from POJOs. The iBATIS framework grew out of a JPetStore Demo in response to an early 2002 Microsoft published paper claiming that .Net was 10 times faster and 4 times more productive than J2EE. Realizing that this was simply not the case, the iBATIS project (which previously had been focused on cryptographic software solutions) quickly responded with the JPetStore 1.0 release. Based on the same Pet Store requirements, JPetStore demonstrated that Java not only could be more productive than .Net, but also could do so while achieving a better, more open architecture than was used in the Microsoft implementation.

JPetStore made use of an interesting persistence layer that quickly captured the attention of the open-source community. Shortly after JPetStore was released, questions and requests for the SQL Maps and Data Access Object (DAO) frameworks spawned the project that would become known as iBATIS Database Layer. The iBATIS Database Layer includes two frameworks that simply happen to be packaged together: SQL Maps and DAO.

Today the iBATIS project is still heavily focused on the persistence layer frameworks known as SQL Maps and Data Access Objects (DAO). JPetStore lives on as the official example of typical usage of these frameworks.

Assimilating the Object Database Counterculture

So far this survey has examined the route that was taken by the traditional ORM vendors and open-source groups as they developed their systems for mapping objects to relational database tables. However, another group of companies took an entirely different approach to persisting objects. These companies held the view that the mapping of objects to relational tables should be avoided completely; that the right way to store objects was directly within the database as objects. To achieve this goal, they needed to rethink the idea of a database, specifically to build an object database.

An early adopter of this object database approach was a company originally called Servio Logic Corporation, which later changed its name to GemStone Corporation. Their product, the eponymous GemStone Object Database, provided direct persistence of Smalltalk objects in an object database. Not only did they support persistent Smalltalk Objects (accessed as persistent Collections), they also introduced many ideas in server-side object programming that were adopted within Java-based services, such as Remote Method Invocation (RMI) and EJB.

ODMG

The object database counterculture began to move toward standardization in 1991 with the formation of the Object Data Management Group (ODMG, later the Object Database Management Group). This group released the ODMG 1.0 standard in 1993, and concluded its work in 2001 with the release of the ODMG 3.0 standard [ODMG].

Some key technical ideas were taken from object databases and the ODMG standards that became important in later standards. In particular, these important ideas were included:

1. Transparent persistence; that is, a developer shouldn't have to be aware that he is making an object persistent. In practice, this means that the developer shouldn't be responsible for writing mapping classes or writing SQL code.
2. Persistence by reachability; meaning that an object becomes persistent when it is related to another persistent object. So you would, for instance, make an Address persistent by adding it to an already-persistent Customer. This process begins with a collection of what are called Persistent Roots that are declared within the Database system itself.
3. Portability; that is, the standard should be portable across a number of different implementations—not only pure object database systems but object-relational mapping systems and hybrid object-relational systems as well.

After the release of the ODMG 3.0 standard, the ODMG was disbanded and its work was taken over by a working group within the OMG [Object Management Group]. However, one of the products of the ODMG continued its lifecycle when the ODMG 3.0 Java binding was submitted to the Java Community Process (JCP) as the basis for the Java Data Objects (JDO) specification [JDO].

JDO

JDO took much of its inspiration from the notions of object databases, and in particular, the ODMG specifications. The JDO 1.0 specification was completed and released through the JCP in April 2002 as JSR 12. Its primary API included the following concepts:

- Any class that implemented the PersistenceCapable interface could be made persistent.
- You can make instances of classes explicitly persistent by invoking a PersistenceManager, or implicitly by relating them to other persistent objects.
- You fetch objects from a PersistenceManager either by object id or through a query. You can also obtain all the persistent instances of a class by asking a PersistenceManager for the extent of the class.

The release of JDO 1.0 resulted in multiple implementations of the JDO interface, with companies like Versant and Xcalia releasing commercial projects that implemented JDO 1.0, and several open-source projects including Apache OJB and JPOX adopting it as well.

JPA

As discussed earlier, by the time EJB 2.0 started to make its way into products, yet another counter-current was building in the Java community that was looking for alternate ways of providing access to persistent data within Java applications. When the EJB 3.0 committee began meeting, it became clear that revisiting persistence would be a key feature of the new specification. The opinion of the committee was that something significant needed to be changed—and as a result, the committee made the following decisions:

- The EJB 3.0 persistence model would be a POJO-based model and would have to address the issue of "disconnected" or detached data in a distributed environment.
- The specification would support both annotations (Introduced in Java 5) and XML descriptors to define the mapping between objects and relational databases.
- The mapping would be complete—specifying not only the abstract persistence of a class, but also its mapping to relational table and mappings of attributes to columns.

So, the EJB committee combined the best ideas from several sources such as TopLink, Hibernate, and JDO to create a new persistence architecture, which was released as a separate part of EJB 3.0 specification and dubbed the Java Persistence Architecture (JPA) [EJB 3 Spec].

There are several vendors with open-source initiatives that have implemented the JPA specification, including JBoss (Hibernate JPA), Oracle (TopLink Essentials), and Apache (OpenJPA). OpenJPA is backed by IBM and BEA.

Service-Oriented Architecture and Beyond

Even though the JPA represents the closing of another chapter in the history of ORM by merging a number of threads, approaches to IT and exploiting Java technology have not stood still. Specifically, the introduction of Service Oriented Architecture (SOA) has changed the way we look at application architectures as well as the way we develop them. For example, more applications are using XML as a canonical form for messages representing requests and responses passed between components of the system exposed as services.

Information as a Service

Applying the SOA paradigm to persistence has resulted in a recent advancement that treats "information as a service." This thought shift aims to free information from the application silos in which it typically resides. With this approach, information is delivered as a service. Applications needing access to the data interact with the service; and the information is exposed via open standards leveraging Web services and XML. Applications can access their data via language neutral technologies such as XQuery and XPath. Because of the use of open, language neutral standards, more applications (even those not based on Java) can have access to the information they need.

IBM's DB2® has been extended to include native storage for XML. This makes DB2 Version 9 the industry's first database designed with both native XML data management and relational data capability. In the past, XML data had to be reformatted or placed into large objects—character or binary large objects (CLOBs or BLOBs). With this approach, data is stored as a single unit or continuous byte string. Such a storage approach unearthed performance challenges when querying for data within the XML document or when one had to update even just a small portion of the XML document. The entire XML document had to be read and parsed before a query could be processed. Another approach commonly used to deal with storing and querying XML documents is the practice of document shredding, in which an XML document is mapped to one or more relational columns. However, this approach does not leave the XML document intact.

The information as a service technology stores XML in a direct form, as a preparsed annotated tree. XML is stored in the database as using a hierarchical node-based model. In this model, each node is linked not only to its parent, but also to its children. This "pure XML" storage capability is an efficient method for accessing and storing entire XML documents, presenting major performance benefits to the consuming application. The capability to deliver information as a service that can be efficiently accessed makes the technology particularly enticing for SOA environments.

DB2 9 allows for the creation of hybrid tables that consist of both relational and XML data. The database supports a new XML data type. Such a hybrid table can be accessed via industry standard extensions to SQL named SQL/XML that allow for `SELECT` statements to retrieve XML documents in whole or in part. Additionally, DB2 supports the XQuery language, which allows for one to use path expressions to navigate through a stored XML document's hierarchical structure.

pureQuery and ProjectZero

In contrast to large companies that could afford to host their own web sites, many smaller companies prefer to outsource their web sites to external companies that provide the infrastructure, such as Yahoo hosting. These external companies relied on scripting languages, like PHP and Perl, with embedded SQL, that provide a quick and easy way to build web sites. These facilities reduced the amount of code one had to write to create a web site, but were not focused on developing reusable business components. Further, with the emergence of AJAX in the browser for rich dynamic content, and community web sites like MySpace and FaceBook, the need to quickly combine web data sources to create new applications came to the forefront. This focus on rapid development led to a new paradigm called "Situational Applications."

Enterprises are now looking to take advantage of this paradigm to create new business opportunities. As such, exposing data through scripting languages using embedded SQL has become popular with enterprise web developers. With the advent of Information as a Service and Web 2.0, companies are looking to exploit these techniques within enterprise Java applications.

To meet this need, pureQuery is an IBM solution for Java data access designed for performance and exploiting SQL. As with iBATIS, the goal is to embrace SQL rather than hide it. But unlike iBATIS, SQL can be bound statically in a mapping file as well as directly in the Java code. pureQuery also embraces the notion of tools to greatly increase developer productivity. pureQuery can be used with a set of Eclipse Java plug-ins that can provide SQL assist inside Java programs. Besides having its own API for direct programmatic access, pureQuery can be layered underneath another framework, such as Hibernate or OpenJPA.

One example of layering on top of pureQuery can be found within ProjectZero. ProjectZero is an IBM incubator project focused on agile development of Web 2.0 applications following the SOA. Web 2.0 applied to SOA allows web artifacts to extend the reach of SOA. This can be thought of as Web Extended SOA.

Summary

In this brief historical survey of some important ORM frameworks (see Figure 1.1 for a graphical timeline view), we've seen how a common set of features evolved through various language-specific frameworks, such as Borland's Delphi (Pascal), Rogue Wave's DBTools (C++), and The Object People's TopLink for Smalltalk. Then we saw how lessons learned from these pioneering efforts came to be part of the "first generation" Java standards, such as JDBC and EJBs. We saw how open-source initiatives like Hibernate emerged to quickly fill the gaps in these standards, and how the object database perspective led to an alternative standards body (ODMG) and approach to Java persistence (JDO).

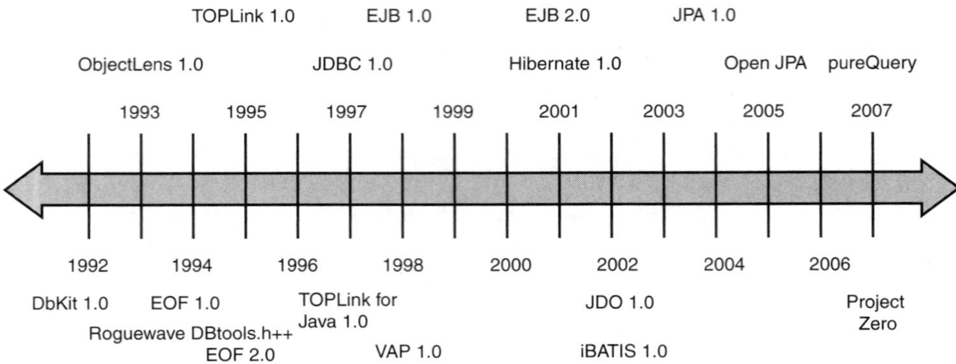

Figure 1.1 The timeline of object-relational mapping technologies we surveyed.

Fortunately, we saw that these paths converged within the JPA standard, proving that a complete, metadata-driven object-relational mapping framework can be defined in such a way that multiple vendors and community development projects like OpenJPA can provide compatible, fully featured implementations. At the same time, newer simplified approaches that don't require a full ORM framework, such as iBATIS and the evolution of information as a service and pureQuery, mean that new ideas will continue to keep the field active and growing.

For the purposes of this book and our architects' point of view, this history lesson helps us to answer this question:

Which mechanisms did you evaluate and why?

From this history, we chose the following five frameworks as representative of various approaches to persistence:

- **JDBC**—Though not really an ORM, JDBC serves as a baseline for comparison as an API used to directly access relational databases with SQL upon which many of the other frameworks are built.
- **iBATIS**—iBATIS serves as a data point for simple frameworks that separate the SQL from the Java code so that it can be easily tuned.
- **Hibernate**—As one of the first, and by far the most popular open-source OR mapping frameworks in existence, and as a major contributor to JPA, Hibernate serves as another good baseline for comparison.
- **OpenJPA**—This demonstrates the JPA standard in an open-source framework that can be tested side by side against the others.
- **pureQuery**—pureQuery provides an early look at one possible future of Java persistence in the context of SOA, Web 2.0, and information as a service.

One chapter is devoted to each of these five frameworks later in the book. First, though, Chapter 2, "High-Level Requirements and Persistence," discusses business and IT requirements around persistence that you should consider; Chapter 3, "Designing Persistent Object Services," covers detailed ORM design issues that will likely impact your choice of persistence mechanisms; and Chapter 4, "Evaluating Your Options," gives a systematic questionnaire-driven approach you can use to evaluate each framework.

References

[Alur] Alur, Deepak, et al. *Core J2EE Patterns. Best Practices and Design Strategies, 2nd Edition.* Sun MicroSystems Press 2003

[Brown] Brown, Kyle, et al. *Enterprise Java Programming with IBM WebSphere, 1st Edition.* Pearson Education 2001

[EJB 2] *JSR 19: Enterprise Java Beans 2.0.* www.jcp.org/en/jsr/detail?id=19

[Fowler] Fowler, Martin et al. *Patterns of Enterprise Architecture,* Addison-Wesley Professional, 2002

[JDO] *JSR 12: Java Data Objects (JDO) Specification.* www.jcp.org/en/jsr/detail?id=12

[ODMG] *Object Database Management Group Homepage.* www.odmg.org/

[Smith] Smith, Donald. *A Brief History of TopLink.* www.oracle.com/technology/tech/java/newsletter/articles/toplink/history_of_toplink.html

High-Level Requirements and Persistence

In Chapter 1, we gave you a brief overview of the history of the most popular persistence mechanisms. Understanding the history of popular persistence mechanisms should help guide your choice of which ones to evaluate. Ultimately, understanding your requirements will drive the selection of which mechanisms to use in your projects.

But we recognize that in today's more "agile" development world, it is not often possible to fully understand all your requirements at the beginning of a project. Thus, the purpose of this chapter is to help you quickly hone in on the most important requirements as they relate to persistence so that you are in a great position to answer this question: Which mechanism(s) do you use to provide access to persistent data in your SOA-style Java application programs and why?

Some "Required" Background

You may be tempted to skip this chapter altogether. Many software architects feel that they already have a solid understanding of how to capture IT requirements. However, it seems that some software architects feel that the needs of the business are not directly associated with the application code, and therefore those requirements will make little or no difference in which persistence framework is chosen.

Understanding Your Stakeholders

But nothing could be further from the truth. Imagine that you have been asked by your CTO to make a build-versus-buy (or even borrow-or-steal) decision about the approach to persistence for a major project. In our experience, you will need to be able to articulate compelling reasons for your choice to various stakeholders in the company who are interested. These stakeholders fall roughly into two groups (as shown in Figure 2.1):

1. **Business Executives**, who will want to understand how the technology decisions, including the choice of persistence mechanism, will impact their ability to support the ***needs of the business***.
2. **Technical Leaders**, who will be wondering how the choice of a framework will change their best practices for designing and implementing ***enterprise quality solutions***.

Figure 2.1 Key concerns of various stakeholders.

It is worth a few pages to get an overview of the requirements that are near and dear to those roles with which you (as an architect) may not be so familiar.

Different Strokes for Different Folks

It is likewise worth noting that there are various techniques to gathering requirements—ranging from traditional waterfall to more modern agile methods. We will not delve too deeply into comparing approaches because there are many good references in the literature on these topics. For example, Robertson & Robertson [Robertson] is a good reference on requirements gathering in the context of traditional methods, whereas [Cohn] or [Ambler] are good references on agile methods.

For the purposes of this book, we think of an approach as "waterfall" if it is phase (or activity) centric with respect to its releases. For example, Figure 2.2 shows an approach in which you gather all the requirements for a release before starting the subsequent design, code, test, and deploy phases in turn after the other completes.

Likewise for this book, we consider an approach "agile" if it is function (or service) centric with respect to the releases. For example, Figure 2.3 shows an approach in which each function (F*n*) is developed in a "depth first" fashion and held until a critical mass of function is ready for final testing and release (R*n*).

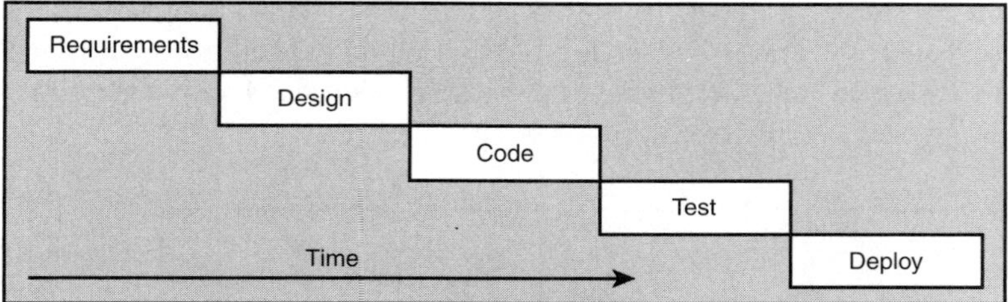

Figure 2.2 Phase-centric waterfall approach.

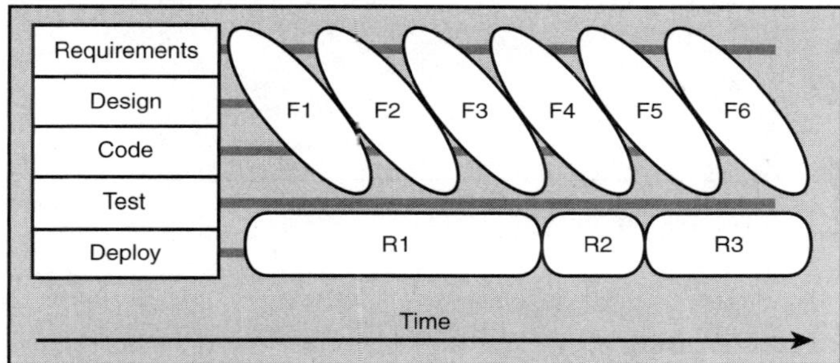

Figure 2.3 Function-centric agile approach.

The common aspect to both approaches is that you first must gather the requirements, then design the solution, then code the design, then test the code, then deploy the application. The real difference is in how much of one activity you complete before going on to the next.

The reasons we prefer agile approaches over waterfall are many. One reason is that we are all part of an organization called IBM Software Services for WebSphere (ISSW), where we help customers exploit IBM WebSphere products and technologies in their enterprise applications—and as quickly as possible. This leads us to prefer short-term projects that lend themselves well to agile approaches. Another reason is summed up in the following "truism":

> *Think before you act—just don't do all of your thinking before acting.*

Executives and the Needs of the Business

When we in ISSW are asked to make recommendations on major architectural components like persistence mechanisms, we like to engage in an evaluation workshop with technical leaders across the organization to gather findings and make specific recommendations.

We also like to "bookend" this workshop with executive participation: first at the beginning with a kickoff session to show commitment by setting the vision and expectations, and then at the end with a review session to have them receive the results. Figure 2.4 shows the timeline of a typical technology evaluation workshop.

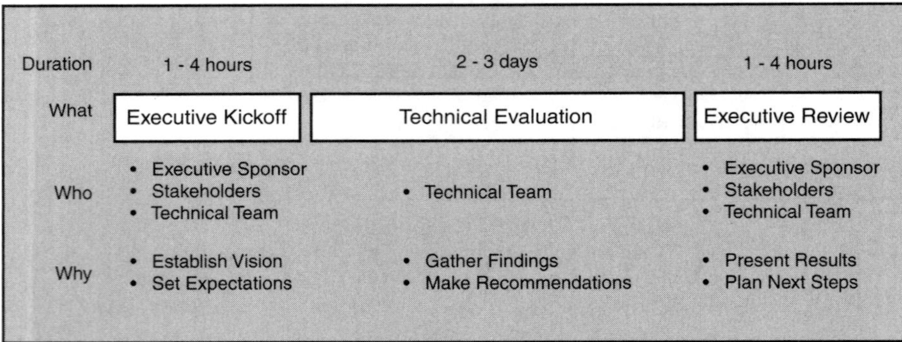

Figure 2.4 Timeline of a technology evaluation workshop.

And where a choice of persistence mechanisms is concerned, those frameworks that can be shown to have the minimum total cost of ownership (TCO) with a maximum Return on Investment (ROI) will usually win over those that do not.

In general, total cost of ownership looks at expenditures and is defined as an aggregate of all the costs incurred in the life cycle of an asset investment, from acquisition to disposal. For example, when considering the TCO of a car, you need to consider not only the purchase price (part of the total cost of acquisition, or TCA), but also the expenses you will incur throughout the life of the car—including expected costs such as gas, tires, oil, and regular maintenance, as well as unplanned expenses such as engine repair and insurance claim deductibles (see Figure 2.5).

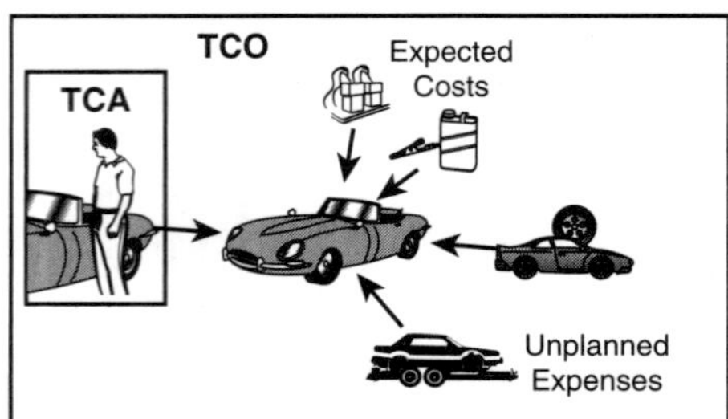

Figure 2.5 Factors to consider in the total cost of ownership of a car.

Unfortunately, many enterprise architects fail to grasp the need to consider TCO when choosing technologies such as persistence frameworks, and instead myopically consider only TCA. Of course, the cost of acquiring a given persistence mechanism should be considered as part of the TCO calculation, but by no means all of it.

And computing TCO for a technology choice such as a persistence mechanism is not always simple because some of the factors that impact TCO are hard to assign specific cost numbers. For example, while hardware and software dependencies are factors you should consider that are somewhat easy to compute, you should also consider intangibles about the framework like those shown in Figure 2.6, such as

- Standards supported
- Number of open-source and community-driven activities
- Number of vendors, types of licenses, and options for support
- Intellectual capital considerations
- Availability of skilled practitioners
- Literature and education
- Development and admin tools

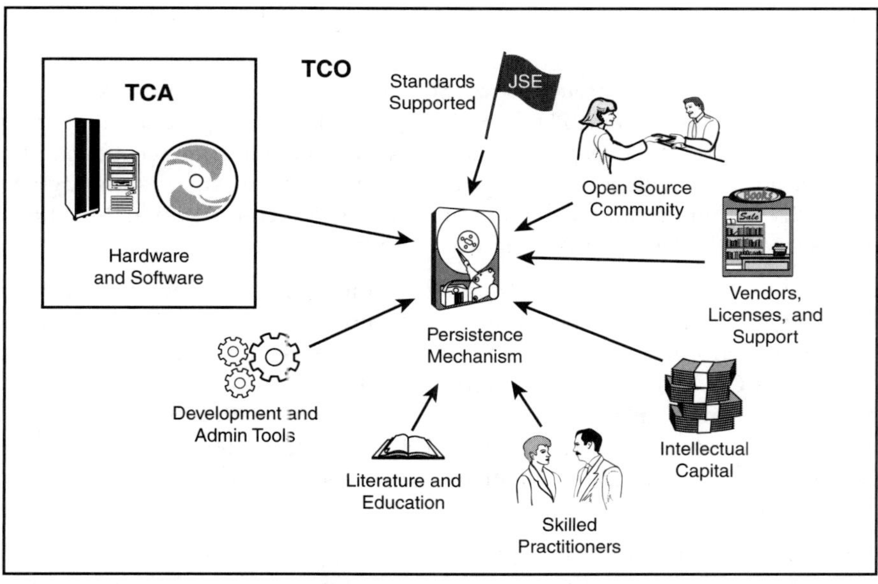

Figure 2.6 Factors to consider in the total cost of ownership of a persistence framework.

Often the cost of selecting your persistence technology may be impacted by choices for other important architectural aspects of the system. For example, you may choose a particular application server runtime that ships with a persistence technology, and therefore reduce the overhead of support.

Before we discuss some of the specific factors to consider, we want to point out that there are downsides to focusing purely on minimizing TCO. For example, although it might seem more cost-effective to use a single vendor for everything, you must also take into account that a particular application will likely outlive the hardware and software platform upon which it is deployed—so you have to factor in the capability to embrace change. In short, it is important to remember that requirements analysis always involves trade-offs.

Hardware and Software Dependencies

One question we almost always hear when presenting a proposal for a persistence framework is this: Do you have to buy additional hardware or software to use it? The reason this question usually gets asked relatively early is that the capital expenses required for new hardware and software make up part of the total cost of acquisition, which tends to get more focus.

Mechanisms that run on existing or multiple platforms are therefore going to be more attractive than those that don't.

Two software platforms that are ubiquitous to most SOA applications based on Java are Java Platform Standard Edition (JSE) and Java Platform Enterprise Edition (JEE). Because Java is a hardware-neutral technology, it allows you to deploy to various hardware platforms. In addition, Java EE platforms provide a full range of enterprise features, such as messaging, clustering, and security. Often platforms are chosen based on the end-to-end architecture, so having your persistence technology integrate with that big picture is important.

Sometimes it is necessary to have a particular persistence mechanism run on both Java SE and Java EE platforms. For example, most companies do not have the resources to install fully configured Java EE platforms on every developer's working environment. These are normally deployed only on QA and stress-test servers, as well as production systems. So the capability to unit test on a Java SE platform (or scaled-down Java EE platform) can help minimize the costs without sacrificing software quality. Figure 2.7 illustrates this approach to testing. Keys Botzum [A.2.1] wrote an excellent in-depth article on this subject that you
A.2.1 should read.

It is worth noting that there are risks in this approach to testing. For example, certain types of application bugs may not show up on Java SE application servers, and therefore may not be found until later in the QA or stress-testing stages, when they are likely to be more expensive to fix.

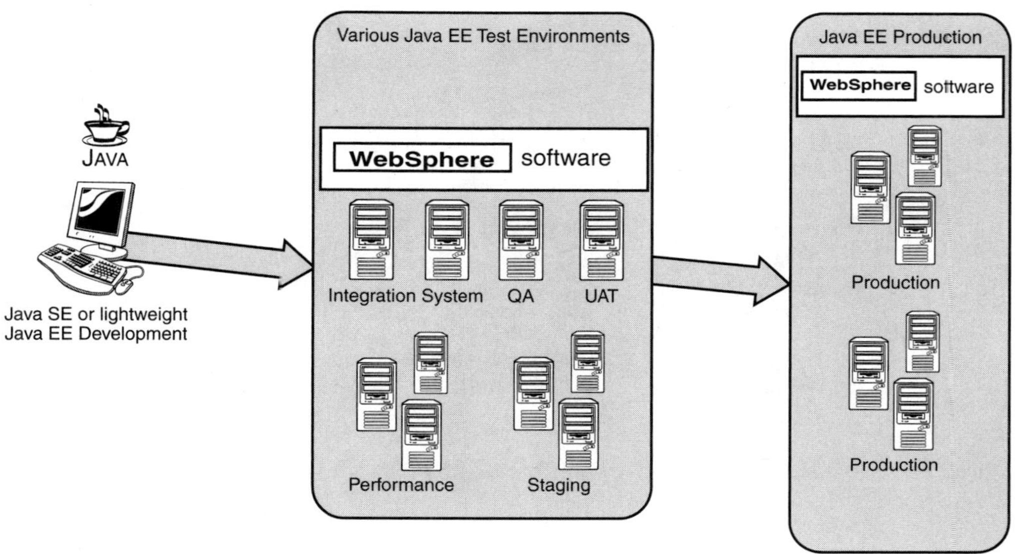

Figure 2.7 Developing, testing, and deploying in JSE and JEE environments.

Standards Supported

Adherence to standards is an equally important high-level requirement to consider. Support for an industry standard indicates that the framework's specification has been scrutinized by a large number of IT professionals who have a vested interest in making sure that it meets their basic requirements. We are big believers in the idea that "two heads are better than one" because synthesizing multiple points of view can result in a whole greater than the sum of the parts, as illustrated by the blind men and the elephant analogy (see Figure 2.8).

As we mentioned in the preceding section, "Hardware and Software Dependencies," standards often allow vendors to create ideal development testing environments separate from their production environment by stubbing out the implementations behind a particular component (allowing for quick and automated execution of test and debug cycles).

Some standards of interest to Java programmers needing access to persistent data include JDBC (Java Database Connectivity), EJB 3 (Enterprise JavaBeans), and JPA (Java Persistence API), the history of which was covered in Chapter 1.

However, there are some downsides to considering only the standards supported by a framework. Standards can be slow to evolve when there are many participants driving a cumbersome consensus-based voting process. And after a consensus has finally been reached, it can take a significant amount of time for reputable vendors to support the new standards—even if just a new version of existing ones. As such, standards almost always lag behind the requirements of cutting-edge-type applications.

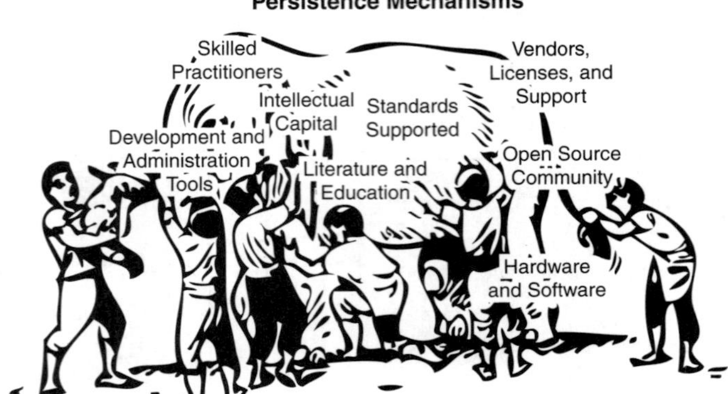

Figure 2.8 Standards can result in a whole greater than the sum of the parts.

Open-Source and Community-Driven Activities

The existence of standards increases the likelihood that a community of practitioners will spring up to create methods and best practices on how to properly exploit the associated technology. And sometimes "open source" projects start up to collectively fill gaps in the standards and associated tools. For example, the Spring Framework often used with Hibernate (another open-source project in its own right) provided "dependency injection" (DI). DI is the capability to proxy dependent services without explicit coding so that the components can be moved easily from one environment to another—such as when unit testing and then stress testing a component.

Thus, open-source software and community-driven development is another aspect that should be considered by executives. It is often the case that a vibrant community can drive certain technologies into "de facto" standard status. And de facto standards will just as often drive an industry standard committee to change direction. For example, the vibrant community behind frameworks like Hibernate drove the Java EE standard to drop the Container Managed Persistence aspect of Enterprise JavaBeans in favor of a new persistence standard called JPA (see Figure 2.9 for a "family tree").

But relying on open-source communities has its own risks, especially if it is one of the "one man" projects that abound, or the community behind it suddenly dies out. The reality is that many standards which appeared to be popular have died out as a new approach wins the hearts and minds of the community. For example, there have been two versions of entity Enterprise JavaBeans components that provided an ORM framework for applications. Unfortunately, "betting on the wrong horse" can cause a great deal of churn in your approach to persistence in the enterprise.

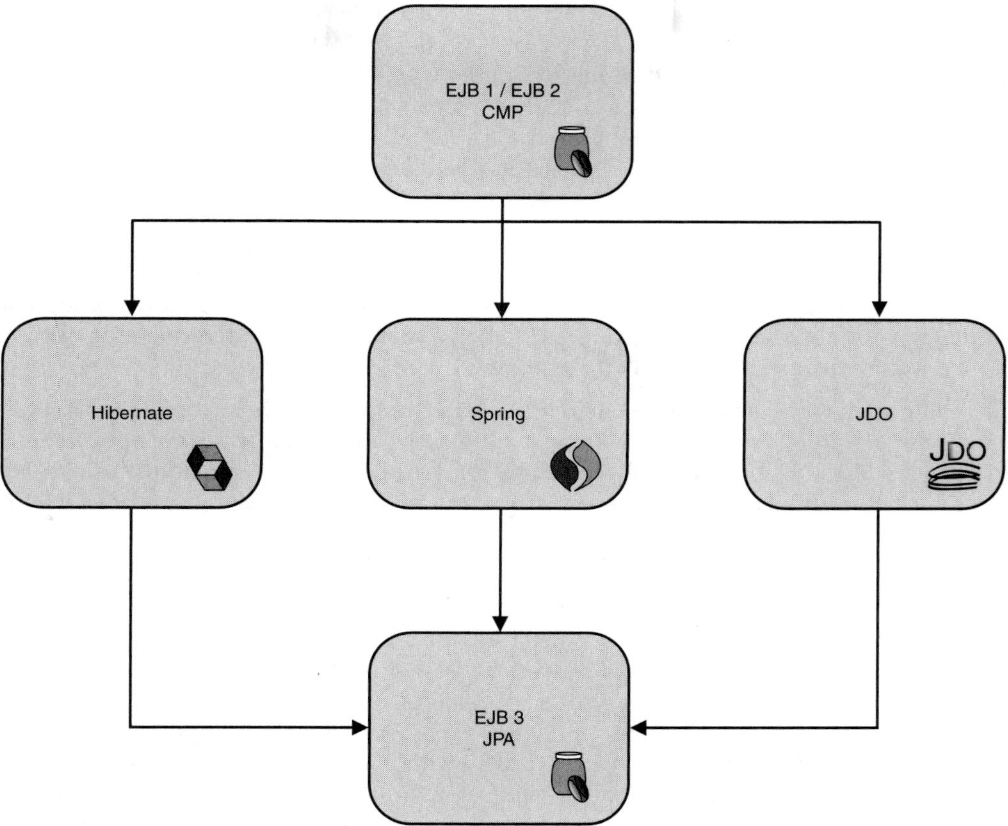

Figure 2.9 How the EJB 3/JPA standard was influenced by Hibernate, Spring, and JDO.

Vendors, Licenses, and Support

Another measure of a vibrant community is whether there is a market for the technology. Specifically, how many vendors provide (and support) the framework? Usually it is "the more the merrier" when it comes to vendors or open-source communities involved with a given technology, because no one wants to be locked into a single source or (maybe worse) an unsupported framework. And open-source communities with big vendors behind them to provide "support for fee" usually do better than others. For example, JBoss owns Hibernate and BEA supports OpenJPA—opening us up to a classic chicken-and-egg situation when considering whether it is the vibrant community that attracts the vendors or vice versa. Regardless, these are definitely strong, active communities.

Most persistence technologies fall under either commercial licenses or open-source licenses. With commercial software licenses, a user pays a fee to obtain a license to use the software. This license defines the terms and conditions under which the user may or may not use the software. For example, some commercial database server software licenses are coupled to the number of processors running on the machine that hosts them. It is paramount that an enterprise be intimately aware of the licensing agreements that they have accepted, because violation of these agreements can be quite costly.

If the persistence technology is backed by a commercial firm, you need to consider whether the commercial vendor charges for support. Also, you must consider (even if it is remote) the possibility of the commercial provider closing shop. Many enterprises often choose a commercial firm for accountability. If there is a bug in the persistence framework, the enterprise typically wants someone to fix it right away.

With some open-source solutions, code fixes and updates can be "philanthropic" with little or no accountability. As such, the enterprise must hope that their own development staff can fix any blocking bugs or that someone in the open-source community can solve the problem at hand. However, the license may restrict you from making changes without contributing that change back to the original source.

Intellectual Property Considerations

Licensing and intellectual property considerations will, of course, vary from project to project within your enterprise. For example, if you are an independent software vendor who specializes in making software to sell to other companies, your ability to patent and sell an application you build that leverages open-source persistence technologies can be greatly affected by the open-source license you are dealing with. On the other hand, if you are using a persistence technology for an in-house application and do not plan on selling or patenting it, your IP staff will likely have less concerns about the license agreement associated with the open-source persistence technology.

Complicating the matter, there are more than 50 types of licenses associated with open-source software to understand. Popular open-source licenses include the General Public License (GPL), Limited GPL (LGPL), the Berkeley Software Distribution License (BSD), the Apache Software License, and the Mozilla license. Many critics of the GPL refer to GPL-style licenses as "viral," in that GPL terms require that all derived works must in turn be licensed under the GPL (see Figure 2.10 for a graphical view, showing how eventually everything becomes "infected" by the GPL). This restriction can be a major concern for enterprises trying to protect the internals of the software applications that they build.

There is a philosophical difference between GPL- and BSD-style licenses; the latter put fewer restrictions on derived works. Other licenses, such as an "Apache" license, have very few restrictions on derivative works, and are usually more popular because of it.

Another interesting IP issue that arises when using a persistence framework based on open-source software is that you are typically dealing with a "product" developed by a community of programmers from around the world. It can be difficult to ascertain whether the open-source code infringes on third-party patents.

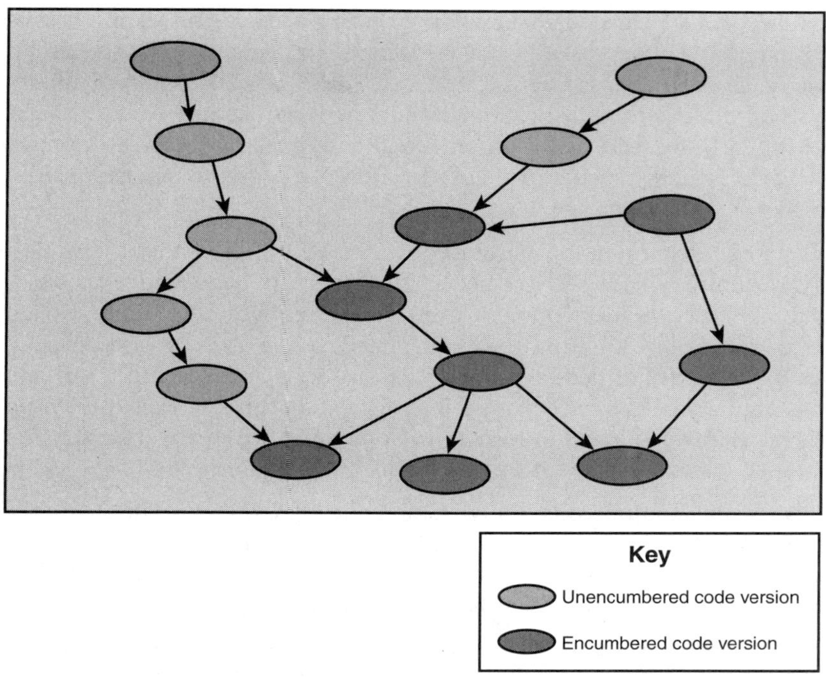

Figure 2.10 The viral nature of a GPL license.

Therefore, an enterprise may need to involve their legal staff to closely analyze the license agreement before selecting a framework based on open-source projects—and this expense should be considered part of its cost of acquisition.

Availability of Skilled Practitioners

We have found that one of the biggest reasons to like frameworks based on standards and vibrant open-source communities is the higher probability that there are enough skilled people available inside the company to design and build applications using that particular persistence technology and approach.

A related question we are often asked is how much skill is needed to successfully use the persistence framework(s) being proposed. Those mechanisms that require a great deal of specialized skill in order to master them are less attractive than those that are simpler to understand and learn.

So before you adopt a new persistence technology, the current skill set of your development team needs to be considered. For example, has anyone on the team worked with the persistence technology being considered? An informal survey to understand what skills you already have in-house can help in the decision-making process.

Many persistence frameworks are considered similar to others; therefore, the learning curve of a developer who is familiar with a similar persistence technology might be less steep than that of one who has never been exposed to similar technologies. The skills survey should perform a gap analysis of the current skill set of the development staff compared to the skills needed to be successful with the technology on an actual enterprise project. For example, developers skilled in a technology such as Hibernate will make an easier transition into another technology like OpenJPA.

When there is a lack of skill regarding a persistence technology in-house, it is a common practice for enterprises to hire outside services—either as temporary consultants or as permanent employees to augment the development team. And a resilient development team should also be able to recover quickly from the unpredicted loss or absence of a development team member. The realities of people getting sick (or just plain sick and tired) and deciding to leave the company need to be considered. Project managers and executives need to consider "what if" scenarios in regard to losing development team members and being able to recover from such losses through hiring of new team members.

An assessment of how easy it is to find skills from outside sources provides yet another measure of the strength of a persistence mechanism with respect to the technical community. This analysis might include a survey of how many resumes are returned in a search of an Internet job search engine for a particular persistence technology.

The lesson here is that picking a brand-new or esoteric technology for your persistence needs can be a costly decision in the long run by making it harder to staff your projects.

Availability of Education and Mentors

To jump-start the learning process and close relatively narrow skill gaps, you should consider providing literature and training about how to best use a particular technology in the context of your enterprise. We have helped many client firms to institute Centers of Excellence (COE) to help evaluate technologies and customize the best practices to better fit with the overall architecture, and then train the development team on how to apply them.

Figure 2.11 shows how these Centers can play a direct role in bringing the rank-and-file developers onboard with a new technology—through mentoring in the context of actual projects. This on-the-job and train-the-trainers approach has proven itself to be "viral" as well, quickly spreading expertise exponentially throughout the organization. With each subsequent "generation," the roles of the COE and development team leads are gradually reversed, until the development team becomes self-sufficient.

Therefore, another gauge of the vibrancy of a persistence technology is the availability of good books or technical articles on the subject. Although not necessarily a measure of simplicity, nor a substitute for having one or more skilled practitioners on the team to serve as mentors, the availability of literature documenting proven best practices can help steer a project toward success even when staffed by novices. The availability of conferences (even if just a track in a more general-interest conference) and education associated with the persistence framework is another good indicator of vibrancy within a technical community that is useful to consider when making your choice.

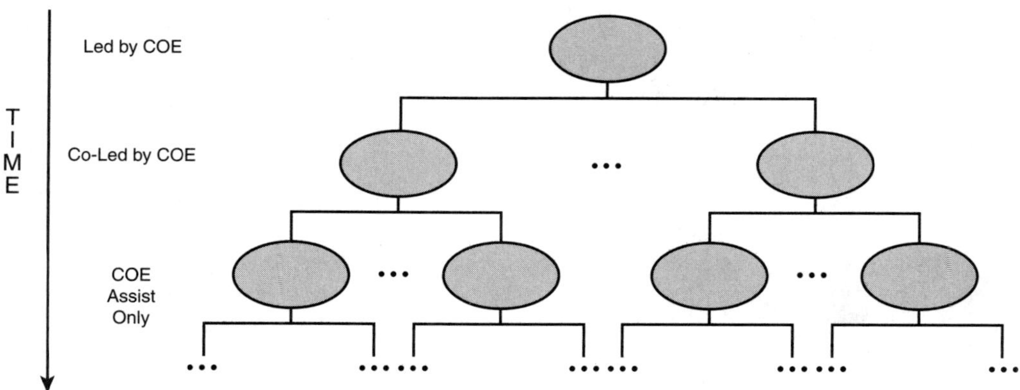

Figure 2.11 The role of a Center of Excellence in educating the development team.

Development and Administration Tools

Modern-day programmers typically use integrated development environments (IDEs) and agile approaches to both speed their development efforts and reduce the complexity (and educational requirements) of using the technology.

Sophisticated visual object-relational mapping (ORM) tools are often available in these IDEs, depending on which persistence technology is adopted. Therefore, an enterprise should consider what ORM tools are available for a particular persistence technology when making a choice.

Of course, building a persistence framework around an ORM tool can cause dependency on the tool and, more problematic, can mask the complexity of the underlying mechanism. We find that the best persistence technologies usually have an easy-to-understand programming model, in which case the ORM tools accelerate development by automating tedious tasks.

Another important tool that is useful for persistence in the enterprise is one that enables tracking the end-to-end path of data during runtime from the application code into the database and back again. For example, sometimes a poorly written SQL statement is tracked down through monitoring tools in the database. Being able to help a developer quickly change the component that issued the SQL could be important to resolving a serious performance issue. And programming models for persistence that separate the SQL from the code so that only a configuration change is required are even better.

End-to-end monitoring is an important aspect of what is now being referred to as Data Governance. Figure 2.12 shows the full life cycle that an architect should be considering with respect to data management.

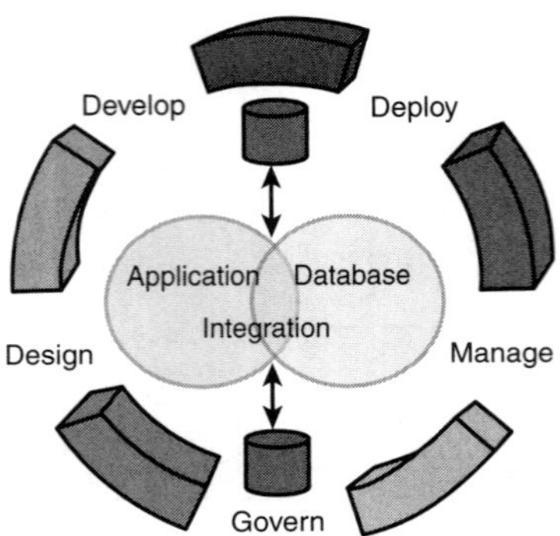

Figure 2.12 Data across the life cycle.

The availability of end-to-end monitoring and other Data Governance tools should be factored into your evaluation of a new persistence mechanism.

Build Versus Buy?

Rather than adopting an existing persistence technology, many enterprises decide to roll out their own persistence frameworks; they, in effect, reinvent the wheel. In our experience, this is a practice that should be avoided because what may seem like a bargain in the short term ends up costing extra in the long run.

Enterprises typically have core competencies in an industry-specific domain, and it is disheartening to see (for example) a financial firm spinning its wheels creating yet another half-baked ORM framework from the ground up when it could be using those same cycles to innovate solutions critical to its core business processes.

What these teams fail to realize (and their enterprise architects fail to point out) is that all the factors contributing to TCO discussed in this section come into play when developing a framework—in addition to the extra TCA expense of building the basic runtime components of a homegrown mechanism. In other words, the need for standards, tools, processes, education, and support do not go away, so the costs just keep adding up. In fact, these costs are often made worse by the fact that when you invent a proprietary framework, you have only a limited community to support the technology and develop these assets crucial to a reasonable TCO.

So unless you are a middleware or database vendor, we strongly recommend that you focus your development team on writing high-quality applications that support the mission-critical business processes of your enterprise.

IT Leaders and Enterprise Quality Solutions

Assume that during the evaluation workshop kickoff, the business executives have (wisely) decided against building a persistence framework. They want your team to choose one or more existing mechanisms that best meet the TCO requirements of the business and the IT requirements of typical applications that will be built over the next two to three years.

It is worth mentioning here that regardless of the time frame, an evaluation of "fitness of use" of a given technology like persistence for a given project should be done on every project. So, what are the technical requirements related to persistence that determine fitness?

Our view is that IT requirements describe the technical constraints within which a software system must operate. So with this in mind, we strive to understand these constraints as objectively measurable characteristics that can be tested. This "test first" approach is essential to agile methods that have you design the simplest thing that can possibly work—and thus avoid the analysis paralysis that can occur with waterfall approaches.

This discussion about the approach to gathering requirements does not directly answer the question about which technical requirements you should consider when choosing a persistence mechanism, except that the focus on testing allows us to recast the question a bit: *What is a good way to classify the objectively measurable characteristics of a system?*

This recasting helps because the ISO 9126 standard [ISO9126] classifies measurable software quality characteristics into the following six categories:

- **Functionality**—A set of attributes that bear on the existence of a set of functions and their specified properties.
- **Reliability**—A set of attributes that bear on the capability of software to maintain its level of performance under stated conditions for a stated period of time.
- **Usability**—A set of attributes that bear on the effort needed for use, and on the individual assessment of such use, by a stated or implied set of users.
- **Efficiency**—A set of attributes that bear on the relationship between the level of performance of the software and the amount of resources used, under stated conditions.
- **Maintainability**—A set of attributes that bear on the effort needed to make specified modifications.
- **Portability**—A set of attributes that bear on the capability of software to be transferred from one environment to another.

We have found these categories very useful, not just because they can be used to define relatively precise requirements, but also because each category can be considered separate aspects (or domains) of the system that can be independently modeled and combined into an enterprise solution. Figure 2.13 shows how these different aspects combine.

We find this factored approach to requirements more suitable for service-oriented applications and agile methods because it follows the world's first recorded best practice: "Divide and Conquer." In keeping with Divide and Conquer, we will look at each category separately in terms of its ramifications on the persistence requirements of applications.

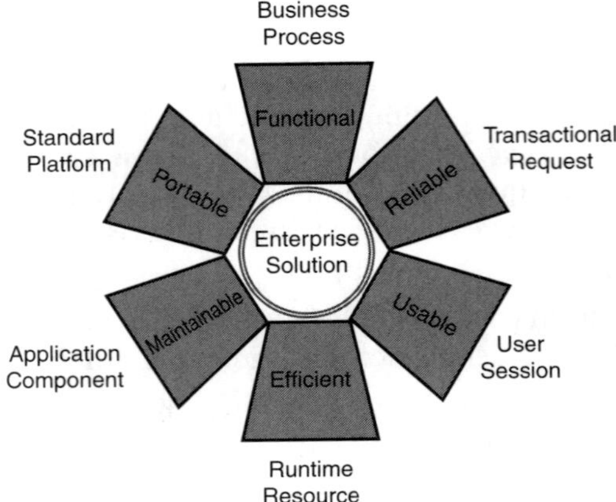

Figure 2.13 ISO 9126 software characteristics used as IT requirement categories.

Functionality and Business Processes

Functionality can be the most important requirement to consider because if an application does not support some aspect of your mission-critical business processes, it is not much good for the enterprise.

One way to capture functional requirements of your business processes is with "use cases." A use case is a fundamental feature of the Unified Modeling Language (UML). UML is a very broad graphical language; because we do not have the space nor the inclination to provide a complete tutorial, we recommend [Booch].

For the purposes of this book, assume that a use case identifies "actors" involved in an interaction with the system and names the interactions so that they can be explored in detail. Figure 2.14 shows an example of a use case diagram.

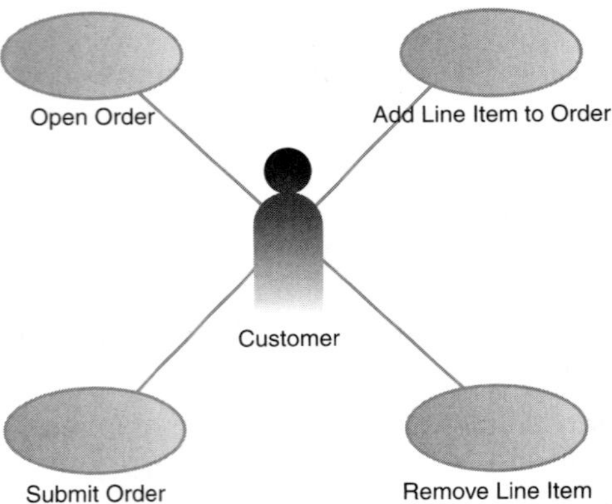

Figure 2.14 Example of a use case diagram.

At this extremely coarse level of granularity, a use case diagram does little more than serve as a graphical index into more precise descriptions of the functional requirements. Good use case descriptions at any level have pre- and post-conditions that specify the state of the relevant components of the system before and after the case, along with functional steps that occur to make the state change. [Cockburn] is a good reference. For example, here is the detailed description of the Open Order Activity of the Place an Order use case:

- **Precondition:**
  - The user is logged into the system.
  - The user triggers a new order use case by one of the following methods:
    - By performing Add Line Item Use Case (#x) when no Order exists.
    - By the submission of a batch order request.
- **Steps:**
  - The system looks up the customer record by using the customer ID stored in the User Authentication Credentials.
  - The system checks whether the user exists.
    - If the user exists, continue to the next step.
    - If the user does not exist, a customer exception is thrown to the UI and activity ends.
  - The system checks whether User contains a current Open Order.
    - If the user does not have an open order, continue to the next step.
    - If the user has an existing open order, an exception is thrown to the UI and activity ends.
  - Create a New Order Record with the following information:
    - New generated ID (nonfunctional requirement #xx: must use database generated key facility).
    - Customer ID.
    - Status set to OPEN.
- **Postcondition:**
  - A current open order is assigned to the user.

For all but the finest granularity use cases with a few linear steps, it can be useful to graphically show the activities that can occur within the use case. These steps can be shown using activity diagrams or state diagrams, depending on the nature of the use case. In our case, because we are operating on a single passive object like an order, it is best to use a state diagram that shows the life cycle. Figure 2.15 shows the state diagram for an Order.

And just as the steps can be graphically documented using state or activity diagrams, one can show the pre- and postconditions of the use case with class diagrams capturing the relationships among domain objects essential to the processing steps. The pre- and postconditions can be considered "states" of the application, and often represent the data that needs to be stored persistently. One reason we like state diagrams is that these states are often common across different functions and use cases.

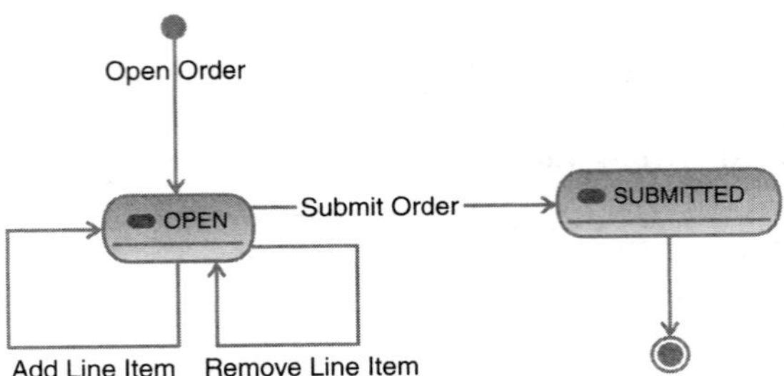

Figure 2.15 State machine diagram of an Order.

The transitions in the state diagram usually include one or more persistent actions in your applications. For example, the open order transition in Figure 2.15 will translate to some create operation that is later realized by an API call to your persistence framework and ultimately some type of SQL Insert. Chapter 3 describes these best practices for domain modeling in more detail, and how these models become the functional endpoints for the OR mapping problem to be tackled during detailed design (with the database schema representing the other endpoint).

Reliability and Transactional Requests

Reliability is considered the next most important requirement because it is not enough to show that your system can perform critical functions only under ideal conditions. If an application system does not work reliably under load or when its subsystems fail, then it doesn't really matter whether it supports the business processes. It is important to ask yourself some tough questions; but we recommend that you ensure they document measurable characteristics of system performance. Here are some examples of such questions, with some slight rephrasing if necessary to get to measurable requirements:

- Can this system run reliably even when there are hardware failures? How much failure can you tolerate?
- What about replication and failover scenarios? How quickly do you need the system to come back up?
- Is manual intervention acceptable, or must the system failover automatically?

Reliability and persistence go hand in hand with transaction management. When you are choosing a persistence framework, it is important to consider how the framework works with the transaction management system you are using. For example, can your persistence mechanism allow persistent actions to run under a "Container Managed Transaction" of your EJB container?

We will not go over transactions in detail, but we will briefly discuss some concepts. A good reference on transactions can be found in [Little]. For the purposes of this book, a transaction is a unit of work that accesses one or more shared resources maintaining the following four basic "ACID" properties:

- They must be **Atomic**: An atomic transaction must execute completely or not at all.
- They must be **Consistent**: Consistency refers to the integrity of the underlying data store and the transactional system as well.
- They must be **Isolated**: The transaction must be allowed to execute without interference from other processes and transactions.
- They must be **Durable**: The data changes made during the course of a transaction must be written to some type of physical storage before the transaction is successfully completed.

Most database systems are specifically designed to maintain the ACID properties of units-of-work accessing the database within a transaction. The persistence mechanisms associated with a given database will have programming model components geared toward starting and committing transactions, and providing basic "CRUD" functions (create, retrieve, update, and destroy functions associated with objects representing persistent data).

Usability and User Sessions

If your application does what you want and does it reliably, but your application's users cannot easily access its functions from the channels they have available to them, then what good is it?

In this context, usability requirements can be characterized by describing the type of session through which a user interacts with the system. There are at least two interesting design patterns associated with user sessions to consider when evaluating persistence mechanisms: (a) online and (b) batch.

Online applications have very different application characteristics than batch applications with respect to a persistence mechanism. For example, batch applications typically perform the following actions:

- Execute a "batch" of functional requests in a single transaction (often a very large number of requests).
- Access the input requests or output results as a "stream" (for example, a DB cursor) for efficiency.
- Emphasize reducing round trips to DB in order to process large amounts of data in as short a time as possible, such as through sorting the input stream.
- Execute the batch application usually by some kind of scheduling scripts like cron.

Figure 2.16 shows the overview of a batch application, in which a batch controller component handles the looping and outer transaction management and invokes business logic that is sometimes shared with online applications.

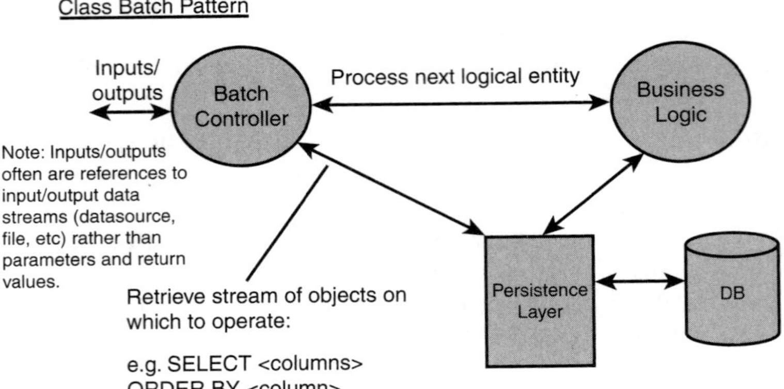

Figure 2.16 Batch streaming.

A good persistence mechanism will enable applications to bulk-read and bulk-update persistent objects mapped to an underlying relational datastore. Also, to get the economies of scale, the framework should enable sorting the data in the batch stream.

Efficiency and Runtime Resources

The most functional, reliable, and usable system will ultimately fail if it does not make efficient use of its resources (such as processors, memory, and disk space)—mainly because TCO and possibly user satisfaction will suffer.

For the purposes of persistence, we will examine two strategies that help minimize response times and maximize throughput, the primary measures of efficiency, by trading one resource for another:

- **Isolation** (an object locking strategy) enables multiple transactions to run concurrently and yet maintain the ACID properties, thus getting better throughput by fully utilizing CPU resources.
- **Caching** (an object preloading strategy) minimizes accesses to external systems by preloading objects in system memory, thus getting better response time at the expense of system memory.

These design strategies require understanding both the response time and throughput requirements and the amount of resources available to the system.

Isolation Levels Trade CPU Utilization for Better Throughput

Isolation is especially important to understand when you are dealing with persistence mechanisms. Developers often must choose the correct isolation levels for each use case to enable the application server to balance CPU utilization and integrity (reliability) requirements. The level of isolation controls how data being accessed is locked from other transactions.

To understand isolation levels, we first need to define *conditions* that happen when two or more application functions operate on the same data:

- **Dirty reads** occur when a transaction is able to read changes made by another transaction before the second transaction has completed.
- **Phantom reads** occur when a new record added to the database is detectable by another transaction that started prior to the `INSERT` that created the record.
- **Repeatable reads** occur when a query is guaranteed to return the same result if read again during the same transaction, even if another transaction has modified the data.

To ensure the preceding conditions, relational databases normally use several different *locking techniques*. The most common techniques are these:

- **Read locks**—Prevents other transactions from changing data read during a transaction until the transaction ends. This prevents nonrepeatable reads.
- **Write locks**—Meant for update. Prevents other transactions from changing the data until the current transaction is complete but allows dirty reads by other transactions and by the current transaction itself.
- **Exclusive write locks**—Meant for updates. Prevents other transactions from reading or changing the data until the current transaction is complete. It also prevents dirty reads by other transactions.

Therefore, the programming model for a good persistence mechanism will allow developers to specify a functional *isolation level*, either through some configuration option or programmatically in their application code. This isolation level can be passed to the database so that the proper locking strategy is applied. The following terms are often used to describe isolation levels:

- **Read uncommitted**—Transactions can read uncommitted data (data changed by a different transaction that is still in progress). This means that dirty reads, nonrepeatable reads, and phantom reads can occur.
- **Read committed**—The transaction cannot read uncommitted data; data that is being changed by another transaction cannot be read. This prevents dirty reads; however, nonrepeatable reads and phantom reads can occur.
- **Repeatable read**—The transaction cannot change data being read by a different transaction. Dirty reads and nonrepeatable reads are prevented, but phantom reads can occur.
- **Serializable**—The transaction has exclusive read and update privileges; different transactions can neither read nor write to the same data. Dirty reads, repeatable reads, and phantom reads are prevented.

The type of isolation is determined by the functional requirements. The stricter the rule, the less performant the application can be. The looser the rule, the greater your chance for data integrity problems. You must have a correct understanding of all the use cases associated with a particular data component so that you can make the correct choice.

Caching Trades Memory for Better Response Times

Even with the weakest isolation levels, you may not be able to meet the response time requirements for accessing your data. Applications may need to cache data in order to minimize the path length. How you cache data will be driven by your IT requirements, including available memory and servers. Certain use cases may require more sophisticated caching solutions than others. Some important questions to consider are these:

1. How many users need to access the same data at the same time?
2. How many units of work are invoked per user session?
3. What data is accessed in each unit of work?
4. How often is a given data item read versus being updated?
5. How many application servers are available?
6. How much memory is available per application server?

The answers to the first four questions help determine how long to cache your data. Specifically, a good persistence framework will provide the capability to bind cached data to one of at least three different scopes:

1. **Transaction (unit of work)**. For example, as a user submits an order, the product quantity data is cached only for the duration of the transaction because it's frequently updated by other application functions and users. The unit of work performs all of its update operations on this data against the transaction cache and then sends all the changes to the database at transaction commit time.
2. **Session**. For example, the related order entry application allows users exclusive access to a "shopping cart" which contains line items that represent a pending (open) order. As long as the user is logged in, the session cache is valid, and the shopping-cart data can be accessed without going to database. When the session ends (through either an explicit logout or an implicit timeout), any changes are committed to the database.
3. **Application**. For example, as the order entry application allows users to add line items to the shopping cart, the rarely updated product catalog data is accessed from the cache for as long as the application server is active. When the server is restarted (or catalog entries are programmatically invalidated), the product catalog cache is reloaded.

The amount of data and its access pattern will often have more impact on caching strategy than the life cycle scope. For example, a given banking application allows users to access their account history as part of their session. This history data is unlikely to change after it has been created (unless you have found a way to change the past). If most of these banking functions access large amounts of history data that prevent it from being effectively cached within a single application server context, then the database itself may become the bottleneck as every request goes to the back end data store.

In this case, you may need a more sophisticated caching solution that partitions the data across hardware and servers based on some mapping associated with the cache data key (for example, user ID). This approach usually requires some equally sophisticated *grid-based caches* such as Object Grid [A.2.2].

A.2.2

A good persistence framework allows a programmer to custom-manage the data maintained in a cache, such as through a pluggable interface point that allows you to integrate with a grid-based cache.

Some use cases may benefit from caching to meet response-time goals, even though the data may periodically change. This scenario is sometimes referred to as "Read Mostly," which requires the mechanism to provide a means to invalidate the cache (as described earlier in the discussion on application scoped cache entries. Of course, you have to be careful—if the data gets updated often, the overhead of asking whether the data is in the cache is valid coupled with the reduced amount of memory available for other purposes begins to outweigh the benefit of occasionally finding valid data in the cache.

Consider also that there are opportunities to cache outside of the scope of the persistence mechanism. For example, you can cache data inside network proxies that sit in front of the application server. Further, you can choose to cache the data inside the user's browser (as is the trend with modern Ajax applications). Although these caches are normally outside the scope of Java-based persistence mechanisms, they should be considered in the context of your end-to-end architecture (and may make those persistence frameworks that support "information as a service" more attractive).

Maintainability and Application Components

Now assume that your application reliably does what you want through the access channels you want, and also assume that it properly balances your available system resources to minimize response time and maximize throughput. In practice, we find that it is usually through numerous iterative cycles of deployment and test that the system matures to this level of stability.

A recent, even more agile, trend in development approaches has emerged in the Web 2.0 world. This approach is a concept called "Perpetual Beta," in which users are providing constant feedback about an application's functions. Based on this feedback, the application is in a constant state of change.

The Perpetual Beta approach allows the quality of the software to drastically improve very quickly based on real-world input. Enterprise applications, such as Yahoo Mail, are beginning to adopt this model, and as such, are choosing frameworks that help adapt to change quickly.

So a good persistence mechanism will enable changes to be made through configuration options without modifying the application code. A great framework will include tools to accelerate definition of persistent objects as well as development, testing, and deployment of services needing access to it. For example, suppose a DBA determines that a particular query will perform much better if you switch the order of the tables being joined. Being able to quickly change the query associated with a given unit of work and deploy the delta to production is essential in this new super-agile business environment in which we find ourselves.

Portability and Standard Platforms

Although last on the list, portability is certainly not the least important of the IT requirements we've explored—especially in the context of all the changes likely to come in both the requirements of an enterprise quality application and the platforms on which they can be hosted. Specific questions concerning portability requirements relate to how easy it is to install, replace, or adapt components of the application.

To put portability into a practical general context, imagine that your company has a division charged with selling basic order entry services to partner product vendors. Of course your company wants to sell these services to as many partners as possible; and to support that goal they want to make as few restrictions as possible on the hardware and software platforms that host the services. By implementing the services in Java that adhere to the Java EE (or even the more lightweight Java SE platform), your company has maximized the potential sales by enabling partners to run the services on IBM WebSphere Application Server, JBoss, or WebLogic, to name just a few of the biggest players.

What Happened to Portable Persistence Promised by Entity EJB Components?

Can we put the portability of a persistence mechanism in a similar practical context? To answer this question, we like to first separate the portability concerns of (a) the application's business logic, and (b) its data access logic. The earliest EJB specifications separated these two types of logic into *session* and *entity* EJB components, respectively.

The **session EJB** component specification (at least the *stateless* one) was very successful and still remains in wide use today. Even the EJB 3 specification leaves the concept relatively unscathed, mainly adding the capability to annotate Java POJOs that capture business logic and reduce the number of artifacts needed to code a Session Bean. One reason for this success is that the programming model for the business logic is basically Java, which has proven to be truly write-once-run-anywhere platforms.

Unfortunately, the **entity EJB** component specification (even the Container Managed Persistence, or CMP, one) has not been nearly so successful. In fact, entity EJB components have fallen into such disuse that the Java Persistence API (JPA) has totally revamped the approach to persistence within a Java SE or Java EE platform. One reason for this lack of success is that CMP components did not deliver on the promise of portability between Java EE platforms. We believe one root cause is that the specification never defined a standard mapping between the object and data layer. Although entity EJB components are designed with the best of intentions to remain database agnostic, this looseness in the specification required a complex and tedious remapping whenever a different vendor or open-source implementation of the platform was chosen.

So while the EJB marketing literature touted the capability to "easily" persist a CMP component in just about any type of persistent store, from relational database tables to flat files, the practical reality was that almost no one needed this high degree of "portability." For the most part, almost all entity EJB components in production use today are stored in relational databases. The portability that most need is the capability to move from vendor to vendor across application servers and relational databases.

Another practical reality is that most entity EJB components have no real data access logic in them anyway. In fact, the EJB 2 specification made it even easier to eliminate any semblance of implementation logic by making CMP "implementations" abstract classes that get converted to concrete classes at deployment time. The implication is that the "real" data access logic associated with an entity CMP component was contained in the vendor-specific mapping files—*which were not portable*. It forced programmers to use a heavyweight component (even when Local interfaces were introduced) that made it much more difficult to unit test CMP components in an automated fashion.

Understanding the Real Portability Requirements for Persistence Frameworks

These unfortunate practical realities left an opening for frameworks such as Hibernate and Kodo Solarmetric to gain in popularity. They could run portably inside both Java SE applications and Java EE applications because they, among other things, defined a standard mapping to relational databases with which any platform providers are expected to comply. Further, they could easily generate data access logic to "hibernate" simple POJO classes through the use of deployment-like tools, greatly simplifying the end-to-end development process.

Taking these lessons to heart, we have learned that good frameworks need to consider varying requirements, from running on JSE, to optimizing access paths. Figure 2.17 enumerates some of these concerns plus a number of others related to maintainability and portability.

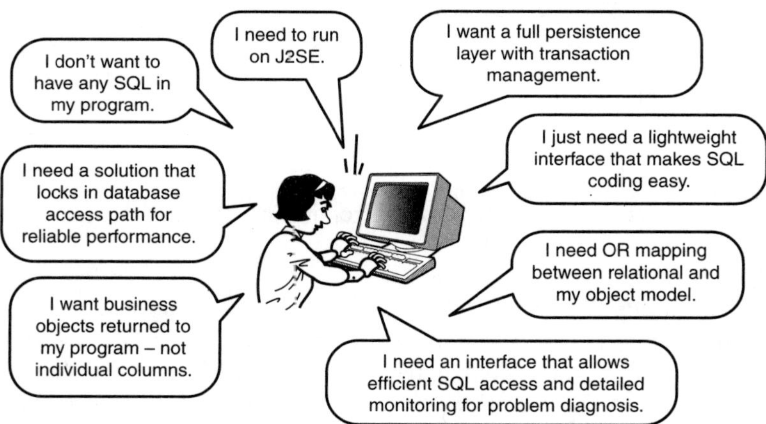

Figure 2.17 Portability requirements gathered from lessons learned with early standards.

You will likely have to compromise on certain decisions and not necessarily expect a mechanism to meet all of these portability requirements. However, rest assured that portability between Java EE and Java SE is achievable, and so should be expected of any persistence framework that you consider.

Interoperability and Enterprise Quality Solutions

We have found that very few applications are implemented totally "from scratch." Most, if not all, development projects we have seen are centered on making various legacy systems communicate with each other and a few new ones (usually providing the "glue") over a network. This network of solution components may also include systems that are hosted in completely different data centers, application server platforms, and data store types. So, in essence, how you share data across applications and domains has a large impact on all the IT requirements discussed in this section from functionality to portability. Figure 2.18 shows an example of two separate applications exchanging data using XML as a standard canonical form for interoperability.

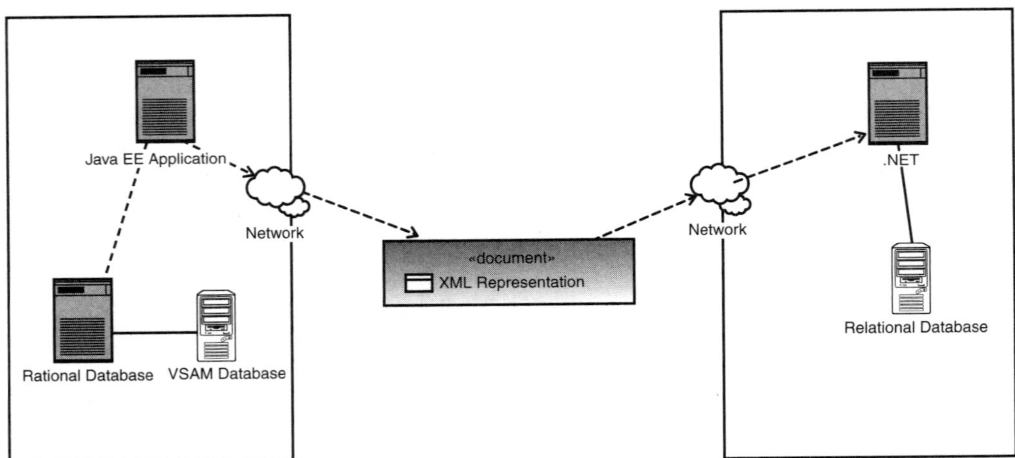

Figure 2.18 Integration of two systems using XML as an interoperability standard.

These same kinds of interoperability requirements and solutions designs apply to persistence frameworks. For example, your persistence framework may need a way to transform data into other formats besides Java Objects. You may need to create an XML representation for a third-party consumer to invoke your service. You may also need a way to have your data render into multiple formats like an ATOM feed to be displayed in your Wiki or JSON (JavaScript Object Notation) to be displayed in some Rich Internet Ajax-based application. We have already discussed standards adherence in the section on TCO as one major aspect of interoperability that should be considered when evaluating persistence mechanisms. This discussion therefore brings us full circle.

This circular reference is appropriate given that we like to illustrate the ISO 9126 software quality characteristics (shown earlier in Figure 2.13) as spokes radiating from a circle representing an enterprise solution that integrates each of these aspects. It implies that each factor is an independent domain of requirements that should be considered when developing an enterprise quality application—and a persistence mechanism can be thought of as a very specialized enterprise application whose "business logic" is to provide persistence for other applications.

Summary

In this chapter, we discussed how both business drivers and IT requirements are the key to defining the needs of your persistence layer, even though most practitioners consider only the IT requirements. Therefore, we stressed that you should consider total-cost-of-ownership issues such as standards adherence, platforms required and other dependencies, vendors and licenses, and available skills and literature.

We then focused on the IT requirements in the context of measurable software characteristics, such as those defined by the ISO 9126 standard. We showed how the pre-/postconditions of use cases and states capture the details of domain objects likely to need access to persistent data, and how these functional requirements need to be considered along with quality of service requirements such as reliability, usability, efficiency, maintainability, and portability requirements when evaluating a given framework.

We looked into the details of ACID properties of transactional requests, isolation levels and their use in tuning applications for concurrent access control, the high throughput requirements of batch applications, and an approach to using XML as an interoperability layer to integrate applications developed according to different standards and hosted on separate runtime platforms.

In the next chapter, we discuss domain models and object-relational mapping as part of detailed application design, and how these detailed programming model aspects also need to be considered when choosing a persistence framework.

 Links to developerWorks

A.2.1 *The Ideal WebSphere Development Environment.*
This article by Keys Botzum and Wayne Beaton serves as a great guide on designing development environments for enterprise applications.
www.ibm.com/developerworks/websphere/techjournal/0312_beaton/beaton.html

A.2.2 *Build a scalable, resilient, high performance database alternative with the ObjectGrid component of WebSphere Extended Deployment.*
This article by Alan Chambers is a great guide for understanding the basic features of the ObjectGrid.
www.ibm.com/developerworks/websphere/techjournal/0711_chambers/0711_chambers.html

References

[Ambler] Ambler, Scott W. *Agile Modeling: Effective Practices for Extreme Programming and the Unified Process; 1st edition*. Wiley, 2002.

[Booch] Booch, Grady et al. *Unified Modeling Language User Guide, 2nd Edition*. Addison-Wesley Professional, 2005.

[Cockburn] Cockburn, Alistair *Writing Effective Use Cases*. Addison-Wesley Professional, 2000

[Cohn] Cohn, Mike. *User Stories Applied: For Agile Software Development*. Addison-Wesley Professional, 2004.

[ISO9126] *The ISO 9126 Standard*. www.issco.unige.ch/projects/ewg96/node13.html

[Little] Little, Mark et al. *Java Transaction Processing: Design and Implementation*. Prentice Hall PTR, 2004.

[Robertson] Robertson & Robertson. *Mastering the Requirements Process*. Addison-Wesley Professional, 1999.

Designing Persistent Object Services

We noted in Chapter 1, "A Brief History of Object-Relational Mapping," that this book is largely about the divide that exists between the world of relational databases and object-oriented programming. This fundamental divide can be bridged (or "mapped") with many different techniques and approaches. The specifics of *how* you bridge this gap is crucial to answering the question about why one persistence framework is better than another for SOA application styles, such as those outlined in Chapter 2, "High-Level Requirements and Persistence." In other words, whereas Chapter 2 is about high-level requirements, this chapter is about detailed design.

This chapter introduces some fundamentals and best practices of domain modeling with respect to persistence, as well as some common strategies of mapping a domain model to a database with an example-driven approach. The primary example showcased—a customer order management system—sets the stage for the evaluations in the rest of this book. The common example's domain model, along with its corresponding database schema, is used in Chapters 5 through 9 to illustrate the details of how to use the object-relational technologies surveyed.

Some Basic Concepts

Chapter 1's historical overview of the evolution of object-relational mapping solutions showed that there are a number of common concepts between the different solutions, and that these same features and concepts have emerged in different languages and products over the years. One of the most important lessons learned over the past two decades in software engineering not discussed in Chapter 1 is that such recurring concepts can be expressed in the form of "patterns"—reusable solutions to common problems.

Pattern Languages

Patterns are described in a context of a problem and the associated forces at play that make the pattern approach the best choice in that situation. Patterns from a related set of problems form a vocabulary that developers can use to discuss concepts in a field; and they also form a basis for comparison of different approaches. For instance, you can describe an ORM product by referring to the patterns that it implements; similarly, you can compare two ORM products by contrasting the different pattern choices that they implement and the trade-offs they make.

The first pattern language describing object-relational mapping was published in the *Pattern Languages of Program Design*, volume 2 [Vlissides]; but for the purposes of this chapter, we will refer to a later pattern catalog covering patterns of ORM: Martin Fowler's *Patterns of Enterprise Application Architecture* [Fowler]. Fowler's patterns have the advantage of being a complete set, while at the same time being easy to understand and to identify when seen in context. Keep in mind that this chapter only introduces these patterns in the context of a survey of the features of ORM, and is not providing a complete coverage of the subject.

The Domain Model Pattern

The most fundamental of these ORM patterns is the Domain Model pattern. Every enterprise system has a context under which it operates. This context is its "domain." A domain can be characterized and modeled as a set of related objects with both behavior and data, each representing a basic concept. We discussed in Chapter 2 how these domains are often organized around various "aspects" of the IT requirements. For example, some "functional" domains are concerned with concrete real-world objects, such as the products that retail customers can buy. Other functional domains are centered around abstract objects that have no physical manifestation, such as the electronic invoices from a shipping company. There are cases in which domains focus on an aspect that is purely technical (or "nonfunctional"). For example, an application component that serves as a connector between a newly developed order entry subsystem and a legacy credit check system has a domain concerned with the interfaces expected by the two systems. Its "function" is to map the interfaces expected by the internal system to those expected by the external one, each modeled separately.

Providing connectivity such as this is the key problem of object-relational mapping in Java applications—how do you relate a domain of objects often modeled as Plain Old Java Objects (POJOs) to a domain of information modeled as tables, rows, and columns of a relational database? Making this connection is the job of a *Data Mapper*, which is a key component of the Domain Model pattern. A Data Mapper is a layer of software (not just a single class or object) that fulfills the responsibility of moving information between the domain objects and the relational database at runtime. Performing this Data Mapper function is the primary role of a persistence mechanism. From one perspective, a Data Mapper is simply a black box—you don't need to look too closely to see how it works; it should just perform its mapping without the need for significant intervention. However, understanding the details of how the Data Mapper function operates is important to both using extensions or advanced features of a particular persistence mechanism, and to comparing different ones.

For example, the simplest technique is to manually populate Java objects with information from relational queries—in effect, hard-coding the object-relational mapping in your application. The majority of systems built with 4GL tooling use this approach, and it is often the quickest solution for small or situational projects. Unfortunately, this approach is nearly always an anti-pattern for a complete enterprise system because the persistence code generated from 4GL tooling is rarely flexible enough to handle the ongoing needs of such a complex system.

Domain Modeling Best Practices

Said another way, we have seen countless projects fail due to poor domain modeling. There seems to be a common misconception that a domain model can be created by an architect and/or business analyst in an afternoon with a graphical drawing tool like Visio, and then thrown over the fence to development to be used unmodified for the remainder of the project. More often than not, these models are completely ignored by development because they do not reflect the nature of the implementation technology and are therefore difficult to map efficiently. Successful model-driven design takes good discipline, and there are some best practices that should be followed to stay on the right path, which are covered in the following sections.

Choose a Modeling Notation to Communicate the Essential Details

Have you ever had to work on a new software project with nothing to learn by except thousands, even millions, of lines of someone else's source code? If so, you have firsthand experience in dealing with the complexity of enterprise software. The only solution to handling this complexity is to abstract away the details. For example, in such a situation, you may write down the interfaces used in a particular Java package in shorthand to learn about the system. This shorthand is one example of a model. In general, a model is a representation of a complex system that abstracts away unnecessary detail so that you can more easily conceptualize the most important characteristics of the system. A city map is a model. A city map does not include the location of every street lamp or traffic signal. These unnecessary details are abstracted so only the most important information is conveyed to the map's reader.

In today's IT world, the Unified Modeling Language (UML) is often used to provide a graphical description of the domain objects and their relationships. Consider the partial domain model of an order management system illustrated in UML, as shown in Figure 3.1.

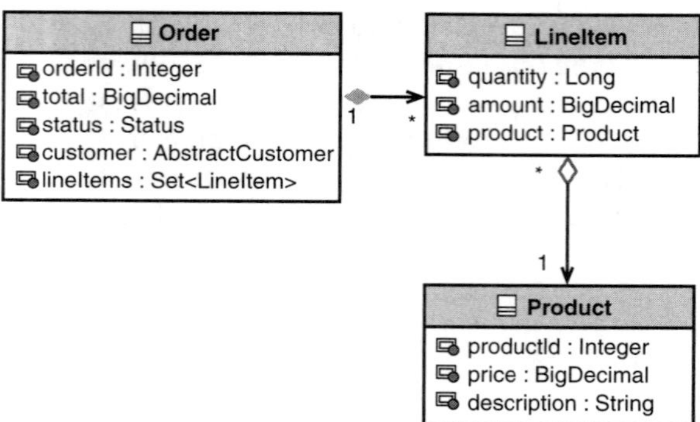

Figure 3.1 Partial domain model of an order management system.

Although this book is not intended to be a complete tutorial on UML (see [Booch] for a good reference), Figure 3.1 shows that a line item belongs to (or is "contained in") an order, and that each line item is associated with (or "refers to") a product. This domain model is an abstraction from the perspective of both a subject matter expert—such as an order packer in the warehouse—and a developer working on the software. From a packer's perspective, the domain model does not include countless details, such as the construction techniques used in the warehouse or the color of the walls. These details are not usually important to a packer in general, so they are omitted from most domain models. Conversely, from a developer's perspective, the domain model does not include countless details about the software implementation, such as code frameworks used or user interface constructs. These implementation details are subject to change and add little value to the domain model.

Figure 3.2 illustrates the nature of the abstraction that occurs when designing a domain model. A domain model lives at the intersection of the domain knowledge of subject matter experts and the implementation knowledge of the development team. In fact, a good domain model becomes a common language for communication. Throughout the lifetime of an enterprise application, all parties involved should use the objects described in the domain model as a language to talk about the project. When a project stakeholder encounters a circumstance where this common language is insufficient or limiting, this is a sure sign that the domain model should be modified to create a deeper, richer model to reflect the needs of the stakeholders in communicating about the application. This approach of keeping a domain model in sync with the application's implementation throughout its lifetime is often referred to as *model-driven design*.

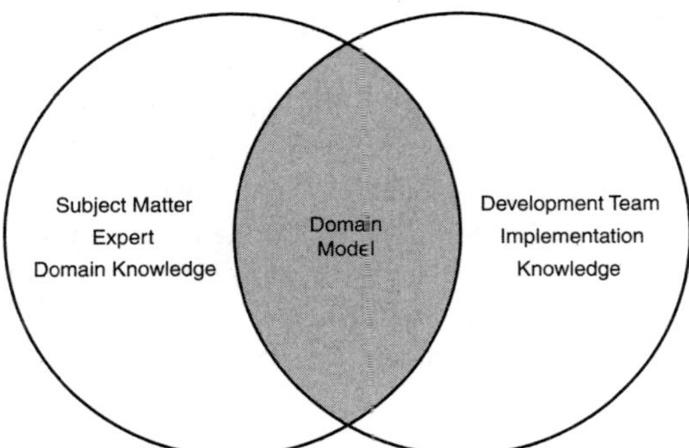

Figure 3.2 Intersection of knowledge that becomes a domain model.

Involve Project Stakeholders in Creating and Modifying the Domain Model

A common anti-pattern is for an architect to create a domain model without consulting anyone outside of the development team. Subject matter experts and end users should be given equal responsibility for the design of a domain model in comparison to the development team. For example, if a new requirement presents itself to track the status of orders that are submitted until they are shipped, the packer should be involved in the modification of the domain model to ensure that it reflects their understanding of this new application function. If this is not done, the domain model can cease to be intuitive to the system's subject matter experts, and it does not provide a common vocabulary. Worse, it is likely that requirements will be communicated incorrectly to the development team.

A Domain Model Is Not a Design Model

We have encountered organizations that attempt to model every single class and interface in their application code to facilitate communication with the development team about the design. This design-specific view is not an effective way to model enterprise applications. Remember that a functional domain model is first and foremost an abstraction to facilitate communication about what the system needs to do. Imagine trying to use a UML class diagram that includes design patterns such as the session facade and helper class, as described by Brown et al. in their book on J2EE design patterns [Brown], to discuss the new order tracking requirement described previously. Would that UML model be useful to the discussion? Would the names of these extra classes provide a practical common language between development and the subject matter experts? Such a diagram quickly becomes cluttered, inflexible, and too complex even for the development team to conceptualize—especially as designs change.

UML that maps directly to application design can be useful for code generation and as a tool for the development team; however, if you want to practice model-driven design, a separate simplified domain model should be maintained that is referenced and utilized by all the stakeholders of the project. Generators can be made to transform each entity and its associations from the domain model to multiple classes and associations in the design model. These kinds of generators are often referred to as *model-to-model (M2M)* transformations. Without going into too much detail, M2M transformations capture design trade-offs and can be modeled independently from the functional aspects to facilitate communication between the design and implementation teams. The generated design models can then be used to drive tools to generate the implementation code; these tools are sometimes referred to as *model-to-text (M2T)* transforms. Having the domain model drive the generation of the design model, and in turn having the design model drive the generation of the implementation, can accelerate development even further. This approach is an application of the Divide and Conquer strategy we discussed in Chapter 2. Furthermore, this process is fundamental to Model Driven Architecture (MDA) and Model Driven Development (MDD). There

are many aspects to consider with MDA and MDD that are beyond the scope of this book. Alan Brown's article [A.3.1] and the Object Management Group's MDA website [MDA] are
A.3.1 good references on this topic for those interested in a deeper dive.

Domain Models Are Not Always Necessary

Formal domain models are not necessary for every project. The most common examples are applications that are small or use a very rigid underlying framework, such as an application that utilizes PeopleSoft or SAP packaged software. In these situations, the development team can do very well with 4GL type tooling and ad hoc development without a formal domain model. And it is worth mentioning that in the Web 2.0 space there has been an increase in these small applications, referred to as situational applications. Unfortunately, when small software projects are successful, there is a tendency to enhance them or extend their functionality. Scaling such projects is an enormous risk, and after a significant software system is built without modeling, it is often not possible to create a workable domain model for more disciplined development in the future unless the system is completely reverse engineered.

Plan for Change

Domain models should change as an application changes. If there is a requirement to change the application in a way that is difficult to represent in the domain model, that usually means the model needs to be changed—perhaps drastically. Making the effort to enhance and deepen the domain model to handle the new requirement will be well worth your time. In the long term, with subsequent releases of the application, the domain model may change so much that it is unrecognizable compared to its original incarnation. This is desirable, as long as it reflects the current requirements and truly serves as the "language of communication" between the stakeholders and the implementers.

The Value of a Common ORM Example

Of course, there are other patterns and best practices related to domain modeling, but many need to be discussed in the context of a concrete scenario for the details to be understood. And for the purposes of this book, we will use a common example as a context for illustrating more specific ORM issues and approaches in this chapter, and reuse this example to evaluate various persistence mechanisms in later chapters.

When choosing a use case, we like to pick one that has enough complexity to illustrate the major features being used in practice or compared. For example, rather than picking a simple "CRUD"-type use case to create, retrieve, update, and destroy a data simple object like a LineItem, it is better to pick some use case that accesses a number of data objects with some interesting business rules, such as processing an Order submitted by a Customer who has poor credit.

The components of a common example and the benefits of each include the following:

- **Common Domain Model and Database Schema, Constraints, and Normalization Approach**—The example should define a domain model and database schema that is strictly followed during the evaluation of the ORM. Having both domain model and database schema defined provides a well-defined set of endpoints. These endpoints ensure an apples-to-apples comparison as the ORM frameworks under evaluation are exercised with the exact same domain objects and database tables. We will use the common example developed here in the second half of this book
- **Common Service Interfaces**—It is also best to provide a clear separation of concerns by exposing an interface with a specific set of services that interact with underlying persistence mechanisms. Separating the underlying implementation from the client with well-defined interfaces illustrates how a particular ORM technology can be encapsulated and componentized. And because all the code examples for the different ORM technologies implement these services, the reader can quickly compare the programming models of the different frameworks.
- **Common Test Cases**—One of the major lessons learned from the Agile community is a discipline sometimes called "test first design." We like to repeat the phrase said by our good friend Stacy Joines in her book on performance [Joines]: "Test early and often." Specifically, after interfaces to a set of persistence services are created and agreed to, the next step is to provide a set of test cases designed to verify that the implementation meets the functional and quality of service requirements of the application (as described in Chapter 2). These test cases become the figurative "voice of the user" for the developer to use during the implementation.

Domain Model

Figure 3.3 introduces the domain model of a customer order management application that serves as a recurring example throughout this book. The intent of this example is to represent the persistence tier of an enterprise Java application. Its domain model is based on real-world object-relational systems we have consulted on across various industries. Although it is necessarily brief, Figure 3.3 provides enough of a domain model to illustrate object-relational mapping concepts throughout the balance of the book. Hereafter, it is referred to as the "common example."

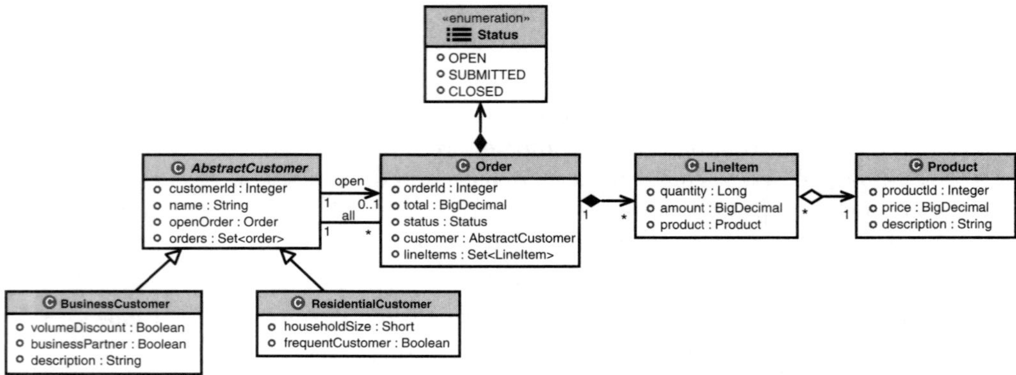

Figure 3.3 Common example domain model.

The domain model stems from a retail business that sells commodity products to end-consumers. The retailer sells to two primary customer segments: business customers and residential customers. Although its products are available to both segments, to entice business customers who tend to place more orders, the system gives special pricing and ordering policies to the business customer segment. A vital business function of the system is to take orders. Accordingly, taking orders is the primary theme for the example application—it stores orders transactionally and provides the functionality to locate and update them.

Specifically, Figure 3.4 shows Abstract Customer as an object that generalizes both business customers and residential customers using UML's generalization association denoted by the triangular shaped arrows. Notice that they are unidirectional and both point to AbstractCustomer, indicating that both residential and business customers share the attributes of AbstractCustomer. More about generalization is discussed in a subsequent section on inheritance.

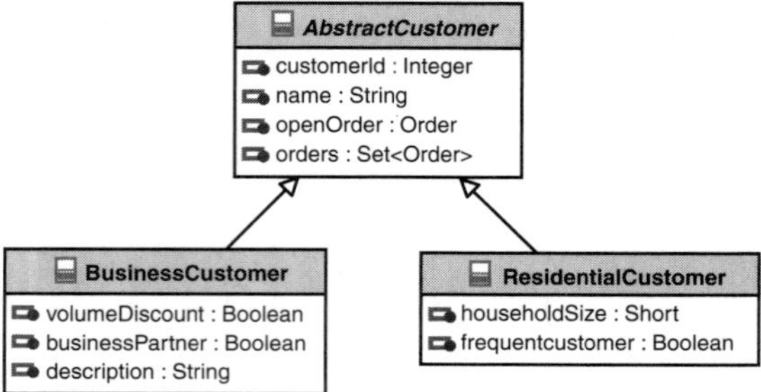

Figure 3.4 Customer inheritance hierarchy.

Figure 3.5 illustrates two different associations between Customer and Order, which is a bit more interesting. Notice that a Customer has a Set of Orders. This Set contains all the Orders in the system for the Customer. It may include Orders in any state (`OPEN`, `SUBMITTED`, or `CLOSED`). Correspondingly, an order within this Set can access its respective Customer by referencing its `customer : AbstractCustomer` attribute. This association between a customer and its orders is denoted by the solid line labeled "all." The customer uses this relationship to access all its orders. It is a UML bidirectional association—both a Customer and an Order can traverse the relationship.

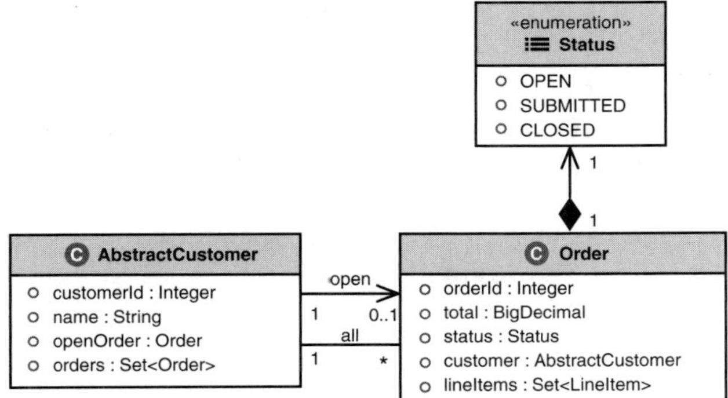

Figure 3.5 Relationship between Customer and Order.

The second relationship, labeled as "open," signifies a customer's reference to an open Order. The Customer accesses its open Order by utilizing the `openOrder : Order` attribute. The cardinality is specified as `0..1` for Order in this association, indicating that it is optional for a Customer to have an associated open Order. The openOrder association is unidirectional and is navigated only through the Customer object. This limitation is reasonable because navigation from Order to Customer is possible through the first relationship.

The reason for modeling the two separate relationships is to help enforce constraints and optimize the access. For example, a web page might always show the customer data and any open order; however, the Set of all Orders might be accessed only by using a history page.

It is a good practice to specify relationships as strictly as possible in domain modeling. We've seen UML diagrams drawn using bidirectional relationships without cardinality, composition, or aggregation, which leaves a lot open to interpretation. Loosely defined domain models often lead to miscommunication and increased implementation complexity. Of course, in practice, having a strictly defined domain model is not always possible—especially if you change your domain model often (as should be the case).

Key Point

Strive to design a domain model with associations and types that are defined as precisely as possible.

The order `status : Status` attribute could easily be modeled as a `String`; however, this would not provide information about the expected values. To define the domain model as precisely as possible, we employed an enumeration with the possible values of `OPEN`, `SUBMITTED`, or `CLOSED`. The model uses the UML notation with a solid diamond referred to as a composition association. The use of composition implies that the Status enumeration is in fact part of the Order, and that the status has no existence outside of the Order. Naturally, because the enumeration belongs to a particular Order, this is a unidirectional 1:1 association.

Unidirectional associations should be used wherever possible to reduce the coupling of the associated types in object systems.

As shown in Figure 3.6, an Order has a Set of LineItem objects representing the products being ordered by the customer. This is again using a UML composition association as all the LineItems are in fact part of or belong to the Order. In object-oriented programming terms, this means that only that particular Order can hold a reference to its LineItem objects. The association is unidirectional and thus can be navigated only through the Order can navigate it. A LineItem has no explicit reference back to its owning Order.

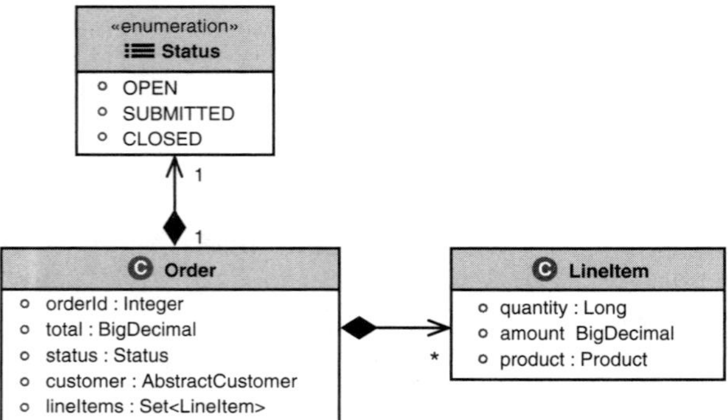

Figure 3.6 Relationship between Order and LineItem.

Figure 3.7 illustrates a new directional association called an *aggregation*—denoted by the hollow diamond. This means that the LineItem is made up of a Product similar to a composition relationship (the solid diamond). The difference from a composition is that the LineItem does not claim ownership over the Product. Should a LineItem be removed from the domain model, the Product remains as it is used independent of the LineItem. Considering that it is a directional association, a LineItem can navigate the aggregation to access its respective Product; however, a Product has no reference to any LineItem instances.

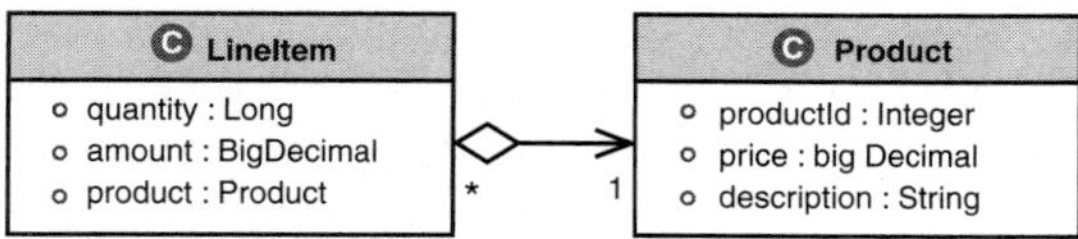

Figure 3.7 Relationship between LineItem and Product.

Database Schema

This section describes the database schema for the common example. As with most enterprise applications, the relational entities used at the database schema layer fundamentally differ from the domain objects used in the domain model.

Figure 3.8 shows an entity-relationship (E-R) diagram that models the database schema for the common example. The data types shown (`SMALLINT`, `VARCHAR`, and so forth) correspond to those supported by Apache Derby. See Appendix A, "Setting Up the Common Example," for more information on Apache Derby and a tutorial detailing how to set up Apache Derby with this database schema.

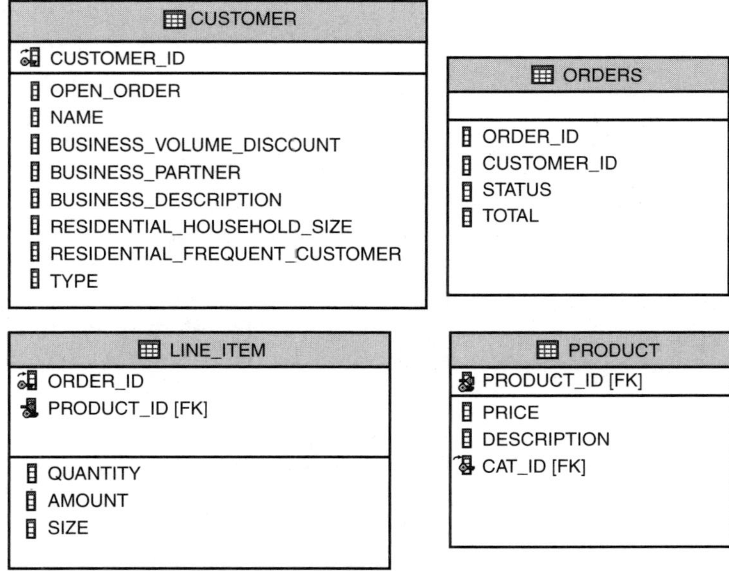

Figure 3.8 Common example entity-relationship diagram.

Although the best of all possible worlds (from both an object and a database modeling perspective) is to have the domain model and the database schema be very closely aligned, this is usually not the case in the real world. Most applications are not "greenfield" ones that allow the designers of the object model and the database schema to start from scratch. It is more common that new applications are built atop existing database schemas. Often these schemas were built from a different viewpoint, with a different domain model. In addition, database design takes factors such as physical storage, servicing multiple applications, and other design-specific issues into account. This difference leads to the necessity of meet-in-the-middle mapping. Meet-in-the-middle object-relational mapping is required to use this database schema while keeping the domain model intact. This topic is covered in detail in the section "Object-Relational Mapping."

The most glaring difference in the E-R diagram compared to the domain model is how the customer information is consolidated into one table. You probably also noticed that there are fewer entities than there were objects in the domain model; for example, there is no direct representation of ProductDirectory or AbstractCustomer. Some more subtle differences are that the LINE_ITEM table has an additional ORDER_ID field referencing its ORDER, the enumeration has been flattened to a `VARCHAR` data type, and all Boolean attributes are represented as single characters denoted by `CHAR(1)`.

The causes and implications of these mismatches are explored in the section titled "The Object-Relational Mapping Impedance Mismatch Revisited." For instance, the superclass inheritance mapping strategy necessary to map the CUSTOMER table to the three Customer objects in our domain model is covered in detail later.

Database Constraints

Utilizing database constraints such as relational constraints, check constraints, and in some cases database triggers, has long been known as a best practice to maintain data integrity [Ramakrishnan]. Although rarely achievable, it should be the goal of a database administrator to configure a database schema such that its data cannot be in an incorrect state. With the help of database check constraints, we have provided some modest protection against data corruption. Check constraint 2 in Figure 3.8 enforces `CHAR(1)` data type fields (representing Booleans in our domain model) to accept only "Y" and "N." For instance, an "A" character should not be inserted into the BUSINESS_VOLUME_DISCOUNT field. Without such constraints, an application can easily insert invalid data into the database—perhaps inadvertently.

All table fields in the schema employ `NOT NULL` constraints except those in the CUSTOMER table. This is because the CUSTOMER table is sparse—meaning it is acceptable for some fields to be `NULL`. The other check constraint on the CUSTOMER table shown in Figure 3.8, check constraint 1, ensures that fields in the CUSTOMER table are inserted or updated to `NULL` appropriately. For example, when a business customer is inserted as a row into the table, the residential fields should be `NULL` and none of the business fields should be `NULL`. The opposite applies when a residential customer is inserted.

Check constraint 3 shown in Figure 3.8 similarly enforces that the STATUS field is restricted to `OPEN`, `SUBMITTED`, or `CLOSED`. There is a copy of the DDL schema in each of the projects of the sample code. You can find instructions for downloading and setting up the example in Appendix A.

Database Normalization Approach

Database normalization emerged out of the work of the famous British database theorist Edgar Frank Codd [Codd]. It prescribes a process of reducing redundancy and anomalies in a relational database schema by following five normal forms (NF). In practice, only the first three normal forms are used. In addition, a stronger variant of the third normal form, called Boyce-Codd normal form, is popular. The fourth and fifth normal forms deal with cases of multivalued dependencies and many-to-many relationships. The customer order database schema is normalized to Boyce-Codd normal form. Before we inspect the normalization of the customer order relational entities, consider the following definitions:

- **First Normal Form (1NF)**—For a schema to be in first normal form, database fields must hold an atomic value, or primitive type, and tables must have a primary key. First normal form prevents redundant rows. It also makes a row identifiable by the primary key.
- **Second Normal Form (2NF)**—A schema is in second normal form if and only if it is in 1NF and all fields are dependent on *all* the primary key fields such that this dependency cannot be reduced.
- **Third Normal Form (3NF)**—Third normal form adds the requirement to 2NF that all nonkey fields are dependent on candidate keys alone and not on any nonkey fields. 3NF was famously described by [Kent] this way: "The relation is based on the key, the whole key, and nothing but the key."
  Note: A candidate key is a type that could serve as an alternate key for the database entity.
- **Boyce-Codd normal form (BCNF)**—Boyce-Codd normal form is a stronger variation of 3NF. A schema is in BCNF if and only if it is in 3NF and the only determinants are the candidate keys. That is, only a key can have a relationship with a nonkey field such that it determines its value.

This is a necessarily brief summary of normal forms; 5NF and 6NF are occasionally used and several other variants exist. For a more complete and detailed introduction to database normalization, see [Date].

The customer order schema is so simple that it is almost intuitively normalized. For instance, most of the tables have a single key for which dependent fields follow naturally. However, it is not very difficult to breach normalization even with such a simple schema. Many database systems allow for a table to be created without a primary key, which breaches 1NF. Organizations often do this in search of performance gains. We strongly discourage this approach because it opens the door to all sorts of data corruption. The difference in performance is often negligible for modern database systems, and there is almost always a better way to improve performance, such as creating indexes, reduction of network latency, or batch processing.

As an example of an entity that breaches 2NF, consider Figure 3.9. Notice that the LINE_ITEM table has a new SIZE field that specifies the size of the purchased product. This may seem like a natural place for it because the size is selected by the end user when the LineItem Object is created for their Order. However, if you look closely, the SIZE field really only depends on PRODUCT_ID and not ORDER_ID (assuming that there is a different PRODUCT_ID for each product size). This breaches 2NF because SIZE is not dependent on the entire key. To remedy this, the SIZE field should be moved to the Product table.

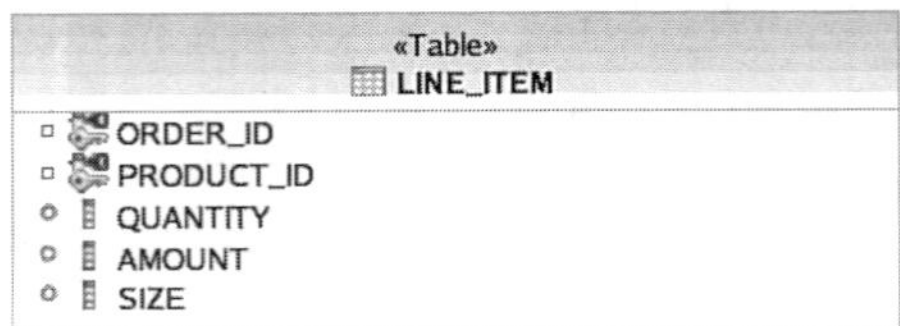

Figure 3.9 LineItem entity with additional SIZE field.

Consider Figure 3.10, which illustrates a modified version of the Customer entity where the NAME field has been expanded to two different fields—RESIDENT_NAME and BUSINESS_NAME. This breaches 3NF and BCNF because the primary key, CUSTOMER_ID, is not a sole determinant of the BUSINESS_VOLUME_DISCOUNT, BUSINESS_PARTNER, and BUSINESS_DESCRIPTION fields. The fields are also determined by the BUSINESS_NAME field, assuming that all business names are unique. To achieve normalization in this situation, the business fields should be separated into their own table with BUSINESS_NAME as the primary key. Notice that this is not the case for the residential fields because residential customers may share the same name. Thus, the residential fields still solely depend on the CUSTOMER key.

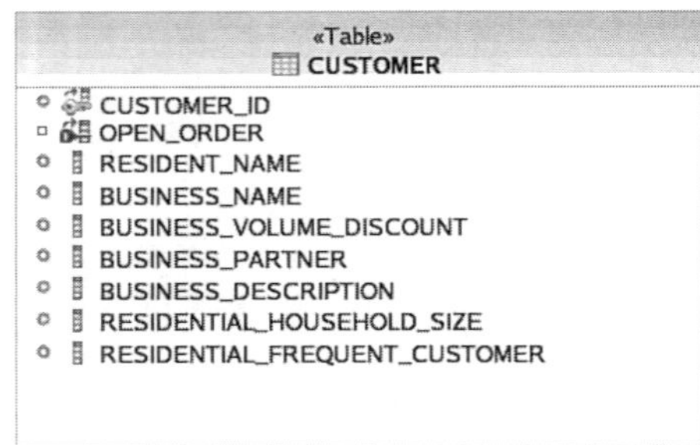

Figure 3.10 Customer entity with more specific name fields.

Service Interfaces

In addition to a database schema and domain model, the common example exposes a series of services from its persistence layer. These services serve as an interface decoupling the persistence tier of the system from presentation and business logic.

Figure 3.11 illustrates the three tiers of well-architected enterprise applications. The purpose of the common example is to showcase an example of a persistence tier that implements the persistence interface. This interface completely abstracts the object-relational technology used, as well as the datastore. Should the business tier of another application need to use the objects from the domain model of the common example, it can do so by using this interface. Thus, the business tier can change without affecting the persistence tier. This is also the case for the interface between the persistence tier and the business tier. If a different user interface is needed, the change can be made without affecting the business tier as long as the interface between the two tiers is honored.

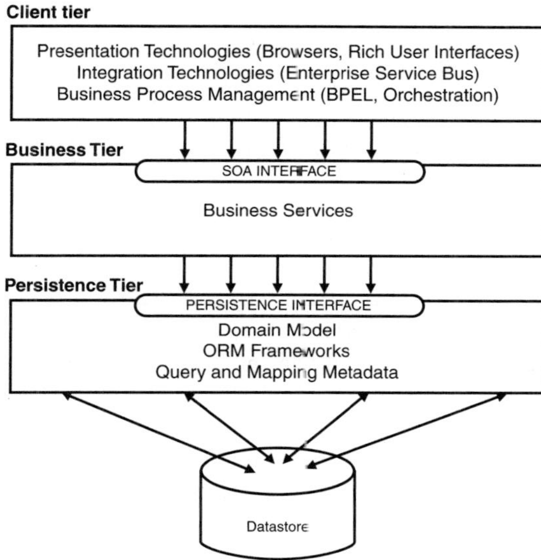

Figure 3.11 Enterprise application tiers.

Listing 3.1 shows an interface exposing five operations from the persistence tier of the common example: `openOrder()`, `addLineItem()`, `removeLineItem()`, `submit()`, and `loadCustomer()`. This is of course only a subset of what is needed for the persistence tier; however, it is suitable for our common example.

Listing 3.1 Java Interface for Common Example

```
public interface CustomerOrderServices {

public Order openOrder(int customerId)
throws CustomerDoesNotExist,
       OrderAlreadyOpen,
       GeneralPersistenceException;

public LineItem addLineItem(int customerId,
                            int productId,
                            long quantity)
```

```
throws CustomerDoesNotExist,
       OrderNotOpen,
       ProductDoesNotExist,
       GeneralPersistenceException;

public void removeLineItem(int customerId,int productId )
throws CustomerDoesNotExistException,
       OrderNotOpenException,
       ProductDoesNotExistException,
       NoLineItemsException,
       GeneralPersistenceException;

public void submit(int orderId)
throws CustomerDoesNotExist, OrderNotOpen, NoLineItems,
       GeneralPersistenceException;

public Customer loadCustomer(int customerId)
throws CustomerDoesNotExist,
       GeneralPersistenceException;

}
```

Figure 3.12 illustrates the usage pattern for three operations of the service. A new Order is created for a given Customer with the `openOrder()` operation. LineItems are added to that Order with the `addLineItem()` operation (`removeLineItem` is similar to `addLineItem`). Then, the Order can be submitted using the `submit()` operation. The `submit()` operation throws an error if there is an attempt to submit an Order without LineItems.

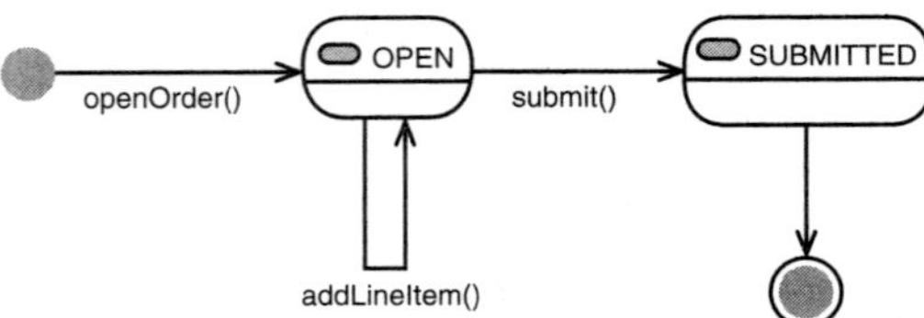

Figure 3.12 State diagram of Order object.

The `loadCustomer()` operation (omitted from the state diagram in Figure 3.12) is used to load the Customer in its current state. For example, if the Customer has an open Order, then it will load that Order as well as any LineItem objects associated with that Order.

Unit Test Cases

Some people like to wait until after the code is completed to begin writing test cases. Some write them in parallel with the code under test, after the interfaces are defined. But because there is no standardized declarative language for describing the formal semantics of a service operation's business logic, we consider test cases an important part of understanding the requirements of an application.

These detailed requirements include the domain model and database schema, which provide fixed reference endpoints for the data used by the application's business logic. The service interfaces provide a fixed reference point for access to the business logic from Java, but by themselves do not describe what each service operation is intended to do. Test cases provide an "operational" semantics that can be verified at runtime to ensure that the code behaves in the required manner.

For the purposes of illustration, we provide one "JUnit" style test case for the `CustomerOrderServices`, with one or more methods used to test each operation.

JUnit is a unit testing framework for the Java programming language. Created by Kent Beck and Erich Gamma, JUnit is one of, and arguably the most successful of, the xUnit family of frameworks that originated with Kent Beck's SUnit. JUnit has spawned its own ecosystem of JUnit extensions. "Junit" is also used as a synonym for "unit tests," as in, "Did you run the junits before you checked in?"

Experience gained with JUnit has been important in the development of test-driven development, and as a result, some knowledge of JUnit is often presumed in discussions of test-driven development, for example in the book by [Beck].

One extension of JUnit is DbUnit. DbUnit is targeted for database-driven projects that, among other things, put your database into a known state between test runs. This is an excellent way to avoid the myriad of problems that can occur when one test case corrupts the database and causes subsequent tests to fail or exacerbate the damage. DbUnit is an open-source framework created by Manuel Laflamme.

DbUnit has the capability to export and import your database data to and from XML datasets. Since version 2.0, DbUnit can work with very large datasets when used in streaming mode. DbUnit can also help you verify that your database data matches the expected set of values.

See Listing 3.2 for the high-level structure of the `CustomerOrderServicesTest` object—a subclass of the DbUnit class `DBTestCase`. We include just enough in the following listings to show the essential details of testing an object service that accesses persistent data; the Download site will include the full code example, and Appendix A describes how to run the test case for each of the five persistence mechanisms under test.

Listing 3.2 High-Level Structure of `CustomerOrderServicesTest`

```
public class CustomerOrderServicesTest extends DBTestCase {

    private CustomerOrderServices customerOrderServices;
    private int customerId = 2;
    private int businessCustomerId = 3;

    public CustomerOrderServicesTest(String name)
    {
        super(name);
        System.setProperty(
            PropertiesBasedJdbcDatabaseTester.DBUNIT_DRIVER_CLASS,
            "org.apache.derby.jdbc.ClientDriver"
```

```
        );
        System.setProperty(
            PropertiesBasedJdbcDatabaseTester.DBUNIT_CONNECTION_URL,
            "jdbc:derby://localhost:1527/PWTE"
        );
        System.setProperty(
            PropertiesBasedJdbcDatabaseTester.DBUNIT_SCHEMA, "APP"
        );
    }
    public void setUp() throws Exception { ... }
    public void testLoadCustomer() { ... }
    public void testLoadCustomerFail() { ... }
    public void testOpenOrder() { ... }
    public void testAddLineItem() { ... }
    public void testSubmit() { ... }
    public void testRemoveLineItem() { ... }
}
```

Listing 3.2 shows the use of a constructor to set properties needed by a setup method to connect to a Java SE environment and invoke database tests within DbUnit. The setup method is called by the JUnit environment during execution to initialize the test environment and instantiate the service being tested.

Listing 3.3 shows the details of getting the `CustomerOrderServices` instance under test using an `InitialContext`. But depending on the framework you use, such as that within Spring or EJB 3, you can annotate the code to have the same effect.

Listing 3.3 Test Case Setup Method

```
public void setUp() throws Exception {
    super.setUp();
    InitialContext ctx = new InitialContext();
    try {
        customerOrderServices = (CustomerOrderServices)
            ctx.lookup("java:comp/env/ejb/CustomerOrderService");
    }
    catch(Throwable e)
    {
       //Code to handle exception
    }
    if(customerOrderServices == null)
    {
        System.out.println("Java SE Version...");
        customerOrderServices = new CustomerOrderServicesJavaSEImpl();
    }
```

The JUnit framework is then configured to run the test case methods to exercise the services and make certain assertions about the expected behaviors. We show one such method implementation in Listing 3.4. See the Wiki for the remainder of the test case method implementations.

Listing 3.4 Load Customer Test Case

```
public void testLoadCustomer() {
    AbstractCustomer customer;
    try {
        customer = customerOrderServices.loadCustomer(customerId);
        assertNotNull(customer);
        assertEquals(customerId,customer.getCustomerId() );
        assertNull(customer.getOpenOrder());
        customerOrderServices.openOrder(customerId);
        customer = customerOrderServices.loadCustomer(customerId);
        assertNotNull(customer.getOpenOrder());
        customerOrderServices.addLineItem(customerId, 1, 1);
        customer = customerOrderServices.loadCustomer(customerId);
        assertNotNull(customer.getOpenOrder());
        assertNotNull(customer.getOpenOrder().getLineitems());
        assertTrue(customer.getOpenOrder().getLineitems().size() > 0);
        customerOrderServices.submit(customerId);
        customer = customerOrderServices.loadCustomer(customerId);
        assertNull(customer.getOpenOrder());

        //Inherit Test
        assertTrue(customer instanceof ResidentialCustomer );
        customer = customerOrderServices.loadCustomer(
            businessCustomerId
        );
        assertTrue(customer instanceof BusinessCustomer);

    }
    catch (CustomerDoesNotExistException e) {
        e.printStackTrace();
        fail("Customer Does Not Exist");
    }
    catch (GeneralPersistenceException e) { ... }
    catch (OrderAlreadyOpenException e) { ... }
    catch (OrderNotOpenException e) { ... }
    catch (ProductDoesNotExistException e) { ... }
    catch (InvalidQuantityException e) { ... }
    catch (NoLineItemsException e) { ... }
}
```

The code in Listing 3.4 shows how the `loadCustomer()` method is called with the expectations (assertions) that

- A customer object was found during the lookup with no exceptions
- The customer ID matched the expected one
- Initially, there is no open order associated with the customer
- An order was opened by the customer with no exceptions
- A second lookup caused no exceptions and found both the customer and an associated open order
- A line item was added to the open order with no exceptions
- A third lookup caused no exceptions and found the customer, an associated open order, and a line item

- The open order associated with the customer was then submitted
- A third lookup caused no exceptions and found the customer without an open order
- A test of the customer found it to be an instance of a residential customer
- A test of a customer loaded using a different ID found it to be an instance of a business customer

Pay special attention to the "catch blocks" for specific exceptions shown in Listing 3.4. Because none of these possible exceptions is expected during this "happy path" test, the processing is similar to that shown for the `CustomerDoesNotExistException` catch block: The stack trace is logged and the test case is declared to have failed. The existence of failure branches implies that to be truly robust, separate test cases should be written to ensure that each expected error condition that could come up is tested and that the proper exception is thrown. We provide only one "error path" test case in the example.

The Object-Relational Mapping Impedance Mismatch Revisited

Given at least two fixed endpoints and an "operational" definition of the method semantics embodied in assertions that can be made about results of invoking the code under test, we are ready to delve deeper into the patterns used to bridge the ORM gap when writing the actual business logic.

As shown in Figure 3.13, the persistence tier of an enterprise application actually maintains two separate, but tightly coupled, models—an object-oriented domain model and a relational model. The fundamental representation of these models is different because they have emerged from different paradigms. The difficulties encountered while trying to map these disparate models is often referred to as the object-relational mapping impedance mismatch. This term originates from electrical engineering systems analysis and is defined as the inability of one system to provide direct input to another.

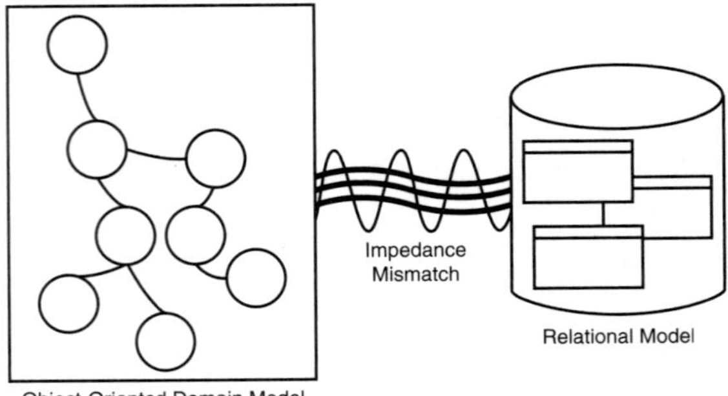

Figure 3.13 Impedance mismatch in object-relational mapping.

Understanding the nature and implications of this mismatch is important when designing the persistence tier of an enterprise application. Certain characteristics of a domain model can drastically increase the complexity of object-relational mapping. This section explores how fundamental object-oriented principles such as inheritance and encapsulation in the domain model affect the mapping process to a relational database schema.

The purpose of this section is to expose the complexity of object-relational mapping and show how beneficial it is to use a framework to handle these problems. Otherwise, the application itself must be designed and maintained to tackle some very nontrivial functionality—especially as it grows—with little quantifiable benefit from a business perspective for all that work on the persistence tier.

Association

Object association is a relationship between two objects such that at least one of the two objects can navigate to the other. We have already seen various associations in the common example's domain model. Domain model associations have a cardinality such as 1:N, 1:1, and the like to indicate whether the relationship is mandatory or optional, or supports multiple object instances. These associations can also be unidirectional or bidirectional.

There also can be more than one association between objects, as shown in Figure 3.14. Associations are naturally modeled in a relational database using foreign key constraints.

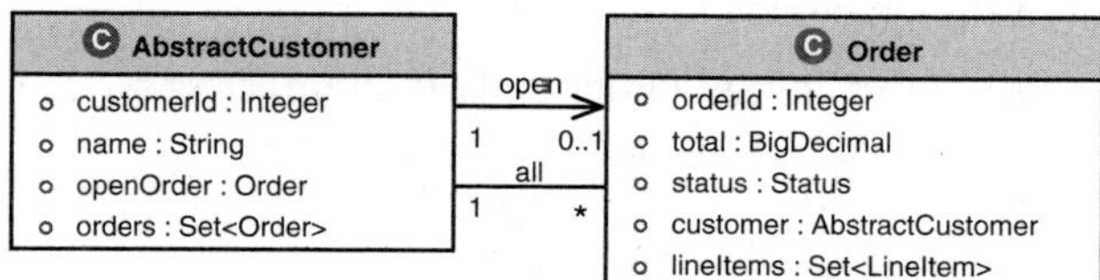

Figure 3.14 Associations between AbstractCustomer and Order.

As shown in Figure 3.15, CUSTOMER has a foreign key constraint associated with ORDER and vice versa. It is clear that CUSTOMER and ORDER have a relationship; however, a lot of information is lost. Modeling the direction of associations is problematic in the database schema when it comes to 1:N cardinality. Shown earlier in Figure 3.3, the domain model, the association labeled as "all" is 1:N and bidirectional. However, in the relational model there is no way to model a field on the CUSTOMER that represents a collection of ORDER data. Instead, ORDER has a foreign key field pointing to CUSTOMER. Starting from the CUSTOMER entity and no prior knowledge, there is no way to determine this relationship.

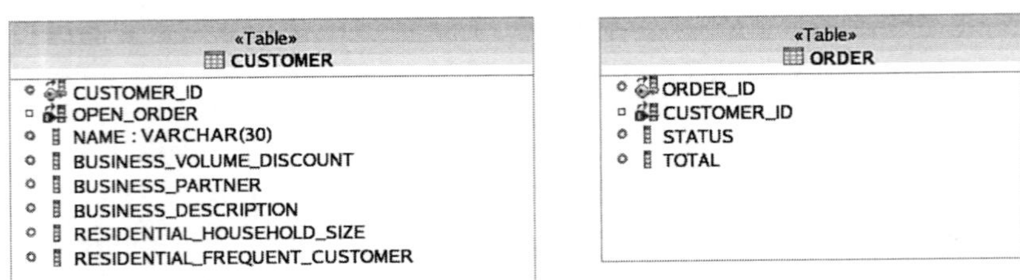

Figure 3.15 Customer and Order in a relational model.

In fact, the association in a relational schema is not completely modeled by just the foreign key constraint—the joins that traverse these foreign keys are needed to define the association. Thus, the static model is not the complete abstraction. The semantics of the database are defined by the structure and the queries (which has some unpleasant implications on encapsulation and thus protection of the semantics is not possible, which is a later topic).

In a database schema, bidirectional 1:N associations cannot be modeled. Only directional cardinality is possible where the entity with the "1" side of the cardinality has a foreign key for the entity corresponding to the "N" side of the cardinality.

This impedance mismatch also occurs if the domain model contains a 1:N directional association where the association is initiated from the single side to the many side of the cardinality.

Our domain model includes such an association between Order and LineItem, as shown in Figure 3.16. Only the Order should have knowledge of this association because the association originates from its side. However, in the relational model an ORDER_ID foreign key field must be contained in LINE_ITEM. It is as if the direction of the relationship is in the exact opposite direction in the relational model.

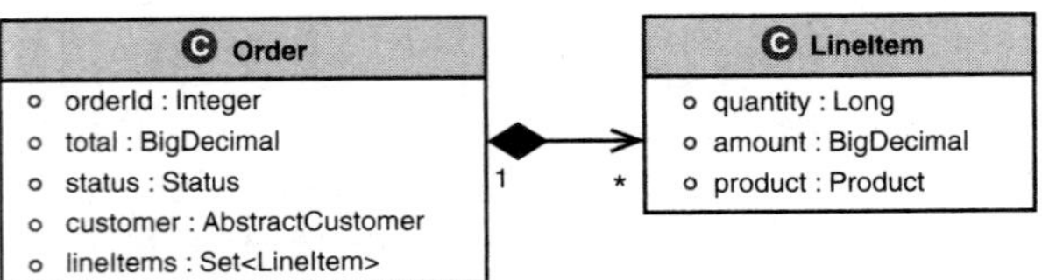

Figure 3.16 Order LineItem directional association.

> **Key Point**
>
> Bidirectional and unidirectional 1:N associations are explicitly modeled in an object-oriented domain model, but are implicitly modeled as unidirectional relationships in the relational model originating from the "N" side of the cardinality. [Fowler] refers to this approach of linking the two models together using the Foreign Key Mapping pattern.

Notice in Figure 3.17 how the ORDER contains no information suggesting that there is a relationship with LINE_ITEM. The Order object in the domain model on the other hand has a reference to a Collection of LineItem objects. The ramification of this mismatch in relationship modeling is significant. Because a relational model can explicitly model only a particular kind of unidirectional relationship, mapping to associations cannot be done automatically. This makes creation of a domain model from a database schema difficult. Metadata, often in the form of comments, must be provided by a developer or database administrator identifying which 1:N relationships are bidirectional and which unidirectional relationships initiate from the "N" side of the cardinality.

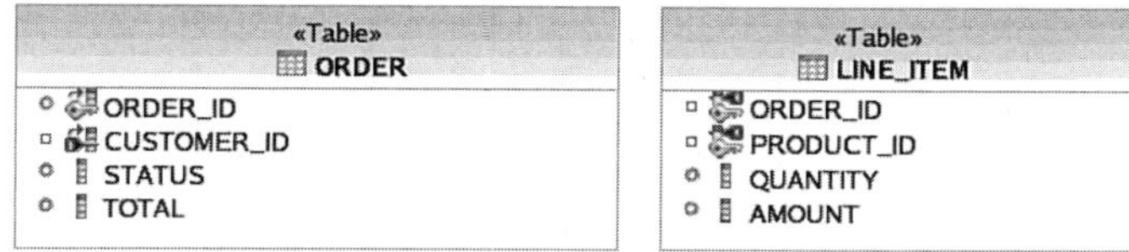

Figure 3.17 `ORDER` and `LINE_ITEM` in a relational model.

Many-to-many (M:N) relationships are modeled differently, as well. This stems from the fact that a relational entity is "flat" and cannot really contain a collection, such as the `Set<LineItem>` on Order in the domain model. Instead, an M:N relationship requires modeling a third entity, often referred to as a join table (also known as an associative table), to hold the foreign keys to the related entities. Sometimes, these join tables can be derived naturally from domain objects. For example, the LINE_ITEM in Figure 3.17 can be considered as a join table that relates ORDER and PRODUCT in a many-to-many fashion. The LINE_ITEM table becomes a convenient place to maintain any attributes unique to the relationship like QUANTITY and AMOUNT.

In many cases, however, there are no attributes associated with the relationship in the domain, so a third table needs to be explicity created during the mapping exercise. Although we did not include such an example in our domain, it is easy to imagine a case where one would be needed.

For example, assume a product can belong to different categories, while a category groups many products. Where the domain model would simply show a many-to-many relationship between Category and Product, the relational model would need to include a third table representing the association. The E-R diagram for this is shown in Figure 3.18.

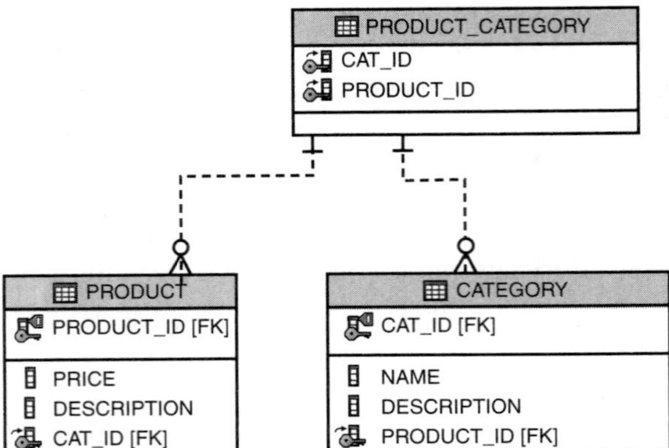

Figure 3.18 Many-to-many join table example.

[Fowler] refers to this approach as the Association Table Mapping pattern. The implicit assumption is that a three-way database join is needed to retrieve both ends of the M:N association from the join table. Navigating this relationship is therefore more costly than 1:1 or 1:N relationships, which need to perform only a single join. When and if this three-way join is performed during processing of a service operation is a significant performance consideration for ORM frameworks and is covered in more detail in the "Object Navigation" section.

Key Point

M:N associations are more costly to traverse in a database than 1:N or 1:1 associations.

M:N associations are not the only associations that require multiple-table joins; in fact, when an object in the domain model is fully populated with its data (when all its attributes are accessed by an application), a join must be performed across all associations. Again, this can have significant performance implications. Thus, when possible, refactor the domain model such that each object has associations to the least number of distinct objects. Multiple associations between the same objects do not require additional joins such as the two associations between Customer and Order.

Key Point

It is a best practice to minimize the number of associations an object has.

One way to minimize associations is to create a separate domain model for each state in the lifecycle of an object, such as shown previously in Figure 3.12, which models the lifecycle of an Order.

Composition

As we've already discussed during the description of the customer order domain model, composition and aggregation are more specific associations. They share all the mapping considerations of a generic association. However, a composition association implies that the associated object is to be discarded should the owner of the association be removed. In Figure 3.19, if the Order is discarded, the LineItem should be as well.

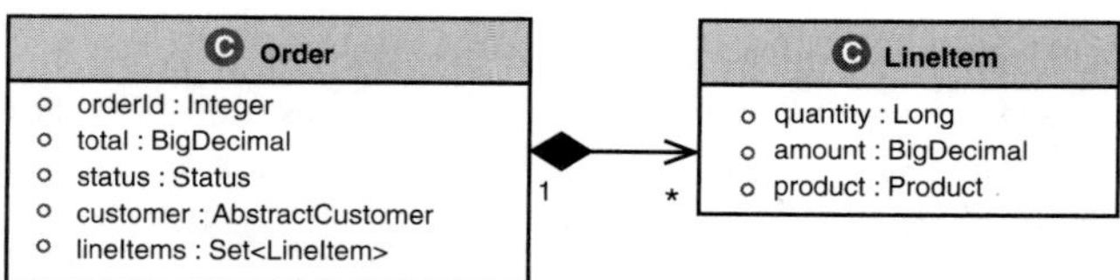

Figure 3.19 Order LineItem composition association.

This distinction is of little concern when using object-oriented languages such as Java because objects are removed from memory when there is no longer a reference to them. However, this is not the default behavior for relational databases. The database administrator often has to explicitly instruct the database to cascade the deletion of database rows across foreign key constraints. In some cases, such as in a 1:1 relationship, this is as easy as appending `DELETE CASCADE` to a foreign key DDL statement.

Unfortunately, using a cascade delete statement is not always possible. This is the case for the 1:N relationship between ORDER and LINE_ITEM shown earlier in Figure 3.17. The ORDER table has no foreign key for LINE_ITEM because of the restrictions on modeling the direction of associations that we already discussed. Instead, the composition must be enforced with a database trigger, such as the Apache Derby trigger shown in Listing 3.5.

Listing 3.5 Database Trigger Example

```
CREATE TRIGGER LINEITEM_CASCADE
AFTER DELETE ON ORDER
FOR EACH ROW
DELETE FROM LINE_ITEM WHERE ORDER_ID = OLD.ORDER_ID
```

Listing 3.5 instructs the database to delete every LINE_ITEM associated with an ORDER when that ORDER is deleted.

Key Point

A composition association often requires a database trigger to enforce data integrity at the database level.

Containment

Containment refers to the object-oriented concept of a data structure especially designed to contain objects. Examples of containers are Collections, Lists, and Sets. Relational databases support only one form of containment, which is containment of database rows within a table. The containment constructs used in object-oriented systems cannot be mapped directly to relational database systems. In fact, in some cases nothing is modeled in the relational model that corresponds to a container in the domain model.

Some containers have a very strong impedance mismatch with the structure of relational data. Collections that do not implement Set are not required to have unique members. For example, Lists with identical members cannot be modeled in a relational database unless a key is generated, which often breaches 3NF if care is not taken.

Suppose that we want to change the `Set<Orders>` attribute on Customer to `List<Orders>` (this makes little sense but we have seen stranger domain models). The ORDER table is consequently changed as shown in Figure 3.20.

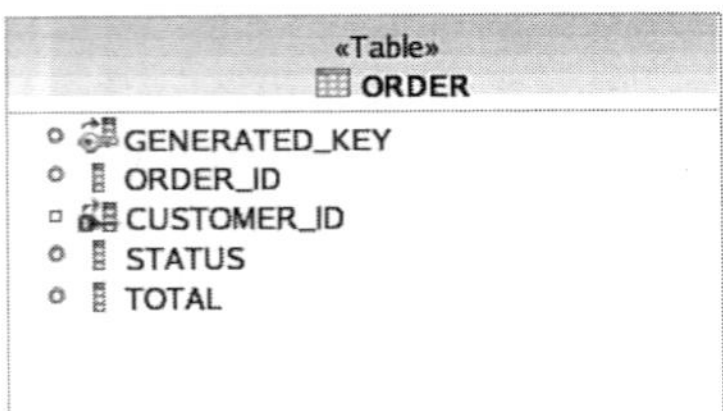

Figure 3.20 ORDER entity modified for duplicates.

The ORDER table in Figure 3.20 can now persist duplicate Order objects with the same ORDER_ID; however, it is not in 3NF. The fields are not determined solely by the primary key—GENERATED_KEY. They are also determined by the ORDER_ID field. Thus, to achieve normalization, a separate table is needed with GENERATED_KEY and ORDER_ID. This is costly because it introduces a Join to populate the Order domain object.

Encapsulation

Encapsulation is the object-oriented concept of reducing the visibility of the implementation for an object in order to provide abstraction to the user of the object. Common encapsulation techniques include utilizing access modifiers (such as `private`, `protected`, and `public` in Java), inheritance, and interfaces. We'll discuss inheritance and interfaces (as part of the section titled "Polymorphism") later. Few of these encapsulation techniques can be natively modeled in a relational schema. It should be noted that database views, privileges, and stored procedures can sometimes be useful, but even with these techniques only some object-oriented encapsulation practices can be modeled practically.

In the case of encapsulation, the fact that a relational database does not support access modifiers is not so much a concern as mapping state information from an object that has encapsulated data. If the domain model has an object that encapsulates internal state information with private, packaged, or protected access, it is difficult to persist that state information unless the object already exposes behavior to persist itself (one trick is to use reflection, but this can be restricted by the Java security manager). Often, there is no alternative course of action other than refactoring the domain model in this situation. Thus, a domain model should not include private information at all (of course, the implementation of the domain model may include private data and behavior).

One reason encapsulation is often used in object-oriented systems is to hide information and behavior that should not be reused by other systems or components. Interface constructs are very popular because they expose only needed behavior and hide unnecessary implementation detail. Databases are not well equipped to do this. In fact, it is very common for an application to share a database with various other systems putting it in a position where it has little control of the data. This can painfully limit refactoring capabilities because changing anything in the database is off-limits. It also means great care must be taken if an application caches data from a database.

Inheritance

Inheritance cannot be modeled natively in a relational database. How to map inheritance is not as straightforward as the object-oriented concepts we have surveyed so far. The three commonly used strategies for mapping inheritance are the class table, concrete table, and single table strategies. These are described in the following subsections using the common example's domain model.

Class Table Inheritance Strategy

The most intuitive inheritance strategy is to create a table per class, whether it is a superclass or subclass, as shown in Figure 3.21. [Fowler] refers to this as the Class Table Inheritance pattern. Although this makes for a database schema that maps directly to the domain model, it has considerable performance implications. Populating an object in an inheritance hierarchy usually requires a database join to load the subclass and superclass data. For example, to populate a `BusinessCustomer` object, a join must be done across both the BUSINESS_CUSTOMER table and the ABSTRACT_CUSTOMER table. The join becomes far more expensive as an inheritance hierarchy grows because more subclasses must be included.

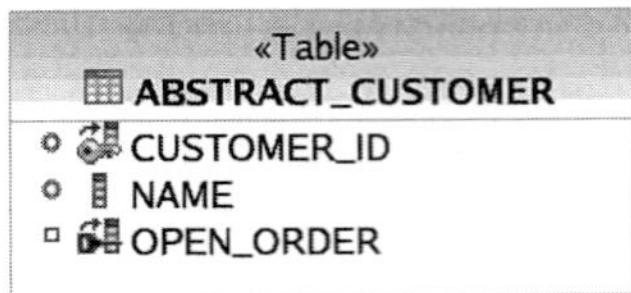

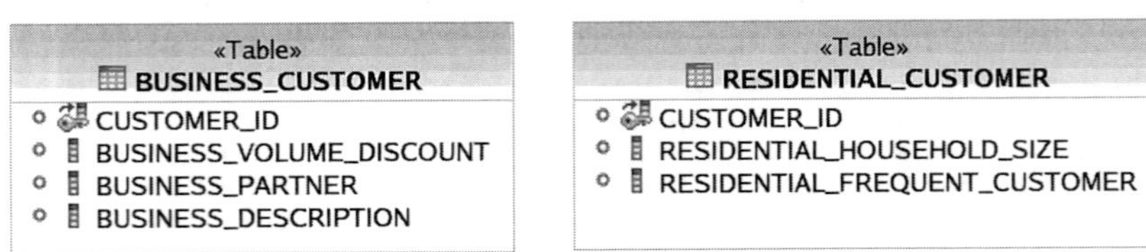

Figure 3.21 Customers modeled with class table strategy.

> **Key Point**
>
> The class table inheritance strategy works best when the domain model has a relatively flat inheritance hierarchy or when "lazy loading" of super- or subclasses can be employed.

Concrete Table Inheritance Strategy

Alternatively, the concrete table inheritance strategy represents only concrete subclass objects in the relational schema, as shown in Figure 3.22. A concrete subclass is a subclass that is not labeled as Abstract, and therefore instances can be created by using the class constructor operation ("new"). In this approach, each concrete subclass table has fields corresponding to the concrete subclasses' fields and those of all of its superclasses in the domain model. [Fowler] refers to this as the Concrete Table Inheritance pattern.

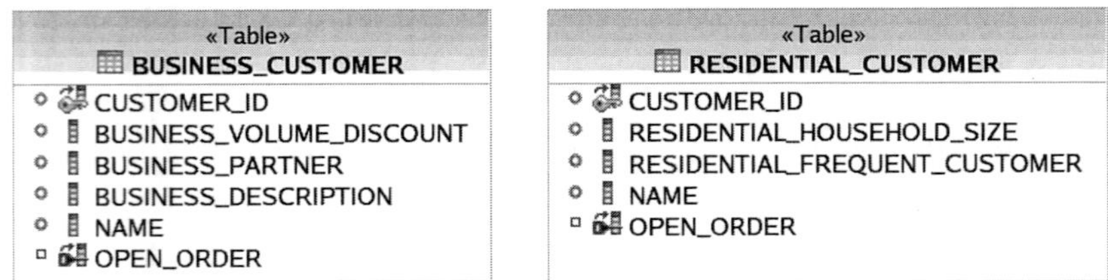

Figure 3.22 Customers modeled with the concrete table strategy.

Although this alleviates the Joins required by the class table strategy, it introduces a data integrity problem. We know from our domain model that each customer should have a unique CUSTOMER_ID; however, with this database schema, it is possible to insert the same

CUSTOMER_ID in both tables (also there are two NAME columns, and a query for all customers would become two queries—one for each table).

To prevent data corruption of CUSTOMER_ID, either a trigger must be employed for all database write operations to the customer tables or a third table must be introduced, as shown in Figure 3.23. Both options incur significant performance costs. The DISCRIMINATOR table is sparse and thus requires check constraints. As with the class table strategy, the concrete subclass strategy forces the persistence tier designer to compromise on either data integrity or performance.

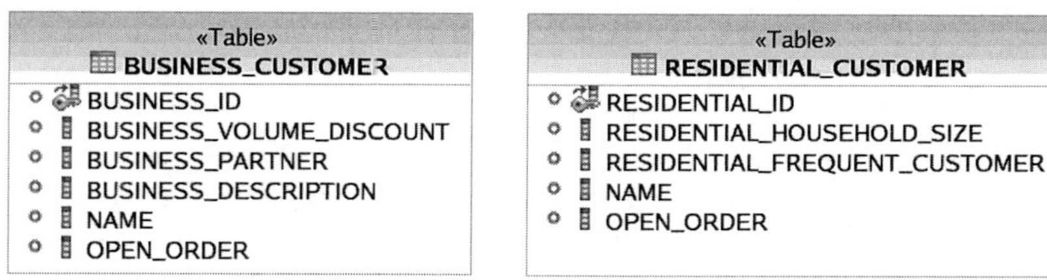

Figure 3.23 Refactored relational model for the subclass table strategy.

> **Key Point**
>
> The concrete subclass table inheritance strategy can performantly map a large inheritance hierarchy; however, this is often at the cost of relational data integrity.

Single Table Inheritance Strategy

The final inheritance strategy commonly employed to map object inheritance to a database schema is the single table strategy (which [Fowler] calls the Single Table Inheritance pattern). This is the strategy employed by the common example, as shown in Figure 3.24. As you've already seen, this creates a sparse table that requires check constraints to enforce. Sometimes a discriminator field is used to signify which subclass a row represents. It is quite rare to have an inheritance hierarchy map to a single table that is normalized. Thus, flatter inheritance structures are more workable for this strategy.

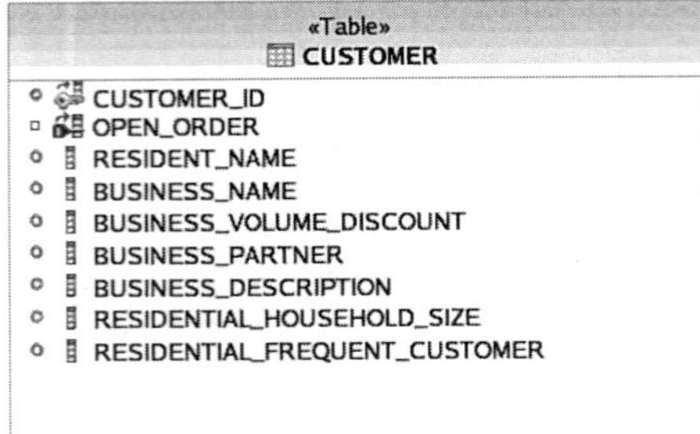

Figure 3.24 Customers modeled with the superclass inheritance strategy.

> **Key Point**
>
> The single table inheritance strategy always requires sparse table check constraints and works best for flat inheritance structures.

Polymorphism

Polymorphism is an object-oriented concept that allows for different types to expose different behavior through the same mechanism or interface. The most common use of polymorphism is to override a superclass method in a subclass. The application code invoking the method does not need to know which type is used at development time, and thus the method to be invoked is not determined until runtime (often referred to as late binding).

There is no native support for behaviors and polymorphism in relational databases; however, the domain model can exploit polymorphism of attributes as part of inheritance. For example, in Listing 3.6, the binding of the `name` attribute to the `AbstractCustomer` reference is considered polymorphic.

Listing 3.6 Example using polymorphism with object attributes

```
AbstractCustomer customer = ...;
if ( java.lang.Math.random() > 0.5 ) {
    customer = new BusinessCustomer("Persistent Enterprises Inc.");
} else {
    customer = new ResidentialCustomer("Eric Harness");
}
Order order = customer.getOpenOrder();
```

In this example, polymorphism of the `getOpenOrder` method would allow loading the open order attribute from a different table or column depending on whether the concrete subclass is a `BusinessCustomer` or a `ResidentialCustomer`, according to one of the techniques discussed in the previous "Inheritance" section, with the same trade-offs to consider.

Object Identity

The identity of an object is handled quite differently in object-oriented languages in comparison to the identity of rows in a database. Most object-oriented languages uniquely identify the instance of an object according to a memory location. Relational databases identify entities using content—relational calculus comes from set theory and thus two entries are identical if their content is identical. Primary keys are a concept on top of this. They are just the subset of attributes that model (or enforce) identity in the real world. This is fundamentally different from object identity. You already saw an example of this impedance mismatch in the "Containment" section, where we attempted to map a List to a database schema.

Our example domain model also has an object identity mismatch. Notice that the LineItem object in Figure 3.25 does not have an attribute corresponding to ORDER_ID in the database schema. This is implied because the only way to access a LineItem is to use the references in Order's `Set<LineItem>`. However, a LineItem with these attributes alone cannot be modeled in the database schema, because the PRODUCT_ID alone cannot be used as a primary key.

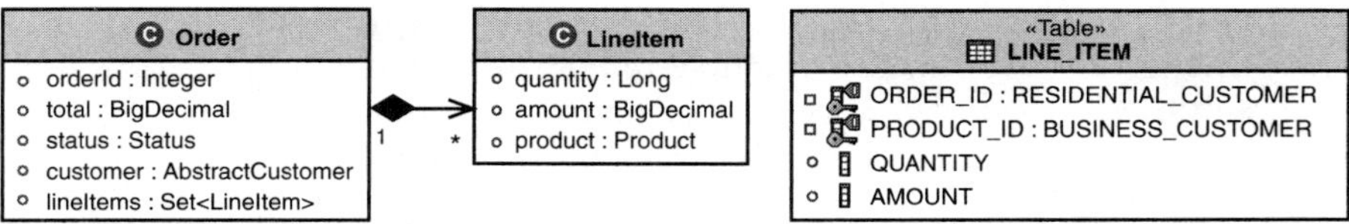

Figure 3.25 Object identity mismatch for LineItem.

This identity mismatch can happen quite frequently because it is natural to minimize the number of attributes on domain objects to keep the model as uncluttered as possible. When one is faced with such a mismatch, there are two fundamental options: either add a unique attribute to the object in the domain model, or create an artificial key on the respective table in the database schema. Most databases have the capability to define a key that is automatically generated using numerical sequences. In the common example schema, we used a combination of the orderId and productId fields to produce a unique key. This approach is discussed in [Fowler] in the Object Identity pattern.

Key Point

When an object in the domain model does not have attributes that uniquely identify the object, an artificial (or surrogate) key column is often required in the database schema.

Even if an object type naturally contains the relational key information from the database, the identity mismatch can cause other problems. For instance, if the same entity is queried twice from the database and populated into two separate object instances, the consequences are severe, including loss of updates, inherent collisions within the same transaction, and the like. These problems can be very difficult to debug in a system at runtime and serve as an excellent example of why object-relational mapping is not trivial.

Key Point

When multiple queries of the same object are performed, the queries should not populate different object instances (unless great care is taken to ensure that these different instances are used in separate transactions).

Object Navigation

There is a very strong impedance mismatch between the implementation of object navigation for an object-oriented language and how you navigate to different table rows in a database schema. Navigating a relationship in an object graph in a Java runtime is as simple as accessing a different memory location. Navigating the data in a database schema often requires joins—or even multistep database queries if the relationships are not explicitly represented. In a client/server environment, multiple queries require costly network round-trips. In Java applications, object navigation is cheap and search is costly. Conversely, in a database system navigation is costly and search can be relatively cheap.

Consider the Order to LineItem directional 1:N association in Figure 3.26. When an instance of Order is retrieved from the database, how many LINE_ITEM rows should be retrieved from the database to populate the `Set<LineItem>`? In-memory object navigation in a Java application accesses the LineItem instances via the references stored in the Set when they are needed individually. But waiting to populate each LineItem from the database with a separate query (called "lazy loading") may not be a suitable solution to iterate through the Set. An alternative approach is to fetch all possible LineItems—however, this "aggressive loading" may also be impractical because the number of rows may be extremely large compared to the available memory to the application, the database's processing resources, or the network's throughput.

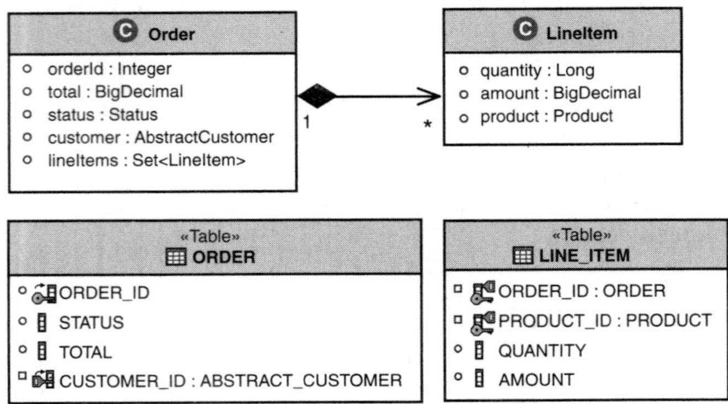

Figure 3.26 Object navigation from Order to LineItem.

In SQL programming, this problem is often solved by retrieving only the LINE_ITEM rows that are needed by the program. For example, perhaps only the LINE_ITEM rows that have an `AMOUNT > 100` are needed. This approach is often not possible for the persistence tier of an application because there is usually no way for it to know what members of the Set will be used by the business tier of the application. If it did know, the domain model could be more specific to reflect this additional constraint. In other words, Order would have a `greaterLineItems : Set<LineItem>` attribute that contains only LineItems with an amount greater than 100.

> **Key Point**
>
> Take care when an object contains collections of other objects. These relationships result in 1:N or M:N relationships in the database, which can have serious performance implications. These relationships should be as constrained as possible to limit the size of the collections that need to be instantiated in the application.

Navigation is therefore at the heart of the impedance mismatch between the object and relational domains. Object-oriented design often tries to factor out any redundancy into separate classes (that is, "One class one concept"—[Gamma]). This approach, using the techniques described in this section, leads to many small classes that get their power from collaboration. In the relational world, this need for factoring is recognized in the concept of normalization, but the cost of navigation is so costly that database design typically leads to fewer and larger tables optimized for the access patterns. ORM frameworks attempt to reconcile these different design goals by using techniques such as caching, paging, and lazy versus aggressive loading; however, these represent trade-offs that are situational, so there isn't one solution that fits all use cases. In short, it is important to be aware of these trade-offs when constructing persistence models for the object and relational domains.

Object-Relational Mapping Approaches

This section covers the three fundamental approaches to object-relational mapping to try and address these trade-offs in design goals: top-down, bottom-up, and meet-in-the-middle. These approaches center around the flexibility of the relational database and schema used. Most of the organizations we've encountered have a legacy database schema in production that cannot be modified because several critical applications still use it. In some cases, data warehousing or federation techniques can be used to, in effect, create a new production schema; however, this increases administration costs and thus total cost of ownership. Thus, for enterprise systems it is most common to see bottom-up and meet-in-the-middle techniques in use. The following sections define these different approaches and the trade-offs they entail.

Top-Down

In a top-down object-relational mapping approach, the domain model dictates the relational schema. That is, the relational schema is optimized for the domain model to minimize the impedance mismatch. This approach often entails generation of a database schema by an ORM framework. Because the schema is generated solely for the domain model and thus a single application, database integrity is often assumed to be enforced at the application level rather than the database level.

Consider Figure 3.27, which shows a possible top-down version of the common example schema. Notice that there are no foreign key constraints. This is handled by the application because it is assumed that no other application will use this database schema. Each table has artificial keys to allow different object instances with the same attributes to be persisted. This removes the necessity to have the ORDER_ID on LINE_ITEM. Although the introduction of the artificial keys breaches 3NF for CUSTOMER, ORDER, and LINE_ITEM, the fact that this database is used only by this application minimizes the ramifications.

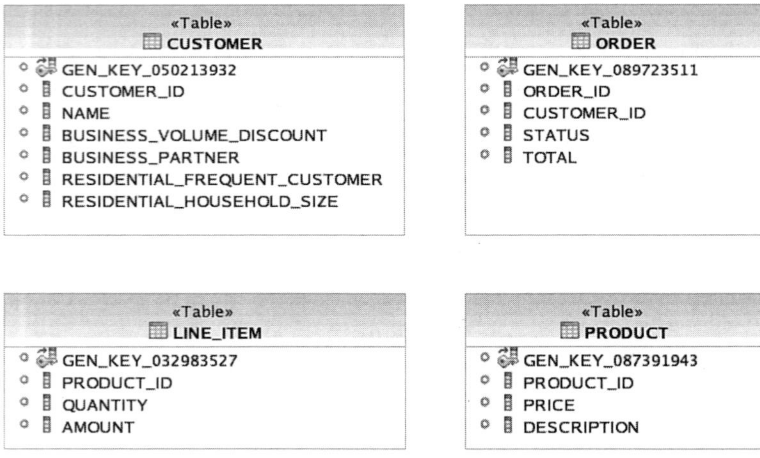

Figure 3.27 Top-down depiction of the customer order schema.

Top-down object-relational mapping is not often seen in enterprise applications that are in production. It is most suitable for applications that use an embedded database (that is, the database is packaged with the code) or in proof of concepts that are testing the functional behavior of the system rather than its performance or maintainability characteristics. In the rare situation where you find yourself building a new enterprise system with top-down schema generation in order to save development time or simplify object-relational mapping, ensure that all stakeholders for the application understand that this oversimplified top-down approach will likely make it impractical for future applications to use the same database schema.

Of course, a more complex mapping that includes primary key columns, foreign keys, and other constraints could be driven "top-down" from the domain model (possibly requiring some additional metadata), so you should carefully look at the top-down mapping features supported by the persistence mechanisms you evaluate.

Bottom-Up

A bottom-up object-relational mapping approach is the exact opposite of top-down—the domain model is optimized for the database schema. A simple pattern for object-relational mapping that applies to bottom-up mapping is the Active Record pattern [Fowler], in which all tables and domain objects have a 1-to-1 mapping. Bottom-up mapping is also closely related to the Data Access Object (DAO) pattern [Alur], in which each table has a 1-to-1 mapping to DAO transfer objects. The bottom-up approach often involves code generation as well; however, in this case domain model classes are generated from an existing database schema according to a specific set of naming conventions. This of course assumes that the domain model and implementation classes are equivalent, and it severely restricts the use of common object-oriented best practices, such as inheritance and encapsulation.

For example, as you can see in Figure 3.28, a bottom-up domain model leaves us with nothing more than containers for database rows. The objects lose their associations; object navigation is done solely through database queries. It is questionable whether this can be considered a domain model at all. Although this domain may be suitable for a simple "CRUD" application to update database rows, the rest of the application is likely to need a richer domain model that can exploit object features like inheritance and direct navigation through references.

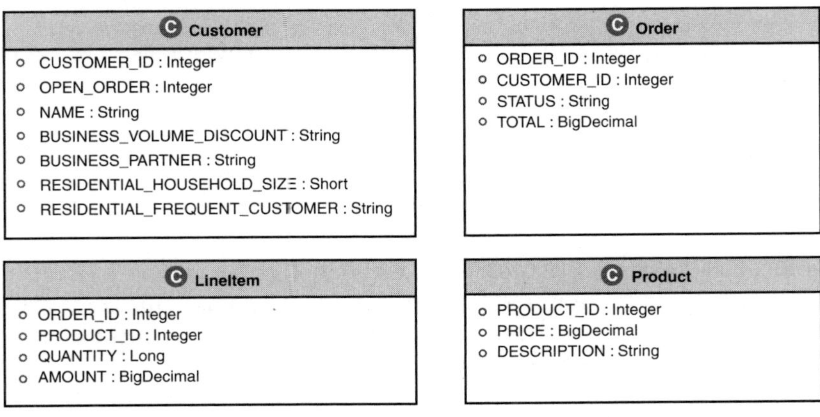

Figure 3.28 Bottom-up depiction of the customer order domain model.

Another key downside to bottom-up mapping is that it forces the use of a domain model that is rarely understandable by the application's stakeholders. Remember that the primary purpose of a domain model is as a means of communication with subject matter experts and developers alike. The table and column names are rarely user friendly and suitable as a common vocabulary. Furthermore, relational types usually are more restrictive than those associated with the domain. It almost would be better to simply teach all the stakeholders DDL!

Of course, exposing the schema directly to the end users, whether as an object diagram, E-R diagram, or DDL, is considered an anti-pattern in most cases. Exposing the schema prevents you from changes—for example, normalizing or denormalizing the tables to best meet the response time and throughput needs of the application.

Finally, consider that even for simple CRUD applications, there is still an impedance mismatch to overcome when using bottom-up mapping—at least between the database specific "data access" objects and the UI logic of the application. Bridging this gap has just been shifted to the application. Thus, the complexity that was eliminated by optimizing the "domain model" for the database schema arises within other parts of the application.

Meet-in-the-Middle

The meet-in-the-middle object-relational mapping is very much like what you would expect: The domain model is optimized for communication with the stakeholders about the application's functionality and usability, and the relational model is optimized for the reliability and efficiency with respect to persistence. The common example we explored in this chapter assumed a meet-in-the-middle approach, not only because it is the most common, but also because it illustrates the problems of mapping from either end.

There are good reasons that meet-in-the-middle object-relational mapping is the most common approach used for enterprise systems. Most businesses have used the same database schemas for years, if not decades; and at the same time, a flexible domain model is needed for applications that must be functional, usable, maintainable, and portable. Most experienced database administrators are reluctant to modify a database schema for a single application because it is likely that the schema will outlast the application. We likewise assume a meet-in-the-middle approach for the examples used in the remainder of the book.

Other Patterns to Consider

This short survey of the mechanics of object-relational mapping has shown how a number of common persistence patterns arise from resolving the object-relational impedance mismatch. There are more patterns, however, that come in handy to map between the objects in an application and the data in a relational database.

Metadata Mapping, Lazy Loading, and Unit of Work

Any framework you choose should provide support not only for the three approaches for mapping objects to relational databases and vice-versa, but also for a number of common implementation patterns that impact the maintainability and efficiency of the mapping.

Perhaps the most common pattern used in implementing persistent objects comes about when you specify additional information (often called metadata) about mapping to enable automatic generation (or interpretation) of the logic used to handle the mapping at run-time. This leads to applying the pattern from [Fowler] referred to as Metadata Mapping, and is common in most commercial and open-source OR frameworks.

Another pattern is often applied when you are traversing a number of linked Foreign-Key Mappings, or loading up a large collection of objects from an Association Table Mapping. In this case, you may find that the amount of time and memory needed to "activate" or "deserialize" the objects is quite expensive. Thus, a common optimization in this case is to apply the lazy loading pattern described in the "Object Navigation" section and obtain related objects from the database only when they are referenced. This lazy loading usually is done using an implementation of the Proxy pattern from [Gamma].

Also, when dealing with a relational database, you need to consider the issue of transactionality. Most ORM systems will implement the Unit of Work pattern to gather together database operations that should occur within the context of a single transaction.

Distributed Façade and Data Transfer Objects

The previously described patterns have been a part of ORM systems nearly since their inception. In [Fowler] another set of patterns dealing with distributed systems and "offline" processing was developed that has had an impact on more modern ORM systems, most notably in the evolution of EJBs into JPA. In particular, Fowler discusses how when you are building a distributed system using technologies like CORBA or EJBs, a common approach is to use the Distributed Façade pattern to encapsulate the interactions among a number of domain objects into a single, large-grained interface that is then published externally. The results of that interaction, and the input into a request for a service, is represented as a set of Data Transfer Objects (DTO) that are then mapped into domain objects, usually using the Data Access Object pattern from [Alur], which is a variant of Fowler's Mapper pattern. The interesting question is whether or not the additional layer of Data Access Objects and Data Transfer Objects is really needed. If a single object can both implement the Data Transfer Object pattern and be a domain object (for example, if a domain object meets all the requirements to be a DTO), then building distributed systems becomes simpler. This approach, in which a persistent domain object can become "disconnected," is an important design principle and major feature of JPA.

Summary

This chapter covered a lot of ground in showing the true complexity of the ORM problem and the demands it will place on a persistence framework. We first discussed the Domain Model pattern and modeling in general as a means for communicating the essential details of a domain, followed by some best practices for modeling that include involving the stakeholders, modeling at the right level of abstraction (or sometimes not creating a domain model at all), and planning for change.

Next we developed a common example that included a domain model and set of associated service operations and unit test cases, as well as a database schema with associated constraints and normalization approach. We used this common example to illustrate the details of the impedance mismatch between the object-oriented world and the relational world, as well as some key patterns for bridging the gap. Some key points that we covered include the following:

- Strive to design a domain model with associations and types that are defined as precisely as possible.
- Bidirectional and unidirectional 1:N associations from a domain model are implicitly modeled as unidirectional relationships in the relational model originating from the "N" side of the cardinality.
- M:N associations are more costly to traverse in a database than 1:N or 1:1 associations, so minimize the number.
- A composition association often requires a database trigger to enforce data integrity at the database level.
- The class table inheritance strategy works best when the domain model has a relatively flat inheritance hierarchy or when "lazy loading" of super- or subclasses can be employed.
- The concrete subclass table inheritance strategy can performantly map a large inheritance hierarchy; however, this performance is often at the cost of relational data integrity.
- The single table inheritance strategy works best for flat inheritance structures.
- An artificial (or surrogate) key column may be required in the database schema if the associated domain object does not have attributes that uniquely identify the object.
- When multiple queries of the same object are performed, the queries should not populate different object instances (unless great care is taken to ensure that these different instances are used in separate transactions).
- Take care when an object contains collections of other objects. These relationships result in 1:N or M:N relationships in the database, which can have serious performance implications. These relationships should be as constrained as possible to limit the size of the collections that need to be instantiated in the application.

Then we explored how applying these basic best practice patterns is impacted by which "endpoint" drives the requirements: top-down (the database schema is driven by the domain model), bottom-up (the domain model is driven by the database schema), or meet-in-the-middle (both the domain model and the database schema are fixed).

Finally, we discussed some other important patterns to consider when developing persistence services, such as Metadata Mapping, Lazy Loading, and Unit of Work, as well as Distributed Façades and Data Transfer Objects.

We will use many of these discussion points next in Chapter 4, "Evaluating Your Options," first to develop a systematic approach to evaluation of the persistence mechanisms, and then apply that approach in the remainder of the book.

 Links to developerWorks

A.3.1 *An Introduction to Model Driven Architecture*

The first of a three part series of articles by Alan Brown, this is essential reading to understand the fundamentals of Model Driven Architecture.

www-128.ibm.com/developerworks/rational/library/3100.html

References

[Alur] Alur, Deepak, et al. *Core J2EE Patterns. Best Practices and Design Strategies, 2nd Edition.* Sun MicroSystems Press 2003.

[Beck] Beck, Kent. *Test Driven Development: By Example.* Addison-Wesley Professional 2002.

[Booch] Booch, Grady et al. *Unified Modeling Language User Guide 2nd Edition.* Addison-Wesley Professional 2005.

[Brown] Brown, Kyle, et al. *Enterprise Java Programming with IBM WebSphere 1st Edition.* Pearson Education 2001.

[Codd] Codd, E. F. *The Relational Model for Database Management: Version 2.* Addison-Wesley 1990.

[Date] Date, C. J. *Introduction to Database Systems: 8th Edition.* Addison-Wesley 2004.

[Fowler]. Fowler, Martin et al. *Patterns of Enterprise Architecture.* Addison-Wesley Professional 2002.

[Gamma] Gamma, Eric et al. *Design Patterns: Elements of Reusable Object-Oriented Software.* Addison-Wesley Professional 1994.

[Joines] Joines, Stacy et al. *Performance Analysis for Java WebSites.* Addison-Wesley Professional 2002.

[Kent] Kent, William. *A Simple Guide to Five Normal Forms in Relational Database Theory.* www.bkent.net/Doc/simple5.htm

[MDA] *OMG Model Driven Architecture.* www.omg.org/mda/

[Ramakrishnan] Ramakrishnan, Raghu. *Database Management Systems.* McGraw-Hill Education Singapore 2002.

[Vlissides] Vlissides, John et al. *Pattern Languages of Program Design 2.* Addison-Wesley Professional 1996.

Chapter 4 Evaluating Your Options

Now that you have a solid understanding of the central role that persistence plays in enterprise architecture and a history of how Java persistence mechanisms and related frameworks have evolved, your next step is to decide which one to use. For purposes of this book, the options you have to consider include Java Database Connectivity (JDBC), iBATIS, Hibernate, Open Java Persistence API (JPA), and pureQuery (a Language Integrated Query for Java). Chapter 1, "A Brief History of Object-Relational Mapping" provides the background on why these five options were chosen. In a nutshell, they represent a good baseline and cross section of the approaches to ORM used by the persistence mechanisms in common use when this book went to press.

This chapter will take you through some best practices for conducting an evaluation based on an objective questionnaire that we will use as a method and template for comparison in the following chapters.

Comparing Apples to Apples

Many people might take the adage about always comparing apples to apples literally, and simply start evaluating each of these five persistence mechanisms against each other to determine which one is best. This "exhaustive" approach to comparison is shown graphically in Figure 4.1.

One problem with an exhaustive comparison is that it is relatively expensive. You would have to make 10 separate comparisons to rank the 5 mechanisms with respect to one another. If you decide to consider another persistence framework, such as SQL for Java (also called SQLJ), which has many excellent articles on how to use it [A.4.1], you would have to evaluate 5 more mechanisms for a total of 15. Consider another on top of that, such as TopLink JPA (see its website for details [Toplink]), and you have to compare 6 more for a

A.4.1

total of 21. The relative effort of the evaluation increases according to the general formula: n(n -1) / 2, where "n" is the number of mechanisms being evaluated. This formula pegs an exhaustive evaluation as an $O(n^2)$ solution—an approach to be avoided if there is any way around it.

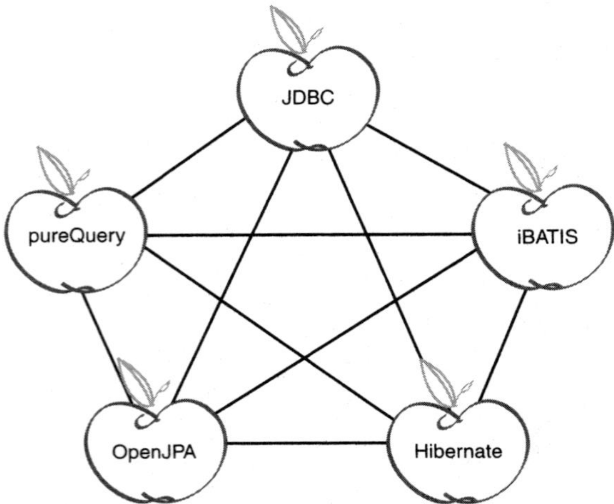

Figure 4.1 An exhaustive apples-to-apples comparison among persistence frameworks.

For those not familiar with the "O" notation, it is a formal way to describe the "order" of computational complexity, and is useful for comparing solutions (as we are doing now with respect to evaluation approaches).

Putting Good, Better, and Best into Context

But this analysis of complexity is somewhat putting the cart before the horse. Labels like "better" and "best" have meaning only within a specific context of measurement and interpretation of the resulting values. This context determines the specifics of how to compare two or more frameworks against each other.

For example, you could simply compare the number of Java methods associated with each API that you can glean from documentation on the assumption that the one with more functions is better.

We do not recommend this approach because it leaves you at the mercy of misleading marketing materials or incomplete documentation. Also, it is not clear that more methods make a framework better. However much people may disagree about the value of a given measurement or its interpretation, within that context there is no argument about which framework is better or best—and therein lies the value of objectivity.

Establish an Independent Standard

The pentagon formed in the center of Figure 4.1 hints at much better context for comparison—if you consider it to represent the union of the features supported by the five options. You can think of each feature in the union as implying a "yes/no" question in a checklist, such as this:

Does the framework support <feature X>?

A union of features is better because you are measuring against a relatively independent standard. An independent standard enables us to establish what an ideal framework should support, and compare what each mechanism actually supports against that ideal.

A helpful side effect is that an evaluation against a standard like a union of features is actually simpler than an exhaustive one—because you do not compare the features of every framework with every other. Instead, you merely compare the features of each mechanism to the checklist (making this an O(n) solution). And the comparison is still among "apples" if you consider the superset of features in the union as the "best" possible example of a persistence mechanism (sometimes called an *archetype*), as shown in Figure 4.2.

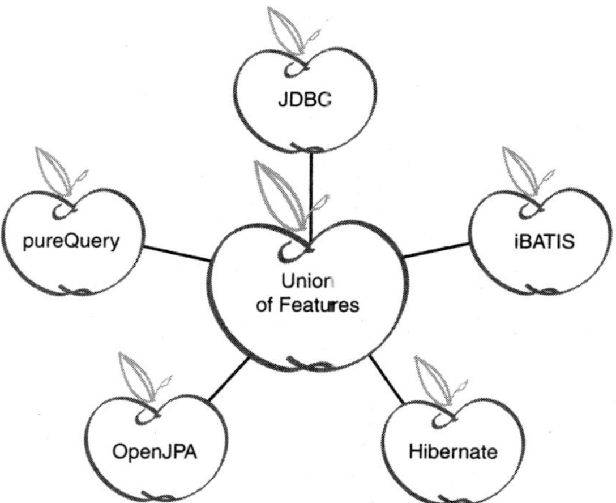

Figure 4.2 Using a union of features as an independent standard for comparison.

Developing a union of features is pretty straightforward. First pick an arbitrary framework and use its features as the starting point for the union. Then examine each other mechanism in turn, enumerating its features and adding any not already found in the current set.

For example, here are some introductory paragraphs about JDBC we found by browsing Wikipedia:

> **JDBC** is an API for the Java programming language that defines how a client may access a database. It provides methods for querying and updating data in a database. JDBC is oriented towards relational databases.

> The Java Platform, Standard Edition, includes the JDBC API together with an ODBC implementation of the API enabling connections to any relational database that supports ODBC. This driver is native code and not Java, and is closed source.

This cursory description leads to some good questions to ask about every framework that you might not have thought to consider, such as these:

Is the framework part of Java Platform Standard Edition (JSE)?

Is there an open-source implementation?

Deeper digging into the materials shows that JDBC supports invoking arbitrary SQL statements and batching multiple statements into one request—providing full functionality and efficiency. Therefore, you should consider asking the following questions as well:

Does the framework support invoking arbitrary SQL statements?

Does the framework support batching multiple statements?

Turning next to iBATIS, its Wikipedia article begins with the following:

> **iBATIS** is a persistence framework which enables mapping SQL queries to POJOs (Plain Old Java Objects). The SQL queries are decoupled from an application by putting the queries in XML files. Mapping of the retrieved objects is automatic or semi-automatic.

These features are important for ease of use and maintainability, and lead to even more questions to think about:

Does the framework support automatic mapping of query data to Java objects?

Does the framework support modifying queries independent of the Java code?

Hibernate, pureQuery, and JPA each add their own features to the union as well; but as you examine each framework in turn, you add fewer and fewer (because most of the features have already been encountered).

Make a List and Check It Twice

After you complete the union from the initial scan of each framework, the next step is to examine each again and determine whether it supports each of the features in the checklist. This second scan is important because it may be that a given mechanism supports a feature but never explicitly documented that fact. The total number of features supported usually increases. At the same time, you find out how many features a framework does *not* support.

It is possible to compare as you go while developing the union as long as you recheck *each* previously evaluated mechanism whenever a new feature is added. However, this approach is functionally equivalent to a second scan.

To illustrate, Table 4.1 summarizes the evaluation against the checklist questions we discussed so far.

Table 4.1 Results of the Evaluation Against the Checklist of Features Derived from the Union

	JDBC	iBATIS	Hibernate Core	OpenJPA	pureQuery
Part of Java SE or EE Standard	Y			Y	
Open Source		Y	Y	Y	
Arbitrary SQL	Y	Y	Y	Y	Y
Batching	Y	Y	Y	Y	Y
ORM		Y	Y	Y	Y
External Queries		Y	Y	Y	Y
Total supported	3	5	5	6	4
Not supported	3	1	1	0	2
Percent	50	83	83	100	66

It is reasonable to consider the framework with the most features supported, or the fewest not supported, or the largest percentage as "the best" within this context. Any of these three measurements used to summarize the table would serve as a more meaningful context for comparison than a simple count of advertised features.

Keep It Real

Comparing to a union of features is not likely to be a satisfactory basis for your choice of mechanism because you are still at the mercy of what the framework documentation has to say about which features are important. Even though you have a collective group of opinions to consider, the basis for comparison is not truly independent.

An even more meaningful context for comparison is to create a list of your project's requirements with respect to persistence features and then evaluate each framework against that checklist. This focus on your project requirements also ensures that the label "best" has a *practical* meaning—it is applied to the mechanism that does the best job of meeting your needs.

One benefit is that even less effort is required than that to compare against a union of features. You do not need to exhaustively research all the frameworks first to develop the union; you simply determine whether a given framework has the required features—which are likely to be a much smaller subset than the complete union, but still another form of "apple," as Figure 4.3 shows.

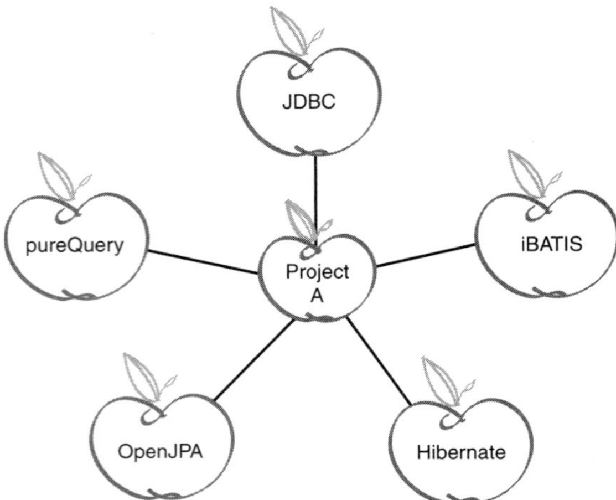

Figure 4.3 Using your project requirements as a more practical standard for comparison.

Focusing on your immediate needs can further simplify an evaluation because you can stop considering an option that fails to meet a "must have" requirement. For example, project "A" may require a robust ORM that allows you to reject JDBC as the mechanism early in the evaluation process.

A more complete approach would be to weight each requirement based on its importance to your project, and then choose the framework with the highest score.

However, this continual comparison to project requirements, even though they are a smaller list than the union, is reminiscent of an exhaustive comparison (Figure 4.4 illustrates the similarity to Figure 4.1). In fact, the long-term costs are likely to be more than for an exhaustive comparison.

But there are other issues with this "every man for himself (or herself)" approach to evaluation. One is that you are spending time evaluating frameworks when you should be implementing applications. Another is that an inexperienced team may not know the right questions to ask. And still another is that you may end up with inconsistent implementations across the enterprise even when the projects are similar.

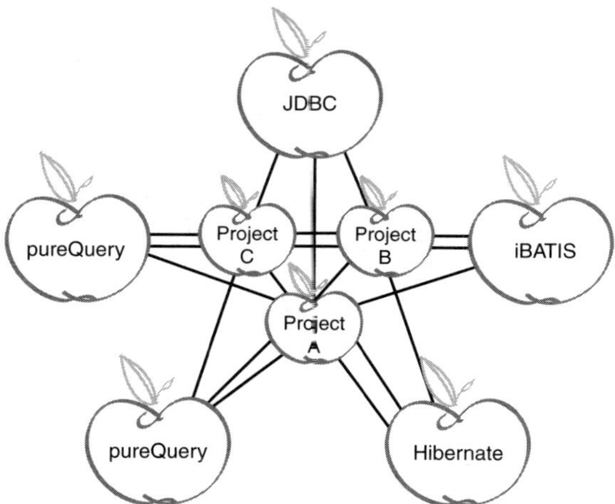

Figure 4.4 Long-term cost of using individual project requirements as a context for comparison.

Persistence in Your Enterprise

The word "enterprise" suggests a solution. Just as it is better to develop an independent standard from a union of advertised features and compare against that, it is better to develop a comprehensive checklist of enterprise requirements from a union of those features needed in previous (or proposed) projects.

Given our previous examples, project "A" would contribute ORM support as an enterprise requirement, project "B" would add the need for dynamic SQL, and project "C" would need both.

Ultimately, your enterprise requirements go far beyond just the technical features usually described in the framework documentation, and include aspects such as business drivers and functional and nonfunctional requirements that we discussed in previous chapters. These aspects lead to additional questions that you should consider in your enterprise wide checklist, such as the following:

> *Are there referenceable projects that have successfully used this framework?*
>
> *Is there a large pool of practitioners skilled in using this framework?*

Another benefit of this broader focus is that only one evaluation of the frameworks against the enterprise requirements is needed to support making your choices later. Your checklist of enterprise requirements becomes the ideal superset of features to compare the frameworks against—still keeping it "apples to apples," as shown in Figure 4.5.

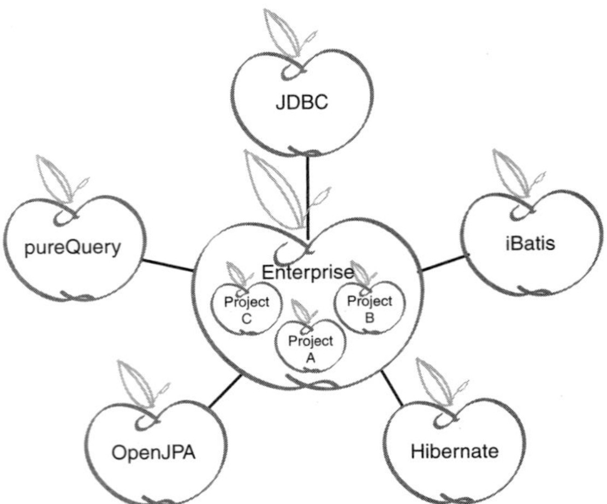

Figure 4.5 Using your enterprise requirements as a standard to drive a single evaluation.

One Size Does Not Fit All

However, you should consider the possibility that you need to choose two or even more frameworks for use within the enterprise—not because they end up with the same objective score in an evaluation, but because there are important underlying differences in the requirements of different *types* of projects.

So when you develop your checklist of enterprise requirements, create a weighted subset for each kind of project that you are likely to encounter, and optimize the choice of framework for each type.

For example, it is likely that highly tuned custom applications such as the order entry system for project "A" (we might call these "compiled" applications) would benefit from an object style programming model provided by Hibernate, or OpenJPA. But it may be that highly dynamic "metadata"-driven applications like the marketing analysis system developed by project "B" would require iBATIS or pureQuery (we might call these "interpreted" applications). Figure 4.6 graphically shows the relationship between these two project types and individual project requirements within the enterprise.

The possibility of choosing multiple frameworks implies that you should ensure that they can work together—adding the ability to integrate with other frameworks, such as JDBC, to your checklist of enterprise requirements to consider. Some requirements, like this one about integration, may be important for a number of project types —implying that a hierarchy of project types would be useful to minimize redundancy.

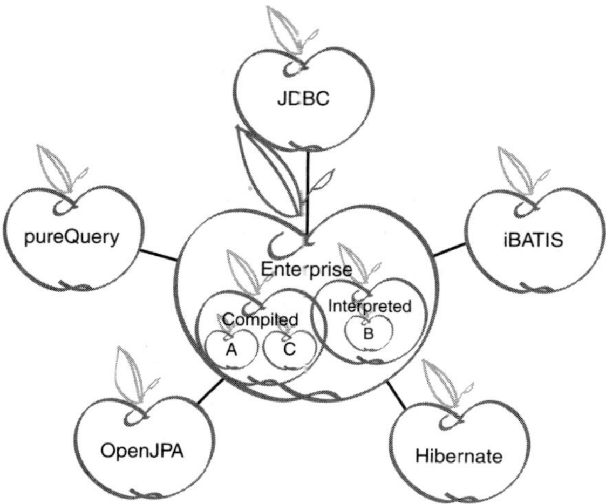

Figure 4.6 Relationship of project types to the enterprise and project requirements.

Ask Not If, but What and Why

But the problem with checklists of features phrased as "yes/no" questions is that for most interesting aspects of persistence (and life in general), the answers are not really black and white. Most of the time there are shades of gray.

For example, consider the question about whether a framework is available under open source. The description about Hibernate found in Wikipedia provides an answer:

> Hibernate is an object-relational mapping (ORM) solution for the Java language. It is free, open source software that is distributed under the GNU Lesser General Public License. It provides an easy to use framework for mapping an object-oriented domain model to a traditional relational database.

The answer was much more specific than just yes, and indicated that it was available under LGPL. We explore LGPL and other license agreements like GPL and Apache with respect to their impact on your ability to sell your applications in Chapter 2 "High-Level Requirements and Persistence." In short, there are usually trade-offs to consider for each one, and most frameworks would answer yes to only one in the set. So rather than asking a number of related "yes/no" questions, like

> *Is the framework distributed under GPL?*
>
> *Is the framework distributed under LGPL?*
>
> *Is the framework distributed under a license from Apache?*

it would be better to ask a single, more open-ended "what" question, such as the following:

> *Under what open-source licenses is the framework distributed?*

This single "what" question not only minimizes the number of questions you have to ask, but also makes it clear that you are evaluating an important aspect of your enterprise requirements.

The Devil Is in the Details

This transformation of many related questions into one that is somewhat open-ended also illustrates that most often, it is not a question of "if" a given framework supports a requirement, but one of "how." In other words, the devil is in the details.

The underlying question we are after concerning the type of license agreements is this:

> *How is the framework distributed?*

A "how" question like this is usually too open-ended for an apples-to-apples comparison—leading us to substitute one or more "what" questions like that given previously. For another example, consider the third sentence from the Hibernate description again (bold italics ours):

> ...it provides an ***easy to use*** framework for mapping an object-oriented domain model to a traditional relational database.

Certainly every framework would like to claim that it is easy to use, so asking a "yes/no" question is rather useless; a completely open-ended "how" question is nearly so:

> *How is the framework easy to use?*

One reason is that the notion of whether a framework is easy to use is a subjective evaluation that applies to the framework as a whole. A better "how" question is specific and objective:

> *How many steps does it take to achieve a given task?*

Within this context, the framework with the fewest steps across all the tasks evaluated would be considered the "best" with respect to ease of use. The questionnaire to drive the data gathering might start with a "what" question around a specific feature, coupled with a very specific question about how that particular feature is used for that task. For example, support for isolation levels could be objectively evaluated with the following two questions:

> *What isolation levels are supported?*
>
> *How are they specified?*

The details provided by the "how" questions make it easy to objectively compare the complexity of the solution with that of others—as long as the same example is used for each framework to minimize the open-endedness.

An evaluation based on this amount of detail allows you to apply Occam's Razor and choose according to its age-old best practice: *"All things being equal, the simplest solution tends to be the best one."*

An Evaluation Template You Can Use

Now that you know how to conduct an objective evaluation and what general kinds of questions to ask, you have all the tools you need to create your own questionnaire and conduct your own evaluation. But because the devil is in the details, we go a step further and extract a questionnaire from enterprise requirements discussed in the previous chapters that you can use as a starting point for your own evaluations.

Our questionnaire is very comprehensive, with the following sections:

- Background
- Architectural Overview
- Programming Model
- ORM Features Supported
- Tuning Options
- Development Process for the Common Example

Each section begins with the major questions that the section is intended to answer, followed by specific subsections with more detailed questions.

Background

This section is most closely related to Chapter 1, "A Brief History of Object-Relational Mapping," where we discuss the various frameworks that you might want to consider in your evaluation. Specifically, you want to be able to answer the following general questions:

Why is the framework is popular enough that you chose it to evaluate?

Type of Framework

What approach to persistence does this mechanism support?

History

How did this framework evolve?

Architectural Overview

This section is derived from the discussion about business drivers in Chapter 2 and is intended to capture some of the more intangible "costs" of moving to that particular mechanism. A reviewer should be able to answer the following questions:

What are the basic components of the framework and how they interact?

Show a high-level diagram that includes development tools and runtime servers.

Standards Adherence

What standards does this mechanism support?

Platforms Required

What software and hardware platforms does this technology require for the runtime?

Other Dependencies

What other Java technologies are needed in order to use this one?

Vendors and Licenses

What vendors or open-source communities currently offer this framework?

For each one listed, what kind of license is available?

For each listed, how can you obtain a trial and/or production download?

Available Literature

What kinds of educational material and reference guides are available? (Provide a link to various sources where available.) Consider using the following table format for clarity:

Title	Source	Description

Programming Model

The purpose of this section is to drill down to see how the framework can be used to support the basic usage patterns found in Java applications needing persistence discussed in Chapter 2.

What is the programming model like in terms of components you have to develop and the language you use for each?

What is the "lifecycle" of a persistent object with respect to framework and application components?

Initialization

What kind of initialization is required to access the framework API within your service implementation?

Show the code required to initialize the framework before a query of Customer with id = 100.

Show how to set up the framework with the Derby JDBC driver and also how to use an application DataSource with JNDI name jdbc/Derby/DataSource.

Connections

What kind of connection model is supported?

Show an example of explicitly creating a connection with the same query used in the initialization section (if supported and not already shown in the initialization section).

Show how to set the database connection pool size to 20.

Transactions

What kinds of transactional control are supported by the framework?

Show an example of grouping two update statements into a single user-defined transaction. If possible, use the following updates:

1. Update a business customer with id = 100 such that businessPartner = false.
2. Update that customer's openOrder such that status = 'SUBMITTED'

Show an example of configuring the framework to use global transactions with an application server (such as with JTA).

What isolation levels are supported?

For each that is supported, show the code required.

Create

Describe the general approach to creating objects within the framework.

Show the code required to create a new ResidentialCustomer.

Show the code required to create a new Order owned by the Customer.

Retrieve

Describe the general approach to queries and object retrieval within the framework.

Specifically, are dynamic queries supported?

Show the code required to retrieve a single Customer that matches a given primary key.

Show the code required to retrieve all Customers that are "active" (specifically all CUSTOMERS that have an OPEN_ORDER).

Update

Describe the general approach to updating objects within the framework.

Show the code required to change the quantity of a LineItem. Specifically, update a LineItem with a given customerId (assume it's already defined) to a quantity of 100.

Show the code required to change the OpenOrder attribute to Null.

Delete

Describe the general approach to deleting objects within the framework.

Specifically, is cascaded delete supported?

Show the code required to delete a LineItem.

Show the code required to delete an Order and all associated LineItems (through a cascaded delete, if supported).

Stored Procedures

Describe the general approach to invoking stored procedures within the framework.

Show the code required to call the following "swap order" Java stored procedure:

```
SwapPojo orderIds = new SwapPojo();
orderIds.setFirst(orderId1);
orderIds.setSecond(orderId2);
dm.update("swap.order",orderIds);
```

Batch Operations

Describe the general approach to supporting batch operations within the framework.

What kinds of update operations are supported in batch mode?

For each operation supported, show an example.

Extending the Framework

Describe any possible extension or plug-in points with brief examples of interfaces/APIs.

If the framework supports plugging into a distributed caching framework, you may want to defer this example to the distributed caching section.

Error Handling

Describe the general approach to handling exceptions in the framework. If possible, consider including a class diagram showing the hierarchy in UML or your favorite notation.

ORM Features Supported

The questions in this section are derived from Chapter 3, "Designing Persistent Object Services," first focusing on the static definitional elements of the ORM problem. Specifically:

How does the framework alleviate the object-relational impedance mismatch problem and make the life of the developer easier?

Are there any ORM features that are unique to this framework for common problems like object identity (such as key generation) or the load-time paradox (navigating large collection relationships)?

Objects

Describe the general approach to mapping objects within the framework.

Show how you would define an Order object.

Inheritance

What types of inheritance does the framework support?

For each type of inheritance supported, show how the framework is used to specify that a ResidentialCustomer inherits from an AbstractCustomer.

Keys

What types of key attributes are supported?

Show how you would define that an Order has an auto-generated key.

Show how you would define that an Order has a simple integer key (if not already covered in the programming model section).

Show how you would define that a LineItem has a compound key consisting of an Order key and a Product key.

What key generation options are available? Specifically, does the framework offer key generation independently of the underlying database (for example, generating a UUID)?

What database-specific methods are supported?

Show how you would define that an Order has an auto-generated key.

Attributes

What types of attributes are supported?

How are they mapped to the underlying database?

Show how you would define that a LineItem has a BigDecimal quantity attribute and how it can be mapped to the Derby type of `BIGINT`

Show how the `Order.Status` enumeration can be mapped to `VARCHAR(9)` of `OPEN`, `SUBMITTED`, and `CLOSED`.

Contained Objects

What kinds of contained objects are supported?

Show how you would define that a Customer contains an Address object.

Relationships

What "directionality" of relationships does the framework support?

What cardinality does the framework support?

Show how to use the framework to specify that an Order is related to a Customer.

Show how to use the framework to specify that a Customer is related to many Orders.

Show how to use the framework to specify that a Customer can reference at most one OpenOrder.

Constraints

What types of constraints on attribute values does the framework support?

Can the framework leverage underlying database constraints?

Show how the framework is used to specify that a Product referred to by a LineItem must be in the Cataloged state. For this example, add a new field to Product called cataloged that is a Boolean.

Derived Attributes

What types of computations are supported for "derived" attributes?

Show how you would define that a LineItem amount attribute is computed by multiplying the price by the quantity.

Does the framework support derived attributes that operate on properties from more than one (related) object?

If so, show how you would define that a LineItem amount attribute is computed by multiplying the Product price by the LineItem quantity.

Does the framework support derived attributes that represent operations across the elements of a collection?

If so, show how you would define that an Order total amount attribute is computed by summing the associated LineItem amounts.

Tuning Options

This section is derived from questions in Chapter 2 concerning quality of service IT requirements. You should be able to answer questions like the following:

How does the framework make tuning at runtime easier without requiring code changes?

Are there any tuning features unique to this framework?

Query Optimizations

What approaches to optimizing queries are supported that do not require changing the Java code?

For example, is it possible to change the number of rows returned by a query?

Caching

What kind of caching strategies are enabled by the framework?

For example, does the framework have its own "single JVM" cache that can be configured?

If so, show how you would cache Products (because they change relatively infrequently).

How do you handle cache invalidation?

Does the framework support integration with a "third-party" distributed cache?

If so, show how that would be done within the framework.

Loading Related Objects

What support does the framework provide for "hydrating" objects related to the target?

Does the framework support "lazy loading" such that specific related objects can be declared to be loaded only when explicitly referenced in the application code?

If so, show how you would configure the framework to indicate that the LineItems are lazy-loaded.

Does the framework support "preloading" such that specific related objects can be declared to be loaded at the same time that the referencing object is loaded (which usually results in a join operation on the database)?

If so, show how you would configure the framework to indicate that the Product related to a LineItem is preloaded whenever the LineItem is loaded.

Locking

Describe the general approach to configuring locks on objects independently of the Java code.

What kinds of configurable locking strategies are supported?

Show how each would be enabled within the framework configuration options.

Does the framework support ordering of operations outside of the code to minimize deadlock conditions?

If so, show how this is done through configuration options.

Development Process for the Common Example

The purpose of this section is to show the end-to-end steps required to develop the services shown in the common example outlined in Chapter 3. The overarching questions include the following:

Are there any development steps that are simplified by or unique to this framework?

Defining the Objects

Describe any steps needed to map the Java objects to the underlying relational stores.

Specifically, are there any specific tools that need to be run?

If so, show when and how they get invoked.

Implementing the Services

Describe any special considerations for implementing services that are unique to this framework that may limit their portability.

Packaging the Components

Describe any special considerations for packaging the code components and the configuration components.

Are there any specific naming or project/directory structure conventions that need to be followed?

Are there any special tools that need to be run to compile or bind components?

If so, show when and how they get invoked.

Unit Testing

Describe any approaches unique to this framework for handling unit testing.

Deploying to Production

Describe any approaches unique to this framework for deploying the applications to production.

Specifically, are there features that make it easy to move from a system test to production environment with little or no configuration changes?

Are there any special tools that need to be run?

If so, show when and how they get invoked.

Making the Most out of Your Experience

Of course you will want to follow our earlier advice to keep it real and customize this questionnaire to the needs of your enterprise, taking into account your unique culture and requirements. For example, you may want to consider adding scenarios that are meaningful to your own enterprise as sections because they will give the best impression of the complexity of a given framework with respect to the functionality it delivers.

Use the Questionnaire Early and Often

To help offset the cost of customizing the questionnaire, we recommend that you reuse it as a starting point for your project requirements. This approach will ensure that your more inexperienced project teams do not overlook a crucial requirement.

Also, constant use of the questionnaire on actual projects gives you lots of opportunity to validate them and keep them current. If a new project represents a new type or comes up with some new requirements, you should first add them to your enterprise questionnaire. Then consider whether to evaluate each project in progress with respect to the new requirements.

Depending on the situation, you may need to revisit your choice of persistence frameworks being used in your production applications—especially if you found a problem during development and testing that led to the new requirements to consider in the future.

We have seen a questionnaire like this one used in other ways, too. In one project, we used it to review the project team's choice of persistence mechanism. This questionnaire helped us to ask the right questions in a systematic fashion and get to the heart of the reasons for their choice.

Record Your History So You Don't Repeat It

Whether you use this questionnaire in practice to conduct your own formal evaluations or review the work of others, make sure to record your answers and choices so that you don't forget them later and have to revisit.

A soft-copy version of the questionnaire in Microsoft Word is available on the download site, ibmpressbooks.com/title/9780131587564. You are welcome to use this template as-is or as a starting point for your own evaluation and review questionnaire.

We use this same template as a starting point for the next five chapters, which evaluate JDBC, iBATIS, Hibernate, OpenJPA, and pureQuery. Feel free to contact any of the authors if you would like to share new questions or reviews of other persistence mechanisms—whether exciting new ones or exciting ones still in common use. In this manner we can all learn from each other and avoid repeating ourselves.

Summary

That said, sometimes it is good to repeat yourself—especially in a summary. This chapter covered a number of best practices to follow when evaluating persistence frameworks for use in your projects. And if you can only remember "top ten lists" (with apologies to David Letterman), here are 10 key points to keep in mind:

1. *Be objective.* Labels like "better" or "best" have meaning only within a specific context of measurement and interpretation of the results.
2. *Be unbiased.* Measure against an independent standard rather than what a given framework chooses to advertise.
3. *Be practical.* With respect to providing an independent standard for evaluation, a union is good but your project requirements are better.
4. *Be comprehensive.* Develop a complete checklist of enterprise requirements as a union of those from previous projects.
5. *Be flexible.* Different project types have different enterprise requirements, so factor a separate checklist to choose the best framework for each project type.
6. *Be open-ended.* It is better to ask a single "what" question about an aspect of the requirements than many related "if" questions.

7. *Be specific.* Follow your "what" questions with a "how" question that clearly defines a scenario so that the details can be compared as well.
8. *Minimize redundancy.* Consider building a hierarchy of project types with common enterprise requirements checklists in the more "abstract" types.
9. *Maximize reuse.* Use your requirements checklists as a starting point for your new projects to minimize your analysis and design costs.
10. *Remain relevant.* Adjust the questions and reevaluate your choices based on actual project experiences.

This chapter also provided a detailed questionnaire that you can use as a starting point for driving and documenting your own formal evaluations and reviews. We use this questionnaire in the remaining chapters of this book.

 Links to developerWorks

A.4.1 *Developing Your Applications using SQLJ*

An article by another ISSW consultant, Owen Cline, which describes practical uses of SQLJ in Java applications, including ones that use EJB components.

www.ibm.com/developerworks/db2/library/techarticle/dm-0412cline/

References

[TopLink] *TopLink JPA*. www.oracle.com/technology/products/ias/toplink/jpa/index.html

Part II

Comparing Apples to Apples

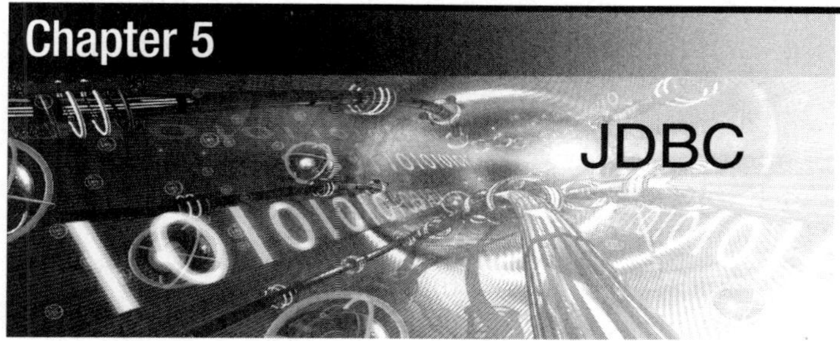

We start our evaluations with Java Database Connectivity (JDBC), not because it is an ORM framework, but because most of the other technologies we evaluate in Chapters 6 through 9 are or can be implemented on top of JDBC. Therefore, JDBC serves as the baseline for the side-by-side comparison we make in Chapter 10, "Putting Theory into Practice."

We will start this chapter with a brief architectural overview—a discussion of the programming model and how you use that programming model to solve the basic issues associated with object-relational mapping (ORM). Then we will show how to build the common example services using JDBC in the context of the end-to-end process for developing that example.

Background

The purpose of this section is to help you understand how JDBC relates to other Java persistence frameworks—by positioning it within history, but more importantly, within a taxonomy of types. These two perspectives illustrate why we are evaluating JDBC in the first place.

Type of Framework

The JDBC library provides an application programming interface (API) to interact directly with relational databases using Structured Query Language (SQL). JDBC is not an ORM framework; its API requires the programmer to have intimate knowledge of SQL and of the database tables with which they interact to provide persistent data for their enterprise applications. The object-relational impedance mismatch becomes blatantly obvious when using JDBC.

Separation of concerns is a primary consideration when developing enterprise quality service-oriented Java applications. Therefore, most Java applications should not directly access data using JDBC, and should instead use a framework like the ones we evaluate in the next chapters. Unfortunately, developers who use JDBC in their applications will almost always build their own framework around it. The Spring JDBC Templates and Apache iBATIS open-source projects are examples of minimalist frameworks built around JDBC that can save a team from going down this treacherous path of reinvention. We will evaluate iBATIS in Chapter 6 to show the specifics of how it provides an ORM solution.

For the purposes of this book and chapter, we will avoid the temptation to invent a framework around JDBC—not only to show you the intricate details of how to use the JDBC API, but also so that you gain a greater appreciation for what a persistence framework must do. And hopefully, after exploring all the aspects that must be implemented, you will see how difficult it really is to build an enterprise quality framework, and you will tend toward a "reuse" versus a "build" decision.

Key Point

Business applications should reuse an existing persistence framework rather than directly using the JDBC API or inventing yet another mechanism.

History

The release of JDK 1.1 in February 1997 included the JDBC 1.0 API classes. This toolkit set the stage for the development of more complex frameworks and the eventual creation of Java Platform Standard Edition (JSE, or Java SE) and Java Platform Enterprise Edition (JEE, or Java EE). JDBC was originally based on database programming interfaces for other languages. In particular, JDBC was influenced by ODBC (Open Database Connectivity), as well as the X/Open SQL CLI (Call Level Interface) specification.

Since its inception, JDBC has been continually updated to address various enterprise-level concerns, including distributed transactions, connection pooling, and batch updates. Since version 3.0, it has been developed under the Java Community Process (JCP) under various Java Specification Requests (JSR). JDBC 4.0 is the current version at the time this book went to press, developed under JSR 221.

Architectural Overview

JDBC is designed to be as standalone as possible. This approach enables it to be used to provide access to persistent data in Java applications running under the basic Java SE platform.

In a Java SE application, the ACID properties of an application service are provided by delegation to the database. So in the programming model section, we will see how direct manipulation of transactions is an important part of your application code when using the JDBC API.

If your applications need to access and update two or more databases in a single unit of work, we strongly recommend that you write the application to use services provided by the Java EE platform rather than inventing your own distributed transaction mechanism. Java EE includes numerous services you will find yourself needing for robust enterprise applications such as these (each followed by a reference to the specification, listed at the end of the chapter, for more details):

- Enterprise JavaBeans [EJB]
- Java Naming and Directory Interface [JNDI]
- Java Transaction API [JTA]
- Java Message Service [JMS)]
- Java API for XML Parsing [JAXP)]
- Java API for XML Web Services [JAX-WS]

Unfortunately, we have seen too many development teams try to invent one or more of these services, especially their own version of Enterprise JavaBeans, to the detriment of their ability to focus on applications crucial to the success of their business.

Key Point

If you need to update more than one database or need other object services in a unit of work, you should code the service to exploit the standard features of JEE.

And as we will see in later chapters, a good framework for persistence will abstract the differences between Java SE and Java EE platforms from the programming model.

Standards Adherence

JDBC represents a specification and set of standards that JDBC library vendors must adhere to in order to be considered compliant. There have been four major versions, with each adding more function than the previous one:

- **JDBC 1.0**—Provided the basic framework for data access using Java via connections, statements, and result sets.
- **JDBC 2.0**—Added scrollable and updatable result sets, batch updates, SQL3 data types, data sources, and custom mappings.
- **JDBC 3.0**—Enhanced existing features and added some new functionality, such as savepoints, auto-generated keys, and parameter metadata.
- **JDBC 4.0**—Provides better code manageability (specifically in the areas of driver and connection management and exception handling) and more complex data type support, such as native XML.

We will focus on JDBC 4.0 in the remainder of this chapter; you can refer to the website for full details of the specification [JDBC].

Platforms Required

Regardless of version, when we say JDBC, we really mean an implementation of the JDBC specification that adheres to (or conforms with) a specific version of the standard. This implementation is called a JDBC Driver, and there are four main types to consider, as shown in Table 5.1.

Table 5.1 JDBC Drivers

Type 1: JDBC-ODBC Bridge	Translates JDBC calls into ODBC calls and sends them to the ODBC driver.
Type 2: A Native API Partly Java Technology-Enabled Driver	Converts JDBC calls into database-specific calls for databases. The driver requires that some binary code be present on the client machine.
Type 3: Pure Java Driver for Database Middleware	Translates JDBC calls into a vendor-specific protocol, which is translated into the database-specific protocol through components installed on the database server.
Type 4: Direct-to-Database Pure Java Driver	Converts JDBC calls into the net-work protocol used directly by DBMSs. The driver allows for a direct call from the client machine to the DBMS server.

The JDK has the basic API (interface classes) and a JDBC-ODBC Bridge Driver bundled inside it. However, we have found that this default driver should be avoided (unless no alternatives exist), because it involves translating every database request from JDBC to ODBC, and then finally to the native database protocol. Furthermore, use of the JDBC-ODBC bridge typically binds one to a Windows platform.

In general, most applications should use a driver built specifically for the database used to store the enterprise data. In the early days when Java was still maturing, native Type 2 drivers were used to boost performance of database applications. But because they only enabled use from Java and were not implemented in Java, they were not portable across operating systems. Now that Java has matured and runs much faster, most drivers are Type 4 and can take advantage of Java's write-once-run-anywhere feature.

Other Dependencies

The JDBC driver being used typically must be added as a JAR to the classpath. When you are dealing with non-Type 4 drivers or managed environments like Java EE, additional software installation or configuration may be required.

Normally, database vendors will provide an optimized Type 4 driver; and it is our experience that the best choice is to use that one. For example, DB2 provides a driver optimized for DB2 databases. That said, there are cases in which one may need to look at a third-party vendor. For example, some database vendors may provide only an outdated driver or none at all.

To make things a bit more complex, many database products have multiple JDBC drivers that application developers can use to interact with their database instances. For example, to interact with MySQL, a popular database among the open-source community, there are free JDBC drivers available as well as commercial options. Some JDBC drivers are optimized for a particular use (for example, reading as opposed to writing to a database).

Vendors and Licenses

The major licensing concern you will have when using JDBC revolves around the JDBC driver libraries used. As mentioned before, this is usually not an issue with Type 4 drivers provided by the database vendor. Further, some Java EE vendors provide the appropriate drivers for all the databases that they support as part of their implementation.

For convenience, Sun has collected a list of more than 200 JDBC driver vendors that can be viewed at their Developer Network (SDN) site that you should check [SDN].

If you will be selling your applications to others, you will need to ensure that your customers can get the appropriate drivers for their back-end databases. If you intend to ship drivers that you use with the installation package of your software, you should carefully scrutinize the licensing agreements of the JDBC drivers to ensure that this is allowed.

Available Literature

A web search on the subject of JDBC yields a huge number of whitepapers, tutorials, and other literature available for reading online. Furthermore, there are lots of books available for purchase online and from brick-and-mortar bookstores. Table 5.2 shows a sampling of the available resources regarding JDBC.

Table 5.2 Available JDBC Resources

Title	Source	Description
JDBC Database Access Tutorial [JDBC 1]	java.sun.com/docs/books/tutorial/jdbc/index.html	Excellent introduction to JDBC by Sun Microsystems
JDBC API Tutorial and Reference, Third Edition [Fisher]	java.sun.com/developer/ Books/jdbc/Fisher/index.html	Great book to have for JDBC API reference
JDBC Technotes [JDBC 2]	java.sun.com/javase/6/docs/technotes/guides/jdbc/	Great collection of links aggregated by Sun regarding the JDBC API
A.5.1 *Getting Started with JDBC 4 Using Apache Derby* [A.5.1]	www.ibm.com/developerworks/edu/os-dw-os-ad-jdbc.html	A developerWorks tutorial on JDBC 4.0 features
A.5.2 *Understand the DB2 UDB JDBC Universal Driver* [A.5.2]	www.ibm.com/developerworks/db2/library/techarticle/dm-0512kokkat/	Good discussion on the difference between Type 2 and Type 4 drivers

Programming Model

In a nutshell, programming with JDBC involves registering a driver by loading a database driver class through a DriverManager class or getting an instance of a DataSource. An application then proceeds by obtaining an instance of a Connection from the DriverManager or DataSource. Using this Connection, the application can obtain Statements for performing actual work with the underlying database. This work includes CRUD (create, read, update, and delete) operations. Many Statement methods, especially queries, return a ResultSet object that provides access to the individual rows and columns associated with the result. Figure 5.1 shows the classes we will use while describing the programming model.

Throughout this section, we will show snippets of code based on the example we introduced in Chapter 3, "Designing Persistent Object Services," to illustrate the basic programming model steps.

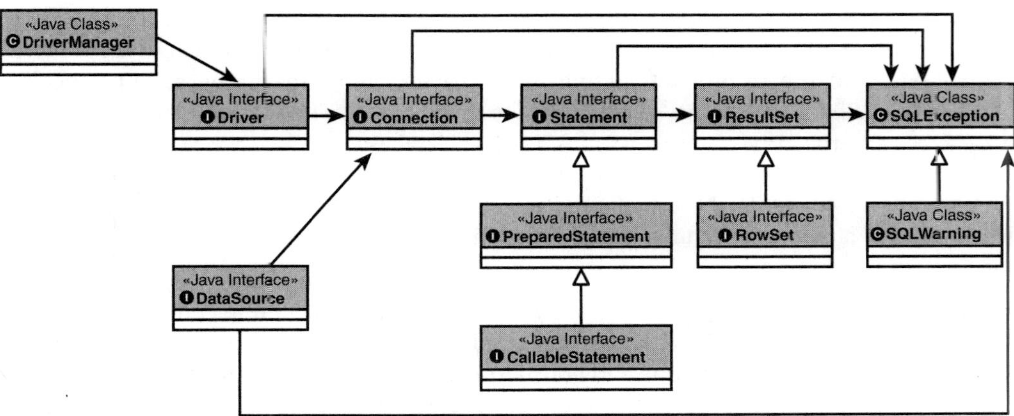

Figure 5.1 JDBC programming model components.

Initialization

Historically, the earliest mechanism for getting a Connection was to use the classloader to bootstrap an instance of a DriverManager. You can simply load the DriverManager class into the runtime environment using a single line of code invoking the Java class loader as shown in Listing 5.1.

Listing 5.1 Programmatic Loading of the JDBC Driver

```
Class.forName("org.apache.derby.jdbc.ClientDriver");
```

The DriverManager class referenced in the statement must be in your classpath, or a runtime exception will occur.

A connection can then be obtained using the DriverManager class. The DriverManager class contains static methods for getting connections. One of these static `getConnection` methods is used in the example of preparation work to obtain a connection shown in Listing 5.2.

Listing 5.2 Obtaining a Connection Using the DriverManager

```
String url = "jdbc:derby://localhost:1527/PWTE";
String username = "myUserName";
String password = "myPassword";
Connection connection = DriverManager.getConnection(
  url, username, password
);
```

The method takes the form `getConnection(String url, String user, String password)`. As seen in the URL used in Listing 5.2, the URL takes on the form of `jdbc:subprotocol:subname:port`. In the case of interacting with Apache Derby, specifying a subprotocol of `derby` in the URL tells the driver manager which driver to use. The subname of `//localhost:1527/PWTE` tells the driver where to look for the database instance we want to use. It is assumed that the database instance is running locally. Depending on whether authentication is required with your database instance (which will be the case for any real production deployment), database username and password information might need to be provided to obtain a connection.

In the early days of Java Applications, using a DriverManager was quite common. However, there are several limitations to this approach. The most glaring one is that you make one connection to a database at a time. Obviously this does not scale within an enterprise application. These applications typically need a mechanism to manage a pool of connections. The JDBC specification came up with an interface called a DataSource that abstracts how you get a database connection. When using a DataSource, the DataSource object takes on the responsibility of connecting an application and the JDBC driver. In Listing 5.3, this role is assumed by a DataSource.

Listing 5.3 Obtaining a Connection Using a DataSource and JNDI

```
//DataSource in a Java EE Environment
InitialContext ic = new InitialContext()
DataSource ds = ic.lookup("java:comp/env/jdbc/Derby/DataSource");
Connection con = ds.getConnection();

//DataSource in a Java SE Environment
DataSource ds = (DataSource) org.apache.derby.jdbc.ClientDataSource();
ds.setHost("localhost");
ds.setUser("myUserName")
ds.setPassword("myPassword");
Connection con = ds.getConnection();
```

In Listing 5.3, we show how a DataSource is used in a Java EE and Java SE environment. In a Java EE environment, the JNDI interface abstracts the DataSource type. Typically, in an Application Server, one would configure a DataSource administratively. Consequently, the need to worry about the connection URL, host, port, username, password, and other database configuration is eliminated from the application. DataSources can be used outside a Java EE environment, as also shown in Listing 5.3. Today, most JDBC drivers provide some implementation of the DataSource interface. Additionally, there are open-source implementations of the DataSource interface offered by the Apache Commons Project (DBCP component), as well as c3p0 (a SourceForge.net project). DataSource objects can provide for such enterprise-level facilities as connection pooling, the capability to participate in distributed transactions, and prepared statement caching. Using the DataSource approach as opposed to the DriverManager approach in Java SE applications makes it easier to use the same code in a Java EE and Java SE environment.

Connections

As shown in Listings 5.2 and 5.3, the onus of obtaining a connection is left up to the Java application programmer, thus constituting an explicit connection model. To minimize the overhead of creating, maintaining, and releasing database connections, connection pooling should be used, effectively avoiding the overhead of creating and destroying database connections. Fortunately, as of JDBC version 2.0, using connection pooling does not require much effort on the application developer's part. The process involves using two objects: `ConnectionPoolDataSource` and `PooledConnection`, both of the java.sql package. As can be seen in the code snippet in Listing 5.4, a `ConnectionPoolDataSource` is looked up. From the object, a `PooledConnection` object is obtained using the `getPooledConnection` method. In turn, to obtain a connection from the pool, the `getConnection` method of the `PooledConnection` object is called. After work is performed using the pooled connection, the connection is returned into the pool by calling the Connection object's `close()` method. It is important to note that not all vendors require the explicit use of the `ConnectionPoolDataSource` object to reap the benefits of pooling. Some application servers abstract a programmer from having to explicitly use the `PooledConnection` and `ConnectionPoolDataSource` objects. Listing 5.4 shows an example of code using the `PooledConnection` and `ConnectionPoolDataSource`.

Listing 5.4 Obtaining a Pooled Database Connection

```
InitialContext ic = new InitialContext()
ConnectionPoolDataSource ds = ic.lookup(
    "java:comp/env/jdbc/Derby/PooledDataSource"
);
PooledConnection pooledConnection = ds.getPooledConnection();
Connection conn = pooledConnection.getConnection(
    ); // get the connection from the pool
// work with the pooled connection
conn.close(); // release the connection back to the pool
```

Setting the database connection pool size is usually an administrative function and varies according to what type of setup is being used. Some vendors may provide an administrative user interface or a scripting interface to configuring connection pools.

After obtaining a connection, the next step is to create a Statement object. There are three types of JDBC Statements:

- **Statement**—The simplest type of SQL operation, where you can pass any SQL String to execute SQL.
- **PreparedStatement**—A subset of the Statement object; unlike a plain Statement object, it is given an SQL statement when it is created. The advantage to this is that in most cases, this SQL statement is sent to the DBMS right away, where it is compiled. As a result, the PreparedStatement object contains not just an SQL statement but an SQL statement that has been precompiled. This means that when the PreparedStatement is executed, the DBMS can just run the PreparedStatement SQL

statement without having to compile it first. Although PreparedStatement objects can be used for SQL statements with no parameters, you probably use them most often for SQL statements that take parameters. The advantage of using SQL statements that take parameters is that you can use the same statement and supply it with different values each time you execute it. Examples of this are included in the following sections.

- **Callable Statements**—A specialized subclass of PreparedStatement used to call stored procedures.

> **Key Point**
>
> Most applications should use PreparedStatements or a subclass of it. The cost of SQL parsing can decrease your application performance. In addition, some application server and database vendors offer prepared statement caches to further performance.

Transactions

Transactions are handled differently depending on whether your code is inside or outside of a Java EE container. When the code is working outside of a Java EE container, transaction control is provided in JDBC via the Connection class of a JDBC driver. Users can demarcate their own transactions, or alternatively opt for the Connection to be in "auto commit" mode. By default, when you obtain a Connection (whether it be from a DriverManager, a DataSource, or a ConnectionPool), the Connection has auto commit enabled. This essentially means that each SQL statement will be treated as a single transaction. When each statement is executed by the database, it will be committed. Sometimes, database transactions consist of multiple statements that must be regarded as a single, atomic transaction. Therefore, after obtaining a Connection, auto commit mode should be turned off, giving control of the transaction to the developer, who can explicitly commit or roll back the transaction. To turn auto commit off, you can call the `setAutoCommit` method of the Connection class with an argument of `false`, as demonstrated in Listing 5.5. Grouping statements into a single, user-defined transaction is relatively straightforward. After calling the `setAutoCommit` method with a `false` argument, the programmer is not required to explicitly demarcate the beginning of a transaction (in fact, there is no way to do so). But it is up to the developer to end a transaction by issuing either the commit or rollback methods on the Connection object.

Listing 5.5 Explicitly Managing a Transaction by Setting Auto Commit to "false"

```
try
{
     Connection connection = DriverManager.getConnection(
        url, username, password
     );
     connection.setAutoCommit(false);
     //operations...
```

```
    conn.commit();
}
catch (SQLException e)
{
    conn.rollback();
}
```

Attention should be made to the process involved in closing the resources (PreparedStatement and Connection objects). Improper cleanup of JDBC resources is often a root of problems in applications leveraging JDBC. This is why so many people use frameworks such as iBATIS or Spring JDBC Templates, which can provide automatic cleanup of these resources.

JDBC is also extensively used in Java EE environments in conjunction with the Java Transaction API. In such settings, where, for example, different EJBs might be involved in a distributed transaction that spans multiple datasources, the responsibility of determining how to commit and/or roll back changes is given to a transaction manager. Classes involved in a distributed transaction are strictly prohibited from calling the `setAutoCommit`, commit, and rollback methods when using container managed transactions, wherein the EJB container sets the boundaries of transactions. This disparity in transaction management in Java SE and Java EE environments often makes it difficult to use the same code between environments.

In Chapter 2, "High-Level Requirements and Persistence," we discussed isolation levels. Databases handle isolation levels in different ways. Which isolation levels are supported by JDBC is all dependent on the JDBC driver and the underlying database. One might dig through the JDBC driver documentation to see which isolation levels are supported. Alternatively, the `DatabaseMetaData` interface can be leveraged to report the transaction support of the database and JDBC driver being used. After a Connection object is obtained, the `getMetaData` method of the object can be called to yield a `DatabaseMetaData` object. It is from this object that general support for transactions and specific support for the various isolation levels can be ascertained. Table 5.3 shows the methods of the `DatabaseMetaData` object that can be used to determine isolation level support.

Table 5.3 Checking for Isolation Levels

DatabaseMetaData Method	Usage
`boolean supportsTransactions()`	Reports whether transactions are supported by the database and/or the JDBC driver
`boolean supportsTransactionIsolationLevel(int)`	Reports whether the database and/or the JDBC driver supports a particular isolation level

The different isolation levels are delineated as static constant integers of the Connection interface and are listed in Table 5.4.

Table 5.4 Isolation Levels

Constant (static int)	Isolation Level Represented
`TRANSACTION_NONE`	Transactions Unsupported
`TRANSACTION_READ_UNCOMMITTED`	Read Uncommitted
`TRANSACTION_READ_COMMITTED`	Read Committed
`TRANSACTION_REPEATABLE_READ`	Repeatable Read
`TRANSACTION_SERIALIZABLE`	Serializable

Since JDBC 3.0, an application developer can mark one or more places in an atomic transaction and perform a partial rollback of the transaction if deemed appropriate. This partial rollback facility is realized with JDBC savepoints. JDBC 3.0 and higher compliant drivers implement the java.sql.Savepoint interface, which facilitates savepoints. To use savepoints, the application developer uses the methods (shown in Table 5.5) of the Connection object.

Table 5.5 Savepoint Related Methods of the Connection Object

Connection Method	Usage
`Savepoint setSavePoint(String)`	Creates a savepoint with a provided name and returns a Savepoint object that will represent it
`Savepoint setSavePoint()`	Creates an unnamed savepoint and returns the Savepoint object that will represent it
`void rollback(Savepoint savepoint)`	Rolls back all the changes made to a database to the point where the specified savepoint was demarcated
`void releaseSavepoint(Savepoint savepoint)`	Removes the specified savepoint from the current transaction (effectively invalidating the savepoint)

Create

After having a Connection properly initialized, you can create, retrieve, update, and destroy data in the associated tables.

Creating data involves issuing an SQL Insert statement. For purposes of an example, assume you have a simple Java object populated by a web application as shown in Listing 5.6.

Listing 5.6 Java Object

```
ResidentialCustomer rc = new ResidentialCustomer();
rc.setFrequentCustomer(true);
rc.setHouseholdSize((short)2);
rc.setName("Kulvir Bhogal");
rc.setCustomerId(39);
```

To persist this object, one approach is to manually transfer its contents into the parameters of a PreparedStatement obtained from the Connection. Listing 5.7 shows how each "?" in the SQL is associated with an ordinal number that can be used with a "set" method on the PreparedStatement.

Listing 5.7 SQL Insert

```
String insertCustomerSQL =
    "insert into CUSTOMER (NAME, RESIDENTIAL_HOUSEHOLD_SIZE," +
    "RESIDENTIAL_FREQUENT_CUSTOMER, CUSTOMER_ID, TYPE ) values " +
    "( ?, ?, ?, ?, ? )";
PreparedStatement insertCustomerPS = conn.prepareStatement(
    insertCustomerSQL
);
insertCustomerPS.setString(1, customer.getName());
insertCustomerPS.setInt(2, customer.getHouseholdSize());
if (customer.isFrequentCustomer())
    insertCustomerPS.setString(3, "Y");
else
    insertCustomerPS.setString(3, "N");
insertCustomerPS.setInt(4, customer.getCustomerId());
insertCustomerPS.setString(5,"RESIDENTIAL");
insertCustomerPS.executeUpdate();
conn.commit();
```

Listing 5.7 also shows how ORM logic is embedded in the code, "mapping" the Java Boolean value to a "Y" or "N" accordingly.

Retrieve

To read data, you can use a PreparedStatement object to issue an SQL Select. The results of an SQL Select are stored in a specialized object called a ResultSet, which will hold a table representation of your results. The ResultSet interface provides methods for retrieving and manipulating the results of executed queries; ResultSet objects can have different functionality and characteristics. These characteristics include type, concurrency, and cursor holdability.

The type of a ResultSet object determines the level of its functionality in two areas: a) the ways in which its cursor can be manipulated, and b) how concurrent changes made to the underlying data source are reflected by the ResultSet object.

These behaviors are determined by the ResultSet type, of which there are three to consider:

- **TYPE_FORWARD_ONLY**—The ResultSet is not scrollable; its cursor moves forward only, from before the first row to after the last row. The rows contained in the ResultSet depend on how the underlying database materializes the results. That is, it contains the rows that satisfy the query either at the time the query is executed or as the rows are retrieved.
- **TYPE_SCROLL_INSENSITIVE**—The ResultSet is scrollable; its cursor can move both forward and backward relative to the current position, and it can move to an absolute position. However, the ResultSet does not reflect any changes made during the transaction.
- **TYPE_SCROLL_SENSITIVE**—As is the case for `TYPE_SCROLL_INSENSITIVE`, the ResultSet is scrollable; its cursor can move both forward and backward relative to the current position, and it can move to an absolute position. However, the ResultSet reflects changes made during the transaction.

Most SOA applications use `TYPE_FORWARD_ONLY`, because services are stateless. Listing 5.8 illustrates a simple query.

Listing 5.8 A Simple SQL Select Invoked Through a PreparedStatement

```
// 2. Retrieve Customer
PreparedStatement customerPS = conn.prepareStatement(
    "SELECT * FROM CUSTOMER"
);
customerPS.setInt(1, customerId);
customerResultSet = customerPS.executeQuery();
while(customerResultSet.next())
{
    Customer c = new Customer();
    customer.setName(customerResultSet.getString("name");
    customer.setAge(customerResultSet.getInt("Age");
    ...
    customerList.add(customer);
}
```

ResultSet objects require that a session has to be maintained while data is manipulated programmatically; furthermore, a ResultSet is tied to the Statement and Connection that created it. Seeing a need for ResultSet objects to be decoupled from these constraints, the javax.sql.RowSet interface was introduced to the Java language in J2SE Version 1.4 as part of JSR 114.

One implementation of the RowSet interface is the CachedRowSet, which shipped as part of the Java 5 SDK. The CachedRowSet object lets you connect to a database, grab data in the form of a ResultSet, release the Connection, manipulate the data locally, and then, when appropriate, reconnect with the database and persist the changes made to the data.

The default implementation of the CachedRowSet object that ships with Sun's SDK assumes optimistic locking. If the data that a client is trying to manipulate was not changed by another application interacting with the database server, the updates will be accepted by the database. If, however, something has changed with the target data in the interim, a synchronization exception will be thrown.

The RowSet specification does not mandate a particular concurrency model. However, the CachedRowSet implementation that ships with the SDK adopts an optimistic concurrency model. Listing 5.9 shows an example of using a CachedRowSet. Notice that it is similar looking to a ResultSet, except it can be disconnected.

Listing 5.9 Using a CachedRowSet with a Dynamic Statement

```
Connection dbconnection = dataSource.getConnection();
// use a statement to gather data from the database
Statement st = dbconnection.createStatement();
String myQuery = "SELECT * FROM CUSTOMER";
CachedRowSet crs = new CachedRowSetImpl();
// execute the query
ResultSet resultSet = st.executeQuery(myQuery);
crs.populate(resultSet);
resultSet.close();
st.close();
dbconnection.close();
```

After a CachedRowSet object has been created, the connection to the database can be severed as was done in the code snippet in Listing 5.9.

Update

Updating a database table requires that an SQL Update statement be issued against the database. Much like the SQL Insert, you can issue an SQL Update using a PreparedStatement as shown in Listing 5.10.

Listing 5.10 Updating Data

```
// 4. Persist the new quantity and amount
updateLineItemPS = conn.prepareStatement(
    "UPDATE LINE_ITEM SET QUANTITY = ?,
     AMOUNT = ? WHERE ORDER_ID = ? AND PRODUCT_ID = ?");
updateLineItemPS.setInt(1, quantity);
updateLineItemPS.setBigDecimal(2, updateAmount);
updateLineItemPS.setInt(3, orderID);
updateLineItemPS.setInt(4, productID);
updateLineItemPS.executeUpdate();
```

Alternatively, when using CachedRowSet, you follow a different pattern to update data. After you have the RowSet loaded, you use its update methods, and then synchronize the changes using the `acceptChanges` method as shown in Listing 5.11. This pattern allows for a client-side application to update a number of rows at once, eliminating the need to "hydrate" and manipulate domain-specific Java objects. Listing 5.11 shows the relevant code to populate a CachedRowSet with a query; then how you can manipulate the CachedRowser; and finally, synchronize it back to the DB.

Listing 5.11 Synchronize Changes to the Database

```
CachedRowSet crs = new CachedRowSet();
String myQuery = "SELECT * FROM ORDER where ORDER_ID = 3";
CachedRowSetImpl();
// execute the query
ResultSet resultSet = st.executeQuery(myQuery);
crs.populate(resultSet);

...

//other logic
if(crs.next())
{
    //update row
    crs.setFloat("total",crs.getFloat()+newQuantity);
}
//Synchronize changes
crs.acceptChanges();
```

Delete

Much like an Update or Insert, deleting involves using a Statement object to issue an SQL Delete, as illustrated in Listing 5.12.

Listing 5.12 Invoking an SQL Delete Using a PreparedStatement

```
// Remove line item
productDeletePS =
conn.prepareStatement(
     "DELETE FROM LINE_ITEM WHERE PRODUCT_ID = ? AND ORDER_ID = ?"
);
productDeletePS.setInt(1, productId);
productDeletePS.setInt(2, orderId);
productDeletePS.executeUpdate();
productDeletePS.close();
conn.commit();
```

Stored Procedures

JDBC allows for the invocation of stored procedures on a database server. Calling stored procedures is made possible by the CallableStatement object described earlier. Listing 5.13 shows a call to a hypothetical `swap_customer_order` stored procedure.

Listing 5.13 Calling the `swap_customer_order` Stored Procedure

```
CallableStatement cs = conn.prepareCall(
    "{call swap_customer_order(?,?)}"
);
cs.setString(1, firstCustomer);
cs.setString(2, secondCustomer);
cs.execute();
```

The use of curly braces ("{...}") in the code in Listing 5.13 is an escape syntax that tells the database driver being used to translate the escape syntax into the appropriate native SQL to invoke the stored procedure named `swap_customer_order`. Setting the parameters for invoking the stored procedure is similar to how the parameters of a PreparedStatement object are populated (that is, via setter methods).

Batch Operations

JDBC allows for batching SQL statements into a Batch Statement to be shipped to the database as one network call. Listing 5.14 shows an example of updating a list of orders in a single batch statement, assuming the IDs to be changed and associated status to change is in an array.

Listing 5.14 Calling Batch Statements

```
try {
...
    connection con.setAutoCommit(false);
    PreparedStatement prepStmt = con.prepareStatement(
        "UPDATE ORDERS SET STATUS=? WHERE ORDER_ID=?"
    );
    for(int I = 0; I < orderIds.length;i++){
        prepStmt.setString(1,orderStatus[i]);
        prepStmt.setString(2,orderIds[i]);
        prepStmt.addBatch();
    }

    int [] numUpdates = prepStmt.executeBatch();
    for (int i=0; i < numUpdates.length; i++) {
       if (numUpdates[i] == -2)
           System.out.println("Execution " + i +
               ": unknown number of rows updated"
           );
       else
           System.out.println("Execution " + i +
               "successful: " numUpdates[i] + " rows updated"
           );
    }
    con.commit();
}
catch(BatchUpdateException b) {
    // process BatchUpdateException
}
```

Extending the Framework

As mentioned earlier, JDBC is the foundational technology of most of the ORM frameworks studied in this book. JDBC is at the heart of most proprietary ORM frameworks as well. The JDBC API has a number of interfaces that can be implemented by vendors or even enterprise application developers when they would like to augment the functionality of the JDBC libraries. The Java Community Process openly publishes the JDBC specification, which vendors can use to build their own, specification-compliant implementations of the JDBC libraries.

Error Handling

Exceptions generated by the Java runtime and DBMS should be printed (or better yet logged) in an associated catch block. Executing the `getMessage` method of the SQLException object can often yield revealing information about what is going awry. However, sometimes you needs more information to diagnose and troubleshoot what may be going wrong. The SQLException object provides three methods: namely, `getMessage`, `getSQLState`, and `getErrorCode`. Vendor error codes are specific to each JDBC driver. Consequently, to determine what the meaning of a particular error code is, you need to reference the driver documentation. Sometimes vendors return multiple exceptions that a developer will iterate through. Listing 5.15 shows an example of a catch block dealing with an SQLException.

Listing 5.15 Using the SQLException to Get Error Information

```
try {
    // Code
}
catch(SQLException ex) {
    while (ex != null) {
        log("Message:    " + ex.getMessage());
        log("SQLState:   " + ex.getSQLState());
        log("ErrorCode: " + ex.getErrorCode());
        ex = ex.getNextException();
    }

}
```

Sometimes when accessing a database via JDBC, SQLWarning objects (a subclass of SQLException) can be generated. Such database access warnings do not halt the execution of an application as would exceptions. This lack of halting execution can sometimes be dangerous, because application developers might not account for such warnings. An example of a warning that might arise is a DataTruncation warning, which indicates that there was a problem when reading or writing data that involved the truncation of data. JDBC warnings can be reported by Connection objects, Statement objects, and/or ResultSet objects by use of the `getWarnings` method. As with the SQLException, the `getMessage`, `getSQLState`, and `getErrorCode` methods can be used to gather more information about the SQLWarning.

ORM Features Supported

The preceding section shows that JDBC is nothing more (or less) than an API for invoking SQL and processing the results. Using the API itself is relatively simple. The complexity emerges when we try to bridge the gap from this purely relational view of data to concepts that programmers using object-oriented languages like Java have come to expect—objects, attributes, relationships, inheritance, and so on. This complexity is due to the ORM impedance mismatch problem described in Chapter 3.

Although JDBC should not by any stretch of the imagination be considered an ORM framework, Table 5.6 shows that it is relatively straightforward to "simulate" concepts from the object domain using those from the relational world.

Table 5.6 Object Domain to Relational Domain

Object Domain	Relational Domain
Object	Row in a table
Inheritance	Root-leaf tables or union/discriminator
Object Identity	Primary key, query
Attribute	Column of various types
Contained Object	Mapped columns, LOBs
Relationship	Foreign key, join
Constraint	Limited, such as `NOT NULL`
Derived Attribute	Limited built-in functions, like `COUNT`, `MAX`, `SUM`; stored procedures

We will look at each of these "mappings" in turn and how the JDBC programming model concepts can then be employed to bridge the gap.

Objects

Table 5.6 shows how a row in a table can be considered as a representation of an "existing" object instance. That said, the mapping is not always one-to-one depending on the approach to normalization used in the database as described in Chapter 3.

Sometimes the data needed to populate a given Java object is spread across more than one table. Hopefully, each table stores data needed by particular applications' functions that are not needed by others. When these logical units of data are separated into their own table like this, the amount of contention on a particular row is reduced. The downside is that when data from two or more tables is needed in a single unit of work, either (a) a relatively expensive join operation must be done, or (b) a separate query must be issued.

But regardless of whether one or more tables are joined, or one or more statements are executed, your job is to transfer data from these objects into the attributes of the associated domain-specific POJO classes. Listing 5.16 shows a code snippet to illustrate.

Listing 5.16 Manual Mapping of Product Object from a ResultSet

```
int productId = 1234;
PreparedStatement productPS = null;
productPS = conn.prepareStatement(
    "SELECT * FROM PRODUCT WHERE PRODUCT_ID = ?"
);
productPS.setInt(1, productId);
ResultSet productResultSet = productPS.executeQuery();
Product product = new Product();
product.setDescription(productResultSet.getString("DESCRIPTION"));
product.setPrice(productResultSet.getBigDecimal("PRICE"));
product.setProductId(productResultSet.getInt("PRODUCT_ID"));
```

When creating a new instance of a persistent object, the ORM mapping problem is reversed—you will use the properties of the newly instantiated Java object to populate the Insert statement values as shown earlier in the "Programming Model" section of this chapter. The main difference here is that if the attributes from the object are maintained in more than one table, an Insert will need to be executed for each table. Remember that to maintain transactional integrity, multiple updates will require autocommit to be turned off, or that you employ batching, as described in the Programming Model section.

Inheritance

Table 5.6 shows how it is possible to simulate inheritance in various ways, and builds off of the discussion of ORM design issues described in Chapter 3.

For example, one popular approach is called *root-leaf* inheritance, which employs a relationship very much like that of inheritance in a UML diagram. When the root-leaf approach is used, the common attributes "inherited" by all subtypes (including the key fields) are maintained in a *root* table, which also includes a column describing the actual type of the row. This type is mapped to a *leaf* table, which in turn maintains the additional persistent attributes of the subtype. The leaf table includes the key field(s) to enable relating the two tables.

Another approach to simulate inheritance is to employ a "union" in which there is only one table with a discriminator describing how to redefine the remaining columns of the table. BLOBs (binary large objects) are sometimes used for the variant data, which are deserialized (when reading) and serialized (when writing) by a Java application based on the type.

The benefit of union over root-leaf style inheritance is that union style does not require a join or multiple updates, as is required in root-leaf style.

That said, root-leaf style inheritance minimizes unused columns in the database, which can occur in union style inheritance when certain subclasses have more attributes to store than others. And whereas BLOBs are used in union style inheritance to minimize the number of table accesses, a root-leaf style is preferred because it does not require serialization or deserialization of the attributes. Additionally, accessing a single table for all attributes as in done in union style inheritance involves a lesser level of normalization than when root-leaf inheritance is used, and can actually cause contention as a negative side effect. Furthermore, when using root-leaf inheritance, most services that operate on "superclasses" do not need to access "leaf" tables; conversely, many behaviors that are unique to the subclass do not need to access the superclass data. Consequently, costly joins can sometimes be avoided in root-leaf inheritance. Finally, it is easier to add additional levels to the inheritance hierarchy when using a root-leaf style—by simply adding new tables with the additional data—whereas modifying the hierarchy with union style inheritance requires modifying existing table definitions.

For these reasons, we tend to prefer root-leaf style inheritance as the mapping strategy.

Keys

There is still some controversy in the object domain concerning the subject of identity. Should each instance have some kind of a generated ID? Or should the key simply be a set of attributes that when taken together uniquely identify an object? This discussion is interesting because it has some interesting ramifications on ORM, especially when coming "from the bottom."

SQL/JDBC queries can refer to any columns (or derived attributes), and return zero or more rows as a result. Indexes on various columns can be declared, which make these queries more efficient. However, it is also possible to declare in the DDL that for a given table, a column or set of columns uniquely identify the row (that is, you can declare key constraints). Doing so serves as a "hint" to the database runtime so that it can, for example, provide a special index to make access to the matching row very efficient.

Unfortunately, when inserting a record into a database table, JDBC does not automatically generate a key field in the database that uniquely identifies that row. Generated keys are a commonly used approach that simplifies building relationships between objects. For example, we require such functionality when we place an order in the ORDER table of the common example described in Chapter 3. To address the requirement for a generated order key, the DDL of the ORDER table was changed to institute auto key generation (see Listing 5.17).

Listing 5.17 Derby DDL Modification for ORDER_ID Auto-Generation

```
CREATE TABLE ORDER  (

    "ORDER_ID" INTEGER NOT NULL generated always as identity,
    "STATUS" VARCHAR(9) ,
        ...
    );
```

With this modification, every time a row is inserted into the ORDER table, a unique ORDER_ID (the key) is generated with an auto-increment. However, it is important to note that not all databases support this type of auto key generation.

Attributes

Whereas, as mentioned earlier in Table 5.6, a single row of a ResultSet (that was produced by issuing a `SELECT` query spanning one or more tables/views) can be thought to represent a domain object, the attributes of these domain objects are persisted as "columns" in tables. The attributes are declared as part of the DDL describing a table. Normally, table columns are retrieved into a ResultSet using the `SELECT` clause of the SQL statement. They also appear in the `WHERE` clause (for queries) and `ORDER BY` clause (for sorting). Similarly, these columns are used in `UPDATE` and `DELETE` statements.

Table 5.7 shows the mapping between types of the Java programming language and the corresponding SQL types.

Table 5.7 JDBC Type Mapping

Java Type	JDBC Type
`String`	`CHAR`, `VARCHAR`, or `LONGVARCHAR`
`java.math.BigDecimal`	`NUMERIC`
`boolean`	`BIT`
`byte`	`TINYINT`
`short`	`SMALLINT`
`int`	`INTEGER`
`long`	`BIGINT`
`float`	`REAL`
`double`	`DOUBLE`
`byte[]`	`BINARY`, `VARBINARY`, or `LONGVARBINARY`
`java.sql.Date`	`DATE`
`java.sql.Time`	`TIME`
`java.sql.Timestamp`	`TIMESTAMP`
`CLOB`	`CLOB`
`BLOB`	`BLOB`

Java Type	JDBC Type
ARRAY	ARRAY
STRUCT	STRUCT
REF	REF
JAVA_OBJECT	JAVA_OBJECT

Contained Objects

Certain complex attribute types can be persisted directly as columns by JDBC/SQL. As illustrated in Table 5.7, Dates and Timestamps get converted automatically into and out of Java types by the JDBC Driver implementation.

Other complex types are only supported indirectly through arbitrarily long VARCHAR, BLOB (Binary Large Object) and CLOB (Character Large Object) column types. These column values must be parsed by the Java application—sometimes through the use of common utility functions (like Java serialization). Say, for example, you would like to persist a domain object into the database "as is." You can do so by leveraging the BLOB type, serializing the domain object when you want to persist it, and deserializing the object when the time comes to gather the domain object. The danger of persisting complex types this way is that an SQL database cannot query within a BLOB.

The most popular approach to handling "contained" objects is to store them as separate fields in the same table, with some naming convention that makes it clear that they are subfields of the same contained object. And, of course, if the back-end database is properly normalized, the "contained" object is maintained in its own table, with the key from the "containing" object being used to identify the contained one. This approach can work well with "contained" objects that are contained in multiple objects, and possibly even many times within the same object—such as when both a billing address and a shipping address are associated with a customer. In this case, a discriminator field is sometimes used in the normalized table to indicate the "role" that the contained object plays—similar to using a field with root-leaf inheritance to indicate the subtype in the common superclass table. This role descriptor can identify the table/class of the containing object as well so that uniqueness of the role across the application domain is guaranteed.

Relationships

Objects can have bidirectional relationships, which can only be simulated in the relational domain as foreign keys. A one-to-many relationship is normally simulated with a foreign key from the "many" side back to the "one" side. For example, where an Order might have many line items, the foreign key back to Order is stored in the LineItem. No update is required to the Order side when a LineItem is created, because there is no column that contains the keys for all the items.

Where a relationship is one-to-one, then, relating the two tables requires updates on both sides, unless the relationship is unidirectional. Updating two tables in the same unit of work will require explicit transactional control or batch updates. We will discuss "preloading" related objects in the upcoming section, "Tuning Options."

Constraints

In the database realm, adding primary and foreign keys to tables is considered an application of a constraint. But these are not the same constraints as those we have in the object domain—which are more related to the cardinality of relationships, ordering, and so on.

In relational database design, a primary key (often referred to as a unique key) is a candidate key that uniquely identifies each row in a table. The primary key comprises a single column or set of columns (that is, a composite primary key). On the other hand, a foreign key is a referential constraint between two database tables. The foreign key identifies a column or a set of columns in one (referencing) table that in turn refers to a column or set of columns in another (referenced) table.

Beyond the constraints of primary and foreign keys, SQL/JDBC also enables a limited set of constraints on columns. These constraints are declared in the DDL. Examples of such constraints include (but are not limited to) the following: indicating that a given column cannot be `NULL`, indicating that a given column's value must be within a certain range of values, and indicating that a given column should be of a certain type (for example, a `DECIMAL` type with a precision of four digits and a scale of two digits). The constraints are checked prior to insert, update, or delete operations.

Derived Attributes

In the `SELECT` and `WHERE` clause of an SQL/JDBC query, certain operators like +, -, *, and / are allowed to return "derived" (or computed) results. Further, certain functions on rows and columns can be executed, like `COUNT`, `SUM`, and `MAX`. For example, the `COUNT` function returns an integer that is the number of rows returned by an associated `SELECT` clause. The `SUM` function returns the sum of the indicated numeric column. The `MAX` function returns the highest value of a selected column, while `MIN` returns the lowest. There are others that vary per database flavor, but the point is that "out of the box" the set is relatively limited. For all intents and purposes, these functions can be treated like virtual columns of the table.

It is important to note that many databases, such as IBM DB2 Universal Database, allow for database developers to supplement the built-in functions supplied by the database with their own functions to, in effect, customize their shop requirements. Case in point, DB2 allows for user-defined functions (UDFs) to be written in Assembler, C, COBOL, PL/I, and Java. For example, let us say that you need for a function to calculate a logarithm of a given number to a given base. You could do so by creating a Java UDF. These UDFs run on the database server. DB2, for example, has its own JVM that could power the hypothetical logarithmic function just mentioned.

And where the database does not have the exact functions desired, stored procedures are sometimes used to allow the database to handle the computation. This is an interesting trade-off to consider and should take into account the amount of data that would have to be passed back to the Java application to compute the data versus the amount of CPU used on the database server.

Tuning Options

The kinds of trade-offs discussed in the previous sections with respect to mapping Java objects to relational tables are exactly what makes programming in JDBC interesting for the developer. The persistence layer of an application is typically the layer that can easily become a performance bottleneck. Consequently, it is paramount that the persistence layer be scrutinized to improve performance where possible. In this section we will examine various tuning options, such as query optimization, caching, loading related objects, and locking.

Query Optimization

Optimizations can be achieved in different areas. SQL statements themselves can be optimized by doing things like reordering the `WHERE` clause. Some optimizations can be achieved in the database, for example, by creating indexes on criteria that is often queried on. JDBC has various knobs and whistles you can use to improve query performance, such as lowering isolation levels on certain use cases, using Prepared Statements, and using various cursors. The JDBC API can also control the amount of data fetched from the database. The JDBC fetch size gives the JDBC driver a hint as to the number of rows that should be fetched from the database when more rows are needed. For large queries that return a large number of objects, you can configure the row fetch size used in the query to improve performance by reducing the number of database hits required to satisfy the selection criteria. Most JDBC drivers default to a fetch size of 10, so if you are reading 1,000 objects, increasing the fetch size to 256 can significantly reduce the time required to fetch a query's results. The optimal fetch size is not always obvious. You can control the fetch size programmatically by setting properties on the ResultSet.

Caching

To minimize access to the database, caching facilities might be leveraged. After the due diligence of transferring data from a ResultSet into a domain object has been performed by an application developer, the domain object can be cached using a caching layer of choice. Domain objects must be cached using the prescribed approach of the caching facility of choice.

Loading Related Objects

Two forms of loading the data are needed to populate a graph of related objects and normalized attributes: "lazy" and "aggressive." Lazy loading generally waits until the objects or properties are accessed to fetch the data with the appropriate query as needed. Of course, this trade-off works well in cases where most of the properties or related objects are never accessed. It does not work so well otherwise, as multiple requests to the database server are made.

Aggressive loading typically is done by issuing SQL joins across various tables to minimize the number of trips to the database server. These joins can be quite complex. Listing 5.18 shows the implementation of a four-way join that demonstrates aggressively loading the data necessary to completely populate an open order associated with a customer. It shows "outer joins" that will load conditionally, so the query will return the data necessary to populate a customer with no open order, a customer with an open order and no line items, or a customer with an open order that contains LineItems. Without a left outer join, you cannot do such a conditional loading. The LineItem, however, has a regular join with the Product because a LineItem will always load with its Product.

Listing 5.18 A Complex Four-Way Join to Get Customer and Order Data

```
customerPS = conn.prepareStatement(
    "SELECT c.CUSTOMER_ID,
            c.OPEN_ORDER, c.NAME, c.BUSINESS_VOLUME_DISCOUNT,
            c.BUSINESS_PARTNER, c.BUSINESS_DESCRIPTION,
            c.RESIDENTIAL_HOUSEHOLD_SIZE,
            c.RESIDENTIAL_FREQUENT_CUSTOMER, c.TYPE,
            o.ORDER_ID, o.STATUS, o.TOTAL,
            l.PRODUCT_ID, l.ORDER_ID, l.QUANTITY, l.AMOUNT,
            p.PRODUCT_ID, p.PRICE,p.DESCRIPTION
     FROM CUSTOMER c
          LEFT OUTER JOIN ORDERS o ON c.OPEN_ORDER = o.ORDER_ID
          LEFT OUTER JOIN (
              LINE_ITEM l
              JOIN PRODUCT p ON l.PRODUCT_ID = p.PRODUCT_ID
          ) ON o.ORDER_ID = l.ORDER_ID
     WHERE c.CUSTOMER_ID = ?"
);
```

The complexity of this SQL query should speak for itself. However, sometimes this level of control is necessary to meet the response time and throughput requirements of a system.

Locking

In the transaction section, we discussed isolation levels supported by JDBC. The proper locking is achieved by setting the desired isolation on a Connection object. Listing 5.19 shows an example.

Listing 5.19 Setting the Isolation Level

```
con.setTransactionIsolation(Connection.TRANSACTION_READ_COMMITTED);
```

A word of caution: Setting the isolation levels can affect performance and data integrity, as we discussed in Chapter 2. Often, these settings can be done at the database or configured on a connection pool from within a Java EE Application Server.

Development Process for the Common Example

One example of the benefits of development with JDBC is that there is not much you need to do before rolling up your sleeves and coding. All that is really necessary is to have the JDBC driver in your classpath. The rest of the dependencies are fulfilled by the Java Development Kit (JDK), which includes the JDBC APIs. We will be showing relevant portions of our common example. You can download the code and read the instructions in Appendix A to run it. In this section, we will show how we implemented our example introduced in Chapter 3.

Defining the Objects

As mentioned earlier, the definition of objects in JDBC is left up to the application developer and must be done programmatically. When using the JDBC approach, you will often apply the Transaction Script Pattern, which avoids mapping to domain objects for the most part and uses simple POJO objects specialized for each request to pass data in and out.

This pattern is often simpler than the Domain Model pattern because the more complex the domain model, the more tedious the code is needed to map object data into and out of Statement parameters and ResultSets.

For purposes of comparison with the other persistence mechanisms, we will use the Domain Model pattern. Listings 5-20 through 5-25 show only the internal property definitions from the Java objects. These properties are all that are necessary for you to understand the code in the next sections, assuming that each property has an associated getter and setter method. The full Java object definitions can be found in the downloadable code on the companion website.

Listing 5.20 shows the essential properties of the AbstractCustomer superclass.

Listing 5.20 The AbstractCustomer Class

```
public abstract class AbstractCustomer implements Serializable
{
    protected int customerId;
    protected String name;
    protected Order openOrder;
    protected Set<Order> orders;
    // getters and setters
```

Listing 5.21 shows the properties defined in the ResidentialCustomer subclass.

Listing 5.21 The ResidentialCustomer Class

```
public class ResidentialCustomer extends AbstractCustomer implements
        Serializable
{
    protected short householdSize;
    protected boolean frequentCustomer;
    //getters and setters
```

In addition to the ResidentialCustomer class, we have a BusinessCustomer class that extends the AbstractCustomer class. Listing 5.22 shows the properties associated with the BusinessCustomer class.

Listing 5.22 The BusinessCustomer Class

```
public class BusinessCustomer extends AbstractCustomer implements
        Serializable
{
    protected boolean volumeDiscount, businessPartner;
    protected String description;
    //getters and setters
```

Listing 5.23 shows the essential properties of the Order class. Notice its association with a Set of LineItem objects as well as with an AbstractCustomer, indicating the customer to which the order belongs.

Listing 5.23 The Order Class

```
public class Order implements Serializable
{
    protected int orderId;
    protected BigDecimal total;

    public static enum Status
    {
        OPEN, SUBMITTED, CLOSED
    }

    protected Status status;
    protected AbstractCustomer customer;
    protected Set<LineItem> lineitems;

    //getters and setters
```

Line items of an order are realized via the LineItem object, the properties of which are shown in Listing 5.24. Notice how the LineItem object has a reference to the Product in it.

Listing 5.24 The LineItem Class

```
public class LineItem implements Serializable
{
    private static final long serialVersionUID = -5969434202374976648L;
    protected long quantity;
    protected BigDecimal amount;
    protected Product product;
    //getters and setters
```

The last of the domain objects is the Product object. Listing 5.25 shows the Product class definition and associated properties.

Listing 5.25 The Product Class

```
public class Product implements Serializable
{
    protected int productId;
    protected BigDecimal price;
    protected String description;
    //getters and setters
```

Implementing the Services

This section shows enough relevant code segments for the service implementation for you to see the complexity that gets introduced into your business logic when using the JDBC API. These code listings assume use of a simple wrapper method to handle the code associated with initialization and getting a Connection as described previously in the "Programming Model" section. See the downloadable code for the details of this wrapper method.

`loadCustomer`

Loading a customer leverages the four-way join we introduced earlier in Listing 5.18. Listing 5.26 shows only a subset of the logic needed to populate an object graph from the result of the joined data.

Listing 5.26 Load Customer

```
public AbstractCustomer loadCustomer(int customerId)
throws CustomerDoesNotExistException, GeneralPersistenceException
{
    PreparedStatement customerPS = null;
    ResultSet customerResultSet = null;
    AbstractCustomer customer = null;
    Connection conn = null;
    try
    {
```

```
        // 1. Setup connection
        conn = getJDBCConnection();
        // 2. Retrieve Customer
        customerPS = conn.prepareStatement(
            // See Listing 5.18 for the 4-way join
        );

    customerPS.setInt(1, customerId);
    customerResultSet = customerPS.executeQuery();
    if (customerResultSet.next()==false) {
        throw new CustomerDoesNotExistException();
    }


    String customerType =
       customerResultSet.getString("TYPE");
    if (customerType.equals("BUSINESS")) {
        BusinessCustomer businessCustomer = new BusinessCustomer();
        String volDiscountEval = customerResultSet.getString(
           "BUSINESS_VOLUME_DISCOUNT");
        if (volDiscountEval.equals("Y"))
            businessCustomer.setVolumeDiscount(true);
        else if (volDiscountEval.equals("N"))
            businessCustomer.setVolumeDiscount(false);
        String businessPartnerEval = customerResultSet.getString(
           "BUSINESS_PARTNER");
        if (businessPartnerEval.equals("Y"))
            businessCustomer.setBusinessPartner(true);
        else if (businessPartnerEval.equals("N"))
            businessCustomer.setBusinessPartner(false);
        customer = businessCustomer;
    }
    else if (customerType.equals("RESIDENTIAL")) {
...
    //Continue to POPULATE 4 Levels of objects...
```

openOrder

In the implementation of the `openOrder`, we first check to see whether an order exists by reusing the `loadCustomer` method and checking whether the Order is loaded into the graph. Assuming no exceptions, we insert the new Order into the Order table. Because the Order table uses a generated ID strategy, we must immediately query the Order table for the new ID, and we update the Customer table with that ID. Listing 5.27 shows the relevant code.

Listing 5.27 Open Order

```
AbstractCustomer customer = loadCustomer(customerId);
Order openOrder = customer.getOpenOrder();
if (openOrder != null) throw new OrderAlreadyOpenException();

order = new Order();
order.setCustomer(customer);
```

```
order.setStatus(Order.Status.OPEN);
order.setTotal(new BigDecimal(0.00));

PreparedStatement insertOrderPS = conn.prepareStatement(
    "insert into ORDERS (CUSTOMER_ID,STATUS,TOTAL)
            values (?,?,?)"
);
insertOrderPS.setInt(1, customerId); // set customerID
insertOrderPS.setString(2,"OPEN"); // set status
insertOrderPS.setBigDecimal(3,new BigDecimal(0.00));  // set total
insertOrderPS.executeUpdate(); // execute update statement
insertOrderPS.close();

PreparedStatement retrieveOrdersIdPS = conn.prepareStatement(
    "select ORDER_ID from ORDERS
     where CUSTOMER_ID=? and STATUS = 'OPEN'"
);
retrieveOrdersIdPS.setInt(1, customerId);
ResultSet rs = retrieveOrdersIdPS.executeQuery();

if(rs.next()){
    int orderId = rs.getInt("ORDER_ID");
    order.setOrderId(orderId);
}
else {
    throw new GeneralPersistenceException(
        "Could not retrieve new order id"
    );
}

PreparedStatement updateCustomerPS = conn.prepareStatement(
    "update CUSTOMER set OPEN_ORDER=? where CUSTOMER_ID=?"
);
updateCustomerPS.setInt(1, order.getOrderId());
updateCustomerPS.setInt(2, customerId);
updateCustomerPS.executeUpdate();
updateCustomerPS.close();

conn.commit();
```

addLineItem

This routine first checks to see whether the Product exists by querying the Product table. It then queries to check whether a LineItem already exists, and updates the quantity if it does. Otherwise, it creates a new instance by inserting a new line item into the table. Listing 5.28 shows the relevant code fragments.

Listing 5.28 Add LineItem

```
PreparedStatement productPS  conn.prepareStatement(
    "select PRICE,DESCRIPTION from PRODUCT where PRODUCT_ID=?"
);
productPS.setInt(1, productId);
productResultSet = productPS.executeQuery();
if (productResultSet==null)
   throw new ProductDoesNotExistException();

customerPS = conn.prepareStatement(
    "select OPEN_ORDER from CUSTOMER where CUSTOMER_ID=?"
);
customerPS.setInt(1, customerId);
customerResultSet = customerPS.executeQuery();

if (customerResultSet == null)
    throw new CustomerDoesNotExistException();

customerResultSet.next();
Object openOrder = customerResultSet.getObject("OPEN_ORDER");
if (customerResultSet.getObject("OPEN_ORDER") == null)
    throw new OrderNotOpenException();

int orderID = (Integer)openOrder;
if (!productResultSet.next())
    throw new ProductDoesNotExistException();

BigDecimal productPrice = productResultSet.getBigDecimal("PRICE");
BigDecimal additionalCost = productPrice.multiply(
    new BigDecimal(quantity)
);
BigDecimal lineItemAmount = new BigDecimal(0.0);

lineItemPS  = conn.prepareStatement(
    "select QUANTITY, AMOUNT from LINE_ITEM
     where ORDER_ID = ? and PRODUCT_ID = ?"
);
lineItemPS.setInt(1, orderID);
lineItemPS.setInt(2, productId);
lineItemResultSet = lineItemPS.executeQuery();
boolean lineItemsCheck = lineItemResultSet.next();
if (!lineItemsCheck) // check if any line items already exist
{
    //Insert new LineItem
}
else
{
    //Update Existing LineItem
}
```

`removeLineitem`

For removing a LineItem, we check to see whether the associated Product exists; if so, then we check whether the associated Order is open. If the Order is open, we delete any LineItem for that Product. We do not check whether the LineItem exists in the table before removing the LineItem because technically, you can examine the value returned by the `executeUpdate` method to see whether the delete occurred. Listing 5.29 shows the relevant fragments of code.

Listing 5.29 Remove LineItem

```
PreparedStatement productPS = conn.prepareStatement(
    "SELECT * FROM PRODUCT WHERE PRODUCT_ID = ?"
);
productPS.setInt(1, productId);
productResultSet = productPS.executeQuery();
boolean productExists = false;
productExists = productResultSet.next();
productResultSet.close();
productPS.close();
conn.commit();
if (!productExists)
    throw new ProductDoesNotExistException();

AbstractCustomer customer = loadCustomer(customerId);
Order openOrder = customer.getOpenOrder();
if (openOrder == null)
    throw new OrderNotOpenException();

int orderId = openOrder.getOrderId();
PreparedStatement productDeletePS = conn.prepareStatement(
    "DELETE FROM LINE_ITEM
     WHERE PRODUCT_ID = ? AND ORDER_ID = ?"
);
productDeletePS.setInt(1, productId);
productDeletePS.setInt(2, orderId);
int deleteCount = productDeletePS.executeUpdate();
productDeletePS.close();
if (deleteCount == 0)
   throw new LineItemDoesNotExist();

conn.commit();
```

submitOrder

The example code for submitting an order using JDBC is shown in Listing 5.30. We check again to ensure that we have an open Order. We also check to see whether we have any LineItems. You cannot submit an order otherwise. If both conditions are met, we update the status of the Order and we set the `OPEN_ORDER` column on the Customer table to `null`.

Listing 5.30 Submit Order

```
AbstractCustomer customer = loadCustomer(customerId);
Order openOrder = customer.getOpenOrder();
if (openOrder == null) throw new OrderNotOpenException();
if ((openOrder.getLineitems() == null) ||
    (openOrder.getLineitems().size() <= 0))
    throw new NoLineItemsException();

PreparedStatement updateOrderStatusPS = conn.prepareStatement(
    "update ORDERS set STATUS ='SUBMITTED'
     WHERE ORDER_ID=?"
);
int orderId = openOrder.getOrderId();
updateOrderStatusPS.setInt(1, orderId);
updateOrderStatusPS.executeUpdate();
updateOrderStatusPS.close();

customerCloseOrderPS = conn.prepareStatement(
    "update CUSTOMER set OPEN_ORDER = NULL
     where CUSTOMER_ID=?"
);
customerCloseOrderPS.setInt(1, customerId);
customerCloseOrderPS.executeUpdate();
```

Packaging the Components

The packaging of components will depend on your deployment environment. JDBC applications on a Java SE platform may require nothing more than specifying the proper JDBC driver JARs in the classpath. Java EE applications may require you to configure a DataSource on an application server by defining references to that DataSource inside a deployment descriptor. Depending on the implementation, you may package your driver with your application or install the driver on a server.

Unit Testing

As we discussed in Chapter 3, we are using JUnit and DbUnit to test our code. The downloadable source contains a test project for each technology. Figure 5.2 shows the Unit Test Project for the JDBC version of the common example.

Deploying to Production

Usually the database URL is different in production than in any of the testing environments. If a DataSource is used, this can be a simple matter of changing the binding; otherwise, don't forget to change the property used to specify the JDBC URL in your configuration file. If you are using a DataSource, you may configure connection pool settings and such as part of a testing process; these settings will likely differ in production.

Figure 5.2 Unit test package.

Summary

JDBC has been part of the Java language almost since its inception. JDBC libraries allow application developers to directly interact with databases by invoking SQL statements within their Java code.

Using JDBC as your persistence mechanism may simplify your dependencies on other components; but, unfortunately, the object-relational impedance mismatch is quickly realized as a developer is forced to try to bridge the chasm between the disparate world of tables, rows, and SQL and the world of objects, classes, and Java.

This assessment does not diminish the importance of JDBC. JDBC 4.0 has become very functional for both online and batch applications, and will continue to evolve to meet the changing requirements of Java applications.

The fact of the matter is that JDBC is the foundation that supports most homegrown, open-source, and commercial ORM frameworks, including those we will study in the rest of this book.

Links to developerWorks

A.5.1 *Getting Started with JDBC 4 using Apache Derby*

This is a DeveloperWorks Tutorial on JDBC 4.0 Features.

www.ibm.com/developerworks/edu/os-dw-os-ad-jdbc.html

A.5.2 *Understand the DB2 UDB JDBC Universal Driver*

This is a good discussion on the difference between Type 2 and Type 4 Drivers.

www.ibm.com/developerworks/db2/library/techarticle/dm-0512kokkat/

References

[EJB] *Enterprise JavaBeans*. java.sun.com/products/ejb/

[Fisher] Fisher *JDBC API Tutorial and Reference, Third Edition*. Prentice Hall PTR 2003

[JAXP] *Java API for XML Processing*. java.sun.com/j2se/1.5.0/docs/guide/xml/jaxp/index.html

[JAX-WS] *Java API for XML Web Services*. https://jax-ws.dev.java.net/

[JDBC] *JDBC 4.0 Specification*. www.jcp.org/en/jsr/detail?id=221

[JDBC 1] *JDBC Database Access Tutorial*. java.sun.com/docs/books/tutorial/jdbc/index.html

[JDBC 2] *JDBC Technotes*. java.sun.com/javase/6/docs/technotes/guides/jdbc/

[JNDI] *Java Naming and Directory Interface*. java.sun.com/javase/6/docs/technotes/guides/jndi/index.html

[JMS] *Java Messaging Service*. java.sun.com/products/jms/

[JTA] *Java Transaction API*. java.sun.com/products/jta/

[SDN] *Sun Developer Network*. developers.sun.com/product/jdbc/drivers

Chapter 6
Apache iBATIS

This chapter provides an overview of Apache iBATIS. It covers how iBATIS implements the object-relational mapping techniques described in the previous chapters. We will briefly survey its history, discuss how it is used, and show several end-to-end examples of its use.

Background

iBATIS is a popular framework for object-relational mapping that makes SQL, stored procedures, and legacy database schemas first-class citizens. The iBATIS philosophy is that SQL is mature, well-known, and tested in industry; thus, SQL and stored procedures are the best mechanism to query for an object with the iBATIS framework. This philosophy is realized in iBATIS with facilities for the direct manipulation of the SQL code. XML-based mapping statements are used to map the arguments and/or results of an SQL statement. Externalizing queries to XML Files makes it easy to be reviewed easily by database administrators.

Type of Framework

iBATIS is a table gateway framework as described in "Patterns of Enterprise Architecture" [Fowler]. An object often represents an entire database table and is associated with inserts, updates, and queries for that type. Although iBATIS can support complex object-relational mapping concepts, such as the java.util.Map type and mapping objects to database joins through the use of advanced SQL, it lacks full object-relational mapping features to make it a Full Data Mapper. Such features include an object-oriented query language and implicit object persistence.

History

What is now iBATIS started as a small body of code that was used primarily as a shortcut to hand-coding JDBC for its author—Clinton Begin [Begin]. In 2002, Microsoft published a paper claiming that a .Net implementation of Sun's Java PetStore application [MSDN] has orders of magnitude in performance improvement. Begin set out to prove this claim wrong by developing JPetStore—an agile Java EE variant complying with the same requirements as a traditional Java EE three-tier architecture (rather than the two-tier architecture allowing ASPs to directly invoke the database introduced by the .Net implementation).

Begin's effort showed that a tiny persistence framework could be used for enterprise quality database access instead of entity EJBs. This library caught the attention of the open-source community as a viable approach to object-relational mapping, resulting in its own open-source project called the iBATIS Database Layer.

Architectural Overview

iBATIS is a simple framework with few dependencies. As shown in Figure 6.1, POJOs can be mapped to input parameters of an SQL statement or to the results of an SQL Statement executing a query. The statements are executed via JDBC. The SQL statements are externalized to XML files and become callable "mapped statements" in your Java code.

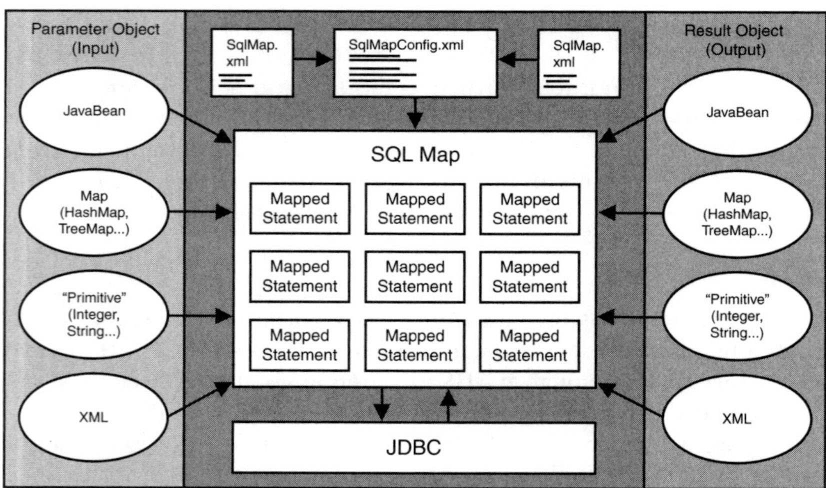

Figure 6.1 iBATIS Data Mapper framework.

Standards Adherence

The iBATIS APIs are not part of any standard or specification. However, iBATIS is designed to be used with two significant standards—JDBC and Java EE. iBATIS utilizes JDBC for underlying database connectivity that is portable. iBATIS also reduces the complexity of using JDBC directly; for instance, it automatically releases JDBC resources for the user. iBATIS is also designed to be used within a Java EE web application, allowing it to use application data sources and transaction management through the Java Transaction API (JTA).

Platforms Required

iBATIS requires J2SE 1.3 or higher, as well as JDBC 2.0 or higher. Nearly all providers of a Java runtime environment (JRE) provide JDBC with their Java distribution. The iBATIS library itself is delivered as a single JAR file (as of version 2.3) with the naming convention of `ibatis-`*`version.build`*`.jar`—for example, `ibatis-2.30.667.jar`.

Other Dependencies

Beyond JDBC 2.0, iBATIS has no dependencies; however, depending on a project's requirements, other libraries may prove useful.

Table 6.1 illustrates some optional dependencies. For example, if you are in an environment where multiple JDBC drivers are used, the Jakarta Commons Database Connection Pool (DBCP) wrapper library can allow for unified pooling.

Table 6.1 iBATIS Dependencies

Description	When to Use	Dependency
Legacy JDK Support	If you're running less than JDK 1.4 and if your app server also doesn't already supply these JARs.	JDBC 2.0 Extensions JTA 1.0.1a Xerces 2.4.0
iBATIS Backward Compatibility	If you're using the old iBATIS (1.x) DAO framework or the old Data Mapper (1.x).	iBATIS DAO 1.3.1
Runtime Bytecode Enhancement	If you want to enable CGLIB 2.0 bytecode enhancement to improve lazy loading and reflection performance.	CGLIB 2.0
DataSource Implementation	If you want to use the Jakarta DBCP connection pool.	DBCP 1.1

continues

Table 6.1 Continued

Description	When to Use	Dependency
Distributed Caching	If you want to use OSCache for centralized or distributed cache support.	OSCache 2.0.1
Logging Solution	If you want to utilize iBATIS debug logs.	Log4J 1.2.8 Jakarta Commons Logging

If your application spans multiple Java Virtual Machines (JVMs), distributed caching can significantly improve performance. iBATIS supports distributed caching with OpenSymphony cache (OSCache), which is also an open-source offering. The Caching section in this chapter discusses caching in detail, including how to plug in any distributed caching service.

A final possible dependency is bytecode enhancement for lazy loading. Bytecode enhancement allows iBATIS to modify application bytecode at runtime. This allows iBATIS to optimize queries—especially large queries—to only the subset of results that are actually used by the end user. iBATIS supports CGLIB 2.0 for bytecode enhancement. Although it is completely optional, it improves the iBATIS implementation of lazy loading and reflection. Utilizing CGLIB is highly recommended if performance is a key requirement for your application.

Vendors and Licenses

In October 2004, iBATIS was voted into Apache and gained Apache incubator status. In May 2005, the project completed its incubation status and became an official Apache open-source project. iBATIS is distributed under the Apache 2.0 license. The latest source code, binaries, and documentation are always available at the iBATIS main site [iBATIS].

Available Literature

iBATIS is designed to be a simple and intuitive framework; however, even the most elegant library should be well documented. The sources in Table 6.2 provide comprehensive documentation about how to use iBATIS in practice.

Table 6.2 Available Literature

Title	Source	Description
iBATIS IN ACTION [Begin]	Manning Publications Co.	Excellent comprehensive resource written by the founder of iBATIS
Developer's Guide [iBATIS 1]	ibatis.apache.org/docs/java/pdf/iBATIS-SqlMaps-2_en.pdf	Comprehensive documentation available in PDF form
iBATIS Tutorial [iBATIS 2]	ibatis.apache.org/docs/java/pdf/iBATIS-SqlMaps-2-Tutorial_en.pdf	An excellent introductory tutorial for getting started
Wiki [iBATIS 3]	opensource.atlassian.com/confluence/oss/display/IBATIS/Home	Excellent for platform-specific notes and information on new undocumented features
Improve persistence with Apache Derby and iBATIS: Part 1	www.ibm.com/developerworks/edu/os-dw-os-ad-ibatis2.html	A developerWorks tutorial on using iBATIS with the Derby Database  A.6.1
Improve persistence with Apache Derby and iBATIS: Part 2	www.ibm.com/developerworks/edu/os-dw-os-ad-ibatis1.html	Part 2 of an article series that shows the JPetStore application written in iBATIS  A.6.2
Improve persistence with Apache Derby and iBATIS: Part 3	www.ibm.com/developerworks/edu/os-dw-os-ad-ibatis3.html	Part 3 of an article series that shows some more advanced iBATIS features  A.6.3
DB2 UDB, WebSphere, and iBATIS	www.ibm.com/developerworks/db2/library/techarticle/dm-0502cline/	Article describing using iBATIS with DB2 and WebSphere Application Server  A.6.4
Tired of hand coding JDBC? Use iBATIS as a data mapping framework instead.	www.ibm.com/developerworks/websphere/techjournal/0510_col_barcia/0510_col_barcia.html	A commentary on iBATIS giving a brief overview  A.6.5

Programming Model

The programming model for iBATIS is a combination of (a) SQL specified in XML files called SQLMaps and (b) calls to instances of special classes, such as SQLMapClient, that invoke the query logic in the XML. iBATIS is designed to be simple to use for the 80% of applications that do not require complex object-relational mapping techniques.

Initialization

The configuration of the iBATIS framework is centered around an XML property file called `SqlMapConfig.xml`. Listing 6.1 shows a basic example.

Listing 6.1 Example SqlMap Configuration File

```
<sqlMapConfig>
  <settings cacheModelsEnabled="true" enhancementEnabled="false"
     maxSessions="64" maxTransactions="8" maxRequests="128"/>
  <transactionManager type="JDBC">
    <dataSource type="SIMPLE">
      <property value="${driver}"
        name="org.apache.derby.jdbc.EmbeddedDriver"/>
      <property value="${url}" name="jdbc:derby:/opt/pwte/EXAMPLE"/>
      <property value="15" name="Pool.MaximumActiveConnections"/>
      <property value="15" name="Pool.MaximumIdleConnections"/>
      <property value="1000" name="Pool.MaximumWait"/>
    </dataSource>
  </transactionManager>

  <sqlMap resource="org/pwte/ibatis/Customer.xml"/>
  <sqlMap resource="org/pwte/ibatis/Order.xml"/>
  <sqlMap resource="org/pwte/ibatis/Product.xml"/>
  <sqlMap resource="org/pwte/ibatis/LineItem.xml"/>

</sqlMapConfig>
```

Setting up the framework in Java before executing a database operation is also quite straightforward. You use an SqlMapClientBuilder to create an instance of an SqlMapClient by loading the SqlMap configuration file. For example, the application code to invoke the query associated with the file shown in Listing 6.1 with a Customer with an ID of 100 is shown in Listing 6.2.

Listing 6.2 iBATIS Initialization in Java

```
SqlMapClient dm = null;
Reader reader = null;
try {
    reader = Resources.getResourceAsReader("SqlMapConfig.xml");
    dm = SqlMapClientBuilder.buildSqlMapClient(reader);
    AbstractCustomer customer =
        (AbstractCustomer) dm.queryForObject("customer.query", 100);

    // perform remainder of logic...

}
catch (IOException ioe) {
    // perform appropriate error handling
}
```

Listing 6.1 illustrates a configuration example for a simple Derby JDBC driver. In practice, JDBC DataSources managed by Java EE application servers are often used. This is fully supported by iBATIS. For instance, Listing 6.3 shows the configuration for a DataSource with the JNDI name of `jdbc/Derby/DataSource`.

Listing 6.3 JNDI DataSource Configuration

```
<sqlMapConfig>
    <settings cacheModelsEnabled="true" enhancementEnabled="false"
        maxSessions="64" maxTransactions="8" maxRequests="128"/>

    <transactionManager type="JTA">
        <property name="UserTransaction"
         value="java:comp/env/UserTransaction" />
        <dataSource type="JNDI">
            <property name="DataSource"
             value="java:comp/env/jdbc/Derby/DataSource" />
        </dataSource>
    </transactionManager>
    ...
</sqlMapConfig>
```

Connections

iBATIS uses a transparent connection model. Connections to the database are allocated and managed for you by the SqlMapClient in an effort to promote simplicity. In fact, iBATIS does not have an API to explicitly create a database connection. However, iBATIS does allow you to access the JDBC Connection object associated with the SqlMap in case you need to configure some advanced settings.

Transactions

All iBATIS statements run inside a transaction. iBATIS supports four types of transactions: local, global, custom, and external. Local transactions use the standard JDBC API for transaction support (Listing 6.1 serves as an example of setting up local transactions). iBATIS can be configured to use other transaction managers, such as a JTA transaction manager for an application server (see Listing 6.3 for an example of configuring transactions with JTA). Another option for Application Servers is to set the transaction type to be External. In this case, iBATIS will assume some other API is handling transactions. This is the preferred option when using iBATIS in an EJB Container with Container Managed Transactions. Finally, iBATIS supports a standard interface to plug in your own custom transaction manager or a third-party transaction manager that is not supported by the SqlMap config.

By default, iBATIS automatically groups each statement into a transaction for you. However, it also supports user transactions—that is, transactions that are explicitly demarcated by the user through methods on the SqlMapClient. Listing 6.4 illustrates a user transaction that groups two updates for a BusinessCustomer. First, the Customer is updated to be a nonpartner; then, its openOrder is updated with a status of `SUBMITTED`. If a runtime exception occurs during either of these operations, the transaction is automatically rolled back. You can also explicitly call the rollback method on the SqlMapClient. When a programmer explicitly calls any transactional operations, iBATIS delegates the call to the underlying API. In the case of JDBC, it will toggle the autoCommit option from true to false and back as appropriate and delegate to the transaction on the underlying Connection. For the JTA option, it will call the corresponding demarcation methods on the UserTransactionOption. If you use the External option, calling those operations will have no effect.

Listing 6.4 User Transaction Example

```
try {
    dm.startTransaction();

    AbstractCustomer customer = new BusinessCustomer();
    customer.setCustomerId(100);
    customer.setPartner(false);

    dm.update(
      "customer.business.update.partner", (AbstractCustomer) customer);

    Map orderUpdateInput = new HashMap();
    map.put("customerId",100);
    map.put("orderStatus","SUBMITTED");

    dm.update("customer.update.order.status", orderUpdateInput);
```

```
    //Other logic that may end badly

    dm.commitTransaction();
}
catch (SomeApplicationExceptionNeedingRollback e) {
    dm.rollbackTransaction();
}
finally {
    dm.endTransaction();
}
```

iBATIS also fully supports standard JDBC transaction isolation levels. iBATIS will use the default for the JDBC driver or the isolation level configured by an application server's datasource. To explicitly set an isolation level before starting a transaction, you can use code like that shown in Listing 6.5.

Listing 6.5 Setting the JDBC Transaction Isolation Level

```
dm.startTransaction(Connection.TRANSACTION_REPEATABLE_READ);
```

See your JDBC driver for the isolation levels associated with the Connection. Some of these are discussed in Chapter 3, "Designing Persistent Object Services" and Chapter 5, "JDBC."

Create

Any database operation accessed through iBATIS requires both an XML SqlMap statement and the Java code to invoke the statement. As an example, let's create a ResidentialCustomer. Listing 6.6 illustrates the XML required.

Listing 6.6 ResidentialCustomer Create SqlMap XML

```
<parameterMap id="customer.residential.map"
   class="org.pwte.example.domain.ResidentialCustomer" >
   <parameter property="name" />
   <parameter property="householdSize" />
   <parameter property="frequentCustomer"
   typeHandler="org.pwte.ibatis.YesNoBoolTypeHandler" />
   </parameterMap>

   <insert id="customer.residential.insert"
    parameterMap="customer.residential.map">
      insert into CUSTOMER ( NAME, RESIDENTIAL_HOUSEHOLD_SIZE,
      RESIDENTIAL_FREQUENT_CUSTOMER ) values ( ?, ?, ? )
</insert>
```

> **Key Point**
>
> Notice that CUSTOMER_ID was not populated. This example assumes that key generation has been put in place such that a primary key is automatically generated. See the "Keys" section, later in this chapter, for a full discussion on key generation.

The `insert` statement contains conventional SQL. The `parameterMap` statement specifies which bean properties from the ResidentialCustomer JavaBean correspond to the statement's parameters. Notice that the `frequentCustomer` property has a customer type handler. This is necessary because our database schema stores booleans as `Y` or `N` characters, and a type handler is needed to convert to and from Java strings. Type handlers are covered in detail in the section "Extending the Framework."

The corresponding Java code to call the `insert` statement is shown in Listing 6.7.

Listing 6.7 Invoking the ResidentialCustomer Create in Java Code

```
ResidentialCustomer customer = new ResidentialCustomer();
customer.setName("Peter Boyce");
customer.setHouseholdSize((short)6);
customer.setFrequentCustomer(true);

dm.insert("customer.residential.insert", customer);
```

Notice how the first argument to the iBATIS `insert` API is the name of the SqlMap. Now consider another example in which we create an Order for this Customer and set the ResidentialCustomer's openOrder attribute. Listing 6.8 illustrates the SqlMap XML needed.

Listing 6.8 Order Create SqlMap XML

```
<parameterMap id="order.open.map" class="org.pwte.example.domain.Order">
 <parameter property="customer.customerId"/>
    <parameter property="status"
      typeHandler="org.pwte.ibatis.StatusEnumTypeHandler"/>
    <parameter property="total"/>
</parameterMap>

<insert id="order.open" parameterMap="order.open.map">
    insert into ORDER_ (CUSTOMER_ID, STATUS, TOTAL) values (?, ?, ?)
</insert>

<update id="customer.open.order" parameterClass="int">
    update CUSTOMER set OPEN_ORDER =
```

```
    (select ORDER_ID from ORDER_ where CUSTOMER_ID = #value#)
  where CUSTOMER_ID = #value#
</update>
```

Notice how the parameter map to create a new order also requires a type handler for the `status` attribute. This is because the `status` attribute is an enumeration and iBATIS requires some extra information to determine how to map the enumeration to the database. Also notice that the `customer.open.order` statement takes in an integer primitive type rather than a JavaBean class and does not require a parameter map. In this case, iBATIS knows how to map the parameters to the database—it knows that the `int` passed in for CUSTOMER_ID should be converted to a JDBC integer type. Thus, because there is no special mapping such as the enumeration in the previous statement, `#argument#` syntax can be used instead of a parameter map.

Listing 6.9 shows the Java code to create a new Order for the ResidentialCustomer.

Listing 6.9 Invoking the Order Create in Java Code

```
Order order = new Order();
order.setCustomer(customer);
order.setStatus(Order.Status.OPEN);
order.setTotal(new BigDecimal(0.00));

dm.insert("order.open", order);
dm.update("customer.open.order", customerId);
```

Retrieve

This section illustrates how read-only queries are performed with iBATIS. Listing 6.10 details the SqlMap statement for a simple retrieval operation of selecting a single customer by customer ID.

Listing 6.10 Customer Retrieve SqlMap XML

```
<select id="customer.select"
 resultMap="customer.select.map"
 parameterClass="int">
      select CUSTOMER_ID, NAME, OPEN_ORDER from CUSTOMER
      where CUSTOMER_ID = #value#
</select>
<resultMap id="customer.select.map" class="business">
  <result property="customerId"/>
  <result property="name"/>
  <result property="openOrder" select="order.select"
   column="OPEN_ORDER"/>
</resultMap>
```

Notice how the ResultMap for the `customer.select` statement has a nested query. The nested `order.select` query populates the customer's openOrder JavaBean. Listing 6.11 shows the corresponding Java code to retrieve a customer and the resultMap section. Because openOrder points to another `select` statement, iBATIS will issue both queries (the `select` to the Customer table and another to the Order table) in response to one API call to the `queryForObject` method to the `customer.select` statement.

Listing 6.11 Invoking the Customer Retrieve in Java Code

```
AbstractCustomer customer = (AbstractCustomer) dm.queryForObject(
   "customer.select", customerId);
```

In Listing 6.11, iBATIS issues two queries; however, suppose you want to populate the Order and Customer based on the result of a single SQL Join between the CUSTOMER and ORDER tables. Listing 6.12 shows the SqlMap for such a query and Listing 6.13 shows the Java code.

Listing 6.12 Active Customer Retrieve SqlMap XML

```
<resultMap id="customer.select.map" class="business">
    <result property="customerId"/>
    <result property="name"/>
    <result property="openOrder"/>
    <result="order.select.map" column="OPEN_ORDER"/>
</resultMap>

<resultMap id="order.select.map" class="order">
    <result property="orderId"/>
    <result property="total"/>
    <result property="status"
     typeHandler="org.pwte.ibatis.StatusEnumTypeHandler"/>
    <result property="lineitems" select="lineitem.select"
     column="ORDER_ID"/>
</resultMap>

<select id="customer.order.select"
 resultMap="customer.select.map"
 parameterClass="customer">
    select CUSTOMER_ID, NAME, OPEN_ORDER
    from CUSTOMER c
    LEFT OUTER JOIN ORDER o
    on c.OPEN_ORDER_ID = ORDER_ID
    where CUSTOMER_ID = #customerId#
</select>
```

If a query returns multiple customer rows, you can use the `queryForList()` method from iBATIS to get a List of Java Objects returned, as shown in Listing 6.13.

Listing 6.13 Active Customer Retrieve SqlMap Java Code

```
List customers = dm.queryForList("customer.active.select");
```

Update

Updating a datasource with iBATIS is very similar to querying data as shown earlier. Consider the use case of changing the quantity of a LineItem. Listing 6.14 and Listing 6.15 illustrate how to change the quantity of a LineItem to 100. In the Update example, we show iBATIS's capability to use "inline" input parameters (named parameters embedded directly in the query). iBATIS also supports the notion of using a parameter map in the XML config file too; we illustrate an example of this approach in Listing 6.22, later in the chapter.

Listing 6.14 Update LineItem SqlMap XML

```
<update id="lineitem.update" parameterClass="java.util.Map">
   update LINE_ITEM set QUANTITY = #quantity#
   where PRODUCT_ID = #productId# and ORDER_ID = #orderId#
</update>
```

Listing 6.15 Invoking the Update LineItem in Java Code

```
// assuming an orderId and productId are given
Map wrapper = new HashMap();
wrapper.put("productId", productId);
wrapper.put("orderId", orderId);
wrapper.put("quantity", 100);
dm.update("lineitem.update", wrapper);
```

Notice that the object passed in as an argument to the `lineitem.update` statement is a Map that is not defined in our domain model (a JavaBean as the key class could have been used just as well). The reason this is necessary is the impedance mismatch between the domain model and the database schema. In the domain model, the LineItem type does not have an `orderId` attribute, but in the database the primary key for the LINE_ITEM table uses both ORDER_ID and PRODUCT_ID. Thus, a custom key class must be used as the argument to our `update` and `insert` statements for LineItem.

As a final update example, suppose a Customer no longer has an openOrder, and thus its open order reference needs to be removed. In terms of our database schema, this means the OPEN_ORDER reference for that CUSTOMER needs to be set to `NULL`. Listing 6.16 and Listing 6.17 showcase how to implement and invoke such an update, respectively.

Listing 6.16 Update Customer Open Order SqlMap XML

```
<update id="customer.close.order" parameterClass="int">
    update CUSTOMER set OPEN_ORDER = NULL where CUSTOMER_ID = #value#
</update>
```

Listing 6.17 Invoking the Update Customer Open Order in Java Code

```
dm.update("customer.close.order", customerId);
```

Delete

As with the other persistence operations, deletion semantics are deferred to standard SQL syntax. iBATIS assumes no responsibility for cascade deletion. It is assumed that cascade delete behavior is configured at the database level.

As an example of a `delete` statement, consider the case in which a LineItem needs to be deleted. Listing 6.18 and Listing 6.19 illustrate this use case, again with the configuration followed by the Java code to invoke it.

Listing 6.18 Delete LineItem SqlMap XML

```
<delete id="lineitem.delete" parameterClass="java.util.Map">
   delete LINE_ITEM
   where PRODUCT_ID = #productId# and ORDER_ID = #orderId#
</delete>
```

Listing 6.19 Invoking the Delete LineItem in Java Code

```
// assuming an orderId and productId are given
Map wrapper = new HashMap();
wrapper.put("productId", productId);
wrapper.put("orderId", orderId);
dm.delete("lineitem.delete", wrapper);
```

Notice the striking similarity to the `update` LineItem use case. Again, a Map object wrapper needs to be used because of the orderId domain modeling mismatch. The only significant difference is the change in the SQL statement.

Now suppose you need to delete an Order and all its associated LineItems, but because of database schema restrictions, you cannot configure the database to perform a cascade `delete`. This use case actually encompasses two iBATIS `delete` statements that manually perform the equivalent of a cascade `delete` as shown in Listing 6.20 and Listing 6.21.

Listing 6.20 Delete Order and LineItems SqlMap XML

```
<delete id="order.delete" parameterClass="int">
     delete ORDER_where ORDER_ID = #value#
</delete>
<delete id="order.lineitem.delete" parameterClass="int">
     delete LINE_ITEM_where ORDER_ID = #value#
</delete>
```

Listing 6.21 Invoking the Delete Order and LineItems in Java Code

```
dm.delete("order.delete',orderId);
dm.delete("order.lineitem.delete",orderId);
```

Stored Procedures

Invoking stored procedures with iBATIS is very similar to other database operations. The only difference is that the SQL is replaced with the name of the stored procedure with its arguments. For instance, consider a stored procedure that swaps the Orders of two Customers. Listing 6.22 and Listing 6.23 illustrate how such a procedure can be invoked.

Listing 6.22 Swap Order Stored Procedure SqlMap XML

```
<parameterMap id="swapParameters" class="map" >
  <parameter property="first" jdbcType="VARCHAR"
   javaType="java.lang.String" mode="INOUT"/>
  <parameter property="second" jdbcType="VARCHAR"
   javaType="java.lang.String" mode="INOUT"/>
</parameterMap>

<procedure id="swap.order" parameterMap="swapParameters" >
  {call swap_customer_order (?, ?)}
</procedure>
```

Listing 6.23 Invoking the Swap Order Stored Procedure in Java Code

```
SwapPojo orderIds = new SwapPojo();
orderIds.setFirst(orderId1);
orderIds.setSecond(orderId2);
dm.update("swap.order", orderIds);
```

Notice that the `update` SqlMapClient API is used because the stored procedure does not return anything. If it did, `queryForObject`, `queryForList`, and the like could be used along with a corresponding result map.

Batch Operations

iBATIS fully supports batch processing through methods on the SqlQueryMap. The `startBatch()` method causes batch mode to be entered, and the `executeBatch()` method causes the batch to be executed, returning the number of rows that were updated as part of the batch.

Listing 6.24 illustrates using batch statement to group two `updates` for a BusinessCustomer. First, the customer is updated to be a nonpartner; then, its OpenOrder is updated with a status of `"SUBMITTED"`. The `executeBatch()` method call should return a value of `2`, representing the number of updated database rows.

Listing 6.24 Batch Statement Example

```
dm.startBatch();
AbstractCustomer customer = new BusinessParnter();
customer.setCustomerId(100);
customer.setPartner(false);
dm.update("customer.business.update.partner",
    (AbstractCustomer)   customer);
Map orderUpdateInput = new HashMap();
map.put("customerId",100);
map.put("orderStatus","SUBMITTED");
dm.update("customer.update.order.status", orderUpdateInput);
int rowsUpdated = dm.executeBatch();
```

Extending the Framework

iBATIS has two special extension points designed for custom type conversion and row processing: type handlers and row handlers. We've seen examples of a TypeHandler, because Boolean types in our domain model, such as `BusinessCustomer.businessPartner`, are represented as characters `Y` and `N` in the database. iBATIS does not provide a default mapping for Booleans to type `CHAR`; thus a TypeHandler must be used, which is an implementation of the `TypeHandlerCallback` interface (part of the `com.ibatis.sqlmap.client.extensions` package) shown in Listing 6.25.

Listing 6.25 TypeHandlerCallback Interface

```
public abstract interface TypeHandlerCallback {
    public abstract void setParameter(
       ParameterSetter setter, Object parameter);
    public abstract Object getResult(ResultGetter getter);
    public abstract Object valueOf(String type);
}
```

The `setParameter` method converts a Java type to a database type, and `getResult` converts a database type to a Java type. `valueOf` is required by iBATIS to compare instances of the type and to test for existence (not null). Listing 6.26 shows how the type handler was implemented for our domain model to convert Boolean Java types to `CHAR` database types.

Listing 6.26 YesNoBoolTypeHandler Implementation

```
public class YesNoBoolTypeHandler implements TypeHandlerCallback {

    private static final String YES = "Y";
    private static final String NO = "N";

    public Object getResult(ResultGetter getter)
    throws SQLException {
        String s = getter.getString();
        if (YES.equalsIgnoreCase(s)) {
            return Boolean.TRUE;
        } else if (NO.equalsIgnoreCase(s)) {
            return Boolean.FALSE;
        } else {
            throw new SQLException(
                "Unexpected value " + s + " found where "
                   + YES + " or " + NO + " was expected.");
        }
    }

    public void setParameter(ParameterSetter setter, Object parameter)
    throws SQLException {
        boolean b = ((Boolean) parameter).booleanValue();
        if (b) {
            setter.setString(YES);
        } else {
            setter.setString(NO);
        }
    }

    public Object valueOf(String s) {
        if (YES.equalsIgnoreCase(s)) {
            return Boolean.TRUE;
        } else {
            return Boolean.FALSE;
        }
    }
}
```

The `com.ibatis.sqlmap.client.event.RowHandler` interface provides an even more versatile extension point since a row handler is executed on every row of the database query. As an example, suppose that `AbstractCustomer` is augmented with a timestamp field. This timestamp field is used by other layers of the application to get an indication of how "fresh" the data is in a Customer POJO. Thus, this timestamp should be automatically generated every time a row for a Customer is loaded. Listing 6.27 shows the RowHandler implementation and Listing 6.28 shows the Java code necessary to execute the query with a row handler.

Listing 6.27 AppendTimestampRowHandler Implementation

```
public class AppendTimestampRowHandler implements RowHandler {

    private AbstractCustomer customer;

    public void handleRow(Object customerPojo) {

        this.customer = (AbstractCustomer) customerPojo;
        customer.setTimestamp(new Date());
    }

    public AbstractCustomer getCustomer() {
        return customer;
    }

}
```

Listing 6.28 Invocation of the Query with a Row Handler

```
AppendTimestampRowHandler handler = new AppendTimestampRowHandler();
dm.queryWithRowHandler("customer.select", customerId, handler);
AbstractCustomer resultingCustomerWithTimestamp = handler.getCustomer();
```

Notice that the same `customer.select` SqlMap statement is used from Listing 6.10. Note that the row handler is just a Java class that you can instantiate, add properties to, and add a complex constructor to. Also notice that after the query is executed, the Customer with the timestamp property is simply fetched from the row handler object with a JavaBean getter.

Error Handling

Figure 6.2 illustrates the various exceptions that the iBATIS framework can throw. The most common type of exception you'll see is a `NestedSQLException`, which contains a nested exception. For example, it may be a `RuntimeSQLException`, which is caused by an error in the SQL or database schema, or an `SqlMapException`, which is caused by an error in an SqlMap. A `NodeletException` is caused by a parsing error for XML. A `TransactionException` occurs when there is an error in a transaction, and a `BatchException` occurs when there is an error in a batch statement.

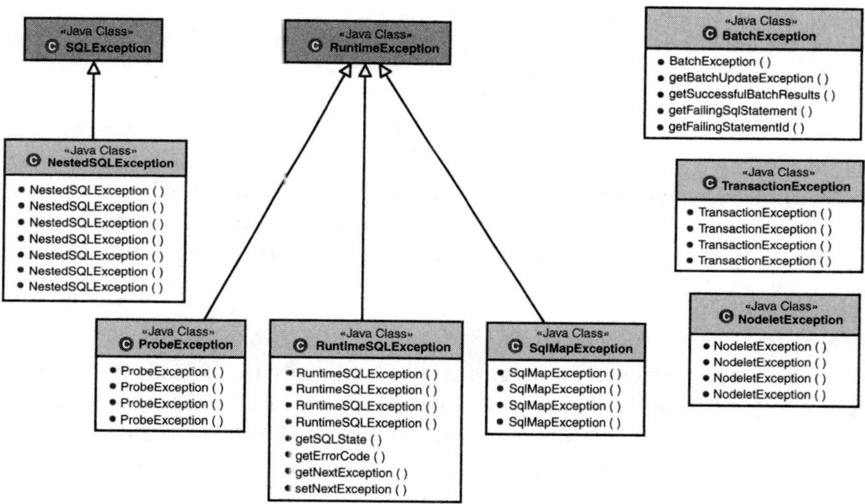

Figure 6.2 iBATIS exceptions hierarchy.

ORM Features Supported

As shown in the preceding section, an iBATIS developer utilizes a combination of Java and XML to implement object-relational mapping. Notice how pure SQL is utilized to define object queries. This section describes how various object-relational mapping fundamentals apply to iBATIS. Some of these were discussed in Chapter 3 when discussing design principles, and again in Chapter 5 when discussing JDBC.

Objects

Objects persisted and queried with iBATIS simply need to be JavaBeans. For example, the Order object is defined, as shown in Listing 6.29.

Listing 6.29 Order JavaBean Class

```
public class Order {
    protected int orderId;
    protected BigDecimal total;
    public static enum Status { OPEN, SUBMITTED, CLOSED }
    protected Status status;
    protected AbstractCustomer customer;
    protected Set<LineItem> lineitems;

    // getters and setters
}
```

Inheritance

All three of the inheritance strategies discussed in Chapter 3—new table, subclass table, and superclass table—can be implemented with iBATIS. However, because iBATIS is simply a tool to bind the input and output of SQL queries to objects, inheritance mapping to the database is largely left up to the developer.

Inheritance Examples

To illustrate how the three inheritance strategies can be realized with iBATIS, this section walks through persisting a ResidentialCustomer for each schema variation. Let's take a look at the Java code required to persist a ResidentialCustomer to the CUSTOMER table. The Java code in Listing 6.30 simply populates a ResidentialCustomer bean and calls an iBATIS mapped statement to persist it.

Listing 6.30 Java Code for Superclass Table Inheritance

```
SqlMapClient dm = ...
    ...
ResidentialCustomer customer = new ResidentialCustomer();
customer.setName("Bill Botzum");
customer.setHouseholdSize((short)4);
customer.setFrequentCustomer(true);

dm.insert("customer.residential.insert", customer);
```

The corresponding iBATIS XML is equally straightforward. The Map XML for the superclass strategy is shown in Listing 6.31.

Listing 6.31 SQLMap for Superclass Table Inheritance

```
<sqlMap>
   <insert id="customer.residential.insert"
     class="org.pwte.example.domain.ResidentialCustomer">
     insert into CUSTOMER(RESIDENTIAL_NAME,
        RESIDENTIAL_HOUSEHOLD_SIZE, RESIDENTIAL_FREQUENT_CUSTOMER)
     values (#name#, #householdSize#, #frequentCustomer#)
   </insert>
</sqlMap>
```

Notice how iBATIS takes care of type conversion automatically. However, iBATIS allows you to override the default Java and JDBC type as well. The developer inserts a bean property from the ResidentialCustomer with the # syntax. There is not much proven here because the insert is to a single table.

Let's move on to the Table-per-class strategy. In this variation, two `insert` SQL statements are required to persist a ResidentialCustomer—one to populate ABSTRACT_CUSTOMER and the other to populate RESIDENTIAL_CUSTOMER. Only one SQL statement can reside in an iBATIS mapped statement, thus the two separate mapped statements must be invoked at the Java level to persist the ResidentialCustomer. This presents a unique challenge—what if one `insert` statement succeeds and the other fails?

Listing 6.32 contains the solution, which is to use the iBATIS transaction API to execute both inserts as a single unit of work. A bit unwieldy, but still less code than the equivalent in JDBC.

Listing 6.32 Java Code for New Table Inheritance

```
ResidentialCustomer customer = new ResidentialCustomer();
customer.setName("Bill Botzum");
customer.setHouseholdSize((short)4);
customer.setFrequentCustomer(true);

try{
    dm.startTransaction();

    dm.insert("customer.abstract.insert", (AbstractCustomer) customer);
    dm.insert("customer.residential.insert", customer);

    dm.commitTransaction();
} finally {
    dm.endTransaction();
}
```

Listing 6.33 shows the two mapped statements called by the Java code. The first inserts the customer's name into the ABSTRACT_CUSTOMER table, and the second inserts the remaining data into the RESIDENTIAL_CUSTOMER table.

Listing 6.33 SQLMaps for New Table Inheritance

```
<sqlMap>
    <insert id="customer.abstract.insert"
     parameterClass="org.pwte.domain.AbstractCustomer">
        insert into ABSTRACT_CUSTOMER ( NAME ) values ( #name# )
    </insert>

    <insert id="customer.residential.insert"
     parameterClass="org.pwte.domain.ResidentialCustomer">
        insert into RESIDENTIAL_CUSTOMER (
            RESIDENTIAL_HOUSEHOLD_SIZE,
            RESIDENTIAL_FREQUENT_CUSTOMER )
        values ( #householdSize#, #frequentCustomer# )
    </insert>
</sqlMap>
```

Finally, we illustrate the subclass table inheritance strategy.

The Java code for this variation is identical to Listing 6.30 for Superclass inheritance. The SQLMap is only slightly different, as shown in Listing 6.34, which simply populates RESIDENTIAL_CUSTOMER.

Listing 6.34 SQLMap for Subclass Table Inheritance

```
<sqlMap>
  <insert id="customer.residential.insert"
   class="org.pwte.example.domain.ResidentialCustomer">
   insert into RESIDENTIAL_CUSTOMER(
       NAME, RESIDENTIAL_HOUSEHOLD_SIZE, RESIDENTIAL_FREQUENT_CUSTOMER)
   values (#name#, #householdSize#, #frequentCustomer#)
  </insert>
</sqlMap>
```

Discriminator Result Mapping

All the examples shown so far have been database inserts. Consider the case in which you need to query a customer by customerId. A problem arises: How can iBATIS determine whether to instantiate the ResidentialCustomer or BusinessCustomer concrete class? Fortunately, iBATIS does have some basic support for this use case by way of the discriminator tag.

A discriminator allows for an iBATIS result map to be resolved at runtime based on a field in a database table called a discriminator field. For example, consider the case in which you retrieve a Map of Customers. Some of these customers are residential and others are business customers. The SQLMap would be as shown in Listing 6.35.

Listing 6.35 Discriminator Inheritance Example

```
<resultMap id="customer.result" class="java.util.HashMap">
    <result property="customerId" column="CUSTOMER_ID"/>
    <result property="name" column="NAME"/>
    <discriminator column="TYPE" javaType="string">
        <subMap value="RESIDENTIAL" resultMap="residential.result"/>
        <subMap value="BUSINESS" resultMap="business.result"/>
    </discriminator>
</resultMap>

<resultMap id="residential.result"
 class="org.pwte.domain.ResidentialCustomer">
    ...
</resultMap>

<resultMap id="business.result"
 class="org.pwte.domain.BusinessCustomer">
    ...
</resultMap>

<select id="customer.select" resultMap="customer.result">
    select * from CUSTOMER
</select>
```

Notice that the result map expects an additional database field called TYPE that should have a value of `RESIDENTIAL` or `BUSINESS`. A different class is instantiated depending on the value of this field.

This is an advanced example of a result map. You may want to look over the Programming Model section to familiarize yourself with iBATIS result maps a bit more before returning to this sample.

Keys

iBATIS has no notion of a key field the same way that SQL has no special semantics for database keys. For example, if you write a map statement that queries a table with a complex key, iBATIS is unaware of this. As far as it is concerned, you've simply mapped a multi-property JavaBean as the parameter for an SQL statement.

The iBATIS framework also does not support the generation of keys itself. It relies on the database to perform any automated key generation. However, it does support a `<selectKey>` construct to retrieve a newly generated key for `insert` statements, because this is such a common task in applications.

As an example of using the `<selectKey>`, let's modify the schema for the ORDER table in the common example such that the orderId is auto-generated with the Derby identity construct as shown in Listing 6.36.

Listing 6.36 Derby DDL Modification for CUSTOMER_ID Auto-Generation

```
CREATE TABLE ORDER  (
   "ORDER_ID" INTEGER NOT NULL generated always as identity,
   "STATUS" VARCHAR(9) ,
         ...
);
```

With this modification, every time a row is inserted into the ORDER table, a unique ORDER_ID is generated with an auto-increment. To illustrate how iBATIS can work with this form of key generation, Listing 6.37 shows the Java code that inserts an Order assuming the setup is complete.

Listing 6.37 Example Java Code for Key Generation

```
SqlMapClient dm = ... ; // standard framework initialization
Order order = ... ; // assume all properties are populated—except orderId

int generatedKey = (int) dm.insert("order.insert", order);
```

Notice how the `insert` statement returns the generated orderId key. The key may be used later by the application in future customer-related queries. How iBATIS is configured to return this generated key can be seen in the corresponding SQLMap shown in Listing 6.38.

Listing 6.38 Example SQLMap Insert for Identity Key Generation

```
<insert parameterClass="org.pwte.domain.Order">
    insert into ( ... ) CUSTOMER values (
        #status#,
        #customerId#,
        #total#
    )
    <selectKey keyProperty="orderId" resultClass="int" type="post">
        select max(ORDER_ID) from ORDER
    </selectKey>
</insert>
```

The selectKey SQL is executed after the insert SQL, which is denoted by type="post". Key generation mechanisms are proprietary to each database provider. In the case of Derby, the identity key generation method is simply an auto-increment; thus, we used a max() function to get the newly generated key. As another example, Oracle and DB2 support key generation via sequences. Listing 6.39 shows the equivalent insert map statement for a sequence called order_sequence.

Listing 6.39 Example SQLMap Insert for Sequence Key Generation

```
<insert parameterClass="org.pwte.domain.Order">
    <selectKey keyProperty="orderId" resultClass="int" type="pre">
        select nextVal('order_sequence')
    </selectKey>
    insert into ( ... ) ORDER values (
        #status#,
        #customerId#,
        #total#)
</insert>
```

Notice how, in this second example, the selectKey SQL is processed first. The nextVal() function is used to determine what the next key will be so it can be returned as the result of the insert mapped statement.

Attributes

iBATIS supports all Java primitive types with the exception of the char type (which is not supported by JDBC, either). Table 6.3 details the type support for iBATIS.

Table 6.3 iBATIS Type Support

Java Type	Type Alias
boolean	Boolean
java.lang.Boolean	Boolean
byte	Byte
short	Short
java.lang.Short	Short
int	int, Integer
java.lang.Integer	int, Iinteger
long	Long

continues

Table 6.3 continued

Java Type	Type Alias
java.lang.Long	Long
float	Float
java.lang.Float	Float
double	Double
java.lang.Double	Double
java.lang.String	String
java.util.Date	Date
java.math.BigDecimal	Decimal

iBATIS has default type aliases for these types, so you don't have to type out the entire package names in a result or parameter map. As an example, consider the case in which a LineItem has a `quantity` attribute with a Java type of `BigDecimal` and has to be mapped to a Derby type of `BIGINT` in the database schema. The SqlMap XML for a `select` by primary key for LineItem is shown in Listing 6.40.

Listing 6.40 Type Mapping Example

```
<resultMap id="lineitem.map" class="lineitem">
    <result property="quantity" javaType="decimal"
     jdbcType="BIGINT"/>
    <result property="amount"/>
    <result property="product" select="product.select"
     column="product_id"/>
    </resultMap>
    <select id="lineitem.select" resultMap="lineitem.map"
     parameterClass="wrapper">
        select * from LINE_ITEM
        where ORDER_ID = #orderId#,
        PRODUCT_ID = #productId#
   </result>
</resultMap>
```

iBATIS can also support custom types through the use of type handlers. For example, Order uses a Java 5 enumeration, called Status, that needs to be mapped to a VARCHAR(9) column in the database with values of `OPEN`, `SUBMITTED`, or `CLOSED`. We've already seen how our `org.pwte.ibatis.StatusEnumTypeHandler` custom type handler can be used to perform this type mapping in Listing 6.8. Listing 6.41 shows the implementation of this type handler class.

Listing 6.41 StatusEnumTypeHandler Implementation

```
public class StatusEnumTypeHandler implements TypeHandlerCallback {

    private static final String
        OPEN = "OPEN",
        SUBMITTED = "SUBMITTED",
        CLOSED = "CLOSED";

    public Object getResult(ResultGetter getter) throws SQLException {
        String status = getter.getString();

        if(OPEN.equals(status)) {
            return Order.Status.OPEN;
        } else if(SUBMITTED.equals(status)) {
            return Order.Status.SUBMITTED;
        } else if(CLOSED.equals(status)) {
            return Order.Status.CLOSED;
        } else {
            throw new SQLException(
                "ORDER STATUS fetched from database is: "
                    +status
                    +" \n STATUS must be OPEN, SUBMITTED, or CLOSED");
        }
    }

    public void setParameter(ParameterSetter setter, Object parameter)
    throws SQLException {
        Order.Status status = (Order.Status) parameter;
        if(status.equals(Order.Status.OPEN)) {
            setter.setString(OPEN);
        } else if(status.equals(Order.Status.SUBMITTED)) {
            setter.setString(SUBMITTED);
        } else {
            setter.setString(CLOSED);
```

```
        }
    }

    public Object valueOf(String s) {
        if(OPEN.equals(s)) {
            return Order.Status.OPEN;
        } else if(SUBMITTED.equals(s)) {
            return Order.Status.SUBMITTED;
        } else {
            return Order.Status.CLOSED;
        }
    }

}
```

For more information on type handlers, see the earlier section titled "Extending the Framework."

Contained Objects

In addition to `java.util.Date`, iBATIS supports nested JavaBeans as well as `java.util.HashMap`. `java.sql.Time` and `java.sql.Timestamp` are also supported, although they are discouraged (using `java.util.Date` is a best practice for portability). iBATIS supports only one collection type—`java.util.List`.

As an example, consider the case in which a Customer contains a nested Address complex type. A result map can have a `<select/>` node that calls a nested query. Listing 6.42 illustrates the retrieval of a Customer object containing an Address.

Listing 6.42 Address Containment Example

```
  <resultMap id="customer.select.map" class="business">
    <result property="customerId"/>
    <result property="name"/>
    <result property="address.city" />
  </resultMap>

<select id="customer.select" resultMap="customer.select.map"
 parameterClass="customer">
     select CUSTOMER_ID, NAME, CITY from CUSTOMER
     where CUSTOMER_ID = #customerId#
  </select>
```

Relationships

iBATIS allows you to match Object graphs with complex relationships. By grouping Result Maps, you can map objects to complex SQL Joins for Eager fetching, or force multiple SQL statements. Listing 6.43 shows an example of issuing a join between the Line Item and Product Table. The properties of the product will automatically populate the object.

Listing 6.43 One-to-One Relationship with Join

```
<sqlMap namespace="PWTE">
    <typeAlias alias="lineitem"
     type="org.pwte.example.domain.LineItem"/>
    <typeAlias alias="product" type="org.pwte.example.domain.Product" />

    <resultMap id="lineitem.map" class="lineitem">
        <result property="quantity" jdbcType="BIGINT"/>
        <result property="amount"/>
        <result property="product.productId"/>
        <result property="product.price"/>
        <result property="product.description"/>
    </resultMap>

    <select id="product.select"
     resultMap="product.select.map"
     parameterClass="int">
        select * from LINE_ITEM as l, PRODUCT as p
        where p.PRODUCT_ID =l.PRODUCT_ID and l.ORDER_ID = #orderId#
    </select>
</sqlMap>
```

The same relationship can be done as shown in Listing 6.44. In this case, the product is defined as an attribute and points to a separate `select` statement.

Listing 6.44 One-to-One Relationship with Multiple Selects

```
<sqlMap namespace="PWTE">
    <typeAlias alias="lineitem"
     type="org.pwte.example.domain.LineItem"/>

    <resultMap id="lineitem.map" class="lineitem">
        <result property="quantity" jdbcType="BIGINT"/>
        <result property="amount"/>
        <result property='product" select="product.select"
```

```
        column="product_id"/>
    </resultMap>

<select id="lineitems.select" resultMap="lineitem.map">
     select * from LINE_ITEM where ORDER_ID = #value#
</select>

<typeAlias alias="product" type="org.pwte.example.domain.Product" />

    <resultMap id="product.select.map" class="product">
        <result property="productId"/>
        <result property="price"/>
        <result property="description"/>
    </resultMap>

    <select id="product.select"
     resultMap="product.select.map"
     parameterClass="int">
        select * from PRODUCT where PRODUCT_ID = #value#
    </select>

</sqlMap>
```

When an application calls the `lineitem.select` statement, its result map calls the `product.select` statement to populate the nested address bean. Notice how the ADDRESS_ID is propagated from the result of the Customer `select` statement to a parameter of the Address `select` statement.

iBATIS supports 1:N and M:N relationships using the join or multiple select as well. Listing 6.45 shows an example of a one-to-many relationship using a Join. M:N would be similar.

Listing 6.45 One-to-Many Relationship with Multiple Selects

```
<resultMap id="order.select.map" class="order" groupBy="orderId">
  <result property="orderId"/>
  <result property="total"/>
  <result property="status"
   typeHandler="org.pwte.example.ibatis.StatusEnumTypeHandler"/>
  <result property="lineitems" resultMap="lineitem.map"/>
</resultMap>

<resultMap id="lineitem.map" class="lineitem">
  <result property="quantity" jdbcType="BIGINT"/>
  <result property="amount"/>
```

```
  <result property="productId"/>
</resultMap>

<select id="order.select"
 resultMap="order.select.map"
 parameterClass="int">
     select o.ORDER_ID, o.TOTAL, o.STATUS,
             l.quantity, l.amount, l.productId
     from ORDERS,LINE_ITEM
     where o.ORDER_ID = #value# and o.ORDER_ID = l.ORDER_ID
</select>
```

In our end-to-end example, we show a more complicated object graph. This can be seen in Listing 6.60. The one-to-many multi-`select` would be similar to the one-to-one multi-`select`.

Constraints

iBATIS is purely a data mapping framework and is not designed to perform validation or integrity logic. Constraints such as value range checks and referential integrity are expected to be implemented at the database layer (below) or application layer (above).

That being said, there are two features of iBATIS that lend themselves to support constraint logic. The first is defining a custom type handler. The custom handler, which ensures that the `Order.Status` enumeration is either `OPEN`, `CLOSED`, or `SUBMITTED`, is an excellent example of enforcing a constraint when a database type is mapped to a Java type with a custom type handler (see the earlier section "Extending the Framework").

The second feature that can be used to enforce constraints is the row handler API. As an example, consider a new Boolean field added to Product called CATALOGUED. A Product referred to by a LineItem must be in a catalogued state. Now suppose that we want to check this constraint on `update` statements. Listing 6.46 details an SQLMap that updates Product.

Listing 6.46 Product Update Statement

```
<update id="product.update"
 parameterClass="org.pwte.example.domain.Product">
    update PRODUCT
    set PRICE = #price#, CATALOGUED = #catalogued#,
        DESCRIPTION = #description#
    where PRODUCT_ID = #productId#
</update>
```

As you can see, this is just a generic `update` statement that allows the application to update any field of a Product. Listing 6.47 shows a row handler designed to be invoked every time an update to a row in the PRODUCT table is executed.

Listing 6.47 Example Row Handler

```
public void handleRow(Object valueObject) {

    Product product = (Product) valueObject;

    // initialize access to framework
    SqlMapClient dm = ...

    // query database for LineItem corresponding to this Product
    List result = dm.queryForList(
        "lineitem.select.byproduct", product.getProductId());

    if(result.size() > 0 && product.getCatalogued() == false) {
        log.error("Product with id="+product.getProductId()
        +" is referred to by at least one LineItem, "
        + "but is not marked as Catalogued.");
    }

    if(result.size() == 0 && product.getCatalogued() == true) {
        log.error("Product with id="+product.getProductId()
            +" is not referred to by at least one LineItem, "
            +"but is marked as Catalogued.");
    }
}
```

Notice that the row handler performs a query for any LineItems associated with the Product. It then checks for invalid states of `Catalogued` and logs errors if an invalid state is found. Listing 6.48 shows the application code used to associate this row handler with the `update` statement shown in Listing 6.46, assuming that the name of the row handler class is `ProductUpdateRowHandler`.

Listing 6.48 Execution of Product Update Statement

```
SqlMapClient dm = getDataMapper();
ProductUpdateRowHandler rowHandler = new ProductUpdateRowHandler();
dm.queryWithRowHandler("product.update", rowHandler);
```

Derived Attributes

As with constraints, iBATIS is not intended to support derived attributes. The iBATIS philosophy is to keep the framework's purpose solely for simple data mapping—derived attributes should be maintained in the database layer (with database triggers or with nested SQL `select` statements) or the application layer. However, as with constraints, a custom row handler can be used to automatically populate a field of a resulting JavaBean. For example, consider the `LineItem.amount` attribute, which is calculated by multiplying the quantity and corresponding price of the Product. Listing 6.49 shows a row handler that performs this calculation and exposes a property to get the resulting LineItem JavaBean.

Listing 6.49 Derived Attribute Row Handler Example

```
public class LineItemRowHandler implements RowHandler {

    private LineItem lineitem;

    public void handleRow(Object valueObject) {

        LineItem lineitem = (LineItem) valueObject;

        BigDecimal price = lineitem.getProduct().getPrice();

        // amount = price * quantity
        BigDecimal amount = price.multiply(
           new BigDecimal(lineitem.getQuantity()));

        lineitem.setAmount(amount);

        // set LineItem property on row handler
        setLineitem(lineitem);
    }

    public LineItem getLineitem() {return lineitem;}

    private void setLineitem(LineItem lineitem) {this.lineitem = lineitem;}
}
```

Notice that after the row handler calculates the amount field for LineItem, it sets a LineItem property on itself. Listing 6.50 shows how the query statement is executed from application code and how the LineItem with the populated amount attribute is retrieved.

Listing 6.50 Derived Attribute Query

```
SqlMapClient dm = getDataMapper();
LineItemRowHandler rowHandler = new LineItemRowHandler();
dm.queryWithRowHandler("lineitem.select", rowHandler);
LineItem lineitem = rowHandler.getLineItem();
```

You may wonder why such a simple calculation should be done in a row handler and not in the application code after a standard SQLMap statement. In the case that the derived attribute calculation is only ever done in one place for the application, this may very well be a more straightforward and maintainable solution. However, having the row handler calculate a derived attribute allows for reuse and allows separation of application code from query logic.

Tuning Options

Although iBATIS focuses on simplicity, it is a feature-rich framework designed to scale well with enterprise applications. Caching, lazy loading, and batching are supported.

Query Optimizations

Because the SQL is external to the Java source code, you can tune the SQL and not need to re-compile the associated Java code that invokes it. An example of tuning an SQL statement is changing the order of conditions in a `where` clause or reordering the joins.

Caching

iBATIS ships with a single JVM cache and allows you to extend to distributed caches.

Single-JVM Caching

iBATIS can be configured to cache the results of mapped statements. A cache model is a configured cache that is defined within SqlMap XML. For example, Listing 6.51 shows how to modify the `customer.select` statement to be cached using a Least Recently Used (LRU) algorithm.

Listing 6.51 Single-JVM Caching Example

```
<cacheModel id="customer-cache" type ="LRU" readOnly="true" serialize="false">
    <flushInterval hours="24"/>
    <property name="cache-size" value="1000" />
</cacheModel>

<select id="customer.select" cacheModel="customer-cache"
resultMap="customer.select.map" parameterClass="int">
    select CUSTOMER_ID, NAME, OPEN_ORDER from CUSTOMER
        where CUSTOMER_ID = #value#
</select>
```

This defines a cache that is flushed every 24 hours and has a depth of 1,000 entries. In addition to LRU, iBATIS supports three other cache types: First-In-First-Out (FIFO), MEMORY, and OSCache. The MEMORY implementation relies on the garbage collector to determine when objects should be flushed from the cache (often a good choice when memory is scarce). Additionally, a fully qualified class name can be used for the cache type, which indicates that a custom cache mechanism should be used. A custom cache and OSCache are covered in the next section.

Distributed Caching

iBATIS fully supports caching in distributed environments. OSCache is supported out-of-the-box. To configure SqlMap statements to be cached with OSCache, set the `type` attribute to `OSCache` in the cache model. Then, all that is required is a standard `oscache.proerties` file in the root of the project classpath. For more information, refer to www.opensymphony.com/oscache/.

As mentioned previously, a custom cache controller can also be used for the `type` attribute of a cache model. The class must implement the CacheController interface (part of the iBATIS cache package). Consider Listing 6.52, which shows the interface.

Listing 6.52 iBATIS CacheController Interface

```
public interface CacheController {

  public void flush(CacheModel cacheModel);

  public Object getObject(CacheModel cacheModel, Object key);

  public Object removeObject(CacheModel cacheModel, Object key);

public void putObject(
    CacheModel cacheModel, Object key, Object object);

  public void configure(Properties props);

}
```

At a high level, an implementation of this interface needs to store objects based on keys and then either remove or retrieve them based on the same key. A CacheModel object is provided that is populated with cache model metadata, such as the `readOnly` attribute. A `java.util.Property` object also can be used as a standard mechanism for additional metadata.

Loading Related Objects

iBATIS supports lazy loading of nested complex types by default. For example, when a Customer is fetched from the database, the nested `select` for its Orders is not invoked until a reference to the nested Set of Orders is made in the application. Lazy loading can be configured at the SqlMapConfig level with the `settings` tag. Listing 6.53 provides an example. These settings are then read by the byte code enhancer to achieve optimized lazy loading semantics.

Listing 6.53 Lazy Loading Configuration

```
<settings
    cacheModelsEnabled="true"
    enhancementEnabled="true"
    lazyLoadingEnabled="true"
    maxRequests="128"
    maxSessions="10"
    maxTransactions="5"
    useStatementNamespaces="false"
    defaultStatementTimeout="5"
/>
```

Locking

iBATIS does not maintain optimistic locking strategies. Implementing optimistic locking is left to the developer, possibly using isolation levels as discussed in Chapter 3. Isolation levels are delegated to the underlying JDBC calls as discussed earlier in the "Transactions" section of this chapter.

Development Process of the Common Example

The iBATIS philosophy is to make development with iBATIS as natural and painless as possible. The addition of iBATIS to a software project should not conflict with an existing development process.

Defining the Objects

iBATIS utilizes Java POJOs that follow the standard JavaBean convention. This makes defining objects with iBATIS seamless because the Java objects can be the very same objects as those in your domain model. If the domain model includes types that are not natively supported by iBATIS, such as the `Order.Status` enumeration in our domain model, type handlers can be employed.

Listing 6.54 and Listing 6.55 illustrate some of the POJOs used for the iBATIS implementation of the common example—AbstractCustomer and ResidentialCustomer. The rest of the POJOs are omitted, considering that they are also literal JavaBean representations of the common example's domain model.

Listing 6.54 AbstractCustomer

```
public abstract class AbstractCustomer implements Serializable {
    protected int customerId;
    protected String name, type;
```

```
    protected Order openOrder;
    protected List orders;
//getters and setters
```

Listing 6.55 ResidentialCustomer

```
public class ResidentialCustomer
extends AbstractCustomer implements Serializable {
    protected short householdSize;
    protected boolean frequentCustomer;
    //getters and setters
```

Several SQLMap XML files corresponding to the POJOs were developed to hold the required SQL queries. Listings 6.56 through 6.59 show the SQLMaps. We have two versions of the load customer: one that issues $2N+2$ Selects where N is the number of LineItems, and another that uses a complex join across the tables. The Select in the *Customer.xml* in Listing 6.56 represents the $2N+2$ Selects, and the `CustomerLoad.xml` in Listing 6.60 represents the Join.

Listing 6.56 Customer.xml

```
<sqlMap namespace="PWTE">
  <typeAlias alias="abstract"
    type="org.pwte.example.domain.AbstractCustomer" />
  <typeAlias alias="business"
    type="org.pwte.example.domain.BusinessCustomer"/>
  <typeAlias alias="residential"
    type="org.pwte.example.domain.ResidentialCustomer"/>
  <typeAlias alias="order" type="org.pwte.example.domain.Order" />
  <resultMap id="customer.select.map" class="abstract">
    <result property="customerId" column="CUSTOMER_ID"/>
    <discriminator javaType="String" column="TYPE">
      <subMap value="BUSINESS" resultMap="customer.business.map"/>
      <subMap value="RESIDENTIAL" resultMap="customer.residential.map"/>
    </discriminator>
  </resultMap>
  <resultMap id="customer.business.map" class="business">
    <result property="customerId" column="CUSTOMER_ID"/>
    <result property="name" column="NAME"/>
    <result property="openOrder"
     select="order.select" column="OPEN_ORDER"/>
    <result property="volumeDiscount" column="BUSINESS_VOLUME_DISCOUNT"
     typeHandler="org.pwte.example.ibatis.YesNoBoolTypeHandler"/>
    <result property="businessPartner" column="BUSINESS_PARTNER"
```

```
      typeHandler="org.pwte.example.ibatis.YesNoBoolTypeHandler"/>
    <result property="description" column="BUSINESS_DESCRIPTION"/>
  </resultMap>
  <resultMap id="customer.residential.map" class="residential">
    <result property="customerId" column="CUSTOMER_ID"/>
    <result property="name" column="NAME"/>
    <result property="openOrder"
      select="order.select" column="OPEN_ORDER"/>
    <result property="householdSize"
      column="RESIDENTIAL_HOUSEHOLD_SIZE"/>
    <result property="frequentCustomer"
      column="RESIDENTIAL_FREQUENT_CUSTOMER"
      typeHandler="org.pwte.example.ibatis.YesNoBoolTypeHandler"/>
  </resultMap>
<select id="customer.select"
 resultMap="customer.select.map"
 parameterClass="int">
      select CUSTOMER_ID, NAME, OPEN_ORDER, TYPE,
          BUSINESS_VOLUME_DISCOUNT,
          BUSINESS_PARTNER, BUSINESS_DESCRIPTION,
          RESIDENTIAL_HOUSEHOLD_SIZE,
          RESIDENTIAL_FREQUENT_CUSTOMER
      from CUSTOMER where CUSTOMER_ID = #value#
  </select>
  <update id="customer.open.order" parameterClass="int">
    update CUSTOMER set OPEN_ORDER =
      (select ORDER_ID from ORDERS where CUSTOMER_ID = #value#)
    where CUSTOMER_ID = #value#
  </update>
  <update id="customer.close.order" parameterClass="int">
    update CUSTOMER set OPEN_ORDER = NULL where CUSTOMER_ID = #value#
  </update>
  <parameterMap id="customer.residential.map" class="residential" >
    <parameter property="customerId" />
    <parameter property="name" />
    <parameter property="householdSize" />
    <parameter property="frequentCustomer"
      typeHandler="org.pwte.example.ibatis.YesNoBoolTypeHandler" />
  </parameterMap>
  <insert id="customer.residential.insert"
   parameterMap="customer.residential.map">
      insert into CUSTOMER (
          CUSTOMER_ID, NAME,
```

```
            RESIDENTIAL_HOUSEHOLD_SIZE,
            RESIDENTIAL_FREQUENT_CUSTOMER )
        values ( ?, ?, ?, ? )
    </insert>
</sqlMap>
```

Listing 6.57 Order.xml

```
<sqlMap namespace="PWTE">
    <typeAlias alias="order" type="org.pwte.example.domain.Order" />
    <typeAlias alias="customer"
     type="org.pwte.example.domain.AbstractCustomer" />
    <parameterMap id="order.open.map" class="order">
        <parameter property="customer.customerId"/>
        <parameter property="status"
           typeHandler="org.pwte.example.ibatis.StatusEnumTypeHandler"/>
        <parameter property="total"/>
    </parameterMap>
    <resultMap id="order.select.map" class="order">
        <result property="orderId"/>
        <result property="total"/>
        <result property="status"
           typeHandler="org.pwte.example.ibatis.StatusEnumTypeHandler"/>
        <result property="lineitems" select="lineitems.select"
         column="ORDER_ID"/>
    </resultMap>
    <insert id="order.open" parameterMap="order.open.map">
        insert into ORDERS (CUSTOMER_ID, STATUS, TOTAL) values (?, ?, ?)
        <selectKey keyProperty="orderId" resultClass="int" type="post">
            select max(ORDER_ID) from ORDERS
        </selectKey>
    </insert>
    <select id="order.select" resultMap="order.select.map"
     parameterClass="int">
        select ORDER_ID, TOTAL, STATUS from ORDERS
        where ORDER_ID = #value#
    </select>

    <update id="order.submit" parameterClass="int">
        update ORDERS set STATUS = 'SUBMITTED' where ORDER_ID = #value#
    </update>
</sqlMap>
```

Listing 6.58 LineItem.xml

```
<sqlMap namespace="PWTE">
    <typeAlias alias="lineitem"
     type="org.pwte.example.domain.LineItem"/>
    <resultMap id="lineitem.map" class="lineitem">
        <result property="quantity" jdbcType="BIGINT"/>
        <result property="amount"/>
        <result property="product" select="product.select"
         column="product_id"/>
    </resultMap>

    <insert id="lineitem.insert" parameterClass="java.util.HashMap">
        insert into LINE_ITEM values (
            #orderId#, #lineitem.product.productId#,
            #lineitem.quantity#, #lineitem.amount#)
    </insert>
    <update id="lineitem.update" parameterClass="java.util.HashMap">
        update LINE_ITEM
        set QUANTITY = #lineitem.quantity#, AMOUNT = #lineitem.amount#
        where PRODUCT_ID = #lineitem.product.productId# and
              ORDER_ID = #orderId#
    </update>
    <select id="lineitems.select" resultMap="lineitem.map">
        select * from LINE_ITEM where ORDER_ID = #value#
    </select>
    <select id="lineitem.select" resultMap="lineitem.map"
     parameterClass="java.util.HashMap">
        select * from LINE_ITEM
        where ORDER_ID = #orderId# and PRODUCT_ID = #productId#
    </select>

    <delete id="lineitem.delete" parameterClass="java.util.HashMap">
        delete from LINE_ITEM
        where ORDER_ID = #orderId# and PRODUCT_ID = #productId#
    </delete>
</sqlMap>
```

Listing 6.59 Product.xml

```
<sqlMap namespace="PWTE">
    <typeAlias alias="product" type="org.pwte.example.domain.Product" />
```

```
    <resultMap id="product.select.map" class="product">
        <result property="productId"/>
        <result property="price"/>
        <result property="description"/>
    </resultMap>
    <select id="product.select"
     resultMap="product.select.map"
     parameterClass="int">
        select * from PRODUCT where PRODUCT_ID = #value#
    </select>
    <select id="product.all" resultClass="java.util.HashMap">
        select * from PRODUCT
    </select>
</sqlMap>
```

Listing 6.60 CustomerLoad.xml

```
<!DOCTYPE sqlMap PUBLIC "-//ibatis.apache.org//DTD SQL Map 2.0//EN"
                        "http://ibatis.apache.org/dtd/sql-map-2.dtd">

<sqlMap namespace="PWTE">
  <typeAlias alias="abstract"
   type="org.pwte.example.domain.AbstractCustomer" />
  <typeAlias alias="business"
   type="org.pwte.example.domain.BusinessCustomer"/>
  <typeAlias alias="residential"
   type="org.pwte.example.domain.ResidentialCustomer"/>

  <typeAlias alias="order" type="org.pwte.example.domain.Order" />

  <resultMap id="customer.with.openOrder.select.map" class="abstract">
    <result property="customerId" column="CUSTOMER_ID"/>
    <discriminator javaType="String" column="TYPE">
      <subMap value="BUSINESS"
       resultMap="customer.with.openOrder.business.map"/>
      <subMap value="RESIDENTIAL"
       resultMap="customer.with.openOrder.residential.map"/>
    </discriminator>
  </resultMap>

<resultMap id="customer.with.openOrder.business.map"
 class="business" groupBy="customerId">
```

```
    <result property="customerId" column="CUSTOMER_ID"/>
    <result property="name" column="NAME"/>
    <result property="volumeDiscount"
     column="BUSINESS_VOLUME_DISCOUNT"
     typeHandler="org.pwte.example.ibatis.YesNoBoolTypeHandler"/>
    <result property="businessPartner"
     column="BUSINESS_PARTNER"
     typeHandler="org.pwte.example.ibatis.YesNoBoolTypeHandler"/>
    <result property="description" column="BUSINESS_DESCRIPTION"/>
    <result property="openOrder.orderId" column="ORDER_ID"
     nullValue="0"/>
    <result property="openOrder.total" column="TOTAL" nullValue="0"/>
    <result property="openOrder.status"
     typeHandler="org.pwte.example.ibatis.StatusEnumTypeHandler"
     column="STATUS" nullValue="null"/>
    <result property="openOrder.lineitems"
     resultMap="lineitem.product.map"/>
  </resultMap>

<resultMap id="customer.with.openOrder.residential.map"
   class="residential" groupBy="customerId">
    <result property="customerId" column="CUSTOMER_ID"/>
    <result property="name" column="NAME"/>
    <result property="openOrder.orderId" column="ORDER_ID"
     nullValue="0"/>
    <result property="openOrder.total" column="TOTAL" nullValue="0"/>
    <result property="openOrder.status"
     typeHandler="org.pwte.example.ibatis.StatusEnumTypeHandler"
     column="STATUS" nullValue="null"/>
    <result property="openOrder.lineitems"
     resultMap="lineitem.product.map"/>
    <result property="householdSize"
     column="RESIDENTIAL_HOUSEHOLD_SIZE"/>
    <result property="frequentCustomer"
     column="RESIDENTIAL_FREQUENT_CUSTOMER"
     typeHandler="org.pwte.example.ibatis.YesNoBoolTypeHandler"/>
  </resultMap>

   <resultMap id="lineitem.product.map" class="lineitem" >
      <result property="quantity" jdbcType="BIGINT"/>
```

```
        <result property="amount"/>
        <result property="product.productId" column="PRODUCT_ID"/>
        <result property="product.price" column="PRICE"/>
        <result property="product.description" column="DESCRIPTION"/>
    </resultMap>

  <select id="customer.with.openOrder.select"
   resultMap="customer.with.openOrder.select.map"
   parameterClass="int">
        SELECT
            c.CUSTOMER_ID, c.OPEN_ORDER, c.NAME,
            c.BUSINESS_VOLUME_DISCOUNT,
            c.BUSINESS_PARTNER, c.BUSINESS_DESCRIPTION,
            c.RESIDENTIAL_HOUSEHOLD_SIZE,
            c.RESIDENTIAL_FREQUENT_CUSTOMER, c.TYPE,
            o.ORDER_ID,o.STATUS,o.TOTAL,l.PRODUCT_ID,
            l.ORDER_ID, l.QUANTITY, l.AMOUNT,
            p.PRODUCT_ID,p.PRICE,p.DESCRIPTION
        FROM CUSTOMER c LEFT OUTER JOIN
          (ORDERS o LEFT OUTER JOIN
            (LINE_ITEM l JOIN PRODUCT p ON l.PRODUCT_ID = p.PRODUCT_ID)
            ON o.ORDER_ID = l.ORDER_ID)
          ON c.OPEN_ORDER = o.ORDER_ID
        WHERE c.CUSTOMER_ID = #value#
  </select>

</sqlMap>
```

Figure 6.3 shows all the Exceptions for our services. See the downloadable sample or refer to Chapter 3 for details.

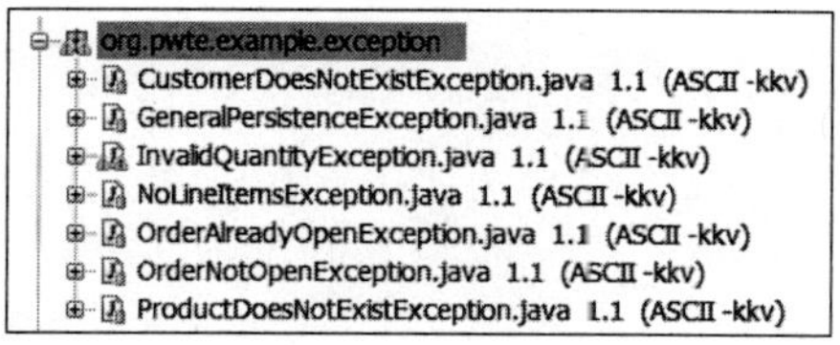

Figure 6.3 Exceptions.

Implementing the Services

This section details the iBATIS implementation of the services from the common example, basically utilizing most of the programming model and ORM features we discussed in the previous sections.

The code for the service interface—`CustomerOrderServices`—is omitted, considering that it is unchanged from the listing in Chapter 3. Nor do we show here the code to initialize the iBATIS SqlMap. The code is basically the same as the code found in the section titled "Initialization." Our service has a special utility for accessing the SqlMap. Examine the downloadable source code for more details. In the next sub-sections, we will look at the iBATIS style implementations associated with the `loadCustomer: openOrder`, `addLineItem`, `removeLineItem`, and `submitOrder` operations.

loadCustomer

The `loadCustomer` method executes the SQL Join defined in the `customer.with.openOrder.select` in `CustomerLoad.xml`. This is shown in Listing 6.61.

Listing 6.61 loadCustomer

```
public AbstractCustomer loadCustomer(int customerId)
throws CustomerDoesNotExistException, GeneralPersistenceException {

    // 1. (Re-)Initialize iBATIS Data Mapper
    SqlMapClient dm = getDataMapper();

    // 2. Retrieve Customer
    AbstractCustomer customer = null;
    try {
        List<AbstractCustomer> list = dm.queryForList(
            "customer.with.openOrder.select",
            customerId
        );
        if(list.size() > 0)
            customer = list.get(0);
        else
            throw new CustomerDoesNotExistException();
    }
    catch(SQLException sqle) {
        throw new GeneralPersistenceException(sqle);
    }

    return customer;
}
```

openOrder

The Open Order service operation implementation creates an `order` Java Object and executes the appropriate named SQL. Listing 6.62 shows the complete method.

Listing 6.62 openOrder

```
public Order openOrder(int customerId)
throws CustomerDoesNotExistException,
       OrderAlreadyOpenException,
       GeneralPersistenceException {

    // 1. (Re-)Initialize iBATIS Data Mapper
    SqlMapClient dm = getDataMapper();
    Order order = null;
    try {
        dm.startTransaction();

        // 2. Retrieve Customer using load routine
        AbstractCustomer customer = loadCustomer(customerId);

        // 3. Ensure Customer does not already
        // have Order in 'OPEN' state
        if(customer.getOpenOrder() != null &&
           customer.getOpenOrder().getOrderId() != 0)
            throw new OrderAlreadyOpenException();

        // 4. Create and persist Order
        order = new Order();
        order.setCustomer(customer);
        order.setStatus(Order.Status.OPEN);
        order.setTotal(new BigDecimal(0.00));
        int orderId = (Integer) dm.insert("order.open", order);
        order.setOrderId(orderId);

        // 5. Update Customer with reference
        // to 'OPEN' Order
        dm.update("customer.open.order", customerId);
        dm.commitTransaction();
        return order;
    }
    catch(SQLException sqle) {
        throw new GeneralPersistenceException(sqle);
```

```
    }
    finally {
        try {
            dm.endTransaction();
        }
        catch(SQLException sqle) {
            throw new GeneralPersistenceException(sqle);
        }
    }
}
```

addLineItem

The `addLineItem` operation implementation first checks to see whether the Product exists by executing the `product.select` statement. It then queries to check whether a LineItem already exists and updates the quantity if it does; otherwise, it creates a new LineItem. Because this code is rather long, we break it into two parts—one that does the validation and the other that does the update. Listing 6.63 shows the implementation of `addLineItem` validations.

Listing 6.63 addLineItem Validation Implementations

```
public LineItem addLineItem(
    int customerId, int productId, long quantity)
throws CustomerDoesNotExistException,
       OrderNotOpenException,
       ProductDoesNotExistException,
       GeneralPersistenceException {
    // 1. (Re-)Initialize iBATIS Data Mapper
    SqlMapClient dm = getDataMapper();
    LineItem lineitem = null;
    try {
        dm.startTransaction();

        // 2. Retrieve Customer and Validate
        AbstractCustomer customer = loadCustomer(customerId);


        // 3. Ensure Customer has an 'OPEN' Order
        if (customer.getOpenOrder() == null ||
            customer.getOpenOrder().getOrderId() == 0)
            throw new OrderNotOpenException();

        // 4. Retrieve Product and Validate
```

```
            Product product = null;
            product = (Product) dm.queryForObject(
                "product.select", productId);
            if(product == null)
                throw new ProductDoesNotExistException();

            // See Listing 6.64 for steps 5-9.
        }
        catch(SQLException sqle) {
            throw new GeneralPersistenceException(sqle);
        }
        finally{
            try {
                dm.endTransaction();
            }
            catch(SQLException sqle) {
                throw new GeneralPersistenceException(sqle);
            }
        }
    }
```

Listing 6.64 continues the implementation logic of the `addLineItem` service operation by populating the appropriate LineItem instance, depending on whether it already exists or not. For readability, the indent is different from it should be if "unrolled" into Listing 6.63.

Listing 6.64 addLineItem Code to Populate an Existing or New LineItem

```
// 5. Check whether Order has existing LineItem
Map keys = new HashMap();
keys.put("orderId", customer.getOpenOrder().getOrderId());
keys.put("productId", productId);
lineitem = (LineItem) dm.queryForObject("lineitem.select", keys);

// 6. If LineItem already exists update quantity and amount
if (lineitem != null) {
    lineitem.setQuantity(lineitem.getQuantity() + quantity);
    lineitem.setAmount(product.getPrice().multiply(
       new BigDecimal(lineitem.getQuantity())));
    Map wrapper = new HashMap();
    wrapper.put("lineitem", lineitem);
    wrapper.put("orderId", customer.getOpenOrder().getOrderId());

    // 7. Update LineItem
    dm.update("lineitem.update", wrapper);
```

```
}
// 8. If LineItem does not exist, create it
else {
    BigDecimal amount = product.getPrice().multiply(
        new BigDecimal(quantity));

    lineitem = new LineItem();
    lineitem.setProduct(product);
    lineitem.setQuantity(quantity);
    lineitem.setAmount(amount);

    // 9. Persist LineItem
    Map wrapper = new HashMap();
    wrapper.put("orderId", customer.getOpenOrder().getOrderId());
    wrapper.put("lineitem", lineitem);
     dm.insert("lineitem.insert", wrapper);
}
dm.commitTransaction();
return lineitem;
```

removeLineItem

The `removeLineItem` service operation implementation must ensure that the LineItem and OpenOrder exist before deleting the associated row. Listing 6.65 shows the Java code that uses iBATIS queries defined earlier in the "Define Objects" section. It also omits the code for validation of the Customer that is the same as in steps 2-3 of the `addLineItem` operation shown in Listing 6.63.

Listing 6.65 removeLineItem

```
public void removeLineItem(int customerId, int productId)
throws CustomerDoesNotExistException,
       OrderNotOpenException,
       ProductDoesNotExistException,
       NoLineItemsException,
       GeneralPersistenceException {
    // 1. (Re-)Initialize iBATIS Data Mapper
    SqlMapClient dm = getDataMapper();

    try {
        dm.startTransaction();

        // 2. Validate as in steps 2-4 of Listing 6.63
```

```
        // 3. Create Key Class for Deletion
        HashMap keys = new HashMap();
        keys.put("orderId", customer.getOpenOrder().getOrderId());
        keys.put("productId", productId);

        // 4. Delete LineItem
        dm.delete("lineitem.delete", keys);
        dm.commitTransaction();

    }
    catch(SQLException sqle) {
        throw new GeneralPersistenceException(sqle);
    }
    finally{
        try {
            dm.endTransaction();
        }
        catch(SQLException sqle) {
            throw new GeneralPersistenceException(sqle);
        }

}
```

submitOrder

Finally, the `submitOrder` method implementation changes the status of the order and removes it from the `openOrder` property of the abstract customer class. Listing 6.66 shows the `submitOrder` implementation.

Listing 6.66 submitOrder

```
public void submit(int customerId)
throws CustomerDoesNotExistException,
       OrderNotOpenException,
       NoLineItemsException,
       GeneralPersistenceException {

    // 1. (Re-)Initialize iBATIS Data Mapper
    SqlMapClient dm = getDataMapper();

    try {
        dm.startTransaction();

        // 2. Validate as in steps 2-4 of Listing 6.63
```

```
        // 3. Ensure Order has LineItems
        if(customer.getOpenOrder().getLineitems() == null ||
           customer.getOpenOrder().getLineitems().size() == 0)
              throw new NoLineItemsException();

        // 4. Update Order status to 'SUBMITTED'
        dm.update("order.submit", customer.getOpenOrder().getOrderId());

        // 5. Remove Customer openOrder reference
        dm.update("customer.close.order", customerId);

        dm.commitTransaction();

    }
    catch(SQLException sqle) {
        throw new GeneralPersistenceException(sqle);
    }
    finally{
        try {
            dm.endTransaction();
        }
        catch(SQLException sqle) {
            throw new GeneralPersistenceException(sqle);
        }
    }
}
```

Packaging the Components

Packaging of iBATIS JavaBeans is straightforward; however, packaging of the SqlMap XML files may require some minor considerations. These files can be packaged anywhere within an application as long as two requirements are met: (1) they are on the classpath, and (2) they are defined in the global iBATIS configuration file. The most common packaging approach is to put an SqlMap XML file in the same package as its corresponding JavaBeans. For instance, in our common example code, `customer.xml` is in same package as `AbstractCustomer.java`.

In the case of the common example, the iBATIS configuration is fairly standard. Listing 6.67 shows the `sql-map-config` file used.

Listing 6.67 sql-map-config.xml

```
<sqlMapConfig>

  <properties resource="database.properties"/>

  <settings cacheModelsEnabled="true" enhancementEnabled="false"
   maxSessions="64" maxTransactions="8" maxRequests="128"/>

  <transactionManager type="JDBC">
    <dataSource type="SIMPLE">
      <property value="${driver}" name="JDBC.Driver"/>
      <property value="${url}" name="JDBC.ConnectionURL"/>
      <property value="${username}" name="JDBC.Username"/>
      <property value="${password}" name="JDBC.Password"/>
      <property value="15" name="Pool.MaximumActiveConnections"/>
      <property value="15" name="Pool.MaximumIdleConnections"/>
      <property value="1000" name="Pool.MaximumWait"/>
    </dataSource>
  </transactionManager>

  <sqlMap resource="org/pwte/example/ibatis/Customer.xml"/>
  <sqlMap resource="org/pwte/example/ibatis/Order.xml"/>
  <sqlMap resource="org/pwte/example/ibatis/Product.xml"/>
  <sqlMap resource="org/pwte/example/ibatis/LineItem.xml"/>

</sqlMapConfig>
```

Unit Testing

iBATIS lends itself well to unit-testing frameworks such as JUnit. For example, if a simple JDBC datasource is used for initial unit testing, switching later to a JNDI-defined datasource is straightforward. iBATIS has no requirements for a container or external libraries. We use the same Unit Test throughout. You can examine the source found on the download site for more details. See Appendix A for instructions on downloading and executing the test cases.

Deploying to Production

In the production environment, it is likely that CGLIB would be employed for performance benefits. If the application runs in a clustered environment (multiple JVMs), plugging in distributed caching, such as OSCache, is a significant consideration.

Summary

iBATIS is an excellent framework to bridge the gap between a legacy database schema and modern object-oriented domain models. iBATIS works well in standalone or contained-based enterprise applications. The learning curve for both a developer and an administrator is not as steep as other frameworks because of its loyalty to standard SQL.

iBATIS can certainly scale to large enterprise applications; however, some advanced features of full object-relational mapping frameworks are left to the developer to implement. For example, every update to the database with iBATIS is explicit. If an object's attribute is changed, the developer must explicitly call another SqlMap statement to synchronize the change with the database. Full ORM frameworks often detect changes to POJOs with reflection or special byte-code enhancement, which implicitly update the database.

iBATIS also lacks an object-oriented query language (OQL), which helps to insulate the developer from needing to know the database schema. With an OQL of some sort, developers can query for objects based on their knowledge of the domain model, which as we discussed in Chapter 3, serves as a common vocabulary for the functional requirements of the application. With iBATIS, the developer needs to understand both the domain model and the database schema, as well as how they are mapped to each other.

However, an advantage of iBATIS is that the queries can be reviewed and optimized by a DBA because they are in a separate XML file.

Looking forward, iBATIS is currently designing the next generation of its framework, which would be version 3.0. It is taking a look at Test Driven Development and the use of Java.

Links to developerWorks

A.6.1 *Improve persistence with Apache Derby and iBATIS, Part 1: Initial configuration, semantics, and a simple test*

This developerWorks tutorial is part one of a three part series that provides specific details on how to use iBATIS with the Derby Database.

www.ibm.com/developerworks/edu/os-dw-os-ad-ibatis1.html

A.6.2 *Improve persistence wit Apache Derby and iBATIS, Part 2: Data definition in Derby*

This is part 2 of the tutorial series that shows the JPetStore application written in iBATIS using the Derby Database.

www.ibm.com/developerworks/edu/os-dw-os-ad-ibatis2.html

A.6.3 *Improve persistence with Apache Derby and iBATIS, Part 3: Transactions, caching, and dynamic SQL*

This is part 3 of the tutorial series that shows some more advanced iBATIS features needed for enterprise applications.

www.ibm.com/developerworks/edu/os-dw-os-ad-ibatis3.html

A.6.4 *DB2 UDB, WebSphere, and iBATIS*

This is an article describing using iBATIS with DB2 and WebSphere Application Server

www.ibm.com/developerworks/db2/library/techarticle/dm-0502cline/

A.6.5 *Comment lines: Roland Barcia: Tired of hand-coding JDBC? Use iBatis as a data mapping framework instead.*

This is a basic commentary on iBATIS that provides a brief overview of the benefits of using the iBATIS framework instead of the JDBC API.

www.ibm.com/developerworks/websphere/techjournal/0510_col_barcia/0510_col_barcia.html

References

[Begin] Begin, Clinton et al. *iBATIS in Action.* Manning Publication Company 2007

[Fowler]. Fowler, Martin et al. *Patterns of Enterprise Architecture.* Addison-Wesley Professional, 2002

[iBATIS] *iBATIS Home Page.* http://ibatis.apache.org/

[iBATIS 1] *iBATIS Data Mapper Developer's Guide.* ibatis.apache.org/docs/java/pdf/iBATIS-SqlMaps-2_en.pdf

[iBATIS 2] *iBATIS SQLMaps Tutorial.* ibatis.apache.org/docs/java/pdf/iBATIS-SqlMaps-2-Tutorial_en.pdf

[iBATIS 3] *iBATIS Wiki.* opensource.atlassian.com/confluence/oss/display/IBATIS/Home

[MSDN] *Using .NET to Implement Sun Microsystems' Java Pet Store J2EE BluePrint Application.* msdn2.microsoft.com/en-us/library/ms954626.aspx

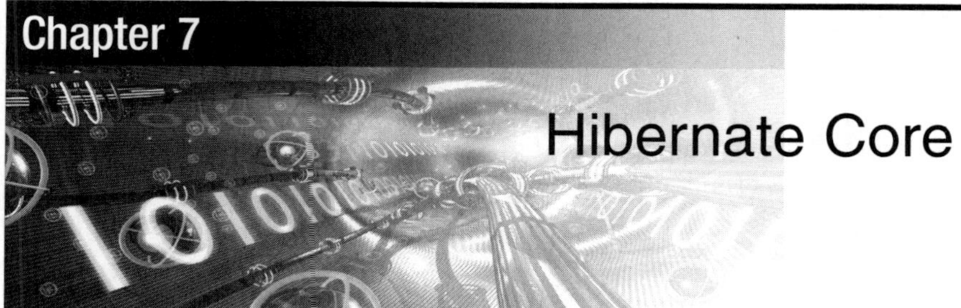

Chapter 7 Hibernate Core

In this chapter we examine Hibernate and how it implements the object-relational mapping techniques described in the previous chapters. We briefly survey its history, discuss how it is used, and show several end-to-end examples of its use.

Background

Hibernate is an open-source, object-relational mapping framework that is available from and supported through www.hibernate.org. Hibernate is relatively lightweight, very powerful, and in the latest (3.2) version a truly general persistence framework that will persist POJOs, XML, or arbitrary Java maps.

Hibernate currently comes in two forms. The first, Hibernate Core (which is the subject of this chapter, and which we will simply refer to as Hibernate), is the original mapping framework API. Hibernate Annotations is the second form—it supports JDK 5.0 annotations and is closely linked to the Hibernate Entity Manager, an implementation of the JPA API built with the Hibernate engine. In both forms, Hibernate is rapidly becoming a de facto standard for persistence across the Java industry. Recent statistics from SourceForge show that Hibernate is being downloaded at a rate between 1,000 and 5,000 times per day. This download rate has been sustained for well over three years, and shows every sign of increasing.

In this chapter we do not show the details of either Hibernate Annotations or Hibernate Entity Manager, because we are focusing on the basic capabilities of Hibernate Core and comparing it to the other frameworks. And because Chapter 8 evaluates JPA in the context of openJPA, we recommend that you read more about Hibernate's Entity Manager [Hibernate 1] for more details on their implementation approach and specific features.

Hibernate Core provides both simplicity and flexibility for developers who need object-relational mapping. It can perform most mapping tasks in a simple, configuration-driven way that does not require the developer to write any SQL code at all. However, if you want to write your own SQL, or use stored procedures for loading and storing data, Hibernate supports that as well. Likewise, it can provide simple connection pooling and caching that would be effective in a JAVA SE environment, or it can integrate with application servers and third-party caching solutions to function effectively in a Java EE environment as well.

Type of Framework

Hibernate is a full object-relational mapping framework that implements the Object Mapper pattern. Although you could implement other pattern types with Hibernate, the fact that it directly supports Object Mapper means that this is the most commonly utilized persistence pattern associated with Hibernate.

History

The following timeline summarizes some of the major events in the evolution of the Hibernate framework. For more information on the background and history of Hibernate, refer to Chapter 1, "A Brief History of Object-Relational Mapping."

- November 2001—Initial SourceForge project opened.
- Mid-2002—Hibernate 1.0 released.
- June 2003—Hibernate 2.0 released.
- October 2003—Hibernate developers hired by JBoss.
- Feb 2005—Hibernate 3.0 released.

Architectural Overview

Hibernate is a fully featured yet small open-source framework for implementing object-relational mapping. It is compliant with most appropriate Java standards in this space and will work within JAVA SE, within most application servers, and within frameworks like Spring.

Standards Adherence

Although there is a version of Hibernate (Hibernate Entity Manager) that fully implements the JPA specification, many Hibernate developers use a POJO (Plain Old Java Objects) model supported through the Hibernate Core API. So strictly speaking, Hibernate Core does not represent or adhere to a specific standard.

However, Hibernate provides a simple API for object-relational mapping that maps Java classes to database tables so that it can be used both within a strict Java SE environment, in which case it handles its own transaction management against a single database, and within a JEE container, allowing the container to manage transactions and issues such as database pooling. Hibernate is compatible with most vendors' JDBC drivers, and will also support most JEE containers.

Platforms Required

Hibernate Core, being a pure Java solution, will run on any hardware platform supporting a Java SE environment. Hibernate Annotations requires Java 5 because it relies upon Java 5 Annotations.

Other Dependencies

Hibernate has a remarkably small code base. The Hibernate Core runtime JAR file is only 2.1MB, and Hibernate relies on only a small set of open-source projects that provide underlying functionality. These include Apache Common Collections and Common logging, ANTLR, DOM4J, ASM (the ObjectWeb open-source bytecode manipulation framework), and the CGLib code generation library. These additional open-source libraries are included in the download for Hibernate. Hibernate requires a JDBC driver for whatever database will be used with Hibernate, which can be obtained from the database vendor.

Hibernate is commonly used with the Spring framework (www.springframework.org) for Aspect Oriented Programming and Dependency Injection, and many Spring projects use Hibernate as their persistence engine. When you use Spring with Hibernate, it simplifies transaction management and also simplifies Hibernate's configuration. However, in this chapter we want to focus on the persistence features of Hibernate and be able to compare it directly with other frameworks like OpenJPA and iBATIS, so we will not use Spring in our examples.

Vendors and Licenses

Hibernate is controlled by the JBoss Group. Although the implementation is handled through the open-source process, many of the key developers are JBoss Group employees, and the JBoss Group certainly sets the priorities of the project. Hibernate has been released under the Lesser Gnu Public License (LGPL). This means that changes to the source code of Hibernate must be made available to the original authors of Hibernate. Given that it is an open-source product, you can obtain production-level downloads directly from www.hibernate.org.

Available Literature

There are many good sources of material for help in understanding Hibernate. Several of the best are listed in Table 7.1.

Table 7.1 Available Literature for Hibernate

Title	Source	Description
Java Persistence with Hibernate [Bauer]	Manning Publications Co.	Excellent introductory resource written by the lead developer of Hibernate.
Hibernate Reference Guide [Hibernate 2]	www.hibernate.org/5.html	Comprehensive reference documentation available in HTML and PDF form.
Wiki [Hibernate 3]	www.hibernate.org/37.html	Excellent for platform-specific notes and information on new undocumented features.
User Mailing Lists [Hibernate 4]	www.hibernate.org/20.htmlh	Resource for advanced questions and debugging.
 A.7.1 *Hibernate Simplifies Inheritance Mapping*	www.ibm.com/developerworks/java/library/j-hibernate/	Article illustrating inheritance with Hibernate
 A.7.2 *Using Hibernate to Persist Your Java Objects to IBM DB2 Universal Database*	www.ibm.com/developerworks/db2/library/techarticle/0306bhogal/0306bhogal.html	This article gives a simple Hibernate overview, illustrating the use of Hibernate with IBM DB2.
 A.7.3 *Using Spring and Hibernate with WebSphere Application Server*	www.ibm.com/developerworks/websphere/techjournal/0609_alcott/0609_alcott.html	This article shows the proper setting to configure when using Hibernate and Spring with WebSphere Application Server.

Programming Model

The Hibernate programming model is simple because it is designed to keep out of the programmer's way. By abstracting the relational details away from the programmer, and moving most of the work of object-relational mapping into XML configuration files, it provides the programmer with a simple, POJO-based approach that makes mapping as easy (in most cases) as calling a method that takes a POJO as a parameter to make it persistent; or receiving a POJO as a method return value to retrieve it from the database.

The Hibernate programming model involves a POJO and an object called Session, which manages the life-cycle of a POJO. A POJO can be in one of three states:

- **Transient**—An object that is not yet associated with a Session, and therefore is not persistent.
- **Persistent**—An object that has just been saved or loaded within the scope of an active Session context.
- **Detached**—An object that has been saved or loaded, but the associated Session context has been closed.

A Transient and Detached object can be made Persistent by being saved, loaded, or merged into an active Session; this cycle can repeat as often as necessary.

Initialization

Hibernate has a very simple initialization mechanism based on the idea of a Hibernate *Session* and a Hibernate *Configuration.* A Configuration is an object that reads a Hibernate Configuration file—the contents of this file determine the configuration options such as the JDBC driver used, how caches and connection pools are configured, and so forth. Configurations are used to build Session Factories, which are then used by methods that use Hibernate persistence (like our service implementations) to obtain Hibernate Sessions. An example of a Session Factory derived from a Configuration is shown in Listing 7.1.

Listing 7.1 Setting Up a Session Factory

```
SessionFactory sessionFactory = new Configuration()
    .configure ("/persistence/my.cfg.xml")
    .buildSessionFactory();
```

The Configuration obtains its information from a configuration file usually named `hibernate.cfg.xml`. This file can be located anywhere, but it is customarily located at the root of the classpath. A sample, very bare-bones configuration file suitable for use in a J2SE environment is shown in Listing 7.2.

Listing 7.2 Hibernate Configuration File for Derby

```
<?xml version="1.0" encoding="UTF-8"?>
<!DOCTYPE hibernate-configuration PUBLIC
  "-//Hibernate/Hibernate Configuration DTD 3.0//EN"
  "hibernate.sourceforge.net/hibernate-configuration-3.0.dtd">
<hibernate-configuration>
<session-factory>
<property name="current_session_context_class">thread</property>
<property name="hibernate.connection.driver_class">
    org.apache.derby.jdbc.EmbeddedDriver
</property>
```

```
<property name="hibernate.connection.url">
    jdbc:derby:c:\eclipse\BookDB;create=true;
</property>
<property name="hibernate.dialect">
    org.hibernate.dialect.DerbyDialect
</property>
<!-- Disable the second-level cache -->
<property name="cache.provider_class">
    org.hibernate.cache.NoCacheProvider
</property>
<!-- Echo all executed SQL to stdout -->
property name="show_sql">true</property>
<!-- Mapping files -->
</session-factory>
</hibernate-configuration>
```

In most cases, the code will be encapsulated into a helper class that is usually named (by convention) HibernateUtil. A simple HibernateUtil class is provided in the documentation of the Hibernate framework. An example of how the HibernateUtil class is used to obtain a Hibernate Session object (and how the Session object is used for transaction management) is shown in Listing 7.3.

Listing 7.3 HibernateUtil Used for Initialization

```
Session session = HibernateUtil.getSessionFactory().getCurrentSession();
session.beginTransaction();
AbstractCustomer retrievedCustomer = (AbstractCustomer)session.load(
    AbstractCustomer.class, new Integer(100)
);
session.getTransaction().commit();
```

In Listing 7.3 we demonstrated how to use the Derby JDBC driver from within Hibernate. In Listing 7.4, we show how to use an application DataSource with JNDI name `jdbc/Derby/DataSource`.

Listing 7.4 Hibernate Configuration File for DataSource

```
<property name="hibernate.connection.datasource">
    java:comp/env/jdbc/Derby/DataSource
</property>
<property name="hibernate.connection.username">admin</property>
<property name="hibernate.connection.password">password</property>
```

This example set of properties (which would replace the `hibernate.connection.driver.class` and `hibernate.connection.url` properties in Listing 7.2) inform the hibernate SessionFactory to use a DataSource, and provide the JNDI name for the datasource, as well as a username and password for authentication to the database.

Connections

Because Hibernate supports a full ORM approach, it uses a transparent connection model. It does not directly support an explicit connection model, meaning that creating a JDBC connection is not one of the standard steps in using Hibernate. When used with an application DataSource as shown previously, Hibernate will use whatever connection pooling is provided by the underlying DataSource. When used with Database drivers that do not support connection pooling, Hibernate also supports third-party connection pooling approaches, such as the C3P0 connection and statement pooling classes. Finally, Hibernate also allows the user to provide his own JDBC Connection object to a Hibernate Session for its use, although the use of this feature is discouraged.

Transactions

Hibernate has been designed to work either inside or outside of a Java EE application server. As such, it supports externally managed JTA transactions, and also can manage its own transaction demarcation with the `org.hibernate.Transaction` API. If no explicit external transaction management is specified or the Hibernate API is not used, it will default to a "pseudo" autocommit for each Hibernate statement. We say "pseudo" because Hibernate does not use the autocommit mode for the underlying database driver, but instead invokes each Hibernate statement its own transaction.

The example in Listing 7.5 shows grouping two updates (setting the business partner attribute to `false`, and updating that customer's open order status to `SUBMITTED`) within a transaction using Hibernate's `org.hibernate.Transaction` API.

Listing 7.5 Using Transactions in Hibernate

```
// note -- assumes customer #100 is in the database and has an open
// order.
Session session = HibernateUtil.getSessionFactory().getCurrentSession();
session.beginTransaction();
BusinessCustomer firstBusinessCustomer = (BusinessCustomer)
   session.load(BusinessCustomer.class, new Integer(100));
firstBusinessCustomer.setBusinessPartner(false);
session.save(firstBusinessCustomer);
Order openOrder = firstBusinessCustomer.getOpenOrder();
openOrder.setStatus(Status SUBMITTED);
firstBusinessCustomer.setOrder(null);
session.save(firstBusinessCustomer);
```

```
session.save(openOrder);
session.getTransaction().commit();
```

Note that in this example we had to perform a `session.save()` on both the customer and the order, because we disconnected the order from the customer when we set the Customer's order to `null` as part of changing the status to submitted (meaning the Customer had no current open order). We discuss the `save()` method throughout this section.

As stated earlier, Hibernate will work with JTA (the Java Transaction API) and you can configure Hibernate to use the JTA within the context of an application server as its transaction manager. You have two choices for using JTA with Hibernate:

- You can let Hibernate use JTA as its underlying transaction manager while still using the Hibernate API for transaction management. This has the advantage of being consistent with programs written that run outside of an application server.
- You can manage transactions external to hibernate with the JTA `javax.transaction.UserTransaction` API. This has the advantage that Hibernate persistence can be tied together in a JTA transaction with operations on other resources like JMS queues.

In either case, setting up Hibernate to use JTA is the same—it simply requires a change to the Hibernate configuration file. In particular, you need to set three elements of this file:

- The property `hibernate.transaction.factory_class` must be set to `org.hibernate.transaction.JTATransactionFactory`.
- You must inform Hibernate of the location of the JTA UserTransaction—for example, in WebSphere this object is found in the JNDI name space at `java:comp/UserTransaction`.
- The property `hibernate.transaction.manager_lookup_class` must be set to the option that is appropriate for your application server environment. For instance, in WebSphere you would set this value to `WebSphereExtendedJTATransactionLookup`.

Note that as of Hibernate 3.2, there was a bug introduced into Hibernate that will not allow you to use the `WebSphereExtendedJTATransactionLookup` class (which is the method supported by IBM). The workaround for this bug was to use the `WebSphereTransactionManagerLookup` class instead, which is not supported by IBM for external use.

A section of a sample configuration file that illustrates setting these elements within this known limitation is shown in Listing 7.6.

Listing 7.6 Hibernate Configuration File for JTA

```
<property name="hibernate.transaction.factory_class">
    org.hibernate.transaction.JTATransactionFactory
</property>
<property name="hibernate.transaction.manager_lookup_class">
```

```
    org.hibernate.transaction.WebSphereExtendedJTATransactionLookup
</property>
<property name="jta.UserTransaction">
    java:comp/UserTransaction
</property >
```

When using Hibernate with JTA, you must also configure it to use DataSources obtained from the application server with JNDI, as was covered previously.

Hibernate supports all the standard JDBC isolation levels, either through the connections it manages on its own, or through the connections provided by the Application Server. For instance, if you are using Hibernate's internal connection pooling, then to set the isolation level on that connection to be "Read Uncommitted" you would use the following property in the Hibernate configuration file:

```
<property name="hibernate.connection.isolation">1</property>
```

The integer 1 refers to the isolation level value for `TRANSACTION_READ_UNCOMMITTED` that is found as a constant having that name in the class `java.sql.Connection`. Note that this should be done only if application isolation is being managed directly, and not through the capabilities of an application server.

Create

Creating a new object in Hibernate is really as simple as creating the POJO with the `new` operator and then using the Hibernate Session `save()` operation to make the object persistent. The example in Listing 7.7 shows how to create a new Customer object in Hibernate. Note that this example sets the primary key (the customer ID) manually rather than using one of Hibernate's automatic key-generation strategies.

Listing 7.7 Create a New Customer

```
BusinessCustomer customer = new BusinessCustomer(
    false, false, "Default Business Partner", "Harry's fast foods",
    null, null
);
customer.setCustomerId(42);
Session session = HibernateUtil.getSessionFactory().getCurrentSession();
session.beginTransaction();
session.save(customer);
session.getTransaction().commit();
```

This approach to setting the key manually is not possible in our common code examples, given the default schema we specified as one of the endpoints in Chapter 3. To make this approach work with the common code examples, you must remove the key generation annotations from the Derby primary key definition for Order. We will discuss this subject again later in the "Keys" section.

The example in Listing 7.8 shows how to take the previously created customer and create an Order that belongs to that customer.

Listing 7.8 Create a New Order for the Previously Created Customer

```
// This assumes customer number 100 (created in the previous example)
// is in the database
Session session = HibernateUtil.getSessionFactory().getCurrentSession();
session.beginTransaction();
BusinessCustomer retrievedCustomer =(BusinessCustomer)session.load(
    BusinessCustomer.class, new Integer(100)
);
Order newOrder = new Order();
newOrder.setCustomer(retrievedCustomer);
newOrder.setOrderId(247);
newOrder.setStatus(Status.OPEN);
retrievedCustomer.setOpenOrder(newOrder);
session.getTransaction().commit();
```

Note that in Listing 7.8 we did not need to explicitly save the Order—this is because by changing the openOrder attribute of the Customer, we rendered this object "dirty," and Hibernate knew to make persistent any objects attached to that object. Hibernate also allows you to specify insert statements using HQL, which we describe in the next section.

Retrieve

In an earlier section we showed how you can use the `Session.load()` method to load a Customer from the database given a particular primary key. Another option you can use that is similar to `Session.load()` is `Session.get()`. It works the same as `Session.load()` except instead of throwing an exception when a row is not found, it returns `null` instead.

A more interesting retrieval mechanism in Hibernate is the ability of programmers to use the HQL (Hibernate Query Language) to specify queries on mapped objects. For instance, the code to retrieve all the Customers that are "active" (that is, that have an open order) is shown in Listing 7.9.

Listing 7.9 Retrieve Active Customers with HQL

```
Session session = HibernateUtil.getSessionFactory().getCurrentSession();
session.beginTransaction();
List activeCustomers = session.createQuery(
    "from org.pwte.example.domain.AbstractCustomer as cust
     where cust.openOrder != null"
).list();
session.getTransaction().commit();
```

The HQL Query used in this example (`from org.pwte.example.domain. AbstractCustomer as cust where cust.openOrder != null`) demonstrates several of the relevant features of HQL. The simplest HQL query is simply `from classname`, which retrieves all instances of a mapped class name from the database. There is an optional `select` clause that precedes the `from` clause that allows you to select individual properties of the mapped object or objects contained within the mapped object as an array or a list. Likewise, the `where` clause allows the specification of which objects to instantiate as part of the list based on the values of the attributes of the mapped object. HQL also supports most standard SQL concepts such as joins, functions, group by, and order by.

For most purposes, though, you will tend to use the power of Hibernate's built-in support for mapping relations between tables to associations between objects, rather than building custom queries in HQL. For instance, the code in Listing 7.10 shows how simple it is to retrieve all the Orders associated with a Customer.

Listing 7.10 Retrieving Orders for a Customer

```
Session session=HibernateUtil.getSessionFactory().openSession();
session.beginTransaction();
BusinessCustomer retrievedCustomer = (BusinessCustomer) session.load(
    BusinessCustomer.class, new Integer(43)
);
Set<Order> orders = retrievedCustomer.getOrders();
session.getTransaction().commit();
session.close();
```

As you can see, Hibernate handles the hard part (querying the tables) for you—you just traverse the existing object relationships established in your POJOs. Likewise, obtaining the singleton open order associated with a customer is a just as simple, as Listing 7.11 shows.

Listing 7.11 Retrieving the Open Order for a Customer

```
Session session=HibernateUtil.getSessionFactory().openSession();
session.beginTransaction();
BusinessCustomer retrievedCustomer = (BusinessCustomer) session.load(
    BusinessCustomer.class, new Integer(100)
);
Order openOrder = retrievedCustomer.getOpenOrder();
session.getTransaction().commit();
session.close();
```

Finally, Hibernate also supports the use of Custom SQL for querying. You can define a SQL (or HQL) query in the mapping document, then name it, and then use that named query. For instance, if we needed to be able to classify Products by some part of the product description, then one way to accomplish that is to place a query in the mapping document for Product, as shown in Listing 7.12.

Listing 7.12 Creating a Named Query in a Hibernate Configuration File

```
<sql-query name="classifiedProducts">
    <return alias="product" class="org.pwte.example.domain.Product"/>
    SELECT product.PRODUCT_ID AS {product.productId},
           product.PRICE AS {product.price},
           product.DESCRIPTION AS {product.description}
    FROM PRODUCT product
    WHERE product.description LIKE :namePattern
</sql-query>
```

You can then use that query with the code given in Listing 7.13, which creates a List of all Product instances that have the word "Gadgets" in their description.

Listing 7.13 Using named queries in Hibernate

```
List products = session.getNamedQuery("classifiedProducts")
        .setString("namePattern", "%Gadgets%")
        .setMaxResults(50)
        .list();
```

Not only does Hibernate support Custom SQL for specifying queries that can then be mapped to the objects defined in a Hibernate mapping file, but Hibernate also supports custom SQL in many other ways. In particular, if you want to specify the SQL to be used for the update, insert, or deletion of an object, that can be specified in the mapping file also. This is done through the use of the `<sql-query>`, `<sql-insert>`, `<sql-update>`, and `<sql-delete>` tags in the Hibernate mapping file. We show the use of these tags later, in the section "Stored Procedures."

Finally, a query mechanism that is truly unique to Hibernate among the ORM products we are evaluating is the Criteria mechanism. The Criteria mechanism allows the developer to construct queries "on the fly" through an implementation of the Interpreter pattern, which you can find in *Patterns: Elements of Reusable Object-Oriented Software* [Gamma 94]. There are two primary classes involved in this interface: the Criteria class and the Restriction class. A Restriction represents a particular comparison or statement to be evaluated against an object. For instance, if you wanted to see whether a Product instance had a particular description (for example, "Widget"), you would use the following method to create an equivalent Restriction that asks whether the attribute name matches the value `Widget`:

```
Restriction.eq("description", "Widget")
```

There are methods in the `Restriction` class that allow for comparisons against `null`, evaluations of whether an attribute is greater than or less than another value, and String comparisons to see whether an object's attribute contains a String, as well as others.

Restrictions are joined together to form Criteria, which are evaluated against a persistent class. So, to find out whether you have a particular AbstractCustomer matching the name "Kyle Brown," you would need the statement shown in Listing 7.14.

Listing 7.14 Abstract Customer Criteria Example

```
AbstractCustomer customer = (AbstractCustomer)
    session.createCriteria(AbstractCustomer.class)
    .add(Restrictions.eq("name", "Kyle Brown"))
    .uniqueResult();
```

Update

One of the ramifications of using a full object-relational mapping tool is that in some cases, making a change to only a single column in a single row of a database may require navigating through several layers of object relationships to first identify the object corresponding to that row before you can make the change. A good example of this is changing the quantity of a line item in a specific order held by a specific customer. The code that's needed to change the line item's quantity is simple—you just invoke the `setQuantity()` method on the appropriate line item. Identifying that line item can be involved, as the code in Listing 7.15 demonstrates.

Listing 7.15 Changing a LineItem Quantity

```
Session session=HibernateUtil.getSessionFactory().openSession();
session.beginTransaction();
BusinessCustomer retrievedCustomer = (BusinessCustomer)session.load(
    BusinessCustomer.class, new Integer(100)
);
Order openOrder = retrievedCustomer.getOpenOrder();
// find Line Item for the specific product having ID = 100
Iterator<LineItem> lineItems = openOrder.getLineitems().iterator();
while (lineItems.hasNext()) {
    LineItem item = lineItems.next();
    if (item.getLineItemId().productId == 100) {
        item.setQuantity(100);
    }
}
session.getTransaction().commit();
session.close();
```

A particular issue with this approach is that depending on the settings of lazy or eager loading, this code may invoke a number of different SQL queries—so this approach should be used with careful attention to the performance details. Finally, some changes are truly trivial, such as that shown in Listing 7.16 to change an open order in a customer to `null`.

Listing 7.16 Setting an Open Order to null in a Customer

```
Session session=HibernateUtil.getSessionFactory().openSession();
session.beginTransaction();
BusinessCustomer retrievedCustomer = (BusinessCustomer) session.load(
    BusinessCustomer.class, new Integer(200)
);
retrievedCustomer.setOpenOrder(null);
session.getTransaction().commit();
session.close();
```

Hibernate also allows you to use HQL `Update` statements to do bulk updates.

Delete

Hibernate supports both explicit and cascaded deletes. The simplest way to delete an object is simply through the `Session.delete()` method, which is roughly the reverse of `Session.save()`. However, deleting a single object is often not as simple as that. Consider the case of removing a LineItem from an Order. First, you have the issue of navigating to the particular LineItem. After you have identified the particular LineItem you are interested in, you can remove it from the collection that contains it, as Listing 7.17 shows.

Listing 7.17 Removing a Line Item

```
Session session=HibernateUtil.getSessionFactory().openSession();
session.beginTransaction();
BusinessCustomer retrievedCustomer = (BusinessCustomer)session.load(
    BusinessCustomer.class, new Integer(100)
);
Order openOrder = retrievedCustomer.getOpenOrder();
// find Line Item for the specific product having ID = 100
LineItem targetItem = null;
Iterator<LineItem> lineItems = openOrder.getLineitems().iterator();
while (lineItems.hasNext()) {
    LineItem item = lineItems.next();
    if (item.getLineItemId().productId == 100) {
        targetItem=item;
    }
}
openOrder.getLineitems().remove(targetItem);
session.save(openOrder);
session.getTransaction().commit();
session.close();
```

Now, this code looks like it should work; and in fact, if you run it, it will *appear* to work while not having the effect you expect. If you look, you will see that a row associated with the LineItem object remains in the database. The reason is that Hibernate needs to be explicitly told how to deal with "orphaned" objects that are removed from Collections. This is a ramification of the way in which Hibernate handles the notion of transient, persistent, and detached objects—as we discussed in the introduction to the "Programming Model" section. This life cycle is so important to understanding the delete operation that we repeat some of the essential details here.

When you remove the object from the collection, you've not changed its persistent nature. In Hibernate an object is first instantiated as transient—right after you've created it with the new operator, but before you've associated it with a Session, it is transient. After you make an object persistent—either by directly making it persistent by using `Session.save()` or by attaching it to a persistent object—it remains persistent. Its state remains in the database until it is removed from the database. In this case, you've just removed one pointer to the object—it could be that other references to the row remain in the database; Hibernate can't know that.

What you can do, however, is to clarify the semantics of the collection. To understand that, examine the snippet from the `Order.hbm.xml` configuration file shown in Listing 7.18.

Listing 7.18 Cascade Attribute in the Mapping File

```
<set name="lineitems" inverse="true" cascade="all, delete-orphan">
  <key column="ORDER_ID' not-null="true"/>
  <one-to-many class="org.pwte.example.domain.LineItem"/>
</set>
```

Notice the attribute `cascade="all, delete-orphan"`. When we have said that attaching a transient object to a persistent object makes the transient object persistent, we've been telling a little white lie. In fact, by default no persistence operations are applied to the objects at the other end of a relationship unless you set the cascade attribute to `all`. Then all the persistence operations you can express through a Session (save, update, delete, and so on) are carried through (cascaded) to the other end of the relationship. The exception to this is `delete-orphan`. This special cascade style is what enables deleting objects when they are removed from a collection. You can either add it as we've shown previously, or use the combination "all-delete-orphan" style in the `cascade` attribute. In fact, we've killed two birds with one stone in setting this to `all` and `delete-orphan`, because now when we delete an Order we find that all the LineItems in the Order are also deleted, as the example in Listing 7.19 indicates.

Listing 7.19 Cascaded Delete of Order and LineItems

```
Session session=HibernateUtil.getSessionFactory().openSession();
session.beginTransaction();
Order order = (Order) session.load(Order.class, new Integer(400));
```

```
session.delete(order);
session.getTransaction().commit();
session.close();
```

Much like in the update scenario, you can use HQL to issue a bulk delete.

Stored Procedures

As noted earlier, in the same way you can specify which SQL to execute for a query, you can specify custom SQL for update, insert, and delete as well. In implementing these processes, you can also specify a stored procedure for the same purpose. So if you wanted to build a hypothetical class "Address" whose SQL would be controlled through stored procedures, its mapping file might look as shown in Listing 7.20.

Listing 7.20 Specifying Stored Procedures in Hibernate

```
<class name="org.pwte.domain.Address">
    <id name="address_id"/>
    <property name="name" not-null="true"/>
    <property name="address" not-null="true"/>
    <property name="city" not-null="true"/>
    <property name="state" not-null="true"/>
    <property name="zip" not-null="true"/>
    <sql-insert callable="true">
      {call createAddress (?, ?, ?, ?, ?, ?)}
    </sql-insert>
    <sql-delete callable="true">
      {? = call deleteAddress (?)}
    </sql-delete>
    <sql-update callable="true">
     {? = call updateAddress (?, ?, ?, ?, ?, ?)}
    </sql-update>
</class>
```

Using this approach, you can still use Hibernate as your object-relational mapping tool even if your database administrators want to maintain strict control over the SQL that executes on the database. Now, Hibernate does put some restrictions on the stored procedures themselves, such as the fact that they have to use the standard SQL92 call form, and not a vendor-specific syntax. These limitations and restrictions are described in the Hibernate documentation. Finally, to specify a SQL query or stored procedure for loading a class (for example, for identity queries using the `load()` method of `Session`), a two-step procedure is followed. First you declare a named SQL query with the `<sql-query>` tag as described previously, and then you specify that it is to be used as the loading query for the class with the `<loader>` tag. Note that this approach lets you define only stored procedures that correspond to inserts, deletes, updates, and queries; there is no predefined way in Hibernate to use stored procedures to implement generic business logic.

Batch Operations

Hibernate allows you to batch updates and inserts into the database; to do so effectively you must set a configuration parameter, and also adjust the application code that triggers the batched updates or inserts. First, you want to make sure that you enable batching by setting the JDBC batch size to a reasonable value in the Hibernate main configuration file (`Hibernate.cfg.xml`):

```
hibernate.jdbc.batch_size 50
```

Likewise, you need to make sure that if you're creating or updating a very large number of objects, you occasionally call the `flush()` and `clear()` methods of `Session` to flush the first-level cache to the database and thus control its size. When you're doing a significant amount of batch processing, it would also probably be useful to entirely disable the second-level cache by setting the CacheMode appropriately because you would not need to store query results when performing batch updates.

In addition, as we mentioned in the "Create," "Update," and "Delete" sections, you can use HQL to run a batch insert, update, or delete.

Extending the Framework

Hibernate has a range of extension points, including the UserType extension point discussed later in "Attributes" and the Cache extension point described in the later "Caching" section.

Error Handling

One of the things that is difficult for people who have had experience only with JDBC to become adjusted to in the Hibernate programming model is the lack of checked exceptions. Hibernate API methods do not (in general) throw checked exceptions—they are all instead declared to throw `HibernateException`, which is a `RuntimeException`. This is a practice that is also present in Spring, and that is preferred by many developers. Thus, in many cases you do not need to encapsulate your code in try-catch blocks as you would in JDBC. There are cases in which you would want to catch specific subclasses of `HibernateException`, though, and we will cover that topic later with detailed examples.

ORM Features Supported

Hibernate supports most standard features required for object-relational mapping. It transparently handles object mapping, key generation, inheritance, relationships, and derived mappings. As we have seen, it also provides flexibility to the user in handling odd cases such as where stored procedures are required, or where special SQL needs to be specified for custom queries. With its strong support for third-party caching facilities, it makes it easier to achieve good runtime performance by alleviating the need to constantly reexecute queries against the database. In short, it tries to cover all the bases in the game of ORM.

Objects

Defining an Order object in Hibernate is no different from defining an Order object in our standard POJO domain model. In Listing 7.21 we show the code of the Order object; as you can see, it does not differ from that presented earlier when the domain model was presented.

Listing 7.21 Defining an Order Object in Hibernate

```
package org.pwte.example.domain;


import java.math.BigDecimal;
import java.util.Set;


public class Order {
    protected int orderId;
    protected BigDecimal total;
    public static enum Status { OPEN, SUBMITTED, CLOSED }
    protected Status status;
    protected AbstractCustomer customer;
    protected Set<LineItem> lineitems;

    //getters and setters
}
```

The key place where development in Hibernate begins to differ from straight POJO development is in the development of the mapping configuration files for each POJO object. Listing 7.22 shows the mapping file for our Order object.

Listing 7.22 Hibernate Mapping File for Order

```
<?xml version="1.0"?>
<!DOCTYPE hibernate-mapping PUBLIC "-//Hibernate/Hibernate Mapping DTD 3.0//EN"
"hibernate.sourceforge.net/hibernate-mapping-3.0.dtd">
<hibernate-mapping>
    <class name="org.pwte.example.domain.Order" table="ORDERS"
     schema="APP">
        <comment></comment>
        <id name="orderId" type="int">
            <column name="ORDER_ID" />
```

```
            <generator class="increment" />
        </id>
        <many-to-one name="customer"
               class="org.pwte.example.domain.AbstractCustomer"
               column="CUSTOMER_ID">
        </many-to-one>
        <property name="status"
         type="org.pwte.example.domain.StatusUserType">
            <column name="STATUS" length="9" not-null="true">
                <comment></comment>
            </column>
        </property>
        <property name="total" type="big_decimal">
            <column name="TOTAL" precision="14" not-null="true">
                <comment></comment>
            </column>
        </property>
        <set name="lineitems" inverse="true" cascade="all" outer-
         join="true">
            <key column="ORDER_ID" not-null="true"/>
            <one-to-many class="org.pwte.example.domain.LineItem"/>
        </set>
    </class>
</hibernate-mapping>
```

There are several features of this mapping file that are worthwhile to point out. The first is the class element inside the hibernate-mapping element. Note that it specifies the basic parts of the mapping between class and table, the fully qualified name of the class, the name of the relational table that it maps to, and the schema that the table is found in.

There are several types of mapping elements contained within the mapping file: they are relationships, collections, and properties. A property represents a single attribute of the class, and shows its map to a corresponding database column. A collection represents an attribute of the class that is represented by a collection; in this case, we see the element declaring that the LineItem class is a member of a Set called `lineitems`. Finally, a relationship describes a relationship between this class and another class, and indicates the cardinality by the name of the element (in this case many-to-one). We will cover each of these features in more depth in the following sections.

Inheritance

Hibernate supports a full set of inheritance mapping options. It supports single table, class table, and concrete table (called "table per class hierarchy," "table per subclass," and "table per concrete class," respectively, in Hibernate terminology) inheritance—as described in

A.7.1

Chapter 3. These options are supported in the Hibernate mapping files by the <subclass>, <joined-subclass>, and <union-subclass> tags, respectively. The structure of the mapping file in this case is a bit different, in that the subclass tags above appear as an element of the <class> tag of the superclass. Property, relationship, and set tags then nest within the subclass tag as usual.

Our schema and code example uses the single-table inheritance model. In Listing 7.23 the section of the Hibernate mapping file for AbstractCustomer shows how the <subclass> tag is used to define that the ResidentialCustomer class inherits from AbstractCustomer and that both use the single table inheritance model. For clarity in this example, we have left out the mapping of BusinessCustomer.

Listing 7.23 Showing Inheritance in Hibernate

```
<?xml version="1.0"?>
<!DOCTYPE hibernate-mapping PUBLIC "-//Hibernate/Hibernate Mapping DTD 3.0//EN"
"hibernate.sourceforge.net/hibernate-mapping-3.0.dtd">
<hibernate-mapping>
    <class name="org.pwte.example.domain.AbstractCustomer"
     table="CUSTOMER" schema="APP">
        <comment></comment>
        <id name="customerId" type="int">
            <column name="CUSTOMER_ID" />
            <generator class="assigned" />
        </id>
        <discriminator column="type" />
        <many-to-one name="openOrder"
         class="org.pwte.example.domain.Order"
         column="OPEN_ORDER"
         insert="false" update="true">
        </many-to-one>
        <set name="orders" inverse="true" outer-join="true">
            <key column="customer_id" not-null="true"/>
            <one-to-many class="org.pwte.example.domain.Order"/>
        </set>
        <property name="name" type="string">
            <column name="NAME" length="30" not-null="true">
                <comment></comment>
            </column>
        </property>
     <subclass
      name="org.pwte.example.domain.ResidentialCustomer"
      discriminator-value="RESIDENTIAL"
      extends="org.pwte.example.domain.AbstractCustomer">
```

```
        <property name="householdSize" type="java.lang.Short">
            <column name="RESIDENTIAL_HOUSEHOLD_SIZE">
                <comment></comment>
            </column>
        </property>
        <property name="frequentCustomer" type="yes_no">
            <column name="RESIDENTIAL_FREQUENT_CUSTOMER" length="1">
                <comment></comment>
            </column>
        </property>
        </subclass>
    </class>
</hibernate-mapping>
```

Notice in this mapping file that you first begin by specifying the superclass (`AbstractCustomer`) and by mapping the properties that are shared by all subclasses (in this case `id`, `openOrder`, `orders`, and `name`). An additional feature that you should pay attention to is the `<discriminator column="type"/>` element. This declares that a discriminator column is used to determine which subclass rows belong to. In the `<subclass>` element you will see the `discriminator-value` attribute, which declares for the `ResidentialCustomer` subclass that the value `RESIDENTIAL` will be used for the value of the discriminator column.

Keys

Hibernate allows you to map the type of the database primary key to a Java type just as with any other attribute. A restriction in the way Hibernate treats key attributes is that once a key attribute has been first assigned, Hibernate does not allow it to be changed—because in that case you would be changing the identity of the object. If you attempt to do so, Hibernate will throw a `HibernateException` when you attempt to commit the transaction. Hibernate supports both composite (compound) and noncomposite primary keys. A simple example of a noncomposite primary key mapping is in the `Order` class, as we have already seen, and as shown in Listing 7.24.

Listing 7.24 Simple Integer Mapping of a Primary Key

```
<id name="orderId" type="int">
  <column name="ORDER_ID" />
  <generator class="increment" />
</id>
```

In this example, you see that the name of the attribute mapped to the database primary key column ORDER_ID is `orderId` and that the Java type that the SQL INTEGER type is to be mapped to is a Java `int`. This example also specifies a generator class, which we will examine shortly.

Composite primary keys should be used when an existing database schema requires the use of a compound key. In most other cases, you should prefer a simple (noncomposite) primary key, because it will generally make the mapping simpler. Hibernate fully supports compound keys. However, to understand the best way to use composite keys, we have to think a while about how key attributes work in Hibernate.

Let's consider the mapping for the `LineItem` class. The LINE_ITEM table has a composite primary key consisting of both ORDER_ID and PRODUCT_ID. However, the `LineItem` class definition does not even contain an `orderId` attribute; and instead of a `productId`, it contains only a reference to an actual product! So, one way of handling this might be to add a `productId` attribute to the class. However, remember how objects are loaded in Hibernate; the `Session.load()` method takes two parameters—the class of the object being loaded, and the primary key value (which may be an Object). There's no easy way to see how both primary key values would be specified. In fact, Hibernate allows a way out of this by permitting you to use a "dummy" instance of the class being loaded as the primary key, but this is not a very elegant solution to our problem. A better solution is to introduce a new class to serve as the primary key of the `LineItem` class. This class, called `LineItemId`, is shown in Listing 7.25.

Listing 7.25 Compound Key Classes in Hibernate

```
package org.pwte.example.domain;

import java.io.Serializable;

public class LineItemId implements Serializable {

    private static final long serialVersionUID = 4790624621686438011L;
    public int productId;
    public int orderId;

    public LineItemId() {
        super();
    }

    //getters and setters

    public boolean equals(Object anObject) {
        // Implement equality logic
    }
}
```

To use this class, we would then have to modify the `LineItem` class to include an attribute of this type, as is shown in Listing 7.26.

Listing 7.26 LineItem Modified to Use LineItemId

```
public class LineItem implements Serializable {

    protected long quantity;
    protected BigDecimal amount;
    protected Product product;
    protected LineItemId lineItemId;

    public LineItem() {
        super();
    }

    public LineItem(long quantity, BigDecimal amount, Product product,
        LineItemId lineItemId) {
        super();
        this.quantity = quantity;
        this.amount = amount;
        this.product = product;
        this.lineItemId = lineItemId;
    }

    public LineItemId getLineItemId() {
        return lineItemId;
    }

    public void setLineItemId(LineItemId lineItemId) {
        this.lineItemId = lineItemId;
    }

    /** Other getter and setter methods omitted for clarity **/
}
```

Now that we've modified the `LineItem` class to contain a `LineItemId`, we can show the section of the `LineItem` mapping file that would allow us to take advantage of this new type, as shown in Listing 7.27.

Listing 7.27 Using LineItemId in Hibernate

```
<composite-id name="lineItemId" class="org.pwte.example.domain.LineItemId">
        <key-property name="productId" column="product_id" type="int"/>
        <key-property name="orderId" column="order_id" type="int"/>
</composite-id>
```

In this example you see that the key columns of the LINE_ITEM table map to the `productId` and `orderId` properties of the `LineItemId` class. This would allow you to use instances of this type as the primary key value in Hibernate.

Now that we've discussed composite keys in Hibernate, we can return to our discussion of the Order primary key. We noted earlier that the `<id>` element contained a `<generator class="increment" /> element` but did not explain it. This element is used to specify the key generation approach that Hibernate should take for autogenerated primary keys.

Hibernate supports both key generation by the database and its own key generation schemes. Table 7.2 summarizes the major key generation schemes supported by Hibernate.

Table 7.2 Key Generation Schemes in Hibernate

Generator Attribute Name	Description
`Identity`	This generator supports identity columns in the database. This option is supported only for certain databases. At the time of writing, this included DB2, MySQL, MS SQL Server, Sybase, and HypersonicSQL.
`Increment`	Hibernate will read the maximum primary key value from the table at startup and then increment an in-memory value by one for each new object created. Should be used only when a single-server instance of Hibernate has exclusive access to the database; good for testing, but not recommended for production.
`Hilo`	Uses a hi-lo algorithm to create a primary key from a retrieved high value and a local low value. This is an approach that can avoid congestion when accessing a single source for inserts. For more information, see the Hibernate documentation [Hibernate].
`Guid`	Uses a globally unique identifier provided by the database. Available only on MySQL and SQL Server.
`sequence`	Creates a sequence in the database. Supported only for DB2, PostgreSQL, Oracle, SAP DB, McKol, and Interbase

Generator Attribute Name	Description
seqhilo	Uses the hi-lo algorithm with a provided database sequence to generate the high value.
uuid.hex	Generates a 128-bit global UUID.
select	Retrieves a primary key generated by a database trigger; i.e., the primary key is generated by the database—Hibernate just reads it.
native	Picks the best identity generator, depending on the capabilities of the underlying database

There are situations in which you would want to use each of these, but detailing all the choices that go into that decision is beyond the scope of this book. The choice we've used for our example (increment), for instance, is a good choice only if you are running Hibernate with a single server accessing the database; because the counter is held in memory, you could potentially get conflicts in a clustered environment. In many cases, either hilo or seqhilo are good choices because they minimize the number of database round-trips. When using these approaches, database round-trips are needed only if a new range of numbers must be requested for the process.

Attributes

The simplest level of mapping in Hibernate is to map individual column values to Java primitives or objects. This is done (as shown in earlier examples) through the <property> tag in the Hibernate mapping file for each class. Hibernate supports mapping attributes of the standard Java primitive types, as well as other Java object types such as Date; String; the Number classes, such as Integer, BigInteger, and BigDecimal; and java.sql types like java.sql.Clob.

A simple example of this can be seen in Listing 7.28, in the mapping of the quantity attribute from LineItem, which maps to a BIGINT type in Derby.

Listing 7.28 Quantity Attribute Mapping

```
<property name="quantity' type="long">
  <column name="quantity' not-null="true" />
</property>
```

An interesting case of attribute mapping to consider is how Hibernate can handle mapping the Order.Status enumeration to the STATUS column (of type varchar(9)) in our Derby schema. To understand how that mapping (shown in Listing 7.29) operates, we will have to take a brief look at the notion of user types in Hibernate.

Listing 7.29 Status Mapping in Hibernate

```
<property name="status" type="org.pwte.example.domain.StatusUserType">
  <column name="STATUS" length="9" not-null="true"/>
</property>
```

Here we see that this looks like a standard Hibernate property element, but the difference comes in on the type—in this type it maps not to a standard Java type but instead to a class we have defined called `org.pwte.example.domain.StatusUserType`.

The issue here is that Hibernate has no standard "out of the box" mapping for Java 5 Enumerations. However, the Hibernate documentation provides an example that can be adapted easily to solve the problem at hand. The way in which this example solves this is by creating a new type that is a subclass of `org.hibernate.usertype.UserType`. UserType is a standard Hibernate extension point that allows a developer to write his own code to specify how to map from any arbitrary Java representation to a database column. It does this through implementing two methods (among a host of others that each UserType subclass must implement). These two key methods are `nullSafeGet` and `nullSafeSet`. The method `nullSafeGet` reads the value of the column from a ResultSet and then returns the Object that represents the property. Correspondingly, the method `nullSafeSet` takes in the object representing that property and then writes an equivalent value to a JDBC PreparedStatement.

There are many other methods of UserType that should also be overridden in a UserType subclass; for more information, we refer the interested reader to the Hibernate documentation, or to the code example provided.

Contained Objects

Hibernate supports the notion of contained objects, which it refers to as Components. In this way, a value type, such as an Address, could be contained within a Customer while both are stored in the same table. To show this example, we will move away from our domain classes, and set up a theoretical "Customer" class that would reference an "Address" class. The class definition of Customer would look as shown in Listing 7.30.

Listing 7.30 Customer Containing Address

```
public class Customer {
    private int id;
    private String name;
    private Address address;
    public Address getAddress() {
        return address;
    }
    public void setAddress(Address address) {
        this.address = address;
```

```
    }
    public int getId() {
        return id;
    }
    public void setId(int id) {
        this.id = id;
    }
    ...

}
```

The definition of Address would be as shown in Listing 7.31.

Listing 7.31 Address Class

```
public class Address {
    private String streetAddress;
    private String city;
    private String state;
    private String zip;

//getters and setters

}
```

You map a Hibernate component into its containing class using the `<component>` element in the Hibernate mapping file, as is shown in Listing 7.32.

Listing 7.32 Customer and Address Mapping File

```
<?xml version="1.0"?>
<!DOCTYPE hibernate-mapping PUBLIC
  "-//Hibernate/Hibernate Mapping DTD 3.0//EN"
  "hibernate.sourceforge.net/hibernate-mapping-3.0.dtd">
<hibernate-mapping>
   <class name="org.pwte.example.domain.hibernate.Customer"
    table="ADDRESSED_CUSTOMER" schema="APP">
      <id name="id" type="int">
          <column name="CUSTOMER_ID" />
          <generator class="assigned" />
      </id>
      <property name="name" type="string">
          <column name="NAME" length="30" not-null="true">
          </column>
```

```
      </property>
      <component name="address"
       class="org.pwte.example.domain.hibernate.Address" >
        <property name="streetAddress" type = "string"
         column="STREET_ADDRESS" not-null="true"/>
        <property name="city" type="string"
         column="CITY"not-null="true"/>
        <property name="state" type="string"
         column="STATE" not-null="true"/>
        <property name="zip" type="string"
         column="ZIP" not-null="true"/>
      </component>
   </class>
</hibernate-mapping>
```

In this case, all the properties of both the Customer class and the Address class are mapped to columns from the ADDRESSED_CUSTOMER table.

Relationships

Relationships are represented in the Hibernate Core POJO model by simple object relationships. A one-to-one relationship or many-to-one relationship is represented by having an object contain an instance variable that holds another object, while a one-to-N relationship is represented through a Java collection type or an array. These object-level relationships are mapped to relations between tables in the Hibernate mapping files.

For instance, to show how an Order is owned by one and only one customer, you declare that there is a many-to-one relationship between Order and AbstractCustomer (for example, many Orders belong to one customer). This is performed in the Hibernate mapping file for Order by the element in the configuration shown in Listing 7.33.

Listing 7.33 Many-to-One Mapping Element for Order to Customer

```
<many-to-one name="customer"
    class="org.pwte.example.domain.AbstractCustomer"
    column="CUSTOMER_ID">
</many-to-one>
```

On the other hand, each customer can own many orders (not only their open order, but all other orders they have placed or abandoned as well). This is done not in the Order mapping file, but in the AbstractCustomer mapping file, with the configuration elements shown in Listing 7.34.

Listing 7.34 Set Mapping Element for Orders in AbstractCustomer Mapping File

```
<set name="orders" inverse="true" outer-join="true">
    <key column="customer_id" not-null="true"/>
    <one-to-many class="org.pwte.example.domain.Order"/>
</set>
```

Here we see that the AbstractCustomer has many orders (of type Order from the common example package), and that they are represented as a Set. The `inverse` attribute relates the fact that this relationship has a mirror image; that each Order also has a corresponding AbstractCustomer. In Listing 7.35, we show how to reference the singleton open order in the AbstractCustomer mapping.

Listing 7.35 Open Order Mapping in AbstractCustomer Mapping File

```
<many-to-one name="openOrder"
    class="org.pwte.example.domain.Order"
    column="OPEN_ORDER" />
```

Finally, as an added example, let's consider the unidirectional, many-to-one relationship between Product and LineItem we saw the Java code for earlier. In this case, the way that this is mapped in the LineItem mapping file is with the element shown in Listing 7.36.

Listing 7.36 Product Mapping for LineItem

```
<many-to-one name="product"
   class="org.pwte.example.domain.Product"
   column="product_id"
   insert="false" update="false">
</many-to-one>
```

We see that the attribute product in LineItem will contain an instance of `org.pwte.example.domain.Product`. The way that this will be mapped is that the product_id column in the LineItem table acts as a foreign key to the table that the `Product` class is mapped to.

Careful readers will notice that we've used two additional attributes: `insert="false"` and `update="false"`. This is because the product attribute maps to part of the primary key of LineItem. This will prevent a developer from trying to change the Product in the LineItem, and thus its primary key value.

Constraints

Hibernate has the capability to support many types of constraints. Hibernate supports column constraints (SQL domains) with the `sql-type` attribute of the `<column>` element in the Hibernate mapping file. More complex column constraints can be specified against some databases through the use of the `check` attribute of the `<column>` element, which allows the use of regular expressions in specifying column value constraints. Table-level constraints can be specified through the `check` attribute of the `<class>` element in the Hibernate mapping file.

Some types of general database constraints, such as foreign key constraints, are picked up automatically through the foreign key attribute of the `<many-to-one>` element. Finally, Hibernate allows you to specify your own general constraints using the `<database-object>` elements. For more information on constraint support in Hibernate, refer to the Hibernate documentation.

Derived Attributes

Hibernate offers comprehensive support for derived attributes. It supports deriving attributes from simple calculations (for example, multiplying two column values together), as well as more comprehensive support that includes deriving an attribute value from properties of the object being loaded, as well as values from other tables. The example in Listing 7.37 shows how you can use a subselect to derive a LineItem's `amount` attribute from the quantity in the LineItem multiplied by the price of the Lineitem's product.

Listing 7.37 Setting the amount Attribute in a Line Item

```
<property name="amount" type="big_decimal"
   formula="(
       select (QUANTITY * p.PRICE) from Product p
       where p.PRODUCT_ID = PRODUCT_ID)" />
```

In addition to simple formulas and subselects, Hibernate also supports using SQL functions like `avg()` and `sum()` in its formulas. The example in Listing 7.38 shows how you could use this support to define that the Order's total property is computed by summing its associated line item amounts.

Listing 7.38 Setting the total Attribute in Order

```
<property name="total" type="big_decimal"
    formula="(
        select SUM(l.AMOUNT) from LINE_ITEM l
        where l.ORDER_ID = ORDER_ID)" />
```

A note to keep in mind about attributes that are derived is that the derived value is originally retrieved from the database when the object is first loaded. You can change the value of the attribute in the object but that will not change the value on the database. Calculating a total is a good example of when this would be applicable; you couldn't know how to update a total value if the value is calculated from a sum of line item amounts. Likewise, if the values in the database change after the object is fetched, it will not be automatically updated with a new calculated value.

Tuning Options

Hibernate is highly optimized for performance, while not sacrificing its simple programming model, and supports a number of different tuning options, as the following sections describe.

Query Optimizations

Hibernate provides a range of options for query optimization, many of which involve reducing either the number of rows returned through batching queries, or the number of queries through joins. The basic range of options on how this is done is discussed in the "Loading Related Objects" section. You can also use specifically tuned SQL statements, including proprietary extensions of the database at hand.

Caching

At one point caching support was a drawback of earlier versions of Hibernate, but the 3.0 and later versions contain very sophisticated support for caches of different scopes. The first level of caching is in the Hibernate Session. Cache entries have a transaction scope by default, but also can be scoped to the lifetime of Session. Actual persistent objects that have been fetched are stored in the first-level cache, which is used not so much for performance reasons, but to guarantee proper object identity within a Session and maintain objects for a particular life cycle scope, such as a transaction. The second-level cache is at the Process Scope/Cluster Scope (which is actually at the SessionFactory Scope). It does not store instances, but instead stores only the state of instances in an internal form to minimize the memory requirements—this cache is the one whose major purpose is to improve performance. Finally, there is a query results cache that is related to the second-level cache. Hibernate enables you to specify how this second-level cache will work by allowing the specification of a cache policy that describes the concurrency strategy, cache expiration policies, and the physical format of the cache.

Hibernate supports several external cache providers that host and implement the second-level cache, including these:

- **EHCache**—Simple support for single-JVM and distributed caching features.
- **OpenSymphony OSCache**—Cache to memory and disk with nice expiration options.
- **SwarmCache**—A cluster cache based on JGroups.
- **JBoss TreeCache**—A fully transactional replicated cache.
- **Custom**—Developers can choose to implement `org.hibernate.cache.CacheProvider`; this is the integration point for many commercial third-party cache products.

Loading Related Objects

When looking at how related objects are loaded, it is a good idea to keep in mind two different questions: *when* the objects are loaded, and *how* they are loaded. Hibernate provides facilities to help specify how both questions should be answered. In the first instance, Hibernate includes a way of specifying different loading modes (lazy or eager) for queries. These are the supported mappings modes:

- **Lazy fetching**—Associated Object is fetched lazily through a proxy (the default).
- **Eager fetching**—Associated Object is fetched immediately with a separate SQL statement.

When tuning a persistent object, sometimes it is most efficient to use a lazy loading technique that defers the loading of a relationship until the time the collection is first referenced. To declare a collection as lazy, you can mark the attribute as being lazy-loaded in the hibernate mapping file for the class, as shown in Listing 7.39.

Listing 7.39 Lazy Loading in Hibernate

```
<set name="lineItems" inverse="true" lazy="true">
    <key>
        <column name="order_id"/>
    </key>
    <one-to-many class="org.pwte.example.domain.LineItem"/>
</set>
```

It should be stated that for collections, lazy loading is the default state; so doing nothing would in this case have the same effect. On the opposite end of the spectrum from lazy loading is eager loading, or retrieving the contents of a relationship in a single SQL statement. How to implement eager loading depends on the type of relationship you want to eagerly load. Consider the following case from `LineItem.hbm.xml`, shown in Listing 7.40.

Listing 7.40 Eager Loading in Hibernate

```
<many-to-one name="product"
    class="org.pwte.example.domain.Product"
    column="product_id"
    lazy="false"
    insert="false" update="false">
</many-to-one>
```

This relationship differs from others you have seen in the addition of the `lazy` attribute to the many-to-one element. The default value of the `lazy` attribute is `proxy`, which means that a proxy is used in place of the Product class until the Product is actually used (when it is accessed). When `lazy` is changed to `false`, the Product instance will be eagerly loaded.

If setting the `lazy` attribute addresses the question of when the relationship is traversed and the object loaded, then the question of how the object or objects are to be loaded is the next issue. Here Hibernate gives us the following options:

- **Join Fetching**—Retrieve the associated object (or collection) in the same select as the outer object using a SQL outer join.
- **Select Fetching**—Use a separate SQL `SELECT` to retrieve the referenced object or collection. This is the default, and unless you specifically set the `lazy` attribute to `false`, this `SELECT` will be executed only when you access the object or collection.
- **Subselect Fetching**—Use a SQL subselect clause to retrieve the referenced object or collection in the same `SELECT` statement as the outer object.
- **Batch Fetching**—A way of improving performance of lazy loading by fetching a set of a specified size with a given set of primary keys; this is especially helpful for very large collections so that not all elements are loaded into memory at once.

Any of these options can be used with lazy or eager loading; the mechanism for choosing them differs. For instance, in conjunction with this last option is the `batch-size` attribute that can be used to tune the number of selects that it takes to load a set of objects into memory. When you apply this attribute to a collection, Hibernate will (effectively) group a set of keys together and then execute a single query that brings back multiple rows. The configuration for this is shown in Listing 7.41.

Listing 7.41 Batch Size Setting for Collections

```
<set name="lineitems" inverse="true"
 cascade="all, delete-orphan" batch-size="10">
   <key column="ORDER_ID" not-null="true"/>
   <one-to-many class="org.pwte.example.domain.LineItem"/>
</set>
```

Join fetching for sets can be seen if we make a small change to the mapping for LineItems from `Order.hbm.xml`, as shown in Listing 7.42.

Listing 7.42 Outer Join in Hibernate

```
<set name="lineItems" inverse="true" fetch="join">
   <key>
      <column name="order_id"/>
   </key>
   <one-to-many class=
    "org.pwte.example.domain.LineItem"/>
</set>
```

What this does is to enable the use of an outer join to combine the retrieval of the containing object (the Order) together with the retrieval of the contained objects (in this case, the LineItems). With one simple attribute change, you can eliminate the "N + 1 SQL statement problem" that has plagued object-relational mapping solutions when dealing with contained collections for many years. This problem occurs when you select a collection of objects that each contain a referenced object; for instance, when a Customer contains an address. In this problem, when you run the single select to obtain a list of "N" Customers, you would find that you would have to execute "N" `SELECT` statements to retrieve all the Addresses that correspond to those Customers. By performing an outer join, we can (as we see in this example) retrieve not only our Order but the referenced LineItems as well. Of course, this opens up the possibility that you may be retrieving too much data—so this is an approach you should consider carefully.

Locking

In persistence programming there are two general notions of how you can provide concurrency on the database: either locking an object on the database (called pessimistic concurrency), or using a versioning scheme that allows you to avoid database locks altogether (called optimistic concurrency). Hibernate provides full support for both concurrency models. We'll consider pessimistic locking first.

Your first option for specifying pessimistic concurrency is to globally set the isolation level for the connections your application is using. As is described in the earlier section "Initialization," you can set the isolation level of a Hibernate-managed connection in the Hibernate configuration file; if a connection is obtained from a DataSource, the isolation level must be configured externally. The issue with simply setting an isolation level on a database connection is that it is a global setting, and may be too restrictive if you only need to specify the behavior of a specific transaction. For that purpose, Hibernate supports the use of database pessimistic concurrency features like `select...for update`. Because these features vary from database dialect to database dialect, Hibernate supports them across dialects by introducing the `Session.lock()` method.

`Session.lock()` takes two parameters, the first being a Hibernate LockMode constant and the second being the object upon which the lock should be obtained. There are several different constants defined in LockMode, but the most common of these for our purposes are `LockMode.UPGRADE` and `LockMode.UPGRADE_NOWAIT`. The `LockMode.UPGRADE` constant specifies that for the specified object Hibernate should perform a version check, and try to obtain a pessimistic upgrade lock using `select...for update` if available. `LockMode.UPGRADE_ NOWAIT` specifies that it should use a `select...for update nowait` instead, which will throw an exception if a lock cannot be obtained immediately.

Up to this point we have considered querying and modifying objects in Hibernate only within the context of a single Hibernate transaction or JTA transaction. However, in the Hibernate model, a persistent object can also act as a Data Transfer Object (DTO), which means that it can be returned from a services method, perhaps displayed in a UI, and then used again as a parameter to another services method. In this case, Hibernate objects can implement the version number pattern so that the same hibernate object used as a DTO can be reassociated with a different Hibernate Session, and it will have optimistic locking semantics. Objects may move from a transient state (not tied to any persistence framework) to a persistent state and back again based on whether they are tied to the Hibernate Session. This is useful, for example, to send an object to a client for modification and then update the database based on the changed object.

Optimistic cases are handled quite differently from pessimistic cases. To handle optimistic locking cases, when persistent objects become transient again, this object is considered a disconnected object. This object can then be reconnected to another Session, and Hibernate can use the Version Number pattern to compare it against the actual data store and check whether the object is still in a valid state. In some situations, a particular layer of your code can be interacting with an object and not know what state it is in. If a persistent object is passed to another method, this method must know its intended behavioral aspects to make sure things are handled correctly.

The way in which Hibernate supports optimistic locking using versioning (or timestamping, which is similar) is that you need to provide a version (or timestamp) attribute in your Java class that will match to a corresponding field in your database schema. So if our `Product` class was to be maintained with optimistic concurrency, we could add a new field `versionNumber` to the definition to correspond to a new database column named VERSION as Listing 7.43 shows.

Listing 7.43 Product Definition with Version Number

```
public class Product implements Serializable {
...
  protected int productId;
    private int versionNumber;
... }
```

Then you would modify the `Product.hbm.xml` configuration file to add the following line after the `<id>` mapping element:

```
<version name="versionNumber" access="field" column="VERSION"/>
```

Development Process for the Common Example

One of the more helpful parts of Hibernate to a developer is that its flexibility allows you to build and test your persistence code however you would like; either you can use an IDE like Eclipse or Rational Software Architect and test your code in an embedded JEE container, or you can simply develop with Notepad and the Java compiler and build and test your code at the command line with Ant, Maven, and JUnit. Thus, the typical development process for Hibernate would be whatever you are comfortable, and familiar with.

Defining the Objects

Because Hibernate uses a POJO-based model, defining objects for persistence with Hibernate is as simple as developing any set of objects that follow the JavaBean naming conventions. The only cases in which you would want to explicitly define an object that is specific to a Hibernate model as opposed to a generic domain model might be when you need to declare a separate ID type to represent a composite primary key, such as we have had to do with the

LineItemId class shown previously. In all other respects, the Java code for the Hibernate persistent classes for the common example are the same as the standard POJO versions of those classes described in Chapter 3, "Designing Persistent Object Services," and shown in Chapter 6, "Apache iBATIS."

As we have also seen already, the other primary action a Hibernate developer has to take is to build a mapping file for each of his persistent objects. Although this can be done entirely by hand in Notepad or in an XML editor, Hibernate also provides Eclipse plug-ins that can help automate this process and make it easier.

In the next few listings we will show the example code for the end-to-end example. First, in Listing 7.44, we show the code for AbstractCustomer.

Listing 7.44 AbstractCustomer

```
package org.pwte.example.domain;

import java.io.Serializable;
import java.util.Set;

public abstract class AbstractCustomer implements Serializable {
    protected int customerId;
    protected String name;
    protected Order openOrder;
    protected Set<Order> orders;

    //getters and setters

}
```

Next, in Listing 7.45, we see the code for BusinessCustomer.

Listing 7.45 BusinessCustomer

```
package org.pwte.example.domain;

import java.io.Serializable;
import java.util.Set;

public class BusinessCustomer extends AbstractCustomer implements Serializable {
    private static final long serialVersionUID = -1210978439928403907L;
    protected boolean volumeDiscount, businessPartner;
    protected String description;

    getters and setters
}
```

Then we see the code for `ResidentialCustomer`, in Listing 7.46.

Listing 7.46 ResidentialCustomer

```
package org.pwte.example.domain;

import java.io.Serializable;
import java.util.Set;

public class ResidentialCustomer
extends AbstractCustomer implements Serializable {
    protected short householdSize;
    protected boolean frequentCustomer;

    //getters and setters
```

All three of these classes (which, as described earlier, are related by inheritance, and for which we have chosen the single-table mapping pattern) are described by the `AbstractCustomer.hbm.xml` mapping file, as shown in Listing 7.47.

Listing 7.47 AbstractCustomer.hbm.xml

```
<?xml version="1.0"?>
<!DOCTYPE hibernate-mapping PUBLIC
  "-//Hibernate/Hibernate Mapping DTD 3.0//EN"
  "hibernate.sourceforge.net/hibernate-mapping-3.0.dtd">
<!-- Generated May 20, 2007 5:19:52 PM by Hibernate Tools 3.2.0.b9 -->
<hibernate-mapping>
    <class name="org.pwte.example.domain.AbstractCustomer"
     table="CUSTOMER" schema="APP" lazy="false">
        <comment></comment>
        <id name="customerId" type="int">
            <column name="CUSTOMER_ID" />
            <generator class="assigned" />
        </id>
        <discriminator column="type" />
        <many-to-one name="openOrder"
         class="org.pwte.example.domain.Order"
         column="OPEN_ORDER"
         lazy="false">
        </many-to-one>
        <set name="orders" inverse="true"
         outer-join="true" lazy="false">
            <key column="customer_id" not-null="true"/>
```

```
        <one-to-many class="org.pwte.example.domain.Order"/>
    </set>
    <property name="name" type="string">
        <column name="NAME" length="30" not-null="true">
            <comment></comment>
        </column>
    </property>
    <subclass
     name="org.pwte.example.domain.BusinessCustomer"
     discriminator-value="BUSINESS"
     extends="org.pwte.example.domain.AbstractCustomer"
     lazy="false">
        <property name="volumeDiscount" type="yes_no">
          <column name="BUSINESS_VOLUME_DISCOUNT" length="1">
            <comment></comment>
          </column>
        </property>
        <property name="businessPartner" type="yes_no">
            <column name="BUSINESS_PARTNER" length="1">
              <comment></comment>
            </column>
        </property>
        <property name="description" type="java.lang.String">
            <column name="BUSINESS_DESCRIPTION">
              <comment></comment>
            </column>
        </property>
    </subclass>
    <subclass
     name="org.pwte.example.domain.ResidentialCustomer"
     discriminator-value="RESIDENTIAL"
     extends="org.pwte.example.domain.AbstractCustomer"
     lazy="false">
        <property name="householdSize" type="java.lang.Short">
            <column name="RESIDENTIAL_HOUSEHOLD_SIZE">
              <comment></comment>
            </column>
        </property>
        <property name="frequentCustomer" type="yes_no">
            <column name="RESIDENTIAL_FREQUENT_CUSTOMER" length="1">
              <comment></comment>
            </column>
        </property>
```

```
        </subclass>
    </class>
</hibernate-mapping>
```

The Order class was previously shown in Listing 7.21. Its mapping file was shown in Listing 7.22. Order uses the class `LineItem`, which is shown in Listing 7.48.

Listing 7.48 LineItem

```
package org.pwte.example.domain;

import java.io.Serializable;
import java.math.BigDecimal;

public class LineItem implements Serializable {
    private static final long serialVersionUID = -5969434202374976648L;
    protected long quantity;
    protected BigDecimal amount;
    protected Product product;
    protected LineItemId lineItemId;

    public LineItem() {
        super();
    }

    //getters and setters
```

Remember that `LineItem` references `LineItemId`, which was previously shown in Listing 7.25. `LineItem` is described by the `LineItem.hbm.xml` mapping file, shown in Listing 7.49.

Listing 7.49 LineItem.hbm.xml

```
<?xml version="1.0"?>
<!DOCTYPE hibernate-mapping PUBLIC
  "-//Hibernate/Hibernate Mapping DTD 3.0//EN"
  "hibernate.sourceforge.net/hibernate-mapping-3.0.dtd">
<!-- Generated May 20, 2007 5:19:52 PM by Hibernate Tools 3.2.0.b9 -->
<hibernate-mapping>
    <class name="org.pwte.example.domain.LineItem"
     table="LINE_ITEM" schema="APP" lazy="false">
        <comment></comment>
        <composite-id name="lineItemId"
         class="org.pwte.example.domain.LineItemId">
           <key-property name="productId"
```

```
            column="product_id" type="int"/>
            <key-property name="orderId" column="order_id" type="int"/>
        </composite-id>
        <property name="quantity" type="long">
            <column name="quantity" not-null="true">
                <comment></comment>
            </column>
        </property>
        <property name="amount" type="big_decimal">
            <column name="AMOUNT" precision="14" not-null="true">
                <comment></comment>
            </column>
        </property>
        <many-to-one name="product"
         class="org.pwte.example.domain.Product"
         column="product_id"
         lazy="false"
         insert="false" update="false">
        </many-to-one>
    </class>
</hibernate-mapping>
```

Finally, we show the implementation of the Product class, in Listing 7.50.

Listing 7.50 Product class

```
package org.pwte.example.domain;

import java.io.Serializable;
import java.math.BigDecimal;

public class Product implements Serializable {
    private static final long serialVersionUID = 2435504714077372968L;
    protected int productId;
    protected BigDecimal price;
    protected String description;

    //getters and setters
```

As with the other classes in the example, the Product class is described by its corresponding `Product.hbm.xml` mapping file, which is shown in Listing 7.51.

Listing 7.51 Product.hbm.xml

```
<?xml version="1.0"?>
<!DOCTYPE hibernate-mapping PUBLIC "-//Hibernate/Hibernate Mapping DTD 3.0//EN"
"hibernate.sourceforge.net/hibernate-mapping-3.0.dtd">
<!-- Generated May 20, 2007 5:19:52 PM by Hibernate Tools 3.2.0.b9 -->
<hibernate-mapping>
    <class name="org.pwte.example.domain.Product"
     table="PRODUCT" schema="APP" lazy="false">
        <comment></comment>
        <id name="productId" type="int">
            <column name="PRODUCT_ID" />
            <generator class="assigned" />
        </id>
        <property name="price" type="big_decimal">
            <column name="PRICE" precision="14" not-null="true">
                <comment></comment>
            </column>
        </property>
        <property name="description" type="java.lang.String">
            <column name="DESCRIPTION" not-null="true">
                <comment></comment>
            </column>
        </property>
    </class>
    <sql-query name="classifiedProducts">
    <return alias="product" class="org.pwte.example.domain.Product"/>
    SELECT product.PRODUCT_ID AS {product.productId},
           product.PRICE AS {product.price},
           product.DESCRIPTION AS {product.description}
    FROM PRODUCT product
    WHERE product.description LIKE :namePattern
    </sql-query>
</hibernate-mapping>
```

Implementing the Services

Implementing services in Hibernate is something that can be accelerated through the flexibility of the Hibernate design. For instance, we've already seen how Hibernate can work easily either with an external transaction manager like JTA or with its own transaction management API. Likewise, it can work just as easily with JTA transactions that are managed through declarative transaction management in an EJB.

The following listings show the implementation of the example service in Hibernate. There are a couple of things to keep in mind about these examples. First of all, each service begins and ends its own transaction; they are not set up to deal with external transaction management, although that could easily be done by removing the transaction management from within the methods and relying on JTA. Second, in these examples we return objects that will then be examined outside of a Hibernate Session (by our JUnit tests). For this reason, we have needed to set the `lazy="false"` parameter on all classes in the configuration files, for all relationships, and for all collections. This can have an adverse effect on performance and would not be recommended for normal operation with Hibernate.

bootstrapping

As shown previously, we simply use the HibernateUtil to get a Hibernate Session.

`loadCustomer`

Listing 7.52 shows how we implement the common `load` method to get the customer. This method is used by various service operation implementations. The assumption made here is that the transaction is already started by the calling routine, so it retrieves only the current Session.

Listing 7.52 loadCustomer

```
public AbstractCustomer loadCustomer(int customerId)
throws CustomerDoesNotExistException, GeneralPersistenceException {
    try {

        // 1. Get a Hibernate Session, but assume tran started
        Session session = HibernateUtil.getSessionFactory()
                .getCurrentSession();
        // 2. Find the customer for this customerId
        AbstractCustomer customer = null;
        customer = (AbstractCustomer) session.load(
                AbstractCustomer.class, new Integer(customerId));
        return customer;
    }
    catch (ObjectNotFoundException e) {
        throw new CustomerDoesNotExistException(
            "No customer exists matching id " + customerId);
    }
    catch (HibernateException e) {
        throw new GeneralPersistenceException(
            "Unexpected Exception " + e);
    }
}
```

openOrder

The `openOrder` service implementation creates an order Java Object and persists it. It then sets the new order onto the customer instance. Listing 7.53 shows the complete example.

Listing 7.53 openOrder in Hibernate

```
public Order openOrder(int customerId)
throws CustomerDoesNotExistException, OrderAlreadyOpenException,
       GeneralPersistenceException {
    try {
        // 1.  Get a Hibernate Session
        Session session = HibernateUtil.getSessionFactory()
                .getCurrentSession();
        session.beginTransaction();

        // 2. Use the Load customer method
        AbstractCustomer customer = loadCustomer(customerId);

        // 3. Check to see if the customer has an open order
        if (customer.getOpenOrder() != null)
            throw new OrderAlreadyOpenException(
                "Order already open for customer matching id "
                                + customerId);

        // 4. Create the new order and save it
        Order myOrder = new Order();
        myOrder.setStatus(Status.OPEN);
        myOrder.setCustomer(customer);
        myOrder.setTotal(new BigDecimal(0));
        session.save(myOrder);

        // 5. Update the open order in the customer
        customer.setOpenOrder(myOrder);

        // 6. Commit the transaction
        session.getTransaction().commit();

        return myOrder;
    }
    catch (HibernateException e) {
        throw new GeneralPersistenceException(
            "Unexpected Exception " + e);
```

```
    }

}
```

`addLineItem`

This is a simple and straightforward implementation that involves only loading a single object (the Customer) from the database and then creating another object (the Order) and adding it to the customer. As we have seen in earlier examples, we need only attach the Order to the customer to make it implicitly persistent. This implementation is so large that we are going to break it into two parts. In Listing 7.54 we set up the service operation and validate the customer and product parameters.

Listing 7.54 addLineItem Part 1—Validate Parameters

```
public LineItem addLineItem(
    int customerId, int productId, long quantity
)
throws CustomerDoesNotExistException, OrderNotOpenException,
       ProductDoesNotExistException, GeneralPersistenceException {
    try {
        // 1.  Get a Hibernate Session
        Session session = HibernateUtil.getSessionFactory()
                .getCurrentSession();
        session.beginTransaction();
        // 2. Load the appropriate instance of the customer
        AbstractCustomer customer = loadCustomer(customerId);
        // 3. Get the Customer's open order
        Order openOrder = customer.getOpenOrder();
        if (openOrder == null)
            throw new OrderNotOpenException(
                "Order not open for customer matching id "
                                + customerId);
        // 4. Get the Product from the product Id
        Product product = null;
        try {
            product = (Product) session.load(
                Product.class, new Integer(productId));
        } catch (ObjectNotFoundException e) {
            throw new ProductDoesNotExistException(
                "No product exists matching id "+ productId);
        }
        // See Listing 7.54 for remainder of logic
    } catch (HibernateException e) {
```

```
        throw new GeneralPersistenceException(
            "Unexpected Exception " + e);
    }
```

Listing 7.55 continues the implementation logic of the addLineItem service operation by populating the appropriate LineItem instance, depending on whether it already exists or not. For readability, the indent is different that it should be if "unrolled" into Listing 7.54.

Listing 7.55 addLineItem Part 2—Populate an Existing or New LineItem

```
// 5. Calculate the amount of the line item from the price and quantity
BigDecimal amount = product.getPrice().multiply(
    new BigDecimal(quantity));

// 6. Create and populate the new LineItemId
LineItemId lineItemId = new LineItemId();
lineItemId.setOrderId(openOrder.getOrderId());
lineItemId.setProductId(product.getProductId());

// 7. Check to see if the line item already exists
LineItem lineItem = null;
try {
    lineItem = (LineItem) session.load(
        LineItem.class, lineItemId);
}
catch (ObjectNotFoundException e) {
    lineItem = new LineItem();
    lineItem.setLineItemId(lineItemId);
    lineItem.setProduct(product);
}

// 8. Update the amount and quantity
lineItem.setQuantity(quantity);
lineItem.setAmount(amount);

// 9. Set the list of line items if needed
// and add the new line Item to the list
if (openOrder.getLineitems() == null) {
    openOrder.setLineitems(new HashSet<LineItem>());
}
openOrder.getLineitems().add(lineItem);
```

```
// 10. Commit the transaction
session.getTransaction().commit();

return lineItem;
```

removeLineItem

This service operation implementation deletes the LineItem by finding the associated record and removing it from the Order Collection. To keep the listing short and focused on the relevant code, we only show "new code" in Listing 7.56, assuming the same basic code for setup and validation as addLineItem Part 1 in Listing 7.54.

Listing 7.56 removeLineItem

```
@Override
public void removeLineItem(int customerId, int productId)
throws CustomerDoesNotExistException, OrderNotOpenException,
       ProductDoesNotExistException, NoLineItemsException,
       GeneralPersistenceException {
    try
    {
        // See addLineItem Part 1, steps 1-4 for setup and validation
        // 5. Create and populate the new LineItemId
        LineItemId lineItemId = new LineItemId();
        lineItemId.setOrderId(openOrder.getOrderId());
        lineItemId.setProductId(product.getProductId());
        // 6. Check to see if the line item already exists
        LineItem lineItem = null;
        try {
            lineItem = (LineItem) session.load(
                LineItem.class, lineItemId);
        }
        catch (ObjectNotFoundException e) {
            throw new NoLineItemsException(e);
        }
        // 7. Remove from Order
        openOrder.getLineitems().remove(lineItem);
        // 8. Commit the transaction
        session.getTransaction().commit();
    }
    catch (HibernateException e) {
        e.printStackTrace(System.out);
        throw new GeneralPersistenceException(
```

```
            "Unexpected Exception " + e);
    }
}
```

In this method, as with the preceding method, we load the `AbstractCustomer`, but this time we use its `openOrder` method to navigate to the open order to which the line item should be added. Likewise, we need to load the product instance that the `LineItem` will reference. There is an interesting difference in this method: If there is already a line item for this product, we do not add another—we merely update the quantity and amount. On the other hand, if a line item does not exist, we create it; then, as in the earlier example, after we have connected the `LineItem` to the Order, it becomes persistent implicitly.

Listing 7.57 shows the relevant details of how to submit an Order in Hibernate, referring back to Listing 7.54 again for code that you have already seen.

Listing 7.57 Submit Order in Hibernate

```
public void submit(int customerId)
throws CustomerDoesNotExistException,
       OrderNotOpenException, NoLineItemsException,
       GeneralPersistenceException {
    try {
        // See addLineItem Part 1, steps 1-3 for setup and validation

        // 4. Throw an exception if the order has no line items
        if ((openOrder.getLineitems() == null) ||
                openOrder.getLineitems().size() == 0)
            throw new NoLineItemsException(
                "No line items for open order");
        // 5. Set the status to submitted
        openOrder.setStatus(Status.SUBMITTED);

        // 7. Set the open order in the customer to NULL and save
        customer.setOpenOrder(null);
        session.save(customer);

        // 8. Commit the transaction
        session.getTransaction().commit();
    }
    catch (HibernateException e) {
        throw new GeneralPersistenceException(
            "Unexpected Exception " + e);
    }
}
```

Packaging the Components

Because Hibernate POJOs are not specific to the Hibernate model, there are no special requirements placed on them with regard to packaging. One concern that you must address, however, is where you place your Hibernate configuration files. You need to make sure that the Configuration implementation knows where they are located; either you can do this by following the standard conventions provided by Hibernate (which states that configuration files are placed on the root of your classpath), or you can use the Configuration constructor shown earlier to explicitly point to the path where your configuration files are located.

For our end-to-end example, in Listing 7.58 we use the `hibernate.cfg.xml` configuration file, which ties together all the other mapping files that you've seen in the previous section.

Listing 7.58 hibernate.cfg.xml Configuration File

```
<?xml version="1.0" encoding="UTF-8"?>
<!DOCTYPE hibernate-configuration PUBLIC
   "-//Hibernate/Hibernate Configuration DTD 3.0//EN"
   "hibernate.sourceforge.net/hibernate-configuration-3.0.dtd">
<hibernate-configuration>
    <session-factory>
        <property name="current_session_context_class">thread</property>
        <property name="hibernate.connection.driver_class">
            org.apache.derby.jdbc.ClientDriver
        </property>
        <property name="hibernate.connection.url">
            jdbc:derby://localhost:1527/PWTE;create=true;
        </property>
        <propertyname="hibernate.dialect">
            org.hibernate.dialect.DerbyDialect
        </property>
        <!-- Disable the second-level cache -->
        <property name="cache.provider_class">
            org.hibernate.cache.NoCacheProvider
        </property>
        <!-- Echo all executed SQL to stdout -->
        <property name="show_sql">true</property>
        <!-- Mapping files -->
        <mapping resource="Product.hbm.xml"/>
        <mapping resource="AbstractCustomer.hbm.xml"/>
        <mapping resource="LineItem.hbm.xml"/>
        <mapping resource="Order.hbm.xml"/>
        <mapping resource="Customer.hbm.xml"/>
    </session-factory>
</hibernate-configuration>
```

Finally, you need to ensure that the hibernate JAR file and the other JAR files on which the hibernate JAR file relies (described in the section "Other Dependencies," at the beginning of the chapter) are on your class path.

Unit Testing

Hibernate is compatible with many unit testing frameworks, such as JUnit, DbUnit, and Cactus. The fact that it will work with either externally managed or internally managed transaction management and DataSources makes it easy to test code either inside a JEE container or outside a container. In fact, we have used JUnit and DbUnit in the internal testing of our code examples for this chapter.

Deploying to Production

Deploying a Hibernate application to production is usually a simple task. The most that one will often do is to make some changes to the `Hibernate.cfg.xml` file to ensure that the Hibernate Session is using the correct database drivers, DataSources, and/or database locations. This is a process that is easy to automate using scripting tools like Ant.

Summary

As you have seen in this chapter, the Hibernate "core" is a fully featured object-relational mapping solution that tries to provide the maximum amount of flexibility for dealing with special cases like difficult legacy schemas while still remaining simple to use for most cases. It facilitates integration with JEE application servers while also allowing the developer to use it from Java SE. It allows for sophisticated performance tuning through query optimization and caching techniques.

Besides having a JPA implementation, other Hibernate projects are being built on top of the "core" to enhance applications. Examples include the following:

- Hibernate Shards Horizontal as a data partitioning framework
- Hibernate Validator for Data integrity annotations and validation API
- Hibernate Search: Hibernate integration with Lucene for indexing and querying data
- Hibernate Tools Development tools for Eclipse and Ant
- NHibernate: The NHibernate service for the .NET framework
- JBoss Seam Framework for JSF, Ajax, and EJB 3.0/Java EE 5.0 applications

In summary, Hibernate is still a de facto standard in many places, and the project continues to grow.

Links to developerWorks

A.7.1 *Hibernate Simplifies Inheritance Mapping*

This article illustrates using Hibernate to implement the various inheritance strategies discussed throughout this book.

www.ibm.com/developerworks/java/library/j-hibernate/

A.7.2 *Using Hibernate to Persist Your Java Objects to IBM DB2 Universal Database*

This article gives a simple Hibernate overview, illustrating the use of Hibernate with IBM DB2.

www.ibm.com/developerworks/db2/library/techarticle/0306bhogal/0306bhogal.html

A.7.3 *Using Spring and Hibernate with WebSphere Application Server*

This article shows the proper settings to configure when using Hibernate and Spring with WebSphere Application Server.

www.ibm.com/developerworks/websphere/techjournal/0609_alcott/0609_alcott.html

References

[Bauer] Bauer, Christian and King, Gavin. *Java Persistence with Hibernate*. Manning Publications Company 2007

[Hibernate] *Hibernate Home Page*. www.hibernate.org

[Hibernate 1] *Java Persistence with Hibernate*. hibernate.org/397.html

[Hibernate 2] *Hibernate Reference Guide*. www.hibernate.org/5.html

[Hibernate 3] *Hibernate Wiki*. www.hibernate.org/37.html

[Hibernate 4] *Hibernate User Mailing Lists*. www.hibernate.org/20.html

Chapter 8

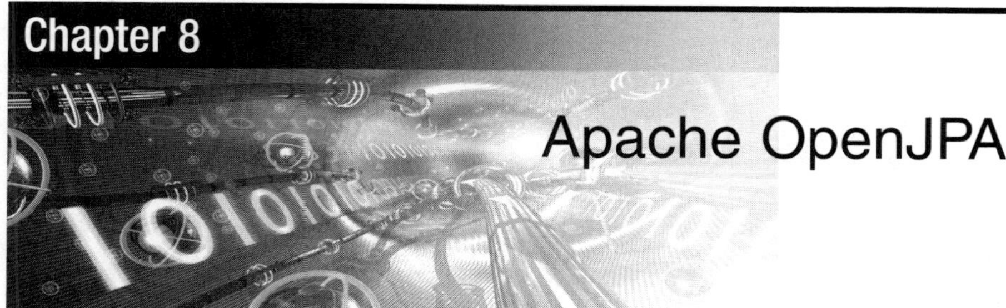

Apache OpenJPA

In this chapter we discuss OpenJPA, an implementation of the Java Persistence API 1.0 specification. We will fill in our evaluation template and implement our common example with OpenJPA. We will discuss OpenJPA extensions to the specification and finish with a brief look forward at JPA 2.0.

Background

In Chapter 1, "A Brief History of Object-Relational Mapping," we gave some history of the Java Persistence space. We discussed the development of the EJB spec from a persistence standpoint, how it grew in developer dissatisfaction over the years, and how open-source frameworks like Hibernate began to grow. We also discussed how this led to the creation of JPA.

As discussed in Chapter 1, by the time version 2 of the Enterprise Java Beans specification started to make its way into products, a counter-current was building in the Java community that began looking for other ways of doing persistence. When the EJB 3.0 committee began meeting, it became clear that revisiting persistence would need to be a key feature of the new specification. The opinion of the committee was that something significant needed to be changed—and as a result, the committee made the following decisions:

- The EJB 3.0 persistence model would need to be a POJO-based model and would have to address the issue of "disconnected" or detached data in a distributed environment.
- The specification would need to support both annotations and XML descriptors to define the mapping between objects and relational databases.
- The mapping would need to be complete—specifying not only the abstract persistence of a class, but also its mapping to relational tables and mappings of attributes to columns.

So the EJB committee combined the best ideas from several sources—TopLink, Hibernate, and Java Data Objects API—to create a new persistence architecture, which was released as a separate part of EJB 3.0 and dubbed the Java Persistence API. JPA represents the confluence of a number of different threads in the Java persistence arena and has since been adopted by all the major persistence vendors and various open-source projects.

In the preceding chapter, we evaluated Hibernate. You will find many features in JPA similar to Hibernate. Hibernate itself has a full-blown JPA implementation as part of its Entity Manager that you can read about for more details [Hibernate]. In this chapter, however, we are going to use Apache OpenJPA.

The Apache OpenJPA project is an Apache-licensed open-source implementation of the Java Persistence API. OpenJPA is focused on building a robust, high-performance, scalable implementation of the JPA specification. You can read more about the Apache Open JPA project at the website [OpenJPA 1].

The original source code contribution was provided by BEA (via their SolarMetric Kodo acquisition, discussed in the "History" section to follow). Several other companies and individuals are participating as committers, contributors, and users in the OpenJPA project, including IBM. The OpenJPA community continues to grow and prosper, with the expectation of graduating from incubation sometime in the near future.

Type of Framework

Much like Hibernate, OpenJPA is a full Domain Mapper, allowing you to map a whole set of objects to your database tables, and abstracting the SQL language from the developer.

History

OpenJPA started its life with another specification called JDO, as discussed in Chapter 1. SolarMetric was one of the first implementers of the JDO specification back in 2001, with a product called Kodo. As the JPA specification began to finalize, SolarMetric began making Kodo both a JPA and JDO implementation. In 2005, BEA purchased SolarMetric and contributed most of the JPA code to Apache as the project OpenJPA. As stated earlier, other vendors like IBM are part of the OpenJPA community. BEA continues to have the SolarMetric Kodo product based on OpenJPA. OpenJPA will be the core persistence engine of BEA WebLogic Server, IBM WebSphere, and the Apache Geronimo Application Server. In May 2007, OpenJPA graduated from the incubator to a top-level project and also passed Sun's Technology Compatibility Kit compliant with the Java Persistence API. In September 2007, OpenJPA released its first GA version.

Architectural Overview

Standards Adherence

OpenJPA is an implementation of the JPA 1.0 Specification that is a subspecification under the SUN EJB 3.0 specification, developed under JSR 220. At the time of this writing, JPA 2.0

is being developed under its own JSR 317, and EJB 3.1 is being developed under JSR 318. The website is the definitive source for the JPA 2.0 specifications [JPA 2].

Platforms Required

Before Java EE 5.0 and EJB 3.0, the persistence layer of the Java EE platform required a full-blown Java EE Application Server. JPA changes this. OpenJPA applications can be written to run in both Java SE and Java EE environments. However, there are some differences in JPA applications hosted inside a Java EE environment as opposed to a Java SE environment. Rather than discuss the differences here, we will highlight them where they exist throughout the remainder of this chapter.

Other Dependencies

OpenJPA comes bundled with several other JARs needed to make it run. Like many Apache projects, it makes use of other Apache licensed packages:

- Several of the Apache Commons projects :`commons-lang`, `commons-logging`, `commons-pool`, and `commons-collections`. Please refer to the Apache Commons website for more information [Apache].
- Apache OpenJPA relies on the Serp project for Java "bytecode enhancement" to add persistence behavior to annotated Java files as a separate step. The Serp JAR comes bundled with OpenJPA. We discuss this step in the later section "Development Process for the Common Example." You can read more about Serp at their website [Serp].
- A valid JDBC database driver.
- For Java EE applications, any JARs required to run OpenJPA in a target Java EE Server.

Vendors and Licenses

OpenJPA is distributed under an Apache License. As mentioned in Chapter 2, an Apache License is more liberal in what you can do with the source because you can change parts of the code, and you don't need to distribute them back to the original authors. In addition, several commercial products ship an OpenJPA implementation, such as IBM WebSphere Application Server and BEA WebLogic Server.

It is worth noting that because JPA is a specification, there are other JPA implementations available beyond the OpenJPA version:

- Hibernate JPA. Refer to Chapter 7, "Hibernate Core," or the Hibernate website [Hibernate] for license information.
- TopLink Essentials, which is an open-source implementation that Oracle built on top of TopLink. We discussed TopLink briefly in Chapter 1. See their website for more information [TopLink].

Available Literature

OpenJPA is very well documented on their website. In addition, there are several articles available. Table 8.1 shows some examples.

Table 8.1 OpenJPA Resources

Resource	Link	Description
OpenJPA Manuals [OpenJPA 2]	openjpa.apache.org/ documentation.html	Comprehensive OpenJPA Module
Integrating OpenJPA with Application Servers [OpenJPA 3]	openjpa.apache.org/ integration.html	List of other articles for integrating OpenJPA with other Application Server.
Building EJB 3 Applications with WebSphere Application Server	www.ibm.com/ developerworks/websphere/ techjournal/0712_barcia/ 0712_barcia.html	Tutorial on using OpenJPA inside the WebSphere EJB 3 Container
A.8.1 *Leveraging OpenJPA with WebSphere Application Server*	www-128.ibm.com/ developerworks/websphere/ techjournal/0612_barcia/ 0612_barcia.html	Tutorial on using OpenJPA inside WebSphere Application Server
A.8.2 *Java Persistence with Hibernate* [Bauer]	www.amazon.com/ Java-Persistence-Hibernate-Christian-Bauer/dp/ 1932394885/ref=pd_bbs_sr_ 1?ie=UTF8&s=books&qid= 1201195747&sr=1-1	Book on using Hibernate JPA API
Enterprise JavaBeans, 5th Edition [Monson-Haefel]	www.amazon.com/ Enterprise-JavaBeans-3-0-Bill-Burke/dp/059600978X/ref= pd_bbs_sr_2?ie=UTF8&s= books&qid=1201195725& sr=8-2	Comprehensive sourcebook on EJB 3
 A.8.3 *Migrating Legacy Hibernate Applications to OpenJPA and EJB 3*	www.ibm.com/ developerworks/websphere/ techjournal/0708_vines/ 0708_vines.html	Techniques useful to migrate a Hibernate Core Application to OpenJPA

Besides OpenJPA, there are many other resources available on the JPA programming model.

Programming Model

OpenJPA is a persistence framework based around persisting common POJOs. It relies on Java Annotations and/or XML to add the persistence behavior. Both options are available. OpenJPA also provides a very rich Object Query Language, batch statement features, and other useful features. As a last resort, OpenJPA allows a developer to drop down to Native SQL.

The basic programming model is relatively straightforward, with an EntityManager (created using an EntityManagerFactory or injected by the environment such as an EJB 3 container) being used to establish a persistent session context in which Plain Old Java Objects (POJOs) can be moved in and out of a persistent context.

It is worth mentioning here that an object association with an EntityManager defines the state in which it is managed. Figure 8.1 illustrates the life cycle of a Java object with respect to persistence in OpenJPA.

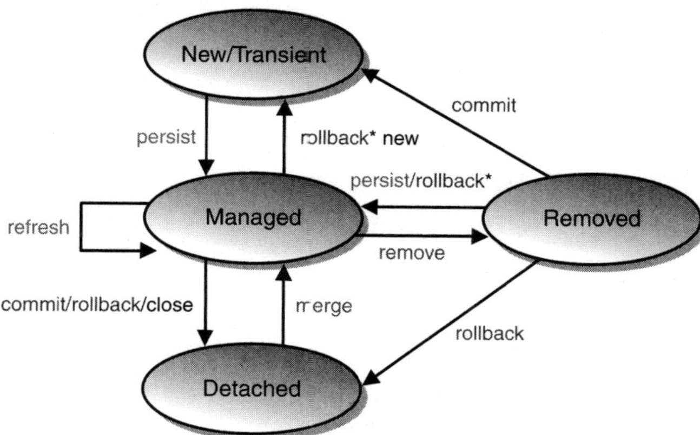

Figure 8.1 OpenJPA life cycle management.

This life cycle is interesting because it brings together the notion of an EntityManager and a POJO, resulting in four states to consider in the programming model:

- **New/Transient**—The Object is instantiated, but there is no relational data in the database.
- **Managed**—The Object is associated with the persistent manager, and therefore the instance has a database record and the Java instance is connected to its record. Executing `getters()` and `setters()` imply database operations.
- **Detached**—The EntityManager is closed but the instance is still around. It is just a Value Object at this point. Executing `getters()` and `setters()` do not imply database updates. You can move a detached instance back to a Managed state by calling `merge` on the EntityManager.

- **Removed**—This is an instance that is no longer in the database because it has been deleted. After the transaction is committed, the object is just like any other transient Java Object.

Within this context, we will consider the specific details of how to do initialization, make connections, create transactions, invoke CRUD methods, and so on.

Initialization

The heart of persisting POJOs relies on a special object called an EntityManager. The goal for a developer is to initialize an EntityManager with the proper mappings and database information necessary. JPA provides several ways to load an EntityManager, depending on the environment.

To initialize the framework, you need to create a file called `persistence.xml`, as shown in Figure 8.1, and define a persistence unit, as shown in Listing 8.1. The listing contains the information necessary for a Java SE Application to configure a persistence unit.

Listing 8.1 Java SE Persistence Unit

```
<persistence-unit name="pie-db-JAVA-SE">
   <provider>
   org.apache.openjpa.persistence.PersistenceProviderImpl
   </provider>
   <properties>
      <property name="openjpa.ConnectionURL"
         value="jdbc:derby://localhost:1527/PWTE"/>
      <property name="openjpa.ConnectionDriverName"
         value="org.apache.derby.jdbc.ClientDriver"/>
      <property name="openjpa.jdbc.DBDictionary" value="derby"/>
      <property name="openjpa.Log"
         value="DefaultLevel=WARN,
         Runtime=INFO,
         Tool=INFO,
       SQL=TRACE"/>
      <property name="openjpa.jdbc.Schema" value="APP"/>
   </properties>
</persistence-unit>
```

The first thing you do is define your provider, which in this case is OpenJPA. Then you use the properties to set up the name of the Driver or DataSource implementation and any additional properties. A full list of properties can be found in the Open JPA Manual referenced earlier [OpenJPA 2l].

In a Java EE environment, the configuration will be slightly different. Application Servers, like WebSphere Application Server, will often provide a default JPA implementation, and it is therefore not necessary to provide a JPA provider. Listing 8.2 shows an example of a `persistence.xml` file in a Java EE environment. In it, you can provide the JNDI name of a configured DataSource. The DataSource implementation is vendor specific. Some Application Server vendors allow for swapping the default implementation.

Listing 8.2 Java EE Persistence Unit

```
<persistence-unit name="pie-db-JAVA-EE">
    <jta-data-source>jdbc/orderds</jta-data-source>
    <properties>
        <property name="openjpa.jdbc.DBDictionary" value="derby"/>
        <property name="openjpa.jdbc.Schema" value="APP"/>
    </properties>
</persistence-unit>
```

Connections

After you configure the persistence unit, JPA will have the necessary information to instantiate a persistence context. A *persistence context* is a set of managed entity instances in which, for any persistent entity identity, there is a unique entity instance. Within the persistence context, the entity's association with the underlying persistence store is managed by the EntityManager (EM). If you are familiar with Hibernate, the EntityManager is similar to the Hibernate Session.

All the connections to the underlying database are encapsulated within the EM. So getting an instance of the EntityManager will get a connection for you as needed without any explicit coding on your part. However, getting an instance of the EntityManager varies between a Java SE and Java EE environment. In a Java SE environment, an *application-managed EM instance* is created by calling the EntityManagerFactory, and the lifetime of that instance is controlled by the application. For each application-managed EM instance, there are one or more corresponding *application-managed persistence contexts*, which are not linked with any transaction and are not propagated to other components. It is important to realize that you must open and close the Entity Manager yourself in an application coded to run in a Java SE environment.

The Persistence class is used as a bootstrap to get access to an EntityManagerFactory for a particular persistence unit configured in a Java SE environment. After you get access to the EntityManagerFactory, you can use that to get an instance of an EntityManager that can be used throughout your code to implement the persistence code. Listing 8.3 shows an example of this process. In this code, we illustrate the three steps just discussed. Notice that in this example, the EntityManager is scoped to each business method. This is one common pattern in a Java SE environment.

Listing 8.3 Look Up Entity Manager Factory

```
public class CustomerOrderServicesJavaSEImpl{
    protected EntityManagerFactory emf  =
        Persistence.createEntityManagerFactory(
        "pie-db-JAVA-SE"
    );
    public Order openOrder(int customerId)throws Exception {
        EntityManager em = emf.createEntityManager();
        em = emf.createEntityManager();
        //Code
        em.close();
    }
...
}
```

It is worth noting that opening and closing an Entity Manager may be slower than keeping an instance around in some scenarios.

In a Java EE environment, the container can "inject" an EntityManagerFactory into a Java EE artifact, such as a Stateless Session Bean or an HttpServlet. Listing 8.4 shows an example of injecting an EntityManagerFactory into a Stateless Session Bean. Once injected, it is used the same way we illustrated earlier. Notice that you still must programmatically close the EntityManager because you used a factory to create the EntityManager. This is because you are still using an application-managed EntityManager.

Listing 8.4 Inject Entity Manager Factory

```
@Stateless
public class CustomerOrderServices {
    @PersistenceUnit (unitName = "pie-db-JAVA-EE")
    protected EntityManagerFactory emf;
    public Order openOrder(int customerId)throws Exception
    {
        EntityManager em = emf.createEntityManager();
        //Code
        em.close();
    }
...
}
```

In an EJB 3 environment, a *container-managed EM instance* is created by directing the container to inject one instance (either through direct injection or through JNDI lookup). The lifetime of that EM instance is controlled by the container; the instance matches the lifetime of the component into which it was injected. Container-managed Entity Managers will also provide automatic propagation of transactions, connections, and other services. We will discuss this further after transactions are discussed.

An EntityManager can be injected directly into an EJB, using a Java annotation called PersistenceContext. Listing 8.5 shows an example of this. In this case, the developer does not have to worry about a factory. Furthermore, you delegate to the container the management of the EntityManager and the propagation of the proper persistence context from EJB component to EJB component. This is a more common pattern in Java EE. If you are using the PersistenceContext in an EJB 3 component, the EJB 3 container will automatically propagate the persistence context for a particular request across components. It is important to keep in mind that an EJB 3 Session Bean is a thread-safe component, and therefore, only one client request is being serviced by the EJB component at a time. This means the EntityManager can safely be used by the instance without fear of another thread accessing it. The container can also take advantage of this and pass the current persistence context which can contain an active transaction.

Listing 8.5 Inject EntityManager

```
@Stateless
public class CustomerOrderServices {
    @PersistenceContext (unitName = "pie-db-JAVA-EE") //Step 1
    protected EntityManager em;
```

To illustrate the object states shown in Figure 8.1 in context of the code to get access to the EntityManager, see Listing 8.6. This listing shows objects in various states and how they move from one state to another. The comments within the listing describe the action.

Listing 8.6 Object States

```
//Set up EM and Transient POJO instance
em = emf.createEntityManager();
Order newOrder = new Order();
newOrder.setStatus(Order.Status.OPEN);
newOrder.setTotal(new BigDecimal(0));

//Make POJO Managed by persisting it
em.persist(newOrder);
newOrder.setTotal(new BigDecimal(1));

//Make POJO Detached by closing
em.close();
newOrder.setTotal(new BigDecimal(2));
```

```
//Make POJO Managed by merging detached instance
em2 = emf.createEntityManager();
em2.merge(newOrder;)
```

As long as a POJO is associated with an EntityManager, updates to the database are implied and the instance is managed. Managed Entities are either (a) loaded by the EntityManager via a find method or query, or (b) associated with the EntityManager with a `persist` or `merge` operation. We discuss this more in later sections on the Create, Retrieve, Update, and Destroy operations.

Transactions

You can demarcate transactions in OpenJPA in the following ways:

- Using a standard programmatic API such as the JTA interfaces
- Using the special `javax.persistence.EntityTransaction` interface provided by JPA
- Using declarative transactions within an EJB 3 Container

We have covered JDBC and JTA transactions in previous chapters. Listing 8.7 shows an example of using the EntityTransaction interface. A developer can get an instance of an EntityTransaction by calling `getTransaction()` on the EntityManager. After they have an instance, you can call begin, commit, or rollback. This is often the norm when using OpenJPA in a Java SE environment or in the web container.

Listing 8.7 Entity Manager Transaction Demarcation

```
public Order openOrder(int customerId)
throws CustomerDoesNotExistException,
       OrderAlreadyOpenException,
       GeneralPersistenceException {
    EntityManager em = null;
    try {
        em = emf.createEntityManager();
        em.getTransaction().begin();
        //use em to manage objects
        em.getTransaction().commit();
        return newOrder;
    }
    catch(CustomerDoesNotExistException e){
        em.getTransaction().rollback();
        throw e;
    }
    //Handle other Exceptions not listed
    finally {
```

```
        if (em != null) em.close();
    }
}
```

If a developer uses an external API like JTA to demarcate transactions and you are using an application-managed EntityManager, you need to have your EntityManager instance "join" the transaction. Listing 8.8 illustrates this situation and shows the code needed to cause the join.

Listing 8.8 Join Transaction

```
@PersistenceUnit (unitName = "pie-db-JAVA-EE")
protected EntityManagerFactory emf;

public Order openOrder(int customerId)throws Exception {
    javax.transaction.UserTransaction tran =
        //code to lookup UserTransaction in JNDI

    EntityManager em = emf.createEntityManager();
    try {
        // Start JTA transaction
        tran.begin();

        // Have em explicitly join it
        em = emf.createEntityManager();
        em.joinTransaction();

        //Code in transaction scope ready to commit
        tran.commit();

        //Code outside of transaction scope
    }
    catch(Exception e) {
        tran.rollback();
        throw e;
    }
    finally {
        em.close();
    }
}
```

When OpenJPA is used in an EJB 3 container, OpenJPA will allow for transactions to be controlled by EJB transaction demarcation. Listing 8.9 shows an example of JPA being used within an EJB 3 Session Bean. The EJB 3 method is marked with a Required transaction. In addition, the EntityManager is injected into the EJB 3 POJO. In this scenario, you get the benefit of having the container manage the EntityManager for you using the container-managed Entity Manager discussed in the preceding section.

Listing 8.9 EJB 3 Transaction Demarcation

```
@Stateless
public class CustomerOrderServicesImpl implements CustomerOrderServices
{
    @PersistenceContext(unitName="pie-db-JAVA-EE")
    protected EntityManager em;

    @TransactionAttribute(value=TransactionAttributeType.REQUIRED)
    public Order openOrder(int customerId)
    throws CustomerDoesNotExistException,
            OrderAlreadyOpenException,
            GeneralPersistenceException {
        // use em
    }
```

For each container-managed EM instance, there are one or more corresponding *container-managed persistence contexts* (PCs). At the time the PC is created, it is linked with the transaction currently in effect and propagated by the container, along with the transaction context to other called components within the same JVM.

The container-managed usage scenario is further subcategorized into transaction-scoped (lifetime is controlled by the transaction) and extended (lifetime is controlled by one or more stateful session bean instances). This means that in the transaction case, inside an EJB 3 container, the persistence context life cycle is governed by the transaction. You get automatic flushing of cache at the end of the transaction. JPA also provides an extended PersistenceContext that will be managed by some greater scope, such as a Stateful Session Bean or perhaps an Http Session. Listing 8.10 shows how you can inject a longer-lived Persistence Context.

Listing 8.10 Extended Persistence Context

```
@PersistenceContext(
    unitName="pie-db-JAVAEE", type=PersistenceContextType.EXTENDED
)
protected EntityManager em;
```

In Chapter 5, "JDBC," we discussed savepoints. Savepoints allow for fine-grained control over the transactional behavior of your application. The JPA specification does not allow for savepoints; however, some vendors, like OpenJPA, may have extensions. OpenJPA's savepoint API allows you to set intermediate rollback points in your transaction. You can then choose to roll back changes made only after a specific savepoint, then commit or continue making new changes in the transaction. OpenJPA's OpenJPAEntityManager (subtype of JPA's EntityManager) supports these savepoint operations:

- `void setSavepoint(String name);`
- `void releaseSavepoint(String name);`
- `void rollbackToSavepoint(String name);`

Savepoints require some configuration, so refer to the OpenJPA documentation for more details.

Create

The EntityManager has most of the methods needed to persist Java objects, or entities. Persistence actions usually occur by passing instances of entities to and from the EntityManager. So for creating data, you would just create an instance of an entity and persist it using the `persist` method of the EntityManager. Listing 8.11 shows an example of this.

Listing 8.11 Persist Data

```
Order newOrder = new Order();
newOrder.setCustomer(customer);
newOrder.setStatus(Order.Status.OPEN);
newOrder.setTotal(new BigDecimal(0));
em.persist(newOrder);
```

This will correspond to an `INSERT` into the database. The Order object in the example is mapped to a table in the database. A POJO mapped to a database is called an Entity in JPA. We will discuss mappings in the "ORM Features Supported" section.

Retrieve

Reading data can be done several ways. The simplest read is to read an object by primary key. The EntityManager `find` method provides an easy way to do this. Listing 8.12 illustrates this. The `find` method takes the name of the class and a primary key value as a parameter. We discuss mapping primary keys in the later section, "ORM Features Supported."

Listing 8.12 Finding Entity Instances

```
AbstractCustomer customer = em.find(AbstractCustomer.class, customerId);
```

Using the `find` methods, OpenJPA can load a whole Object Graph. Listing 8.13 shows an example of accessing the Order Object after loading the customer. If the Order Object is mapped as a relationship and the proper fetching strategies are set, OpenJPA will load more than the root object with the `find` method. Later in the chapter, fetching is discussed.

Listing 8.13 Related Entity Instances

```
AbstractCustomer customer = em.find(AbstractCustomer.class, customerId);
Order existingOpenOrder = customer.getOpenOrder();
```

JPA also comes with a rich query language called EJB-QL (sometimes called JPQL). You can issue queries against the object model. We will not provide a detailed tutorial on the query languages, and instead recommend that you read the reference guide [JPQL]; but the query language provides syntax to execute complex queries against related objects. Listing 8.14 shows an example of executing a query. As a developer, you can create a query using the `createQuery` against the EntityManager. Notice you can use `:name` to mark places where you want to use parameters. OpenJPA also supports using the `?` approach used by JDBC Prepared Statements. However, both approaches will translate to Prepared Statements.

Listing 8.14 Executing JPA Queries

```
Query query = em.createQuery(
     "select l from LineItem l
      where l.productId = :productId and l.orderId = :orderId "
);
query.setParameter("productId", productId);
query.setParameter("orderId", existingOpenOrder.getOrderId());
LineItem item = (LineItem) query.getSingleResult();
```

OpenJPA also supports the capability to externalize queries from the code using the "named query" concept, which allows you to associate a query to a name using an annotation or the XML mapping file. Listing 8.13 shows how you annotate a POJO with the NamedQuery. The rest of the annotations in the listing are explained in the later section, "ORM Features Supported." After you define the NamedQuery, you can execute somewhere else in your code, as shown in the second part of Listing 8.15. It is worth mentioning that if you want to truly externalize the queries, you should use the XML deployment descriptor.

Listing 8.15 Executing JPA Queries

```
@Entity
@Table(name="LINE_ITEM")
@IdClass(LineItemId.class)
@NamedQuery(
    name="existing.lineitem.forproduct",
    query="
        select l from LineItem l
        where l.productId = :productId
        and l.orderId = :orderId"
)
```

```
public class LineItem {
    ...
    Query query = em.createNamedQuery("existing.lineitem.forproduct");
    query.setParameter("productId", productId);
    query.setParameter("orderId", existingOpenOrder.getOrderId());
    LineItem item = (LineItem) query.getSingleResult();
```

With EJB-QL, when you are querying for Objects, you can load related objects as well, depending on the mapping. You can also load objects using joins. OpenJPA also extends EJB-QL with some value adds.

For the majority of the cases, you should be able to get data you need. There are cases when you need to drop down to native SQL. This could be to call a Stored Procedure, to get an optimized SQL, or because you cannot get OpenJPA to generate the correct SQL needed for the use case. OpenJPA supports the notion of native queries. You can execute SQL and project onto a POJO. An example is shown in Listing 8.16.

Listing 8.16 Native SQL

```
Query query = em.createNativeQuery(
    "SELECT * FROM LINE_ITEM", LineItem.class
);
List<LineItem> items = query.getResultList());
```

You can also have Native Named Queries if you want to externalize the SQL.

Update

OpenJPA supports updating existing data in a few ways. Figure 8.1 showed you the life cycle of a POJO with respect to the EntityManager. Any field updated on a POJO that is associated with the EntityManager implies a database update. Listing 8.17 shows an example of code finding an instance of LineItem and executing an update.

Listing 8.17 Updating Persistent Entities

```
LineItem existingLineItem = em.find(LineItem.class,lineItemId);
existingLineItem.setQuantity(existingLineItem.getQuantity() + quantity);
existingLineItem.setAmount(existingLineItem.getAmount().add(amount));
```

Any update to related objects also implies an update. In Listing 8.18, we show that after finding the customer Entity, you can traverse to the Order. Because the customer is still being managed by the EntityManager, so is the Order.

Listing 8.18 Updating Related Entities

```
AbstractCustomer customer = em.find(AbstractCustomer.class, customerId);
Order existingOpenOrder = customer.getOpenOrder();
BigDecimal amount = product.getPrice().multiply(new BigDecimal(quantity));
existingOpenOrder.setTotal(amount.add(existingOpenOrder.getTotal()));
```

OpenJPA also supports updating of detached Entities using the `merge` method. Listing 8.19 shows an example of a detached case. In the first part of the listing, you can see a fragment of Servlet code calling a service. The Service implementation is shown in the second part of the listing. A web request first reads the data using an HTTP `GET`, which gets access to the data and stores it in sessions. The service implementation uses a `find` to access the data and finish the request. Then an HTTP `POST` comes in to update the data in session. The Servlet `doPost` passes the detached instance into the `updateLineItem` method. The implementation of `updateLineItem` will attempt to merge the instance to the EntityManager.

Listing 8.19 Updating via merging

```
public void doGet(
    HttpServletRequest request, HttpServletResponse response)
{
    String customerId = populateFromRequest(request);
    LineItem li = customerService.getLineItem(li);
    writeToSession(li);
}

public void doPost(
    HttpServletRequest request, HttpServletResponse response
)
{
    LineItem li = populateFromSession(request);
    customerService.updateLineItem(li);
}
...

public LineItem getLineItem(int liId) throws GeneralPersistenceException
{
    EntityManager em = //Get Entity Manager
    LineItem li  = emf.find(LineItem.class,liId);
    return li;
}
```

```
public void updateLineItem(LineItem li) throws GeneralPersistenceException {
    EntityManager em = //Get Entity Manager
    em.merge(li);
}
```

OpenJPA allows you to use EJB-QL to issue updates as well, such as shown in Listing 8.20. This feature enables you to update many instances with one statement. You also avoid hydrating objects in certain scenarios where performance is important.

Listing 8.20 Updating via Query Language

```
Query query = em.createQuery(
    "UPDATE CUSTOMER c
     SET o.discount = :discount
     WHERE c.type = 'RESIDENTIAL'"
);
query.setParameter("discount", discount);
query.executeUpdate();
```

Delete

You can delete data several ways using OpenJPA. A managed instance can be removed by calling `remove` on the EntityManager, as shown in Listing 8.21. (Listing 8.23 shows an even better option.)

Listing 8.21 Deleting via EntityManager Remove

```
LineItem existingLineItem = em.find(LineItem.class,lineItemId);
if(existingLineItem != null){
    em.remove(existingLineItem);
}
```

You can configure OpenJPA to propagate deletes along an object graph. We will show you mapping relationships later; however, in Listing 8.22, you can see that Order has a relationship to a Set of LineItem instances. On the relationship, you can see that we have set the cascade to `REMOVE`. This means that when you delete an Order, all associated Lineitem instances will be deleted as well.

Listing 8.22 Deleting via Cascading

```
@Entity
@Table(name="ORDERS")

public class Order implements Serializable {
```

```
...
@OneToMany(cascade=CascadeType.REMOVE, fetch=FetchType.EAGER )
@ElementJoinColumn(
    name="ORDER_ID",referencedColumnName="ORDER_ID"
)
protected Set<LineItem> lineitems;
```

Finally, much as with Updates, OpenJPA allows you to delete, using EJB-QL Queries. Listing 8.23 shows an example of deleting via a query. This approach is useful if you want to delete many rows with one network call.

Listing 8.23 Deleting via a Query

```
Query query = em.createQuery(
    "DELETE FROM LineItem l
     WHERE l.productId = :productId
     and l.orderId = :orderId"
);
query.setParameter("productId", productId);
query.setParameter("orderId", existingOpenOrder.getOrderId());
query.executeUpdate();
```

Stored Procedures

We already showed how you can use native queries in OpenJPA. Native queries can be used to call stored procedures as shown in Listing 8.24.

Listing 8.24 Using a Native Query to Call a Stored Procedure

```
Query query = em.createNativeQuery("CALL SHIP_ORDER(?)");
query.setParameter(1, orderId);
query.executeUpdate());
```

Batch Operations

As we showed in the Update and Delete sections, OpenJPA supports batching updates and deletes using EJB-QL. The Apache version of OpenJPA (1.0.0) currently does not support automatic statement batching for persistent operations. However, vendors that build on top of OpenJPA sometimes provide this function. The EJB 3 implementation of WebSphere Application Server provides an enhanced version of OpenJPA. They provide a configuration option for deferring update operations to commit time and batching them together. Other vendors may provide similar optimizations. The optimizations can make mass updates several orders of magnitude faster; see also the "Batch Operations" section in Chapter 5 for details of how this approach works.

Extending the Framework

When writing OpenJPA plug-ins or otherwise extending the OpenJPA runtime, however, you will use OpenJPA's native APIs. OpenJPA allows you to extend the framework in various ways, including these:

- You can extend the default EntityManager or EntityManagerFactory. This is often done by Vendors offering enhanced JPA implementations on top of OpenJPA.
- You can extend the query engine. This is usually done to provide optimized solutions, such as integrating with cache technologies.
- Data Caches can be added to back the OpenJPA cache.
- Other areas support extending behavior, such as fetch and primary key generation strategies.

The OpenJPA implementation shows the specific interfaces and classes that need to be extended to provide your own extensions.

Error Handling

JPA Exceptions are unchecked. Figure 8.2 shows the JPA Exception Architecture. JPA uses standard exceptions where appropriate, most notably IllegalArgumentExceptions and IllegalStateExceptions. These exceptions can occur when you perform persistence actions without the proper setup—for example, sending an Entity to an EntityManager that is not managing it.

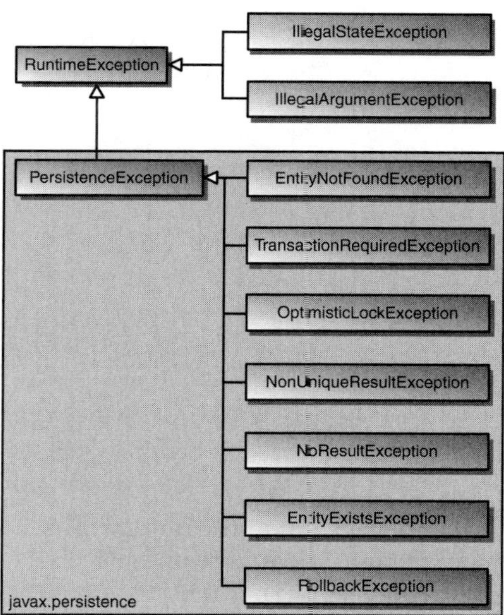

Figure 8.2 JPA exception class diagram.

The specification also provides a few JPA-specific exceptions in the `javax.persistence` package. Listing 8.25 shows an example of catching an EntityNotFoundException. Alternatively, because the exceptions are unchecked, you can choose to not catch it and handle it at a higher level.

Listing 8.25 Exception Example

```
{   try
    AbstractCustomer customer = em.find(
        AbstractCustomer.class, customerId
    );
    ...
}
catch(javax.persistence.EntityNotFoundException e)
{    throw new GeneralPersistenceException(e);

}
```

All exceptions thrown by OpenJPA implement `org.apache.openjpa.util.ExceptionInfo` to provide you with additional error information. Figure 8.3 shows the class diagram of the ExceptionInfo interface.

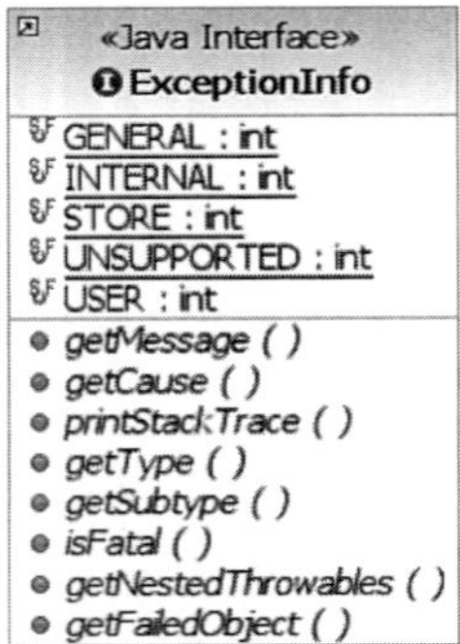

Figure 8.3 ExceptionInfo interface.

ORM Features Supported

We have shown you how a programmer would use Entities to perform the runtime persistence operations. We will now show you how to map Entities to a database using OpenJPA. OpenJPA allows mapping Entities via Java Annotations and XML. The choice is up to the developer and usually depends on whether you want to expose the underlying relational database details into the code; or in some cases, whether you have “legacy” Java objects that are not easy to change.

Objects

Throughout this book, we have been showing meet-in-the-middle Mapping. OpenJPA supports top-down, bottom-up, and meet-in-the-middle. It is worth mentioning that the JPA spec defines a common standard for top-down generation of database schemas. Listing 8.26 shows the minimum annotation needed to make a POJO a JPA Entity. Simply by marking a class with the `@Entity` annotation, you have a persistent capable class. If your database schema follows the JPA naming convention, or if you want to have the database schema generated, then the class can be used. In this case, OpenJPA will look for a table named Customer. The table will have two columns: id and name. The table names and column names will match whether they contain upper- or lowercase spellings.

Listing 8.26 Creating an Entity with Java Annotations

```
@Entity
public class Customer
{
    private String name;
    private int id;

    public getName(){return name;}
    public setName(String name){this.name=name;}

    public getId(){return id;}
    public setId(int id){this.id = id;}
}
```

As mentioned earlier, you can also use XML as an alternative to Java Annotations. Listing 8.27 shows an XML entity mapping for the same Customer. As noted previously, some developers prefer to externalize their database mappings to keep the Java code "pure." Some other developers prefer to use Annotations together with XML. In some cases XML and Annotations can be used. In this case, XML will serve as an override for Annotations. This might not make sense when an entity is always mapped to a relational table; however, in other cases XML overrides can provide benefits (for example, enabling you to change a schema name or optimize a query without changing the Java code).

Listing 8.27 Creating an Entity with XML

```
<entity-mappings
    xmlns="java.sun.com/xml/ns/persistence/orm"
    xmlns:xsi="www.w3.org/2001/XMLSchema-instance"
    xsi:schemaLocation=
       "java.sun.com/xml/ns/persistence/orm orm_1_0.xsd"
```

```
    version="1.0"
>
    <entity class=" Customer" />
</entity-mappings>
```

OpenJPA does a lot of defaulting for you; as long as you match the naming conventions, things will fall into place. This includes naming conventions for relationships and other complex types. For the rest of the section, though, we will show explicit mappings to illustrate the important concepts. In addition, it is often the case that the database schema will not always match the Object model, and will require a meet-in-the-middle mapping—as occurs in our example throughout the book.

Mapping Entities to tables with different names is easy. Listing 8.28 shows the Order Entity mapped to a table called ORDERS. You use a simple annotation called `@Table`.

Listing 8.28 Mapping an Entity to a Table

```
@Entity
@Table(name="ORDERS")
public class Order implements Serializable {
```

Similarly, you can map Entities to a table using XML, as shown in Listing 8.29.

Listing 8.29 Mapping an Entity to a Table with XML

```
<entity-mappings xmlns="java.sun.com/xml/ns/persistence/orm"
    xmlns:xsi="www.w3.org/2001/XMLSchema-instance"
    xsi:schemaLocation=
        "java.sun.com/xml/ns/persistence/orm orm_1_0.xsd"
    version="1.0"
>

<entity class=" Order ">
    <table name="ORDERS"/>
...
</entity>
```

The Table annotation and XML both let you specify a schema name as well.

Inheritance

OpenJPA fully supports inheritance in persistent classes. It allows persistent classes to inherit from nonpersistent classes, persistent classes to inherit from other persistent classes, and nonpersistent classes to inherit from persistent classes. It is even possible to form inheritance hierarchies in which persistence skips generations. There are, however, a few important limitations:

- Persistent classes cannot inherit from certain natively implemented system classes such as `java.net.Socket` and `java.lang.Thread`.
- If a persistent class inherits from a nonpersistent class, the fields of the nonpersistent superclass cannot be persisted.
- All classes in an inheritance tree must use the same identity type. Identifiers will be covered in the next section.

OpenJPA supports three strategies for Inheritance:

1. Single Table
2. Joined
3. Table Per Class

We described each of these in detail in Chapter 3, "Designing Persistent Object Services."

Single Table Strategy

All JPA providers have to provide an implementation of the Single Table and the Joined strategy. Table Per Class is optional. Single Table mandates all classes in the inheritance hierarchy map into one table. In our book example for OpenJPA, this is our default implementation.

The `AbstractCustomer` superclass contains a type discriminator. This discriminator will be used to create the correct type at runtime. All the fields are mapped into a single table. Listing 8.30 shows how this mapping would look in OpenJPA.

Listing 8.30 Superclass Mapping with a Single Table

```
@Entity
@Inheritance(strategy=SINGLE_TABLE)
@Table(name = "CUSTOMER")
@DiscriminatorColumn(name="TYPE", discriminatorType = STRING)
public abstract class AbstractCustomer implements Serializable {

    @Id
    protected int customerId;
    ....
```

The subclasses would then specify a discriminator value. Listing 8.31 shows the mapping for ResidentialCustomer (each subclass would have a similar mapping). Notice that you do not have to specify a table mapping because the superclass handles the mapping.

Listing 8.31 Subclass Mapping with a Single Table

```
@Entity
@DiscriminatorValue("RESIDENTAL")
public class ResidentialCustomer
extends AbstractCustomer
```

```
implements Serializable {
    protected short householdSize;
    protected boolean frequentCustomer;
```

In Listing 8.32, the same mapping is shown in XML. We show it here just to highlight that mappings can be done in XML.

Listing 8.32 XML Mapping for Single Table

```
<entity class=" org.pwte.example.domain.AbstractCustomer ">
    <table name="CUSTOMER" />
    <inheritance strategy="SINGLE_TABLE"/>
        ...
</entity>
<entity class=" org.pwte.example.domain.ResidentialCustomer ">
    ...
</entity>
```

Single table inheritance mapping is the most performant of all inheritance models because it does not require a join to retrieve the persistent data necessary to populate the class hierarchy of a single instance from the database (it still may require a join to retrieve related objects, of course). Similarly, persisting or updating a single persistent instance can often be accomplished with a single `INSERT` or `UPDATE` statement. Finally, relations to any other class within a single table inheritance hierarchy are just as efficient as relations to a base class.

However, the larger the inheritance model gets, the "wider" the mapped table gets—in that for every field in the entire inheritance hierarchy, a column must exist in the mapped table. This may have undesirable consequences on the database size, because a wide or deep inheritance hierarchy will result in tables with many mostly empty columns. In addition, changes to any class in the hierarchy would result in changes to the table. This issue is significant because after systems are deployed, it is generally very difficult to change database schemas of existing tables.

Joined Strategy

The Joined Strategy is really the table per class strategy we discussed in Chapter 3. Here, every class in the inheritance chain gets its own table. Each subclass's primary key would also be a foreign key to the primary key table.

Listing 8.33 shows the `AbstractCustomer` with the Inheritance strategy of `Joined`. Notice it is mapped to an ABSTRACT_CUSTOMER table.

Listing 8.33 Mapping Superclass with the Joined Strategy

```
@Entity
@Inheritance(strategy=JOINED)
```

```
@Table(name = "ABSTRACT_CUSTOMER")
public abstract class AbstractCustomer implements Serializable {

    @Id
    protected int customerId;
    protected String name;
    protected String type;
```

In Listing 8.34, you will notice that the `Residential` subclass is mapped to its own table. Notice the use of the `@PrimaryKeyJoinColumn` annotation to link the primary key to the superclass. The Business Customer class will be similar.

Listing 8.34 Mapping Subclass with the Joined Strategy

```
@Entity
@Table(name = "RESIDENTIAL_CUSTOMER")
@PrimaryKeyJoinColumn(name="CUSTOMER_ID",
referencedColumnName="CUSTOMER_ID")

public class ResidentialCustomer
extends AbstractCustomer implements Serializable {
    protected short householdSize;
    protected boolean frequentCustomer;
```

The joined strategy has the following advantages:

- Using joined subclass tables results in the most *normalized* database schema, meaning the schema with the least spurious or redundant data.
- As more subclasses are added to the data model over time, the only schema modification that needs to be made is the addition of corresponding subclass tables in the database (rather than having to change the structure of existing tables).

Relations to a base class using this strategy can be loaded through standard joins and can use standard foreign keys, as opposed to the machinations required to load polymorphic relations to Table-per-Class base types, described next. The joined strategy is often the slowest of the inheritance models, unless provisions are made to "lazily load" levels of the hierarchy. Retrieving any subclass can require one or more database joins, and storing subclasses can require multiple `INSERT` or `UPDATE` statements.

Table-per-Class Strategy

The Table-per-Class strategy is what we defined as the Concrete Table Inheritance Strategy in Chapter 3. In this model, each concrete subclass will have its own table, and the superclass information is repeated in each of the tables. Listing 8.35 shows how you would configure the `AbstractCustomer` superclass with the `TABLE_PER_CLASS` strategy option. All that is needed is setting the inheritance type because the class is Abstract Class.

Listing 8.35 Mapping Superclass with Table-per-Class

```
@Entity
@Inheritance(strategy=TABLE_PER_CLASS)
public abstract class AbstractCustomer implements Serializable {

    @Id
    protected int customerId;
    protected String name;
    protected String type;
```

Listing 8.36 shows both subclasses, each mapping to its corresponding table.

Listing 8.36 Mapping Subclass with Table-per-Class

```
@Entity
@Table(name = "RESIDENTIAL_CUSTOMER")
public class ResidentialCustomer
extends AbstractCustomer implements Serializable {
    protected short householdSize;
    protected boolean frequentCustomer;

...

@Entity
@Table(name = "BUSINESS_CUSTOMER")
public class BusinessCustomer
extends AbstractCustomer implements Serializable {
    protected boolean volumeDiscount;
    protected boolean businessPartner;
```

As mentioned in Chapter 3, you need a way to manage the primary keys across the various concrete classes. Some databases support the notion of a sequence to generate keys across tables.

The Table-per-Class strategy is very efficient when operating on instances of a known class. Under these conditions, the strategy never requires joining to superclass or subclass tables. Reads, joins, inserts, updates, and deletes are all efficient in the absence of polymorphic behavior. Also, as in the joined strategy, adding new classes to the hierarchy does not require modifying existing class tables, as is required in the Single-Table strategy.

Polymorphic relations to nonleaf classes in a Table-per-Class hierarchy have many limitations. When the concrete subclass is not known, the related object could be in any of the subclass tables, making joins through the relation impossible. This ambiguity also affects identity lookups and queries; these operations require multiple SQL `SELECT`s (one for each possible subclass), or a complex `UNION`.

Table-per-Class inheritance mapping has the following limitations:

- You cannot traverse polymorphic relations to nonleaf classes in a Table-per-Class inheritance hierarchy in queries.
- You cannot map a one-sided polymorphic relation to a nonleaf class in a Table-per-Class inheritance hierarchy using an inverse foreign key.
- You cannot use an order column in a polymorphic relation to a nonleaf class in a Table-per-Class inheritance hierarchy mapped with an inverse foreign key.
- Table-per-Class hierarchies impose limitations on eager fetching. We will discuss fetching later in the section on "Tuning Options."

A more serious issue with the Table-per-Class strategy is what happens when a non-leaf (superclass) in the hierarchy is changed. In this case, every concrete class that inherits from that class—either directly or indirectly—must change. Therefore, you should only use the Table-per-Class strategy when the hierarchy is relatively stable.

Keys

Any Entity instance is uniquely identified by an ID in JPA. The ID property is then mapped to the primary key. You can mark a field on your entity as an ID using the `@Id` annotation. Listing 8.37 shows an example.

Listing 8.37 ID Field

```
@Entity
public class Product implements Serializable {
    private static final long serialVersionUID = 2435504714077372968L;

    @Id
    protected int productId;

    protected BigDecimal price;
    protected String description;

...
```

It some cases, primary keys need to be generated at Entity Creation Time. OpenJPA supports a number of mechanisms to do this.

JPA includes the `GeneratedValue` annotation for this purpose. It has the following properties:

- **`GenerationType.AUTO`**—The default. Assign the field a generated value, leaving the details to the JPA vendor.
- **`GenerationType.IDENTITY`**—The database will assign an identity value on insert.
- **`GenerationType.SEQUENCE`**—Use a datastore sequence to generate a field value.
- **`GenerationType.TABLE`**—Use a sequence table to generate a field value.

OpenJPA also offers two additional generator strategies for non-numeric fields, which you can access by setting `strategy` to `AUTO` (the default), and setting the `generator` string to one of the following:

- **`uuid-string`**—OpenJPA will generate a 128-bit UUID unique within the network, represented as a 16-character string. For more information on UUIDs, see the IETF UUID draft specification at www1.ics.uci.edu/~ejw/authoring/uuid-guid/.
- **`uuid-hex`**—Same as `uuid-string`, but represents the UUID as a 32-character hexadecimal string.

Listing 8.38 shows an example of using the Identity mapping. In this case, OpenJPA will defer to the database's implementation of generating an identity. The Sequence and Identity columns require that your database support these features.

Listing 8.38 Generating an ID Using the Identity Strategy

```
@Entity
@Table(name="ORDERS")
public class Order implements Serializable {
    private static final long serialVersionUID = 7779370942277849463L;


    @Id
    @GeneratedValue(strategy=GenerationType.IDENTITY)
    @Column(name="ORDER_ID")
    protected int orderId;
    protected BigDecimal total;
```

For the Table Generator Strategy, you must define a table in the database. (The OpenJPA documentation contains details on the schema for this table.) Listing 8.39 shows an example of using the Table Strategy. In this case, you define a specific generator that points to a table. Then you point your generated strategy to the table. The Sequence would work in a very similar fashion. Sequence and table generators usually work better when you have to define an ID across several tables. For example, when using the Table-per-Concrete method of mapping Inheritance, all of your subclasses may need to share a common sequence or generator to ensure data integrity across instances.

Listing 8.39 Generating an Identity with the Table Strategy

```
@Entity
@Table(name="CUSTOMER")
public class Customer {


    @Id
    @GeneratedValue(
```

```
        strategy=GenerationType.TABLE, generator="AuthorGen"
    )
    @TableGenerator(
        name="AuthorGen", table="AUTH_GEN", pkColumnName="PK",
        valueColumnName="AID"
    )
    @Column(name="AID", columnDefinition="INTEGER64")
    private long id;

    ...
}
```

The JPA specification requires you to declare one or more identity fields in your persistent classes. OpenJPA fully supports this form of object identity, called application identity. OpenJPA, however, also supports datastore identity. In datastore identity, you do not declare any primary key fields. OpenJPA manages the identity of your persistent objects for you through a surrogate key in the database.

You can control how your JPA datastore identity value is generated through OpenJPA's `org.apache.openjpa.persistence.DataStoreId` class annotation. This annotation has `strategy` and `generator` properties that mirror the same-named properties on the standard `javax.persistence.GeneratedValue` annotation just described.

To retrieve the identity value of a datastore identity entity, use the `OpenJPAEntityManager.getObjectId(Object entity)` method. Listing 8.40 shows an example of using this method.

Listing 8.40 Using an Application Managed Identity in OpenJPA

```
import org.apache.openjpa.persistence.*;

@Entity
@DataStoreId
public class LineItem {

    ... no @Id fields declared ...
}
```

If you choose to use application identity, you may want to take advantage of OpenJPA's application identity tool. The application identity tool generates Java code implementing the identity class for any persistent type using application identity. The code satisfies all the requirements the specification places on identity classes. You can use it as-is, or simply use it as a starting point, editing it to meet your needs. Refer to the OpenJPA documentation for more details.

When your entity has multiple identity fields, at least one of which is a relation to another entity, you must use an identity class. You cannot use an embedded identity object. Identity class fields corresponding to entity identity fields should be of the same type as the related entity's identity.

Your identity class must meet the following criteria:

- The class must be public.
- The class must be serializable.
- The class must have a public no-args constructor.
- The names of the nonstatic fields or properties of the class must be the same as the names of the identity fields or properties of the corresponding entity class, and the types must be identical.
- The `equals` and `hashCode` methods of the class must use the values of all fields or properties corresponding to identity fields or properties in the entity class.
- If the class is an inner class, it must be `static`.
- All entity classes related by inheritance must use the same identity class, or else each entity class must have its own identity class whose inheritance hierarchy mirrors the inheritance hierarchy of the owning entity classes.

Listing 8.41 shows an example of an ID class that can be used as an Identity. This class can be used then in the find operation as input.

Listing 8.41 An ID class in OpenJPA

```
@Embeddable
public class LineItemId implements Serializable{
    private static final long serialVersionUID =
        2160402020032769707L;

    private int orderId;
    private int productId;

    //getters and setters
    @Override
    public int hashCode() {
        //calculate hash
    }
    @Override
    public boolean equals(Object obj) {
        //implement equals
    }
}
```

After you do this, you can use the `@IdClass` annotation to specify the class, as shown in Listing 8.42. The ID fields on the Entity must match that on the ID class.

Listing 8.42 IdClass Annotation Usage

```
@Entity
@Table(name="LINE_ITEM")
@IdClass(LineItemId.class)
@NamedQuery(
    name="existing.lineitem.forproduct",
    query="select l from LineItem l
           where l.productId = :productId
           and l.orderId = :orderId"
)
public class LineItem implements Serializable {

    @Id
    @Column(name="ORDER_ID")
    private int orderId;

    @Id
    @Column(name="PRODUCT_ID")
    private int productId;
```

Alternatively, you can use the `@EmbeddedId` annotation and have the ID class as a member of the entity. This is assuming the ID class is annotated as embeddable, as in Listing 8.40. We will discuss embeddable classes later in the chapter. Listing 8.43 shows an alternative implementation of the LineItem Entity with the EmbeddedId.

Listing 8.43 Embeddable ID

```
@Entity
@Table(name="LINE_ITEM")
public class LineItem implements Serializable {

    @EmbeddedId
    private LineItemId lineItemId;
```

The JPA specification limits identity fields to simple types. OpenJPA, however, also allows `ManyToOne` and `OneToOne` relations to be identity fields. To identify a relation field as an identity field, simply annotate it with both the `@ManyToOne` or `@OneToOne` relation annotation and the `@Id` identity annotation. Listing 8.44 shows an example of how this looks.

Listing 8.44 Entities as ID

```
@Entity
@IdClass(LineItemId.class)
```

```
public class LineItem {

    @Id
    private int lineItemId;

    @Id
    @ManyToOne
    private Order order;

    ...
}
```

OpenJPA allows you to specify an ID through XML mapping as well. For details, we again refer you to its extensive documentation [OpenJPA 2].

Attributes

A field on an Entity is a primitive Java type. By default, all fields on an Entity are persistent. Therefore, all you have to do is declare a POJO as an entity and define its Ids. Listing 8.45 shows an example of a persistent Product class.

Listing 8.45 Persistent Fields

```
@Entity
public class Product implements Serializable {
    @Id
    protected int productId;

    protected BigDecimal price;
    protected String description;
    //getters and setters
}
```

Alternatively, you can use the `@Basic` annotation to denote that a field is persistent. That `@Basic` annotation is usually not used because fields are persistent by default; however, if you need to override the default handling, you can use it. You will see an example later. To map the field to a column, you can use the `@Column` annotation. An example is shown in Listing 8.46. Notice that you do not have to specify a column annotation for attributes whose name matches that of the column. OpenJPA will map each field to the column with the same name.

Listing 8.46 Mapping Columns

```
public class LineItem implements Serializable {

    @Id
    @Column(name="ORDER_ID")
    private int orderId;

    @Id
    @Column(name="PRODUCT_ID")
    private int productId;
    ...
```

You can express the same mappings using XML, as shown in Listing 8.47.

Listing 8.47 XML Mapping for Attributes

```
<entity-mappings>

    <entity class="Order">
        <attributes>
            <id name="orderId">
                <column name="ORDER_ID"/>
            </id>
            <basic name="total"/>
            <basic name="tax">
                <column name="TAX_FIELD">
            </basic>
        </attributes>
    </entity>
...
</ entity-mappings>
```

Fields that you do not want to persist can be marked as transient using the `@Transient` annotation. An example is shown in Listing 8.48. It is left up to the developer to populate this field. We will discuss derived fields later.

Listing 8.48 Declaring a Field to be Transient

```
@Entity
@Table(name="ORDERS")
public class Order implements Serializable {

    @Id
    protected int orderId;
    protected BigDecimal total;
    protected BigDecimal tax;
    @Transient
    protected BigDecimal totalAndTax;
```

The JPA specification defines default mappings between Java Types and Database types. It will handle most basic conversions between Strings and VARCAR and even Strings to number types. The `@Column` annotation and XML equivalent have additional attributes to customize the mapping.

- **`String name`**—The column name. Defaults to the field name.
- **`String columnDefinition`**—The database-specific column type name. This property is used only by vendors that support creating tables from your mapping metadata. During table creation, the vendor will use the value of the `columnDefinition` as the declared column type. If no `columnDefinition` is given, the vendor will choose an appropriate default based on the field type combined with the column's length, precision, and scale.
- **`int length`**—The column length. This property is typically used only during table creation, though some vendors might use it to validate data before flushing. `CHAR` and `VARCHAR` columns typically default to a length of 255; other column types use the database default.
- **`int precision`**—The precision of a numeric column. This property is often used in conjunction with `scale` to form the proper column type name during table creation.
- **`int scale`**—The number of decimal digits a numeric column can hold. This property is often used in conjunction with `precision` to form the proper column type name during table creation.
- **`boolean nullable`**—Whether the column can store `null` values. Vendors may use this property both for table creation and at runtime; however, it is never required. Defaults to `true`.
- **`boolean insertable`**—By setting this property to `false`, you can omit the column from SQL `INSERT` statements. Defaults to `true`.
- **`boolean updatable`**—By setting this property to `false`, you can omit the column from SQL `UPDATE` statements. Defaults to `true`.
- **`String table`**—Sometimes you will need to map fields to tables other than the primary table. This property allows you to specify that the column resides in a secondary table. We will see how to map fields to secondary tables later in the chapter.

The JPA specification also helps deal with more complicated mapping like dates. The `@Temporal` annotation allows you to map a Java Date field to the appropriate database date type. Listing 8.49 shows an example of mapping a Java Date to a `TIMESTAMP` using the `@Temporal` annotation.

Listing 8.49 Declaring a Date Field to be Temporal

```
@Entity
@Table(name="ORDERS")
public class Order implements Serializable {

    @Id
    protected int orderId;
    protected BigDecimal total;
    protected BigDecimal tax;
    @Transient
    protected BigDecimal  totalAndTax;
    @Temporal(TemporalType.TIMESTAMP)
    protected java.util.Date orderCreated;
```

OpenJPA also supports mapping fields to CLOB or BLOB columns using the `@Lob` annotation. Listing 8.50 shows an example of using `@Lob` to map a JPEG of the picture into a database column.

Listing 8.50 Declaring a Lob Mapping Type

```
@Entity
public class Product implements Serializable {
    @Id
    protected int productId;
    protected String name;
    protected String description;
    @Lob
    protected JPEG picture;
```

In Java 5, you can use Enumerations. You can mark your mapping to say which value (ordinal or String) you want to persist. Listing 8.51 shows how you can mark the status enumeration to be treated as the String value in the mapping.

Listing 8.51 Declaring Enumerated Field Mapping Types

```
@Entity
@Table(name="ORDERS")
public class Order implements Serializable {
```

```
    @Id
    @GeneratedValue(strategy=GenerationType.IDENTITY)
    @Column(name="ORDER_ID")
    protected int orderId;
    protected BigDecimal total;

    public static enum Status { OPEN, SUBMITTED, CLOSED }
    @Enumerated(EnumType.STRING)
    protected Status status;
```

The default is Ordinal, but you can change the default value using OpenJPA-specific settings.

JPA supports customizing the fetch option of a field as well. You can fetch any field eagerly (loaded when the object is loaded) versus lazy (loaded when a field is accessed on the managed object). Eager is the default setting. Listing 8.52 shows an example of mapping the JPEG field with a fetch pattern of lazy.

Listing 8.52 Declaring the Fetch style

```
@Entity
public class Product implements Serializable {

    @Id
    protected int productId;
    protected String name;
    protected String description;

    @Lob
    @Basic(fetch=FetchType.Lazy)
    protected JPEG picture;
```

OpenJPA provides an `@ExternalValues` annotation for extending the default mapping. In addition, you can create custom types. See the OpenJPA documentation for more details.

Contained Objects

JPA supports contained objects, which are called embedded objects. For example, suppose there is an Address object associated with a Customer object in our domain model, but the database has only the Customer table with the address fields in it. Figure 8.4 shows this mapping.

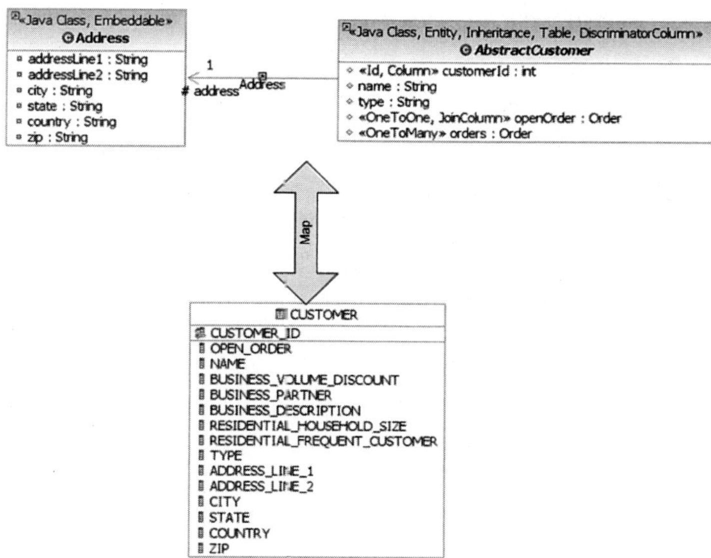

Figure 8.4 Component mapping.

When creating the Address class, you would annotate it as `@Embeddable`. You can add column mappings on that class as well. Listing 8.53 shows the Address class.

Listing 8.53 Marking an Object as Embeddable

```
@Embeddable
public class Address implements Serializable{
    @Column(name="ADDRESS_LINE_1")
    private String addressLine1;

    @Column(name="ADDRESS_LINE_2")
    private String addressLine2;
    private String city;
    private String state;
    private String country;
    private String zip;
```

Then you can declare an address instance as a member of the class and mark it as `Embedded`, as shown in Listing 8.54.

Listing 8.54 Embedding an Embeddable Object

```
@Entity
@Inheritance(strategy=SINGLE_TABLE)
@Table(name = "CUSTOMER")
@DiscriminatorColumn(name="TYPE", discriminatorType = STRING)
public abstract class AbstractCustomer implements Serializable {

    @Id
    @Column(name="CUSTOMER_ID")
    protected int customerId;
    protected String name;
    protected String type;

    ...
    @Embedded
    protected Address address;
```

The Embedded annotation also allows you to override the mapping in case you want to embed the Address into another object where the column names in the associated relational table are likely different. You would use special override annotations to do this; refer to the OpenJPA specification for more details.

OpenJPA supports the reverse scenario as well—in which you may have a single object but multiple tables. Suppose that this time your domain model has a Customer object with the address information declared as properties rather than as a separate Address object, but in the relational database there were a CUSTOMER table and an ADDRESS table. Figure 8.5 shows the mapping.

In this case, the ADDRESS table's primary key is also a foreign key to the CUSTOMER table. The mapping for the Customer object will look as shown in Listing 8.55. In JPA, you use the `@SecondaryTable` annotation to denote the address table. Then you add the table attribute to each `@Column` annotation you want mapped to the secondary table. You can have several secondary tables allowing you to map several tables that share a primary key to a single object.

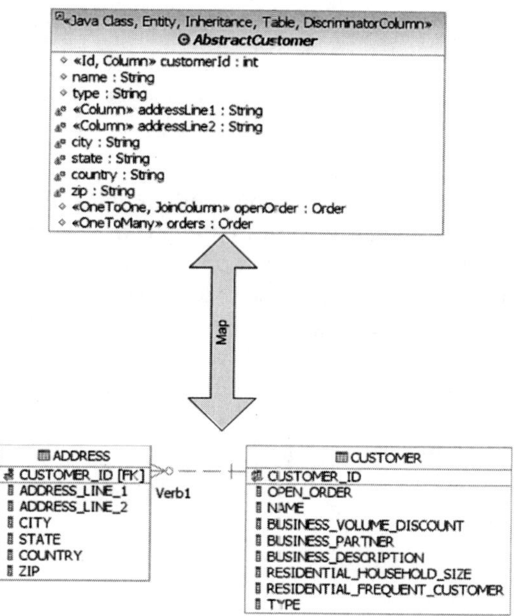

Figure 8.5 Secondary table.

Listing 8.55 Secondary Table Annotation

```
@Entity
@Inheritance(strategy=SINGLE_TABLE)
@Table(name = "CUSTOMER")
@SecondaryTable(name="ADDRESS")
@DiscriminatorColumn(name="TYPE", discriminatorType = STRING)
public abstract class AbstractCustomer implements Serializable {

    @Id
    @Column(name="CUSTOMER_ID")
    protected int customerId;
    protected String name;
    protected String type;

    @Column(name="ADDRESS_LINE_1",table="ADDRESS")
    private String addressLine1;

    @Column(name="ADDRESS_LINE_2",table="ADDRESS")
```

```
    private String addressLine2;

    ...
```

Relationships

OpenJPA supports mapping one-to-one, one-to-many, many-to-one, and many-to-many relationships. It allows relationships to be either unmanaged (unidirectional) or managed (bidirectional). The annotations or XML match the type of relationship: `@OneToOne`, `@OneToMany`, `@ManyToOne`, and `@ManyToMany`. Without any database mappings, the default mapping will use a naming convention for foreign keys. However, you can specify the keys by using the `@JoinColumn`, as shown in Listing 8.56. This listing shows an example of a One-to-One relationship between Customers. You can also define the fetch behavior much like you can with a field, and the behavior for operations against the root object. Cascading operations were shown earlier in the chapter.

Listing 8.56 One-to-One Relationship

```
@Entity
@Inheritance(strategy=SINGLE_TABLE)
@Table(name = "CUSTOMER")
@DiscriminatorColumn(name="TYPE", discriminatorType = STRING)
public abstract class AbstractCustomer implements Serializable {

    @Id
    @Column(name="CUSTOMER_ID")
    protected int customerId;
    protected String name;
    protected String type;

    @OneToOne(
        fetch=FetchType.EAGER,
        cascade = {CascadeType.MERGE,
                   CascadeType.REFRESH},
        optional=true
    )
    @JoinColumn(name="OPEN_ORDER", referencedColumnName = "ORDER_ID")
    protected Order openOrder;
```

In our example, the Customer also has a one-to-many relationship with all the Orders, as shown in Listing 8.57. You will notice that no Join Column is specified. Instead, the `mappedBy` attribute is used to define a bidirectional relationship.

Listing 8.57 One-to-Many Relationship

```
@Entity
@Inheritance(strategy=SINGLE_TABLE)
@Table(name = "CUSTOMER")
@DiscriminatorColumn(name="TYPE", discriminatorType = STRING)
public abstract class AbstractCustomer implements Serializable {

    @Id
    @Column(name="CUSTOMER_ID")
    protected int customerId;
    protected String name;
    protected String type;

    @OneToOne(
        fetch=FetchType.EAGER,
        cascade = {CascadeType.MERGE,
                   CascadeType.REFRESH},
        optional=true
    )
    @JoinColumn(name="OPEN_ORDER", referencedColumnName = "ORDER_ID")
    protected Order openOrder;

    @OneToMany(mappedBy="customer",fetch=FetchType.LAZY)
    protected Set<Order> orders;
```

Listing 8.58 shows the other side of the relationship. The Order has a reference to Customer and it has a many-to-one relationship. Notice it defines all the metadata for the bidirectional relationship.

Listing 8.58 Many-to-One Relationship

```
@Entity
@Table(name="ORDERS")
public class Order implements Serializable {
    private static final long serialVersionUID = 7779370942277849463L;


    @Id
    @GeneratedValue(strategy=GenerationType.IDENTITY)
    @Column(name="ORDER_ID")
    protected int orderId;
    protected BigDecimal total;
```

```
    public static enum Status { OPEN, SUBMITTED, CLOSED }
    @Enumerated(EnumType.STRING)
    protected Status status;

    @ManyToOne
    @JoinColumn(
        name="CUSTOMER_ID", referencedColumnName="CUSTOMER_ID"
    )
    protected AbstractCustomer customer;
```

Listing 8.59 shows Order's one-to-many relationship to LineItems. This is a unidirectional relationship because LineItem does not have a reference to Order. In this case, notice the use of a special `@ElementJoinColumn`. This is an OpenJPA extension that allows you to define the metadata for a one-to-many one-way mapping.

Listing 8.59 One-to-Many Relationship

```
@Entity
@Table(name="ORDERS")
public class Order implements Serializable {

    // Removing code that is the same as in Listing 8.58

    @OneToMany(cascade=CascadeType.REMOVE,fetch=FetchType.EAGER )
    @ElementJoinColumn(
        name="ORDER_ID", referencedColumnName="ORDER_ID"
    )
    protected Set<LineItem> lineitems;
```

Another way to map relationships in OpenJPA is through a join table, as described in Chapter 3. This is actually used for many-to-many relationships, but it can also be used for one-to-many and many-to-one relationships. As a matter of fact, join tables are the only implementation of unidirectional one-to-many relationships that the JPA specification demands for compliance. In Chapter 3 we show a PRODUCT_CATEORGY table that defines both keys for the product and category tables. A Product can belong to different categories, and a category groups many products.

Listing 8.60 shows a bidirectional relationship between products and categories.

Listing 8.60 Many-to-Many Relationship

```
@Entity
@NamedQuery(name="product.all",query="select p from Product p")
public class Product implements Serializable {
```

```
    @Id
    @Column(name="PRODUCT_ID")
    protected int productId;

    protected BigDecimal price;
    protected String description;


    @ManyToMany
    @JoinTable(name="PRODUCT_CATEGORY",
            joinColumns={@JoinColumn(name="PRODUCT_ID")},
            inverseJoinColumns={@JoinColumn(name="CAT_ID")}
    )
    protected Collection<Category> categories;

...


@Entity
public class Category implements Serializable {

    @Id
    protected int CAT_ID;
    protected String name;

    @ManyToMany(mappedBy="categories")
    protected Collection<Product> products;

    public int getCAT_ID() {
        return CAT_ID;
    }

...
```

Collection-based Entities can also be ordered using the `@OrderBy` annotation, as shown in Listing 8.61.

Listing 8.61 Order Constraint

```
@Entity
@Inheritance(strategy=SINGLE_TABLE)
@Table(name = "CUSTOMER")
@DiscriminatorColumn(name="TYPE", discriminatorType = STRING)
public abstract class AbstractCustomer implements Serializable {
```

```
    @Id
    @Column(name="CUSTOMER_ID")
    protected int customerId;
    protected String name;
    protected String type;

    @OrderBy("status")
    protected Collection orders;
```

Constraints

OpenJPA allows you to define constraints on various mappings as well as work with database constraints. Some constraints have special annotations, whereas others are attributes on another annotation. Listing 8.62 shows an example of a unique constraint that declares the field as suitable for a key.

Listing 8.62 Unique Constraint

```
@Entity
@Inheritance(strategy=SINGLE_TABLE)
@Table(name = "CUSTOMER")
@DiscriminatorColumn(name="TYPE", discriminatorType = STRING)
public abstract class AbstractCustomer implements Serializable {

    @Id
    @Column(name="CUSTOMER_ID")
    protected int customerId;
    protected String name;
    protected String type;

    @Unique
    protected String ssID;
```

Refer once again to the associated OpenJPA documentation for a list of other constraints supported [OpenJPA 2].

Derived Attributes

Earlier, we showed that we can make a field transient with annotations in the code or XML mapping file. Often, you need to calculate transient fields based on other persistent fields. To do this properly, you need to know when data is loaded and persisted to manage the state of the object. Although Entities are just POJOs in OpenJPA, you can define Entity Listener methods on the POJO, or attach an `EntityListener` class to the POJO. Listing 8.63 shows an example of marking a method with the `@PostLoad` annotation, which causes the method to be invoked after the data is loaded.

Listing 8.63 Life Cycle Methods

```
@Entity
@Table(name="ORDERS")
public class Order implements Serializable {


    @Id
    protected int orderId;
    protected BigDecimal total;
    protected BigDecimal tax;
    @Transient protected BigDecimal totalAndTax; //Not persisted

    @PostLoad
    protected void calculateTotal() {
        totalAndTax =
        total+tax;
    }
}
```

As you can see from Listing 8.63, the `totalAndTax` field will not be set until the object is loaded and the persistent fields have been set.

JPA also supports the following callbacks for life cycle events and their corresponding method markers:

- **`PrePersist`**—Methods marked with this annotation will be invoked before an object is persisted. This could be used for assigning primary key values to persistent objects. This is equivalent to the XML element tag `pre-persist`.
- **`PostPersist`**—Methods marked with this annotation will be invoked after an object has transitioned to the persistent state. You might want to use such methods to update a screen after a new row is added. This is equivalent to the XML element tag `post-persist`.
- **`PostLoad`**—Methods marked with this annotation will be invoked after all eagerly fetched fields of your class have been loaded from the datastore. No other persistent fields can be accessed in this method. This is equivalent to the XML element tag `post-load`.
- **`PreUpdate`**—This is the complement to `PostLoad`. While methods marked with `PostLoad` are most often used to initialize nonpersistent values from persistent data, methods annotated with `PreUpdate` are normally used to set persistent fields with information cached in nonpersistent data.
- **`PostUpdate`**—Methods marked with this annotation will be invoked after changes to a given instance have been stored to the datastore. This is useful for clearing stale data cached at the application layer. This is equivalent to the XML element tag `post-update`.

- `PreRemove`—Methods marked with this annotation will be invoked before an object transactions to the deleted state. Access to persistent fields is valid within this method. You might use this method to cascade the deletion to related objects based on complex criteria, or to perform other cleanup. This is equivalent to the XML element tag `pre-remove`.
- `PostRemove`—Methods marked with this annotation will be invoked after an object has been marked as to be deleted. This is equivalent to the XML element tag `post-remove`.

You can also externalize the callback methods to a different class using the `@EntityListener` annotation on the class. Refer to the OpenJPA documentation for more details.

Tuning Options

Query Optimizations

Some vendors allow an option to compile the associated SQL at build time, which can greatly improve performance. Also, it is possible to create named queries that enable specifying the SQL in the external configuration file. The SQL can then be tuned separately from the code.

Caching

The JPA specification defines two levels of caching: one that is scoped to the Entity Manager and another that is scoped to the Persistent Unit. The Entity Manager level cache is associated with a current transaction unless you are using the Extended Context—in which you can scope the cache to the life cycle of a Stateful Session Bean. We discussed this life cycle earlier in the "Programming Model" section. The JPA Entity Manager has a flush method you can invoke to clear the cache and push changes to the database.

The Entity Manager cache is there is for keeping data around during a multi-request flow, often called a "conversation;" however, the persistence unit cache is meant to really be a performance booster for read-only or read-mostly data. OpenJPA provides a data-level cache at the persistence unit level. OpenJPA provides a Single JVM cache provider. This may be ideal for read-only data that is initialized during the startup of an application. To use it, you can configure a cache provider on the persistence unit. Listing 8.64 shows an example of configuring the single JVM cache.

Listing 8.64 Caching

```
<persistence-unit name="pie-db-JAVA-SE">
    <provider>
    org.apache.openjpa.persistence.PersistenceProviderImpl
    </provider>
```

```
    <properties>
        <property name="openjpa.MaxFetchDepth" value="5"/>
        <property name="openjpa.jdbc.MappingDefaults"
            value="StoreEnumOrdinal=false"/>
        <property name="openjpa.ConnectionURL"
            value="jdbc:derby://localhost:1527/PWTE"/>
        <property name="openjpa.ConnectionDriverName"
          value="org.apache.derby.jdbc.ClientDriver"/>
        <property name="openjpa.jdbc.DBDictionary" value="derby"/>
        <property name="openjpa.jdbc.Schema" value="APP"/>
        <property name="openjpa.DataCache" value="true"/>
    </properties>
</persistence-unit>
```

After you configure the cache, you can configure whichever entity you need to cache. For example, in Listing 8.65 we cache the product data. In the listing, the timeout attribute of the annotation specifies when the provider should invalidate the cache from when the data was first created.

Listing 8.65 Life Cycle Methods

```
import org.apache.openjpa.persistence.DataCache;

@Entity
@NamedQuery(name="product.all",query="select p from Product p")
@DataCache(timeout=6000000)
public class Product implements Serializable {

        @Id
        @Column(name="PRODUCT_ID")
        protected int productId;
```

A single JVM often will not work for read-mostly cases or distributed cache facilities meant to deal with large volumes of data in a distributed fashion to alleviate database contention. There are some distributed cache technologies that specialize in these situations. IBM WebSphere Extended Data Grid [DataGrid] also allows you to work with distributed cache technologies as a second-level cache to OpenJPA, as well as supporting other patterns for using JPA with cached data.

A.8.4

OpenJPA also supports a QueryCache to cache the results of queries so that they can be reused without going back to the database. See the OpenJPA documentation for more details.

Loading Related Objects

OpenJPA supports both eager and lazy loading. We showed in the "Attributes" and "Relationships" sections that you can mark a field or relationship with a fetch *type*. In addition, OpenJPA supports fetch *groups* that allow you to link objects that are logically linked together in your application. If you have a class with two lazy fields, but you know in your application that when you load one, you will most likely load the other, you can configure a fetch group. Listing 8.66 shows how to load Customer and LineItem objects together whenever the other is accessed in the context of a lazily loaded Order.

Listing 8.66 Fetch Groups

```
@Entity
@FetchGroups({
    @FetchGroup(name="detail", attributes={
        @FetchAttribute(name="lineItems"),
        @FetchAttribute(name="customers")
    })
class Order
```

This `FetchGroups` feature can be very important to minimize the number of round trips to the database at the same time that you minimize the initial load time of an object.

Locking

A.8.5

OpenJPA provides both configuring and an API option for affecting the desired locking level. For more details on database locking, see the paper titled *"Locking Strategies for Database Access."*

In addition, because OpenJPA supports disconnected patterns, you can use the `@Version` annotation to map a particular version column to a database. Listing 8.67 shows how simple this task can be.

Listing 8.67 Version Number

```
@Entity
public class Order {

    @Id private String orderId;
    @Version private int version;
```

Remember that when an object becomes disassociated with its EntityManager, it becomes disconnected. When the object is reattached, OpenJPA will check whether the version number has changed in the database before performing the updates. When the JPA runtime detects an attempt to concurrently modify the same record, it throws an exception to the transaction attempting to commit last. This prevents overwriting the previous commit with stale data.

A version field is not always required, but without one, concurrent threads or processes might succeed in making conflicting changes to the same record at the same time.

Development Process of the Common Example

Now that we have gone through OpenJPA in detail, we will show you the steps required to develop a complete application. To run it yourself, follow the directions in Appendix A, "Setting Up the Common Example." Keep in mind that Chapter 2, "High-Level Requirements and Persistence," and Chapter 3, "Designing Persistent Object Services," describe the requirements and design of our example. This section focuses on the details related to developing OpenJPA applications after you understand the requirements and settle on a design.

Defining the Object

When developing an OpenJPA application, you define your objects by coding Java Classes with annotations, and then coding XML mapping files. The following listings show our domain model implemented in Java with OpenJPA annotations being used to specify the mapping metadata. We only show subsets of the classes to illustrate the mapping. You can examine all the code by downloading the sample as shown in Appendix A. Listing 8.68 lists the `AbstractCustomer` superclass. It is mapped using a Single Table Strategy. Besides the defaulted primitive value fields, we explicitly map the open order field as a one-to-one relationship to the ORDERS table because a Customer object may have at most one open order, and we map the orders field as a one-to-many relationship with respect to the ORDERS table because a Customer might refer to more than one in any state, including `open`. The orders field is declared a bidirectional relationship, and therefore additional details are defined on the Order side. We also define an Eager fetching strategy, because we want to fetch the open order record whenever the customer is accessed. We use a `Lazy` option to load the orders collection only when we specifically access the history.

Listing 8.68 Abstract Customer

```
@Entity
@Inheritance(strategy=SINGLE_TABLE)
@Table(name = "CUSTOMER")
@DiscriminatorColumn(name="TYPE", discriminatorType = STRING)
public abstract class AbstractCustomer implements Serializable {

    @Id
    @Column(name="CUSTOMER_ID")
    protected int customerId;
```

```
    protected String name;
    protected String type;


    @OneToOne(
        fetch=FetchType.EAGER,
        cascade = {CascadeType.MERGE,CascadeType.REFRESH},
        optional=true
    )
    @JoinColumn(name="OPEN_ORDER", referencedColumnName = "ORDER_ID")
    protected Order openOrder;
    @OneToMany(mappedBy="customer",fetch=FetchType.LAZY)
    protected Set<Order> orders;

    ... //Gettters and Setters...
}
```

Listing 8.69 shows the `ResidentialCustomer` subclass. Notice we used the `DiscriminatorValue` to determine the type. We described this in the Inheritance section of the template.

Listing 8.69 Residential Customer

```
@Entity
@DiscriminatorValue("RESIDENTAL")
public class ResidentialCustomer
extends AbstractCustomer implements Serializable {
    @Column(name="RESIDENTIAL_HOUSEHOLD_SIZE")
    protected short householdSize;
    @Column(name="RESIDENTIAL_FREQUENT_CUSTOMER")
    protected boolean frequentCustomer;
    //Getters and Setters...
}
```

Listing 8.70 shows the `BusinessCustomer` subclass, which is similar to the `ResidentialCustomer` subclass.

Listing 8.70 Business Customer

```
@Entity
@DiscriminatorValue("BUSINESS")
public class BusinessCustomer extends AbstractCustomer implements Serializable {
    @Column(name="BUSINESS_VOLUME_DISCOUNT")
```

```
    protected boolean volumeDiscount;
    @Column(name="BUSINESS_PARTNER")
    protected boolean businessPartner;
    @Column(name="BUSINESS_DESCRIPTION")
    protected String description;
    //Getters and Setters...
}
```

Listing 8.71 shows the `Order` object. We elected to generate the Order ID using the Identity Strategy because this primary key is bound to a single table. We also map a relationship back to the `AbstractCustomer` using `ManyToOne`. The detail of this bidirectional relationship is defined on the `Order` object.

The `Order` object also has a Set of LineItems for the Order that implements a unidirectional relationship between the Order and LineItem classes. We have no requirement to navigate from a LineItem to an Order; defining a single-sided relationship will make the underlying SQL optimal.

Listing 8.71 Order Object

```
@Entity
@Table(name="ORDERS")
public class Order implements Serializable {
    @Id
    @GeneratedValue(strategy=GenerationType.IDENTITY)
    @Column(name="ORDER_ID")
    protected int orderId;
    protected BigDecimal total;
    public static enum Status { OPEN, SUBMITTED, CLOSED }
    @Enumerated(EnumType.STRING)
    protected Status status;
    @ManyToOne
    @JoinColumn(
        name="CUSTOMER_ID", referencedColumnName = "CUSTOMER_ID"
    )
    protected AbstractCustomer customer;

    @OneToMany(cascade=CascadeType.REMOVE,fetch=FetchType.EAGER )
    @ElementJoinColumn(name="ORDER_ID",referencedColumnName="ORDER_ID"
    )
    protected Set<LineItem> lineitems;

    //getters and setters
}
```

Listing 8.72 shows the LineItem class. You will notice that the LineItem class is a composite key. This choice was made to illustrate how to map to certain legacy schemas. ORM technologies tend to work better with generated keys. The LineItem also has a one-to-one relationship to the Product. This is also a unidirectional relationship because there is no requirement to navigate from a Product instance to the LineItem objects that reference it. Product instances also usually are cached because the product catalog changes infrequently.

Listing 8.72 LineItem

```
@Entity
@Table(name="LINE_ITEM")
@IdClass(LineItemId.class)
@NamedQuery(name="existing.lineitem.forproduct",
    query="select l from LineItem l
           where l.productId = :productId and l.orderId = :orderId"
)

public class LineItem implements Serializable {
    @Id
    @Column(name="ORDER_ID")
    private int orderId;

    @Id
    @Column(name="PRODUCT_ID")
    private int productId;
    protected long quantity;
    protected BigDecimal amount;

    @ManyToOne(fetch = FetchType.EAGER)
    @JoinColumns({
        @JoinColumn(name="PRODUCT_ID",
            referencedColumnName = "PRODUCT_ID"
        )}
    )
    protected Product product;

    //getters and setters
}
```

Listing 8.73 shows the composite primary key for the `LineItem` Entity.

Listing 8.73 Line Item ID

```
@Embeddable
public class LineItemId implements Serializable{
    private int orderId;
    private int productId;
    //getters and setters
    @Override
    public int hashCode() {
        //unique hashcode
    }
    @Override
    public boolean equals(Object obj) {
        //equals
    }
}
```

Listing 8.74 shows the Product. The Product is a simple class that is mapped to the PRODUCT table. It has no relationships. (Real products usually have many more details and belong to categories and such.) We have added a `NamedQuery` to the Product annotations to specify a query that retrieves the list of products. As noted previously, we also cache the Product. This example should not be considered complete and is for demonstration purposes only; products in real enterprise systems are usually indexed, categorized, and related to extensive catalog and inventory management systems.

Listing 8.74 Product

```
@Entity
@NamedQuery(name="product.all",query="select p from Product p")
@DataCache(timeout=6000000)
public class Product implements Serializable {
    @Id
    @Column(name="PRODUCT_ID")
    protected int productId;
    protected BigDecimal price;
    protected String description;
    //getters and setters
}
```

We did not employ the option to provide XML mapping files. OpenJPA is meant to reduce the number of artifacts one has to develop. We could have chosen to minimize the annotations and specify the mapping inside XML descriptors. For example, in a real application, we recommend externalizing the cache period and the named query so that the code need not change to modify these parameters.

Key Point

It is a best practice to externalize named queries and cache configurations in EJB XML deployment descriptors and not to place them in the source.

Implementing the Services

This section shows the implementation of the Service. For OpenJPA, we provided both an EJB 3 version of the service and a Java SE version. Because EJB 3 Session Beans are Java classes, the Java SE version just extends the proper EJB 3 class and bootstraps the EntityManager as described earlier. Figure 8.6 shows all the exceptions for our services. See the downloadable sample or refer to Chapter 3 for details.

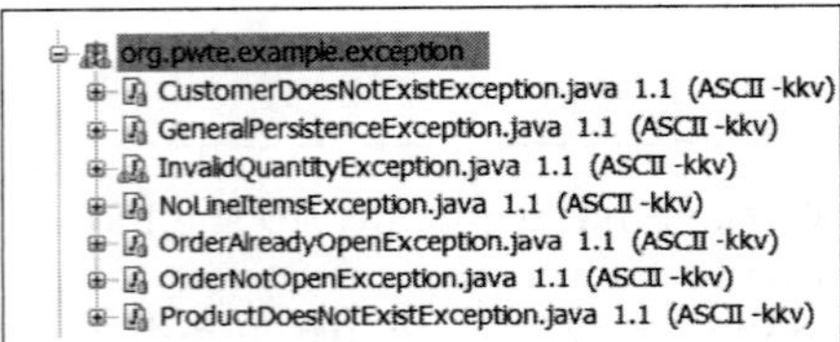

Figure 8.6 Exceptions from the common example.

We have two implementations of our service: one for Java SE using OpenJPA and another using IBM JPA (built on OpenJPA) for EJB 3. The interface for the service was introduced in Chapter 3, so refer to the details there. For the EJB 3 version, the service interface has an extra `@Local` annotation to denote a Local EJB. The service implementations vary slightly from a bootstrapping standpoint with Java SE.

Specifically, the Java SE version of the application looks up the EntityManager using the EntityManagerFactory, as illustrated earlier in Figure 8.3. The EJB 3 version is illustrated earlier in Figure 8.5.

The `loadCustomer` operation uses the EntityManager `find` method to look up the customer. Because the mapping file defined the proper eager loading, it will load the customer record, an open order if it exists, and any line items for that order. The Inheritance is also automatic; based on the type, it will return the correct subclass. All this happens with one call. Listing 8.75 shows the `loadCustomer` method as implemented in the EJB 3 version. The Java SE version uses transaction demarcation. You can examine the downloadable source to see the difference. Appendix A shows how to load the code into your Eclipse-based development environment.

Listing 8.75 The loadCustomer Implementation

```
public AbstractCustomer loadCustomer(int customerId)
throws ExistException,GeneralPersistenceException {
    AbstractCustomer customer = em.find(
        AbstractCustomer.class, customerId
    );
    return customer;
}
```

The `openOrder` operation creates an order Java Object and persists it. It then sets the new order onto the customer instance. The transaction is implied because of the nature of EJBs. The openOrder routine will check if an order is open and throw an exception if it is. Listing 8.76 shows the implementation.

Listing 8.76 The openOrder Implementation

```
public Order openOrder(int customerId)
throws CustomerDoesNotExistException, OrderAlreadyOpenException,
       GeneralPersistenceException{
    AbstractCustomer customer = loadCustomer(customerId);
    Order existingOpenOrder = customer.getOpenOrder();
    if(existingOpenOrder != null) {
        throw new OrderAlreadyOpenException();
    }
    Order newOrder = new Order();
    newOrder.setCustomer(customer);
    newOrder.setStatus(Order.Status.OPEN);
    newOrder.setTotal(new BigDecimal(0));
    em.persist(newOrder);
    customer.setOpenOrder(newOrder);
    return newOrder;
}
```

The implementation for the addLineItem operation first checks to see whether the Product exists using the EntityManager `find` method as seen in the other examples. It then queries to check whether a Line Item already exists, and updates the quantity if it does. Otherwise, it creates a new instance. Again, the transaction is implied due to the EJB 3 method. Listing 8.77 shows the implementation of `addLineItem`.

Listing 8.77 The addLineItem Implementation

```
public LineItem addLineItem(
    int customerId,
```

```
    int productId,
    long quantity)
throws CustomerDoesNotExistException,
       OrderNotOpenException,
       ProductDoesNotExistException,
       GeneralPersistenceException,
       InvalidQuantityException {
    Product product = em.find(Product.class,productId);
    if(quantity <= 0 ) throw new InvalidQuantityException();
    if(product == null) throw new ProductDoesNotExistException();
    AbstractCustomer customer = loadCustomer(customerId);
    Order existingOpenOrder = customer.getOpenOrder();
    if(existingOpenOrder == null) {
        throw new OrderNotOpenException();
    }
    BigDecimal amount = product.getPrice().multiply(
        new BigDecimal(quantity)
    );
    existingOpenOrder.setTotal(
        amount.add(existingOpenOrder.getTotal())
    );
    LineItemId lineItemId = new LineItemId();
    lineItemId.setProductId(productId);
    lineItemId.setOrderId(existingOpenOrder.getOrderId());
    LineItem existingLineItem = em.find(LineItem.class,lineItemId);
    if(existingLineItem == null) {
        LineItem lineItem = new LineItem();
        lineItem.setOrderId(existingOpenOrder.getOrderId());
        lineItem.setProductId(product.getProductId());
        lineItem.setAmount(amount);
        lineItem.setProduct(product);
        lineItem.setQuantity(quantity);
        em.persist(lineItem);
        return lineItem;
    }
    else {
        existingLineItem.setQuantity(
            existingLineItem.getQuantity() + quantity
        );
        existingLineItem.setAmount(
            existingLineItem.getAmount().add(amount)
        );
```

```
        return existingLineItem;
    }
}
```

The `removeLineItem` operation simply deletes the LineItem by finding the record and removing it. Listing 8.78 shows the implementation.

Listing 8.78 The removeLineItem Implementation

```
public void removeLineItem(
    int customerId,
    int productId
)
throws CustomerDoesNotExistException,
       OrderNotOpenException,
       ProductDoesNotExistException,
       NoLineItemsException,
       GeneralPersistenceException {
    Product product = em.find(Product.class,productId);
    if(product == null) throw new ProductDoesNotExistException();
    AbstractCustomer customer = loadCustomer(customerId);
    Order existingOpenOrder = customer.getOpenOrder();
    if(existingOpenOrder == null ||
       existingOpenOrder.getStatus() != Order.Status.OPEN)
        throw new OrderNotOpenException();
    LineItemId lineItemId = new LineItemId();
    lineItemId.setProductId(productId);
    lineItemId.setOrderId(existingOpenOrder.getOrderId());
    LineItem existingLineItem = em.find(LineItem.class,lineItemId);
    if(existingLineItem != null) {
        em.remove(existingLineItem);
    }
    else {
        throw new NoLineItemsException();
    }
}
```

The `submitOrder` operation is almost as simple—it changes the status of the order and removes it from the `openOrder` property of the abstract customer class. Listing 8.79 shows the `submitOrder` implementation.

Listing 8.79 The submitOrder Implementation

```
public void submit(int customerId)
throws CustomerDoesNotExistException, OrderNotOpenException,
       NoLineItemsException,
       GeneralPersistenceException {
    AbstractCustomer customer = loadCustomer(customerId);
    Order existingOpenOrder = customer.getOpenOrder();
    if(existingOpenOrder == null ||
       existingOpenOrder.getStatus() != Order.Status.OPEN)
        throw new OrderNotOpenException();
    if(existingOpenOrder.getLineitems() == null ||
       existingOpenOrder.getLineitems().size() <= 0 )
        throw new NoLineItemsException();
    existingOpenOrder.setStatus(Order.Status.SUBMITTED);
    customer.setOpenOrder(null);
}
```

Packaging the Components

The environment you deploy to will affect how the application is packaged. A Java SE environment may require you to copy files, or package the code into a JAR. You most likely have to write some deployment scripts. Figure 8.7 shows the Java Project in Eclipse. It is a plain Java Project with the `persistence.xml` defined in the `meta-inf` directory. The `persistence.xml` is necessary to obtain the connection.

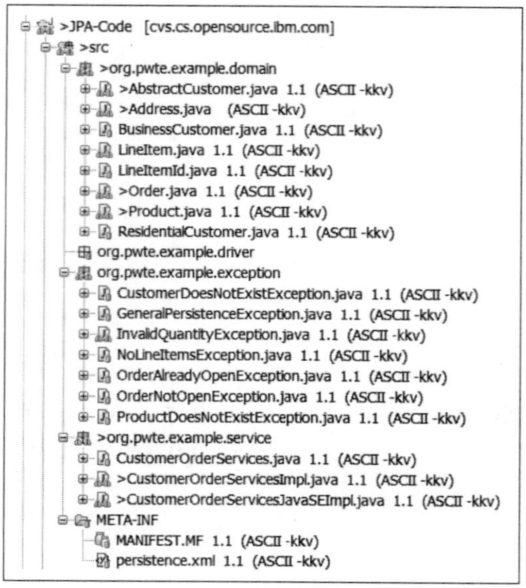

```
>JPA-Code [cvs.cs.opensource.ibm.com]
  >src
    >org.pwte.example.domain
      >AbstractCustomer.java 1.1 (ASCII -kkv)
      >Address.java (ASCII -kkv)
      BusinessCustomer.java 1.1 (ASCII -kkv)
      LineItem.java 1.1 (ASCII -kkv)
      LineItemId.java 1.1 (ASCII -kkv)
      >Order.java 1.1 (ASCII -kkv)
      >Product.java 1.1 (ASCII -kkv)
      ResidentialCustomer.java 1.1 (ASCII -kkv)
    org.pwte.example.driver
    org.pwte.example.exception
      CustomerDoesNotExistException.java 1.1 (ASCII -kkv)
      GeneralPersistenceException.java 1.1 (ASCII -kkv)
      InvalidQuantityException.java 1.1 (ASCII -kkv)
      NoLineItemsException.java 1.1 (ASCII -kkv)
      OrderAlreadyOpenException.java 1.1 (ASCII -kkv)
      OrderNotOpenException.java 1.1 (ASCII -kkv)
      ProductDoesNotExistException.java 1.1 (ASCII -kkv)
    >org.pwte.example.service
      CustomerOrderServices.java 1.1 (ASCII -kkv)
      >CustomerOrderServicesImpl.java 1.1 (ASCII -kkv)
      >CustomerOrderServicesJavaSEImpl.java 1.1 (ASCII -kkv)
    META-INF
      MANIFEST.MF 1.1 (ASCII -kkv)
      persistence.xml 1.1 (ASCII -kkv)
```

Figure 8.7 Packaging.

In a Java EE application, you usually have to package an application in an EAR file. Figure 8.8 shows the layout of the EAR file, which is made up of other files, such as EJB-JAR files for EJBs or WAR files for web applications. See the Java EE specification for details. Notice that we can use the same Java SE JAR as an EJB 3 module as well.

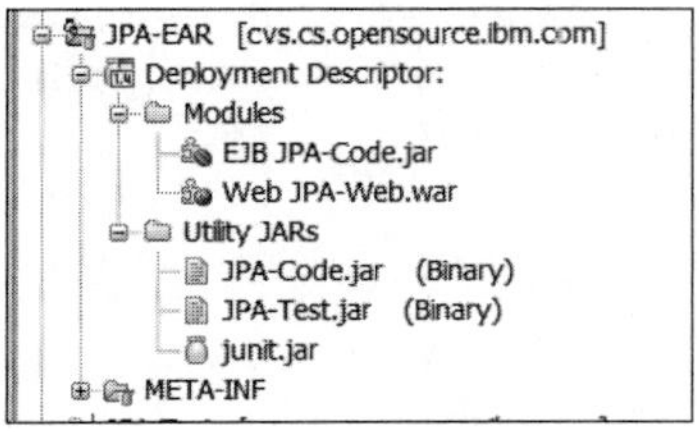

```
JPA-EAR [cvs.cs.opensource.ibm.com]
  Deployment Descriptor:
    Modules
      EJB JPA-Code.jar
      Web JPA-Web.war
    Utility JARs
      JPA-Code.jar (Binary)
      JPA-Test.jar (Binary)
      junit.jar
  META-INF
```

Figure 8.8 Java EE EAR.

The `persistence.xml` file is packaged in the `meta-inf` directory and contains our persistence units. We illustrated the format earlier. As with the operation implementations, you can examine the downloadable source for more details.

Unit Testing

Depending on the methodology, you may have coded your unit test before or after implementing the service operations. Agile methods usually push a test-driven approach and encourage coding test cases first. Regardless, our OpenJPA example contains the unit test to run the application. Figure 8.9 shows the Unit Test project for the common example.

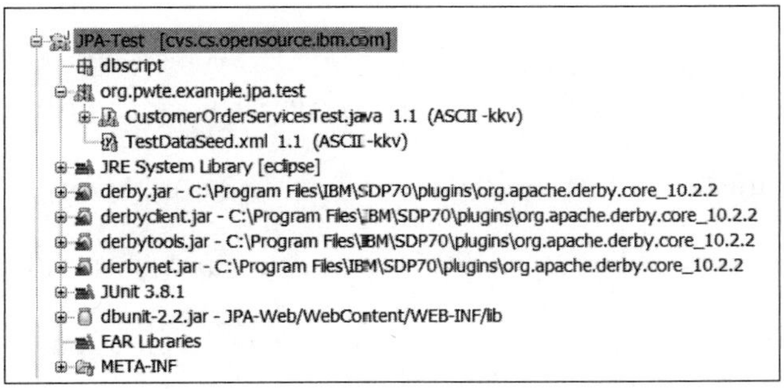

```
JPA-Test [cvs.cs.opensource.ibm.com]
  dbscript
  org.pwte.example.jpa.test
    CustomerOrderServicesTest.java 1.1 (ASCII -kkv)
    TestDataSeed.xml 1.1 (ASCII -kkv)
  JRE System Library [eclipse]
  derby.jar - C:\Program Files\IBM\SDP70\plugins\org.apache.derby.core_10.2.2
  derbyclient.jar - C:\Program Files\IBM\SDP70\plugins\org.apache.derby.core_10.2.2
  derbytools.jar - C:\Program Files\IBM\SDP70\plugins\org.apache.derby.core_10.2.2
  derbynet.jar - C:\Program Files\IBM\SDP70\plugins\org.apache.derby.core_10.2.2
  JUnit 3.8.1
  dbunit-2.2.jar - JPA-Web/WebContent/WEB-INF/lib
  EAR Libraries
  META-INF
```

Figure 8.9 Unit Test package.

Chapter 3 explains the aspects of the unit test that are the same regardless of the persistence mechanism used (as it should be). The only difference with OpenJPA is that we also provide the option to look up the Session Bean in the Java EE case and use JUnitEE to run it. There is no JPA-specific information within the unit test, but there is EJB information. As long as you have the Java EE API JARs, this unit test can run in both a Java SE environment and a standard Java EE environment. Examine the downloadable source for details and Appendix A for instructions on how to run them.

Deploying to Production

Deploying to production involves setting the proper configuration values for the target environment. Other than the common testing needed to move an application to production, there are no additional considerations other than those already specified in this section. In a Java SE environment, you have to run the bytecode enhancer yourself. In a Java EE container, like WebSphere Application Server, the bytecode enhancer is run automatically when the installation tools are run, so it will not be an explicit step.

Summary

OpenJPA is a very capable persistence technology. In addition to providing much function, it is based on a standard. Products like WebSphere Application Server provide enhanced versions of OpenJPA, and caching technologies like ObjectGrid can provide enterprise-quality applications. In this chapter, we showed you how to code against the OpenJPA APIs, map entities, and configure the system for your applications. The OpenJPA documentation can provide you with many more details. In addition, we showed you how to implement the services from the common example.

The JPA 2.0 specification was being written at the time of this writing. Some extensions from OpenJPA, Hibernate, and others may eventually be included in the specification. The Specification group is looking at the following items:

- Expanded object/relational mapping functionality, including greater flexibility in combining existing mapping options, support for collections of embedded objects, multiple levels of embedded objects, ordered lists, combinations of access types, and so forth.
- Additions to the Java Persistence query language.
- An API for "criteria" queries. Hibernate contains a Criteria API we covered in the previous chapter.
- Standardization of sets of "hints" for query configuration and for Entity Manager configuration.
- Standardization of additional metadata to support DDL generation and "Java2DB" mapping.
- Expanded pluggability contracts to support efficient passivation and replication of extended persistence contexts in Java EE environments.
- Standardization of additional contracts for entity detachment and merge, and persistence context management.
- Support for validation.

You should keep an eye on the progress of this specification and see which of these features actually get added to the standard.

Links to developerWorks

A.8.1 *Building EJB 3.0 applications with WebSphere Application Server*

This article shows you how to create EJB 3 style applications with IBM's JPA provider, which is built on OpenJPA.

www.ibm.com/developerworks/websphere/techjournal/0712_barcia/0712_barcia.html 2007

A.8.2 *Leveraging OpenJPA with WebSphere Application Server*

This article discusses configuring Apache OpenJPA with WebSphere Application Server version 6.1 when the EJB 3 Feature Pack is present.

www.ibm.com/developerworks/websphere/techjournal/0612_barcia/0612_barcia.html

A.8.3 *Migrating legacy Hibernate Applications to OpenJPA and EJB 3*

This article discusses best practices for migrating a Hibernate Core Application to OpenJPA

www.ibm.com/developerworks/websphere/techjournal/0708_vines/0708_vines.html

A.8.4 *Build Grid-Ready Apps with ObjectGrid*

Tutorial on building application for IBM ObjectGrid (renamed WebSphere XD DataGrid)

www.ibm.com/developerworks/edu/wes-dw-wes-objectgrid.html

A.8.5 *Locking Strategies for Database Access*

Excellent paper on database locking.

www.ibm.com/developerworks/websphere/techjournal/0603_ilechko/0603_ilechko.html

References

[Apache] *Apache Commons*. commons.apache.org/

[Bauer] Bauer, Christian and King, Gavin. *Java Persistence with Hibernate*. Manning Publications Company 2007

[DataGrid] *WebSphere Extended Deployment Data Grid*. www-306.ibm.com/software/webservers/appserv/extend/datagrid/

[Hibernate] *Java Persistence with Hibernate*. hibernate.org/397.html

[JPA 2] *JSR 317: Java Persistence 2.0*. jcp.org/en/jsr/detail?id=317

[JPQL] *JPQL Language Reference*. openjpa.apache.org/builds/1.0.1/apache-openjpa-1.0.1/docs/manual/jpa_langref.html

[Monson-Haefel] Burke, Bill and Monson-Haefel, Richard. *Enterprise JavaBeans 5th Edition*. O'Reilly 2006

[OpenJPA 1] *Apache Open JPA Home Page*. openjpa.apache.org/

[OpenJPA 2] *Open JPA Documentation*. openjpa.apache.org/documentation.html

[OpenJPA 3] *Open JPA Integration Index*. openjpa.apache.org/integration.html

[Serp] *Serp Homepage*. serp.sourceforge.net/

[TopLink] *TopLink JPA*. www.oracle.com/technology/products/ias/toplink/jpa/index.html

Chapter 9

pureQuery and Project Zero

Throughout this book, we have evaluated various persistence technologies. Up until now, the mechanisms we examined in this book have been standards based or open-source Java solutions—or both. In this chapter, we are going to deviate from this pattern and evaluate pureQuery, a commercial solution from IBM that represents a different approach. There are a number of reasons we think you should find it worthwhile to examine pureQuery:

- You may want to exploit new languages or new architectures. For example, in Chapter 2, "High-Level Requirements and Persistence," we discussed the emergence of Web 2.0 and how data access patterns are different. You may want a persistence solution that is optimized around the Web 2.0 style of development (sometimes called Web Oriented Architecture or Web Extended SOA). Today's Java standards and solutions are geared toward enterprise applications.
- Often, solutions use scripting languages such as Ruby on Rails; and a simplified persistence solution that exploits these languages will be required. In this chapter, we illustrate the use of a Java-based scripting language called Groovy and how pureQuery can be used in such a scripting environment.
- Performance may be the most important factor you consider in your requirements. In this case, a solution that is optimized for SQL or even a particular vendor's database product that you already use may be ideal.
- You will likely find that monitoring the end-to-end data access paths is required. Sometimes, persistence technologies optimized for a database can contain opportunities to inject (either through tooling or code) entry-points to data access monitoring features provided by the vendor. In this chapter, we explore the ability to monitor within pureQuery.

Background

pureQuery is an IBM solution for Java data access designed for performance and exploiting SQL. As with iBATIS evaluated in Chapter 6, the goal is to embrace rather than hide SQL. Unlike iBATIS, SQL can be embedded directly in the Java application code (as was done with SQL for Java), rather than specified indirectly in an annotation or a separate mapping file. To make this even easier, pureQuery can be used with a set of Eclipse Java plug-ins that can provide SQL assist inside your programs.

Type of Framework

At the core, pureQuery is a table gateway framework. However, all the patterns we have examined in this book can be implemented to some degree within pureQuery because it has multiple layers. For example, you can use the runtime API directly and implement the transaction script pattern. Using the pureQuery tools, you can generate a set of data objects based on SQL statements and database schemas and implement the gateway pattern. Finally, pureQuery can be used as an underlying layer to another ORM, which then can implement a full Domain Mapper—in this case, you might be using pureQuery indirectly through another mechanism and not even know it!

History

Java persistence has been dominated primarily by ORM frameworks. History has shown that since Java EE was created, there have been various attempts at ORM (CMP, JDO, Hibernate, and so on.). JPA seems to be the current emergent winner in that space. However, as stated, there is a considerable amount of time invested in tuning ORM-based applications for performance. In addition, there is a class of applications that use SQL directly for reasons we stated in the introduction to this chapter. Beyond these reasons, enterprise customers were explicitly asking IBM for a persistence framework to meet a number of additional requirements that we discussed briefly in Chapter 2. Figure 9.1 (repeated from Chapter 2) illustrates some of these requirements.

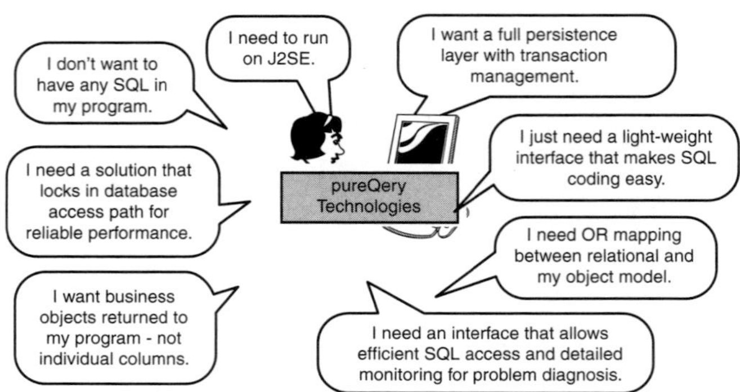

Figure 9.1 Persistence requirements considered in developing pureQuery.

IBM decided to create pureQuery as a common query engine that could be used in various environments to meet these and other requirements.

Architectural Overview

pureQuery is a high-performance Java data access platform focused on simplifying the tasks of developing and managing applications that access data. Its goal is to improve the life cycle of Java applications that access data. pureQuery takes an end-to-end view of the data access life cycle, from Java code to the relational database. Figure 9.2 illustrates this life cycle.

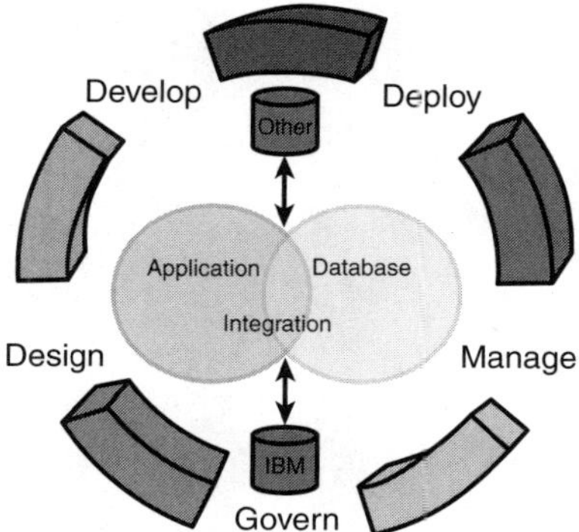

Figure 9.2 Persistence l fe cycle considered by pureQuery.

At each life-cycle stage, pureQuery attempts to meet several requirements and design goals:

- **Design**
  - Enable querying of different data sources, including Database, Cache, Collections, XML
  - Multiple API "styles" to integrate well with popular Java frameworks, including JPA
  - Minimize path length from application code to data access, including passing application SQL directly to the database
- **Develop**
  - Provide tools to embed SQL in a Java source file
  - Expose SQL APIs that are easy to invoke and extend
- **Deploy**
  - Generate code automatically when metadata styles are used
  - Optimize both dynamic and static SQL access paths for efficiency
- **Manage**
  - Make packaging as simple as possible
  - When data access problems occur, track SQL back to individual application source code components quickly across the application tiers

- **Govern**
  - Align with enterprise change control processes
  - Make security and access control to the data as simple as possible

From an architectural point of view, pureQuery is designed as a very thin layer on top of JDBC so that it can be used with many JDBC-compliant databases and serve as an implementation engine for other frameworks. Figure 9.3 shows an overview of pureQuery's layered architecture. It is worth noting that running pureQuery under a different ORM such as Hibernate and JPA is shown in the figure to illustrate what is possible. However, at the time of publication, these implementations are not yet available to the general public.

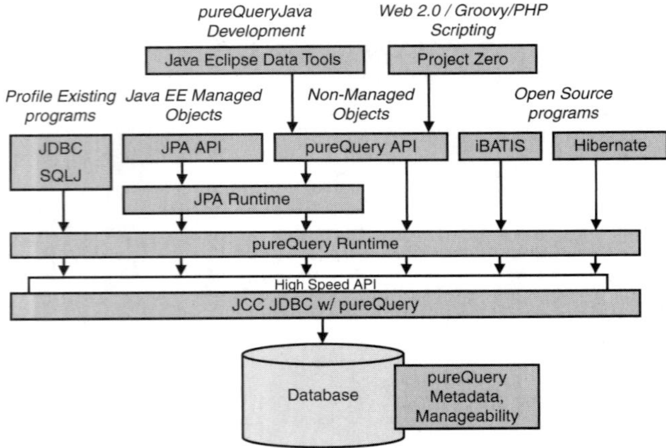

Figure 9.3 pureQuery architecture showing its layered approach.

This architecture enables pureQuery to meet the requirements listed for most databases, especially in the Design, Develop, and Deploy life cycle stages. However, because pureQuery is optimized to work with IBM DB2, it can exploit enhancements in the IBM DB2 JCC driver to achieve additional benefits, such as the following:

- Single API for joins in-memory across cache, relational, and in-memory objects. Joins in-memory across XML documents.
- Static SQL for better performance.
- Access path locked in at deployment for more reliable production runtime behavior.
- Multiple versions of the access path and the ability to easily revert to prior versions.
- Tooling to gather performance metrics, including historical trends at both the application and statement level.
- All SQL statements and access paths recorded in the DB2 server, which helps DBA with problem determination and capacity planning.
- Application origin captured for all SQL statements for rapid problem source identification across the application tiers and runtime stack.

Standards Adherence

The pureQuery technology itself is currently not part of a standard. That said, pureQuery-based applications can run inside Java SE and Java EE environments, and can be used in scripting environments such as Groovy. With pureQuery, your code will work with most JDBC-compliant databases, so you will not lose portability. In addition, if you use pureQuery under another framework, you can achieve better development productivity and runtime performance without your end users needing to know about it.

pureQuery was built by the IBM Information Management team in response to these requirements and is being extended by ProjectZero as needed to support Web 2.0 applications. Project Zero is an IBM incubator project focused on agile development of Web 2.0 applications based on Service Oriented Architecture (SOA). Web 2.0 applied to SOA allows Web artifacts based on HTTP and RESTful principles to extend the reach of SOA. This new architecture is referred to as *Web Extended SOA*. We will discuss these principles throughout this chapter. Fielding is the definitive source for more information on RESTful principles [Fielding].

The way the two are related is that pureQuery is used as a query engine for Project Zero. In addition to using the data APIs, Project Zero provides the capability to make use of scripting languages to access data directly through SQL. Project Zero allows for executing pureQuery using Groovy and PHP. Additionally, Milestone 2 includes a Resource Mapping for creating a standard mapping between RESTful services and data that exploits pureQuery.

Another thing that makes ProjectZero very exciting is its exciting new development approach called *Community-Driven Commercial Development* (CD/CD, or CD^2). CD^2 enables the user community to observe and influence technical decisions for ProjectZero (also called "Zero"). Furthermore, users have direct access to the Zero development team and the source code itself.

This approach should not be confused with Open Source, where the community can contribute to any aspect of the technology. Although you can contribute requirements, prototypes, and extensions to Zero, you cannot contribute directly to the core.

But similar to Open Source and Standards bodies, Project Zero's goals are both technical and social in nature.

The technical goals are to provide a scalable platform that simplifies Web Extended SOA application development in three important dimensions:

- **Create**—Simplify development with support for scripting languages (currently Groovy and PHP), conventions that promote RESTful patterns, and catalogs of reusable assets.
- **Assemble**—Enable rapid access and aggregation of disparate services into unified applications, including data flows, orchestrations, and custom mediations.
- **Deploy**—Provide an application-centric runtime environment based on the well-known and stable Java VM, and optimized for agile development (small footprint; fast restart).

The social goals relate to the CD^2 process itself. In keeping with CD^2, all the information about Zero is "open" and available at www.projectzero.org. At the time we wrote this chapter, Project Zero had released Milestone 1 and was close to releasing Milestone 2. We expect the platform to evolve as time goes on, and may even become a de facto standard in its own right.

Platforms Required

The pureQuery runtime requires an underlying JDBC driver like most persistence frameworks. You can use it to build Java SE applications. Other dependencies will be specific to the environment in which pureQuery is used. For example, when using pureQuery inside of Project Zero, you need to download its platform from the website [Zero 1].

Other Dependencies

Besides the JDBC drivers and environment-specific dependencies, there are no other dependencies for the pureQuery runtime. The pureQuery technology also includes tools to generate code and optimizations. They are based on the Eclipse Platform and require an Eclipse runtime with Data Tool support. The IBM Data Studio contains the pureQuery tools. We show examples of this tooling throughout the chapter. See the IBM Data Studio web page for more details [IBM DS].

Vendors and Licenses

The pureQuery technology is licensed by IBM, and its runtime and tools ship with the IBM Data Studio product. Please refer again to [IBM DS] for details on the license. The pureQuery runtime also comes with Project Zero. For details on the Project Zero license, see the FAQ page [Zero 2].

Available Literature

The pureQuery technology is a fairly new technology. However, some practiced articles and tutorials are already available. Table 9.1 lists some examples.

Table 9.1 Available Literature

	Title	Source	Description
 A.9.1	"Overview of pureQuery Tools"	www.ibm.com/developerworks/db2/library/techarticle/dm-0709surange/	General overview of the pureQuery tools
 A.9.2	"pureQuery: IBM's New Paradigm for Writing Java Database Applications"	www.ibm.com/developerworks/db2/library/techarticle/dm-0708ahadian/	General introduction to pureQuery

Title	Source	Description	
"Detect and Fix SQL Problems Inside Java Program"	www.ibm.com/developerworks/db2/library/techarticle/dm-0709surange2/	Article showing how to use the pureQuery tools to detect SQL problems with your application	 A.9.3
"Configuring Data Access with Project Zero" [Zero 3]	www.projectzero.org/wiki/bin/view/DocumentationMilestoneOne/DataAccess	Developer Guide for using Data Access APIs with Project Zero	
"Building RESTful Services for your Web Application with Project Zero"	www.ibm.com/developerworks/ibm/library/i-zero1/	Tutorial on Project Zero showing Data APIs in Action	 A.9.4
"RESTful applications in an SOA: Part 2"	www.ibm.com/developerworks/ibm/library/i-zero2/	Follow-on tutorial on Project Zero showing Data APIs and ZRM in Action	 A.9.5
"Use Project Zero's data access APIs to build a simple wiki"	www.ibm.com/developerworks/web/library/wa-pz-wiki/	Article illustrating the data access API's in Project Zero in the context of building a Wiki.	 A.9.6

Programming Model

In this section, we examine three distinct patterns for application development using pureQuery technology:

- **Direct use of the Data API**—pureQuery provides a complete set of Java methods for executing queries and update operations. These methods take an SQL statement and associated parameters as input and, where applicable based on the statement type, return results in numerous forms including: (a) scalar and primitive types, (b) Java collection types, and (c) user-defined Bean types. With this Data API style pattern, the SQL query or update statement can be embedded directly in the application code and appears as a parameter on the associated method invocation. This approach, sometimes referred to as "Inline Method Style," offers simplicity and tight integration between the SQL and the Java languages.

- **Annotated Method Style**—pureQuery allows Data access and update methods to be declared in a user-created Java interface using annotations that express the specific query or update operations in standard SQL. Using Java-annotated class definitions (often on classes that follow the conventions for Java Beans [Java Beans]), a code generator automatically creates the implementation of the specified methods. The Annotated Method style offers the advantage of separating the data access declarations and the associated SQL from the application's business logic. The application simply invokes the methods defined in the interface and uses familiar Java objects, beans, and collections for providing parameters to the method and for receiving query results. In essence, this approach is tooling that hides the details of the Data API from the developer.
- **Indirectly**—Sometimes the pureQuery API is used underneath another platform, such as the Groovy wrappers available in Project Zero.

Throughout this chapter, we emphasize the Data API and wrappers through Project Zero; however, in certain sections of the template, we will show examples of the underling Java API.

When discussing Project Zero, we use the Groovy scripting language as the concrete example. Groovy is a scripting language for Java developers. The Groovy website [Groovy] defines it like this:

- An agile and dynamic language for the Java Virtual Machine
- Builds upon the strengths of Java but has additional power features inspired by languages like Python, Ruby, and Smalltalk
- Makes modern programming features available to Java developers with an almost-zero learning curve
- Supports Domain-Specific Languages and other compact syntax so your code becomes easy to read and maintain
- Makes writing shell and build scripts easy with its powerful processing primitives, OO abilities, and an Ant DSL
- Increases developer productivity by reducing scaffolding code when developing web, GUI, database, or console applications
- Simplifies testing by supporting unit testing and mocking out-of-the-box
- Seamlessly integrates with all existing Java objects and libraries
- Compiles straight to Java bytecode so you can use it anywhere you can use Java

Initialization

We will show pureQuery initialization both for the pureQuery API and for the Groovy extensions. It is worth noting that the pureQuery Data API can be used directly in Project Zero based applications.

Data API

The Data API is the core of the pureQuery API. It provides the methods you need to execute queries. To access it, you need to execute one of the `get` Data methods of a DataFactory. pureQuery allows you to pass in a JDBC Connection or a DataSource. It leaves it up to the developer to create a connection or DataSource. Listing 9.1 shows an example of using JDBC to create a connection.

Listing 9.1 Getting an Instance of Data with a JDBC Connection

```
Class.forName("org.apache.derby.jdbc.EmbeddedDriver");
String url = "jdbc:derby://localhost/test";
String username = "myUserName";
String password = "myPassword";
Connection connection = DriverManager.getConnection(
    url, username, password
);
Data data = DataFactory.getData (connection);
```

The decision to delegate the initialization to the application context allows it to be reusable in various environments. Listing 9.2 shows how you can pass a DataSource into the DataFactory.

Listing 9.2 Getting an Instance of Data with a JDBC DataSource

```
InitialContext ic = new InitialContext()
DataSource ds = ic.lookup("java:comp/env/jdbc/Derby/DataSource");
Data data = DataFactory.getData (ds);
```

Frameworks built on top of pureQuery provide their own style of bootstrapping, as we will see in the discussion of Project Zero.

Project Zero

Project Zero provides query wrappers that enable you to invoke queries within the Groovy and PHP scripting languages. To do this, it provides a scripting abstraction to the Data API. In Milestone 1 of Project Zero, this is called a Manager. This Manager wraps the pureQuery Data API and provides extensions for executing queries using Groovy programming constructs, such as GString, where you can declare regular expressions that refer to other parts of your code. We show examples later in the sections on Create, Retrieve, Update, and so on. A Manager is configured in a Zero configuration file. For details on how Zero configuration works, see the Project Zero website [Zero 4].

Listing 9.3 shows an example of a Zero configuration file. In Milestone 1, Project Zero used "stanzas" in their configuration file. As of Milestone 3, the configuration syntax changed to use a JSON format instead. The example in this book works with Milestone 1. Each stanza starts by declaring a Global Context where all state is maintained in a Project Zero application. The Global Context has zones into which you can store data. The zone defines the scope and life cycle for the data. A configuration key takes the following format: `/app/db/`*`<manager_name>`*`/config`. You will use the *<manager_name>* to create an instance of a Manager in your code, as we will see in the "Connections" section.

Listing 9.3 Zero Configuration for Manager

```
[/app/db/pie/config]
class=org.apache.derby.jdbc.ClientDataSource
serverName=localhost
portNumber=1527
databaseName=PWTE
connectionAttributes=create=true
```

The Project Zero website has a specific page that contains more information on the Global Context [Zero 5].

Connections

In this section, we show how to access connections using both the Data API and Project Zero.

Data API

We showed in the "Initialization" section how the Data API makes a connection. After you bootstrap Connections or DataSource objects into your application context, all you need to do is get an instance to a data object. This was shown earlier in Listings 9.1 and 9.2. The Data Interface contains the query method necessary to execute SQL. Figure 9.4 shows the Interface for the Query API.

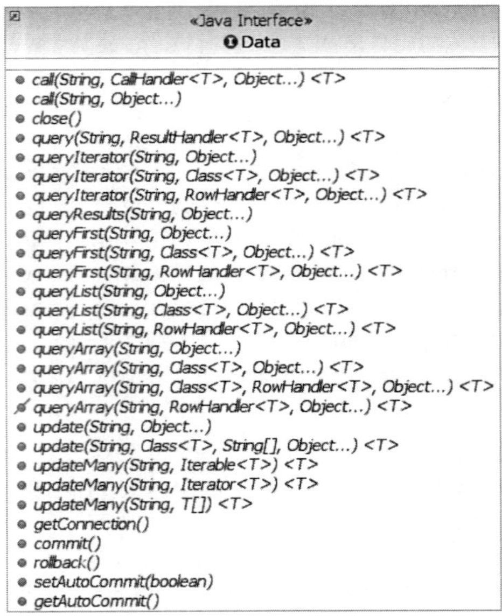

Figure 9.4 Data Interface.

Project Zero

In Project Zero, rather than asking for a Data instance, you can get an instance of the Manager to use within your Groovy scripts. All you have to do is call the `create` method on the Manager, as shown in Listing 9.4.

Listing 9.4 Creating a Manager Instance

```
Manager db = Manager.create("pie");
```

This is the pattern for creating an instance in Milestone 1. Future milestones may provide a slightly different API. The Manager Object wraps the Data API and adds some more convenient methods for patterns in a Web 2.0 environment. Some of these patterns are shown later in the chapter.

Transactions

In this section, we show how to handle transactions using pureQuery's data API and Project Zero.

Data API

Transactions can be managed in pureQuery using methods on the Data API. PureQuery will then delegate to the underlying JDBC Connection object. If you want to use pureQuery in a distributed transaction rather than use the Data API to demarcate transactions, you must manage your transactions using the JTA API or Container Managed Transactions in an EJB container. When getting an instance of the Data API, you just pass in the DataSource. Listing 9.5 shows an example.

Listing 9.5 Demarcating Local Transactions with the Data API

```
Data data = DataFactory.getData (connection);
data.setAutoCommit(false);
...  //Execute Code
data.commit();
```

Project Zero and Transaction Closures

Keep in mind that Project Zero is an environment for writing Web 2.0-based applications where you normally do not concern yourself with managing distributed transactions. However, the Manager class provides convenient methods for starting, committing, rolling back, and ending transactions. It will delegate to the underlying pureQuery API. Listing 9.6 shows an example of the typical sequence of calls to explicitly manage a transaction.

Listing 9.6 Explicitly Demarcating Local Transactions in Project Zero

```
db.startTransaction();
try {
```

```
    db.update("INSERT...");
    db.update("UPDATE...");
    db.update("DELETE...");
    db.commitTransaction();
}
catch (Exception e) {
    db.rollbackTransaction();
} finally {
    db.endTransaction();
}
```

Scripting languages like Groovy have programming constructs, called *closures*, that are like parameterized macros that get defined and "unrolled" inline when used. A closure can greatly simplify your code by handling housekeeping functions that normally must be coded explicitly. Fully explaining Groovy closures can take an entire chapter by itself; the website devotes a whole section to it [Groovy 2].

In any event, the Manager API provides a transaction closure called `inTransaction` that allows you to wrap a piece of code inside a transaction and automatically handle the commit and rollback logic. Listing 9.7 shows an example.

Listing 9.7 Transaction Closure with Groovy

```
public Order openOrder(int customerId)
throws CustomerDoesNotExistException, OrderAlreadyOpenException {
    Order newOrder = new Order();
    db.inTransaction
    {
        db.update("INSERT...");
        db.update("UPDATE...");
        db.update("DELETE...");

    }
    return newOrder;
}
```

Zero provides similar abstractions in the PHP language. A specific section is devoted to PHP on the Project Zero website [Zero 6], so we will not show the details here.

Create

Now that we have the bootstrapping completed, the connection made, and the transaction started, we are ready to create some persistent data. We will start with the Data API and then examine how you can create data in Project Zero applications.

Data API

As stated earlier, there are two styles of development in pureQuery: the inline code style and the annotated method style. The inline code style requires you to use the Data API where you can use the special `:<property_name>` convention to insert variables from a specified bean into the queries. This saves you from having to explicitly map fields. Listing 9.8 shows an example that creates an Order in a bean and uses an insert statement.

Listing 9.8 Create Order

```
Order newOrder = new Order();
newOrder.setCustomer_id(1);
newOrder.setStatus("OPEN");
newOrder.setTotal(new BigDecimal(0));
db.update (
    "insert into ORDERS (CUSTOMER_ID, STATUS, TOTAL)
            values( :customer_id, :status, :total)",
    newOrder
);
```

The other style of development is the annotated method style. In this style, you create a Java Interface that contains a method prefaced with an `@Update` annotation that contains the SQL insert statement. Listing 9.9 shows an example.

Listing 9.9 Create an Order with the Annotated Method style

```
public interface OrderData {
@Update(
    sql="insert into ORDERS (CUSTOMER_ID, STATUS, TOTAL)
              values( :customerId, :status, :total)"
)
int createOrder(Order order);
...
```

To create an order anywhere in your code, you simply invoke the `createOrder` method with an Order bean as specified. This annotated interface is then used to generate the actual code using the pureQuery tooling. Figure 9.5 shows an example of the generated artifacts.

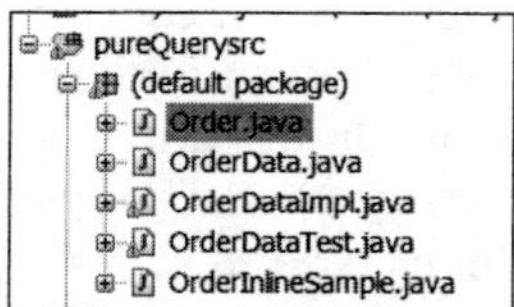

Figure 9.5 Generated code.

For more detail on the pureQuery tools, refer to the developerWorks website.

Like OpenJPA, pureQuery also allows you to externalize the SQL into an XML file and run
A.9.1 the generator against the interface and XML file. As a matter of fact, pureQuery uses the JPA syntax for naming native queries so that they can be used in your code. Listing 9.10 shows an example of the XML syntax.

Listing 9.10 Native Query Method

```
<entity-mappings xmlns="java.sun.com/xml/ns/persistence/orm">
  <named-native-query
     name="org.pwte.domain.OrderData#createOrder(Order)"
  >
    <query>
        insert into ORDERS (CUSTOMER_ID, STATUS, TOTAL)
               values( :customerId, :status, :total)
    </query>
  </named-native-query>

  <entity class="Order">
  </entity>
</entity-mappings>
```

If you prefer to create fewer artifacts and do not mind modifying the SQL directly in your code, you will likely prefer the annotated style. Otherwise, if you prefer to externalize your SQL so that it can be reviewed and maintained separately, then you will likely prefer the XML approach.

Project Zero

Project Zero extends the query APIs to enable you to use scripting advantages. For example, Groovy supports the notion of GString, which allows you to enter an expression within a string. Listing 9.11 shows an example of inserting a LineItem. Strings that are declared inside double quotes in Groovy can contain arbitrary expressions inside them, as shown in Listing 9.11 using the `${expression}` syntax in a similar way to JSP EL, Velocity, and JEXL. Any valid Groovy expression can be enclosed in the `${...}`, including method calls and such. GStrings are defined the same way as normal Strings would be created in Java.

What actually happens is whenever a string expression contains a `${...}` expression, then rather than a normal `java.lang.String` instance, a GString object is created that contains the text and values used inside the String. GString uses lazy evaluation, so it's not until the `toString()` method is invoked that the GString is evaluated. More information on GStrings can be found in a special section of the Groovy website [Groovy 3]. The Project Zero API will take the handle to the GString object, get an array of items, and replace the expression with `?` needed for a prepared statement. (Keep in mind that anything that causes the GString to evaluate to a String, like the + concatenation in Java, will not allow for using the GString substitution.)

Listing 9.11 Insert Using GStrings

```
LineItem lineItem = new LineItem();
lineItem.setOrderId(openOrder.getOrderId());
lineItem.setProductId(product.getProductId());
lineItem.setAmount(amount);
lineItem.setProduct(product);
lineItem.setQuantity(quantity);
db.update(
  "INSERT INTO LINE_ITEM (ORDER_ID,PRODUCT_ID,amount,quantity)
   VALUES (
      ${lineItem.orderId},
      ${lineItem.productId},
      ${lineItem.amount},
      ${lineItem.quantity}
    )"
);
```

Project Zero also supports other scripting patterns that allow you to bind properties from multiple objects into the SQL with a `?#.property` syntax, where # is the number of the object passed as input. These are inherited from pureQuery. Listing 9.12 shows an example.

Listing 9.12 Binding Properties from Multiple Objects into an Update

```
Object order = // obtained perhaps through defaultJsonInput
Customer customer = // obtained somehow through another source

data.update(
    "INSERT INTO
         orders (
             orderId, customerId, itemId, quantity, price, address
         )
         VALUES (
              ?1.orderNum, ?2.custId, ?1.itemNum, ?1.quantity,
              ?1.price, ?2.address
         )
    ",
    order, customer
);
```

Retrieve

As we did with create, we will first examine approaches to retrieve data enabled by the pureQuery Data API, and then examine those enabled by ProjectZero.

Data API

Also as in the "Create" section, you can enter any SQL and use the `:<propertyName>` or `?` pattern for issuing queries. Listing 9.13 shows an example of getting an instance of a customer using the `?` pattern and the `queryFirst` method. The `queryFirst` method takes three parameters. The first is the query itself. The second parameter is the class the result will be mapped to. And the third parameter is the id value that maps to the `?` parameter. The later "ORM Features Supported" section describes the details of how the mapping is done. The default is to match the column name to the fields on the class by name.

Listing 9.13 Retrieving Customer

```
Customer getCustomer = db.queryFirst (
    "select
         CUSTOMER_ID, OPEN_ORDER, NAME, BUSINESS_VOLUME_DISCOUNT,
         BUSINESS_PARTNER, BUSINESS_DESCRIPTION,
         RESIDENTIAL_HOUSEHOLD_SIZE, RESIDENTIAL_FREQUENT_CUSTOMER,
         TYPE
     from CUSTOMER where CUSTOMER_ID = ?
    ",
    Customer.class, customerId
);
```

The Data API also allows you to retrieve Lists and Arrays with the `queryList` and `queryArray` methods. You can even get an iterator directly, as shown in Listing 9.14.

Listing 9.14 Retrieving Many Customers

```
Iterator<Customer> getCustomers = db.queryIterator (
    "select * from CUSTOMER", Customer.class
);
```

You also can use the `@Select` annotation or native query method in the same way as we illustrated in the "Create" section.

Project Zero

Exactly as we did in the create scenario, you can use GString to get results. Listing 9.15 shows an example of getting Product data.

Listing 9.15 Getting Product Data

```
Product product = db.queryFirst(
    "select * from Product where product_id = ${productId} ",
    Product.class
);
```

Besides retrieving JavaBeans, you can retrieve a Java Map or primitives. You can also retrieve Lists of JavaBeans, Maps, or primitives. Project Zero is optimized for passing JSON objects, XML, or Data Feeds. Listing 9.16 shows an example used by a Project Zero application to extract XML out of a result. You will see another use of a closure associated with the Manager—this time called `eachRow`. The `Select` statement is the parameter to the left of the arrow, and the closure statement is to the right of the arrow.

Listing 9.16 XML Results

```
def data = zero.data.groovy.Manager.create('mydb')
def xml = new groovy.xml.MarkupBuilder(request.writer)

xml.records() {
        data.eachRow('SELECT * FROM table'){ row ->
          item(id: row['id'], name: row.name)
        }
}

// creates the following XML:
// <records>
//   <item id="10" name="Geoff" />
//   <item id="11" name="Roland" />
//   <item id="15" name="Kyle" />
// </records>
```

Update

Again, we will look at how to update persistent objects using the pureQuery Data API followed by examples using ProjectZero and Groovy.

Data API

You can execute update statements to modify data using the pureQueryAPI exactly as you can execute insert and select statements. Listing 9.17 shows an example of using the inline style to update the CUSTOMER database row from properties in a Customer instance.

Listing 9.17 Executing Updates

```
Customer customer = // get instance.
db.update(
    "update CUSTOMER
         set CUSTOMER_ID = :customer_id, OPEN_ORDER = :open_order,
             NAME = :name,
             BUSINESS_VOLUME_DISCOUNT = :business_volume_discount,
             BUSINESS_PARTNER = :business_partner,
             BUSINESS_DESCRIPTION = :business_description,
             RESIDENTIAL_HOUSEHOLD_SIZE = :residential_household_size,
             RESIDENTIAL_FREQUENT_CUSTOMER =
                 :residential_frequent_customer,
             TYPE = :type
     where CUSTOMER_ID = :customer_id
    ",
    customer
);
```

As with the other CRUD operations we have examined so far, all the coding styles are supported. Listing 9.18 shows the annotated query style being used to update an Order.

Listing 9.18 Annotated Update

```
// Update one ORDERS by Order object
@Update(
    sql="update ORDERS
             set CUSTOMER_ID = :customer_id,
                 STATUS = :status,
                 TOTAL = :total
         where ORDER_ID = :order_id"
)
int updateOrder(Order o);
```

Project Zero

Listing 9.19 shows code from the implementation of the `submit` method from the common example that highlights the use of the Groovy GString style and the `inTransaction` closure.

Listing 9.19 Use of Update in Project Zero using GString style

```
public void submit(int customerId)
throws CustomerDoesNotExistException,
       OrderNotOpenException, NoLineItemsException {
```

```
    db.inTransaction
    {
        //Code to get and make changes to openOrder
        db.update(
            "UPDATE ORDERS
                SET STATUS = ${Order.Status.SUBMITTED.toString()}
             where ORDER_ID = ${openOrder.orderId}"
        );
        db.update("UPDATE CUSTOMER SET OPEN_ORDER = NULL");
    };
}
```

Delete

This section shows that deleting data in the pureQuery Data API or Project Zero and Groovy is no different from the other CRUD methods.

Data API

Listing 9.20 shows an example of using the Data API to delete an order with a given status.

Listing 9.20 Delete Order

```
Order order = //
db.update("delete from ORDERS where ORDER_ID = :order_id", order);
```

Listing 9.21 shows how you can use the `@Update` annotation to cause two methods to be generated that you can use in your code. The first method has a parameter for passing the order id; the second has a parameter for passing an Order object, from which the ID is extracted.

Listing 9.21 Annotated Style of Delete

```
// Delete ORDERS by parameters
  @Update(sql="delete from ORDERS where ORDER_ID = ?")
  int deleteOrder(int order_id);

  // Delete one ORDERS by Order object
  @Update(sql="delete from ORDERS where ORDER_ID = :order_id")
  int deleteOrder(Order o);
```

Project Zero

Listing 9.22 shows part of the `removeLineItem` method from the common example. You can see that we use the Groovy Pattern of GString in much the same way we do with other patterns.

Listing 9.22 Delete in removeLineItem

```
public void removeLineItem(int customerId,int productId )
throws CustomerDoesNotExistException, OrderNotOpenException,
       ProductDoesNotExistException, NoLineItemsException,
       GeneralPersistenceException {
    db.inTransaction
    {
        //Code to retrieve and determine object can be deleted
        db.update(
            "DELETE FROM LINE_ITEM
             WHERE PRODUCT_ID = ${productId} AND
                   ORDER_ID = ${customer.openOrder.orderId}"
        );
    }
}
```

Stored Procedures

The Data API enables you to invoke stored procedures using the call statement, much like you can call any other SQL statement. Listing 9.23 shows an example.

Listing 9.23 Invoking a Stored Procedure using the Data API

```
Connection con = DriverManager.getConnection(...);
Data db = DataFactory.getData(con);

StoredProcedureResult spr = db.call(
    "CALL shipOrder(?)", orderId
);
spr.close();
```

This same method is used to call stored procedures in Project Zero.

You can also cause a method to be generated using the special `@Call` annotation, as shown in Listing 9.24.

Listing 9.24 Creating a Method to invoke a Stored Procedure Using Annotations

```
@Call(sql="CALL CALL shipOrder(?)")
public StoredProcedureResult shipOrder(int orderId);
```

You then use this method in your application code, effectively separating the SQL from the code that uses it. The Manager API can be used to call stored procedures in a similar fashion.

Batch Operations

The Data API in pureQuery has an `updateMany` method that enables you to send a batch of statements to the database. Listing 9.25 shows an example of passing an ArrayList of LineItems into the `updateMany` statement. Project Zero's DataManager API has a version of this method as well.

Listing 9.25 Batch Updates

```
ArrayList<LineItem>  lineItems = //
rowsAffected = data.updateMany(
     "INSERT INTO lineItems (LINE_ITEM_ID, PRODUCT_ID,  QUANTITY)
      VALUES (:lineItemId, :productId, :quantity)",
     lineItems
);
```

Extending the Framework

There are various ways of extending pureQuery. Project Zero is an example of extending pureQuery to support various additional patterns. One of the most common ways to extend pureQuery is with ResultHandlers and RowFactories. Figure 9.6 shows the relationship between the Data Interface and the handlers.

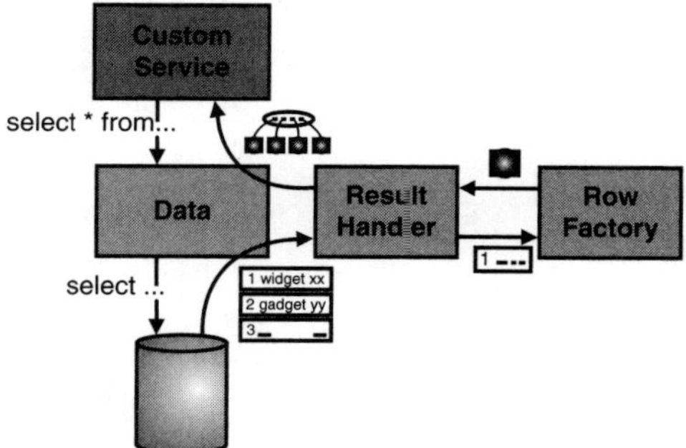

Figure 9.6 Extending the handlers.

The most common scenario is to write your own handlers to provide custom result formats. For example, pureQuery provides result handlers to return specialized results. Listing 9.26 shows an example of using a JSONResultHandler to create a custom JSON result handler. Notice that you have to pass the ResultHandler into the generic query method.

Listing 9.26 Custom ResultHandler

```
//code that uses the custom handler
String json = d.query(
```

```
    "select * from Customer", new JSONResultHandler()
);
...
//Definition of Handler...
class JSONResultHandler implements ResultHandler
{
    String handle(ResultSet rs)
    {
        sb.append("{");
        for (int x=1; x<=cols; x++) {
          sb.append("\""+ m.getColumnName(x) +"\"=\"");
          sb.append(rs.getString(x) +"\"");
          if (x<cols) sb.append(",");
          }
        sb.append("}");
    }
}
```

You can also use a RowHandler to create custom results a row at a time within the context of the queryFirst method, as shown in Listing 9.27. Unlike a ResultHandler, which gets passed to the generic query method, The RowHandler can be passed into the various query methods, such as queryFirst or queryList. After the RowHandler, you can add any of the inputs necessary, like the hard coded 100 in Listing 9.27.

Listing 9.27 Custom RowHandler

```
CustomClass myCustCls = data.queryFirst(
    "SELECT column1,column2 FROM sometable WHERE id=?",
    new RowHandler() {
        public CustomClass createNext(
            ResultSet resultSet, CustomClass obj
        )
        {
            CustomClass custom = new CustomClass();
            custom.customProp1 = resultSet.getString(1);
            custom.customProp2 = resultSet.getDate(2);
            return custom;
        }
    },
    100
);
```

Error Handling

The Data API throws an unchecked `DataRuntimeException` for most errors. This exception is shown in class diagram notation in Figure 9.7.

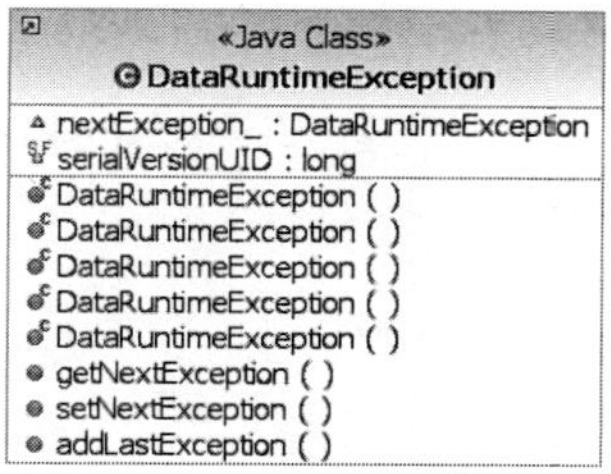

«Java Class»
DataRuntimeException
nextException_ : DataRuntimeException
serialVersionUID : long
DataRuntimeException ( )
DataRuntimeException ( )
DataRuntimeException ( )
DataRuntimeException ( )
DataRuntimeException ( )
getNextException ( )
setNextException ( )
addLastException ( )

Figure 9.7 Exception class.

ORM Features Supported

The pureQuery framework is optimized for relational database queries. However, as we have shown, you can pass Objects into and out of queries through various shortcuts. pureQuery provides a set of Java Annotations that can be used to add extra metadata in case your table names do not match the class. The goal is not to be a full Domain Mapper, but to provide flexibility in class names.

Objects

Class names that match table names do not need to be mapped. However, pureQuery provides Java Annotations to override default mappings. The annotations are very similar to those of the JPA specification. Listing 9.28 shows the use of the `@Table` annotation.

Listing 9.28 `@Table`

```
@Table(name="PRODUCT", schema="APP")
public class Product implements Serializable {
    ...
}
```

Inheritance

pureQuery can populate objects that are part of an inheritance hierarchy based on a query; however, you have to determine the type of mapping as described in Chapter 3. There is no specific support for a particular inheritance mapping. Listing 9.29 shows the `AbstractCustomer` and `ResidentialCustomer` used in our example, using the `@Table` annotation to map both to the same table. The listing shows how you would map using the single table inheritance style. Listing 9.30 shows how you would populate the Objects.

Listing 9.29 Inheritance

```
@Table(name="CUSTOMER")
public abstract class AbstractCustomer implements Serializable {

    ...

}

@Table(name="CUSTOMER")
public class ResidentialCustomer
extends AbstractCustomer implements Serializable {
    ...
}
```

In Listing 9.30, we first query the type to check what instance to populate when we load a Customer from the database.

Listing 9.30 Populate Inheritance Chain

```
public AbstractCustomer loadCustomer(int customerId)
throws CustomerDoesNotExistException {
    String customerQuery = "
        SELECT
            c.CUSTOMER_ID, c.NAME, c.BUSINESS_VOLUME_DISCOUNT,
            c.BUSINESS_PARTNER, c.BUSINESS_DESCRIPTION,
            c.RESIDENTIAL_HOUSEHOLD_SIZE,
            c.RESIDENTIAL_FREQUENT_CUSTOMER, c.TYPE,
            o.ORDER_ID, o.STATUS, o.TOTAL,
            l.PRODUCT_ID, l.QUANTITY, l.AMOUNT,
            p.PRICE,p.DESCRIPTION
        FROM CUSTOMER c
        LEFT OUTER JOIN ORDERS o ON c.OPEN_ORDER = o.ORDER_ID
        LEFT OUTER JOIN (
            LINE_ITEM l JOIN PRODUCT p ON l.PRODUCT_ID = p.PRODUCT_ID
        ) ON o.ORDER_ID = l.ORDER_ID
        WHERE c.CUSTOMER_ID = ${customerId}
    ";

    def typeRow = db.queryFirst(
        "SELECT type FROM CUSTOMER c
         WHERE c.CUSTOMER_ID = ${customerId}
        "
    );
```

```
    AbstractCustomer customer = null;
    if(typeRow == null)
        throw new CustomerDoesNotExistException();
    else if (typeRow.type.equals(CustomerType.RESIDENTAL.toString())) {
        customer = db.query(
            customerQuery,
            new JoinResultHandler(ResidentialCustomer)
        ).get(0);
    else if (typeRow.type.equals(CustomerType.BUSINESS.toString()))
        customer = db.query(
            customerQuery,
            new JoinResultHandler(BusinessCustomer)
        ).get(0);
    else
        throw new CustomerDoesNotExistException();

    if (customer == null)
        throw new CustomerDoesNotExistException();

    return customer;
}
```

Using this technique, we must issue an extra query each time we load an object. Another technique is to write your own RowHandler and check the type first as you traverse the ResultSet. We leave this as an exercise to the interested reader using similar techniques as described in the section "Extending the Framework."

Keys

Because pureQuery exposes SQL, you do not need to explicitly create keys; however, pureQuery provides the `@Id` annotation for use in your POJO class, as shown in Listing 9.31. The pureQuery tools do not make use of it directly, but extensions can make use of it for optimizations. We show an example in the "Relationships" section.

Listing 9.31 @Id

```
@Table(name="PRODUCT", schema="APP")
public class Product implements Serializable {
    private static final long serialVersionUID = 2435504714077372968L;

    @Id
    @Column(name="PRODUCT_ID")
    protected int productId;
```

In Project Zero, there is a specialized insert method that extends the pureQuery support for keys. In cases in which tables generate the key, the insert method will return that key to the program. Listing 9.32 shows an example of this.

Listing 9.32 Special Insert Method for Project Zero applications

```
newOrder.setStatus(Order.Status.OPEN.toString());
newOrder.setTotal(new BigDecimal(0));
newOrder.setCustomer(customer);
def orderId = db.insert(
    "INSERT INTO ORDERS (STATUS,TOTAL,CUSTOMER_ID)
     VALUES (
        ${Order.Status.OPEN.toString()},
        ${new BigDecimal(0)},
        ${customerId}
     )",
    ['ORDER_ID']
);
newOrder.setOrderId(orderId.intValue());
```

Attributes

You can use the `@Column` annotation to map attributes to columns. Listing 9.33 shows this pattern.

Listing 9.33 @Column

```
@Table(name="PRODUCT", schema="APP")
public class Product implements Serializable {
    private static final long serialVersionUID = 2435504714077372968L;
    @Id
    @Column(name="PRODUCT_ID")
    protected int productId;
    @Column(name="PRICE")
    protected BigDecimal price;
    @Column(name="DESCRIPTION")
    protected String description;
    //setters and getters
```

Contained Objects

There is no direct support for contained objects. However, you can easily populate a contained object using a RowHandler.

Relationships

The pureQuery runtime currently does not support populating an object graph; however, the Project Zero extension does. In Listing 9.34, you can see the use of the special `@Join` annotation and JoinResultHandler to populate Object graphs from joins.

Listing 9.34 @Join

```
@Table(name="ORDERS")
public class Order implements Serializable {
    private static final long serialVersionUID = 7779370942277849463L;
    @Id
    @Column(name="ORDER_ID")
    protected int orderId;
    protected BigDecimal total;

    public static enum Status { OPEN, SUBMITTED, CLOSED }
    protected String status;
    protected AbstractCustomer customer;
    @Join
    protected Set<LineItem> lineitems;
```

After you have defined which fields you want to Join, you can issue a query and pass in the JoinResultHandler, as shown in Listing 9.35. The JoinResultHandler will use the `@Id` annotation of the related class to determine the foreign key.

Listing 9.35 JoinResultHandler

```
String customerQuery = "
    SELECT
        c.CUSTOMER_ID, c.NAME, c.BUSINESS_VOLUME_DISCOUNT,
        c.BUSINESS_PARTNER, c.BUSINESS_DESCRIPTION,
        c.RESIDENTIAL_HOUSEHOLD_SIZE,
        c.RESIDENTIAL_FREQUENT_CUSTOMER, c.TYPE,
        o.ORDER_ID, o.STATUS, o.TOTAL,
        l.PRODUCT_ID, l QUANTITY, l.AMOUNT,
        p.PRICE, p.DESCRIPTION
    FROM CUSTOMER c
    LEFT OUTER JOIN ORDERS o ON c.OPEN_ORDER = o.ORDER_ID
    LEFT OUTER JOIN (
        LINE_ITEM l JOIN PRODUCT p ON  l.PRODUCT_ID = p.PRODUCT_ID
    ) ON o.ORDER_ID = l.ORDER_ID
    WHERE c.CUSTOMER_ID = ${customerId}
";
```

```
AbstractCustomer customer = db.query(
    customerQuery,
    new JoinResultHandler(ResidentialCustomer)
).get(0);
```

Constraints

Constraints in a full ORM framework are hints to the persistence framework from metadata specified in various ways. These hints are often used to either (or both) generate application code to enforce the constraints, or to generate DDL with constraints in the underlying datastore. Because you deal directly with SQL in pureQuery and Project Zero, they do not have any special meta data considerations for constraints beyond those already discussed.

Derived Attributes

And because all objects are "disconnected" in pureQuery and Project Zero, there is no special transient field. You can calculate any field with SQL functions or custom Java logic associated with a get method—depending on which is most natural to the application.

Tuning Options

Because pureQuery is a gateway framework that exposes the SQL in one or more of your application artifacts, you can get the exact SQL you want. The thinness of the pureQuery Data API is optimized for getting your queries and updates from your application code to the database as efficiently as possible. Therefore, tuning generally involves optimizing the SQL for the exact usage pattern needed in the service operation.

To maximize the maintainability of your applications, we recommend separating any SQL from the business logic that uses it through encapsulation. As you have seen throughout this chapter, pureQuery and Project Zero provide many techniques for this—including through annotations, which enable you to separate the SQL into service interface classes that are then used in your code, or through the use of the XML mapping files to provide the mapping metadata. Either approach is excellent and has its advantages and disadvantages.

In the remainder of this section, we discuss some common approaches used with pureQuery and Project Zero to optimize queries, cache data, load related objects, and handle locking. See Chapter 3 for additional discussion of best practices associated with these design trade-offs.

Query Optimizations

Using the Annotated method of development, you can choose to generate a static SQL implementation of the services. Using the pureQuery API with the JCC DB2 drivers, the static SQL is stored in the DB2 catalog. Figure 9.8 shows the benefits of using static SQL optimization.

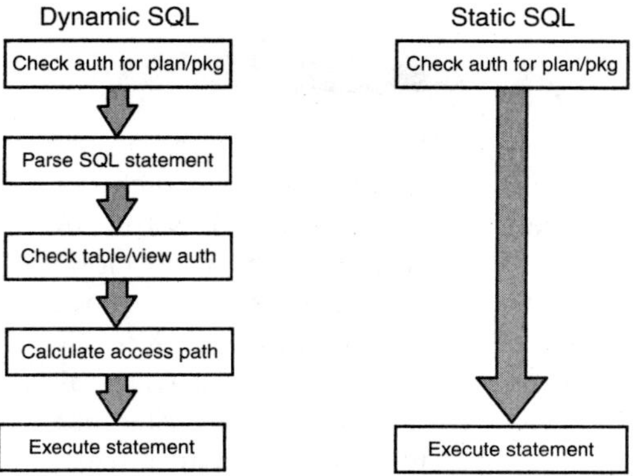

Figure 9.8 Dynamic versus static SQL.

It is worth noting that similar performance enhancements can be achieved with dynamic SQL and a prepared statement cache solution. However, static SQL can be significantly faster because the optimization happens at compile time and can create elaborate plans for processing the associated statements on the database. A PreparedStatement cache for dynamic SQL is somewhat slower, because the plan must be re-created during the first invocation or whenever the cache is invalidated. In addition, the memory requirements in the application and the database to maintain the cache can be significant, especially if there are a huge number of queries to be cached. Table 9.2 gives some more details to consider between static SQL and dynamic SQL.

Table 9.2 Dynamic Versus Static SQL Comparison

	Dynamic SQL	Static SQL
Performance	It is possible to approach static SQL performance with help from dynamic SQL caches. However, cache misses are costly.	All SQL parsing and catalog access is done at BIND time, resulting in fully optimized execution at runtime.
Access Path Reliability	Any prepare can result in a new access path plan as statistics or host variables change, resulting in nondeterministic performance characteristics, even for queries you may have optimized.	The access path is locked in at BIND time. All SQL is available ahead of time for analysis by EXPLAIN. The result is much more deterministic performance characteristics.

continues

Table 9.2 continued

	Dynamic SQL	Static SQL
Authorization	Privileges are handled at object level. All users or groups must have privileges to every table that could be accessed in a Statement, which can either be a security exposure, an administrative burden, or both.	Privileges are based on the Java package in which the SQL appears. Only the DB administrator needs table access. Users and Groups have authority to access a specific package. This makes it easier to administer and to prevent nonauthorized SQL execution.
Monitoring, Problem Determination	There is no easy way to tell where any particular SQL statement came from in the application, except by manually examining a stack trace.	Knowing the class and package where the SQL originated at compile time makes it simple to record as part of the plan, and track back to the SQL statement location in the application at runtime.
Capacity Planning, Forecasting	It is difficult to summarize performance data at program level.	The Package Level Accounting feature provides a view of the workload to aid accurate forecasting.
Tracking Dependent Objects	There is no record of which objects are referenced by a compiled SQL statement.	Object dependencies are registered in database catalog.

Caching

You can use an external cache like ObjectGrid to cache resultsets and write a customer handler. In Project Zero, you can cache data inside the Global Context.

Loading Related Objects

In the relationship section, we showed the use of the `@Join` annotation to load related objects "eagerly" as part of your query. Judicious use of this feature, balancing it with lazy loading approaches, is important to your application performance.

Locking

Locking can be achieved through the underlying JDBC or database settings concerning isolation levels. There is no explicit support for this in pureQuery or Project Zero.

Development Process for the Common Example

The purpose of this section is to show how the programming model, ORM mapping, and tuning features come together in the context of the end-to-end development process. This end-to-end view provides a relatively complete picture of how the framework will be used in practice. As stated earlier, pureQuery supports various development modes, each of which will have an impact on the approach to development and deployment. The style you select will determine the artifacts you build and the tooling you use.

pureQuery is probably most productive using a style of development where you drive to the details of the database very quickly (the "endpoints" of the ORM problem associated with design discussed in Chapter 3). Then you think about exploiting the database as efficiently as possible in your application code—akin to the Transaction Script style discussed in Chapter 5. The reason that pureQuery is most productive with this approach is that its Java development environment is strongly integrated with the database you are coding against. Figure 9.9 gives you an example.

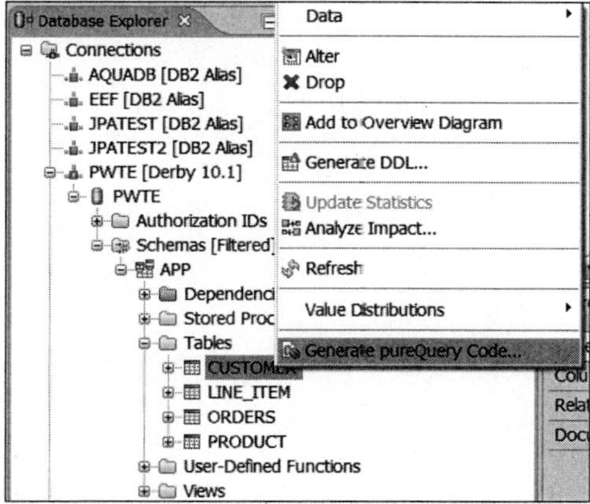

Figure 9.9 Generating pureQuery code.

The pureQuery tooling gives you options to generate domain objects, annotated interfaces, and test query methods (using both the Data API and annotated interface). The pureQuery tooling also allows you to migrate existing SQL-based applications into pureQuery applications. You can highlight any SQL and generate annotated interfaces against it, as shown in Figure 9.10.

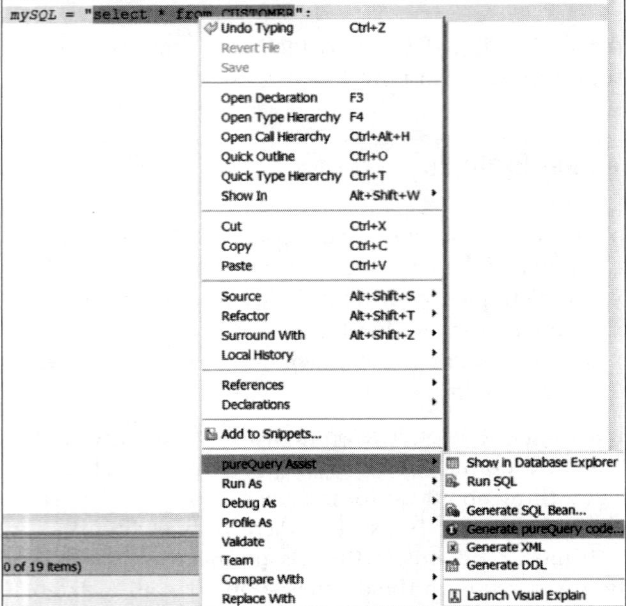

Figure 9.10 Generating from SQL.

The Java Editors have been enhanced to support SQL assist as well. Figure 9.11 shows an example.

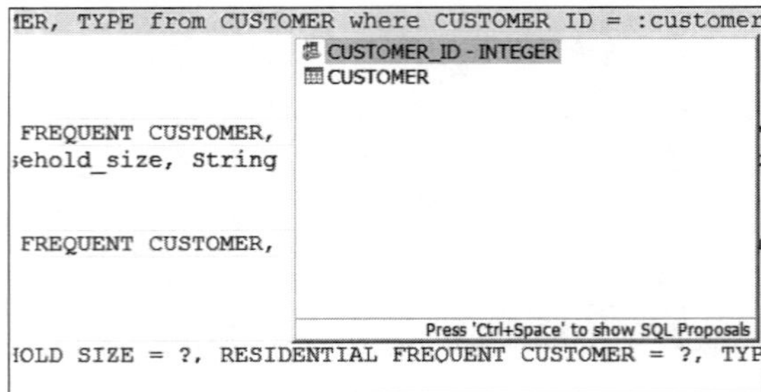

Figure 9.11 SQL assist.

Taken together, the pureQuery tooling greatly increases productivity when you are building database applications.

We chose to implement the common example using the Project Zero platform. The Project Zero platform by default does not utilize some of the pureQuery tools, specifically because Project Zero is based on scripting languages. We will use the same Java Domain Model and Java

Interface, but we implemented the service as a Groovy class. The remaining sections discuss how you can use Project Zero on top of pureQuery to define the objects, implement the associated services, package the components, unit test the application, and deploy it to production.

Defining the Objects

In this section, we show the domain objects in our common example. We have used some of the pureQuery annotations to map attributes to tables. Next, we show our domain objects. The domain objects themselves are still Java objects. At the time we wrote and reviewed the bulk of this chapter, Project Zero was based on Groovy 1.0, so no Java Annotations were available. Project Zero now supports Groovy 1.5, which allows for Java Annotations.

It is worth saying that you may not choose to implement a Domain Model this way in Project Zero because the goal for Web 2.0-based applications is to create RESTful services. Project Zero provides the capability to query directly into JSON objects that can be consumed by AJAX style browser applications. We kept the example the same for the evaluation purposes. We show a short listing of the Zero Resource Model as a "forward look" in the Summary section.

For now, Listing 9.36 shows the `AbstractCustomer` class. Notice the use of the annotations to substitute names. You will also notice we use the `@Join` annotation for the current order that will allow a Join statement to populate the object graph correctly.

Listing 9.36 AbstractCustomer

```
@Table(name="CUSTOMER")
public abstract class AbstractCustomer implements Serializable {

    @Id
    @Column(name="CUSTOMER_ID")
    protected int customerId;
    @Column(name="NAME")
    protected String name;
    @Column(name="TYPE")
    protected String type;
    @Join
    protected Order openOrder;
    protected Set<Order> orders;

    //Insert setters and getters
```

The `ResidentialCustomer` class is shown in Listing 9.37. We annotate the table name to Customer.

Listing 9.37 ResidentialCustomer

```
@Table(name="CUSTOMER")
public class ResidentialCustomer
extends AbstractCustomer implements Serializable {
    @Column(name="RESIDENTIAL_HOUSEHOLD_SIZE")
    protected short householdSize;
    @Column(name="RESIDENTIAL_FREQUENT_CUSTOMER")
    protected boolean frequentCustomer;

    //Insert setters and getters
```

Similarly, Listing 9.38 shows the `BusinessCustomer` class.

Listing 9.38 BusinessCustomer

```
@Table(name="CUSTOMER")
public class BusinessCustomer
extends AbstractCustomer implements Serializable {
    @Column(name="BUSINESS_VOLUME_DISCOUNT")
    protected boolean volumeDiscount;
    @Column(name="BUSINESS_PARTNER")
    protected boolean businessPartner;
    @Column(name="BUSINESS_DESCRIPTION")
    protected String description;

    //Insert setters and getters
```

The `Order` class is shown in Listing 9.39. You will notice we use the `@Join` annotation for the collection of LineItems. The `@Join` annotation can be used on collections as well as single valued objects.

Listing 9.39 Order

```
@Table(name="ORDERS")
public class Order implements Serializable {
    @Id
    @Column(name="ORDER_ID")
    protected int orderId;
    protected BigDecimal total;
    public static enum Status { OPEN, SUBMITTED, CLOSED }
    protected String status;
    protected AbstractCustomer customer;
```

```
    @Join
    protected Set<LineItem> lineitems;

    //Insert setters and getters
```

The `LineItem` object is shown in Listing 9.40. It uses the substitution annotations in the same way as the other objects. It also uses the `@Join` annotation to load the Product.

Listing 9.40 LineItem

```
@Table(name="LINE_ITEM")
public class LineItem implements Serializable {
    @Id
    @Column(name="ORDER_ID")
    protected int orderId;
    @Id
    @Column(name="PRODUCT_ID")
    protected int productId;
    @Column(name="QUANTITY")
    protected long quantity;
    @Column(name="AMOUNT")
    protected BigDecimal amount;
    @Join
    protected Product product;

    //Insert setters and getters
```

Listing 9.41 shows the `Product` object for our example.

Listing 9.41 `Product`

```
@Table(name="PRODUCT")
public class Product implements Serializable {
    @Id
    @Column(name="PRODUCT_ID")
    protected int productId;
    @Column(name="PRICE")
    protected BigDecimal price;
    @Column(name="DESCRIPTION")
    protected String description;

    //Insert setters and getters
```

Implementing the Services

The Service Implementation is a Groovy class that implements the common Java Interface we used throughout the book. The code in Listing 9.42 assumes you have created an instance of the Zero Manager for the class using the configuration shown earlier in Listing 9.3 and code shown in Listing 9.4.

loadCustomer

The `loadCustomer` method uses the data manager to execute the desired SQL. There is some extra logic in that we need to check the type first by issuing a query just for the type to instantiate. We could have implemented a row handler, but the code would have been more complex. Notice we can issue complex SQL. Listing 9.42 shows the example.

Listing 9.42 loadCustomer

```
public AbstractCustomer loadCustomer(int customerId)
throws CustomerDoesNotExistException {
    def typeRow = db.queryFirst(
        "SELECT type FROM CUSTOMER c WHERE c.CUSTOMER_ID = ${customerId}"
    );
    String customerQuery =
        "SELECT c.CUSTOMER_ID, c.NAME, c.BUSINESS_VOLUME_DISCOUNT,
             c.BUSINESS_PARTNER, c.BUSINESS_DESCRIPTION,
             c.RESIDENTIAL_HOUSEHOLD_SIZE,
             c.RESIDENTIAL_FREQUENT_CUSTOMER, c.TYPE,
             o.ORDER_ID, o.STATUS, o.TOTAL,
             l.PRODUCT_ID, l.QUANTITY, l.AMOUNT,
             p.PRICE, p.DESCRIPTION
         FROM CUSTOMER c
         LEFT OUTER JOIN ORDERS o ON c.OPEN_ORDER = o.ORDER_ID
         LEFT OUTER JOIN (
             LINE_ITEM l JOIN PRODUCT p ON  l.PRODUCT_ID = p.PRODUCT_ID
         ) ON o.ORDER_ID = l.ORDER_ID
         WHERE c.CUSTOMER_ID = ${customerId}
    ";
        AbstractCustomer customer = null;
        if(typeRow == null)
            throw new CustomerDoesNotExistException();
        else if (typeRow.type.equals(
                    CustomerType.RESIDENTAL.toString()))
                customer = db.query(
                    customerQuery,
                    new JoinResultHandler(ResidentialCustomer)
                ).get(0);
```

```
        else if (typeRow.type.equals(CustomerType.BUSINESS.toString()))
                customer = db.query(
                    customerQuery,
                    new JoinResultHandler(BusinessCustomer)
                ).get(0);
        else
            throw new CustomerDoesNotExistException();

        if (customer == null)
            throw new CustomerDoesNotExistException();
        return customer;
    }
```

openOrder

The openOrder method executes all code within a Groovy closure for transaction demarcation. Listing 9.43 illustrates again how Groovy GStrings are used as input in a more complete example.

Listing 9.43 openOrder

```
public Order openOrder(int customerId)
throws CustomerDoesNotExistException, OrderAlreadyOpenException {
    Order newOrder = new Order();
    db.inTransaction
    {
        AbstractCustomer customer = loadCustomer(customerId);
        if (customer.getOpenOrder() != null )
            throw new OrderAlreadyOpenException();

        newOrder.setStatus(Order.Status.OPEN.toString());
        newOrder.setTotal(new BigDecimal(0));
        newOrder.setCustomer(customer);
        def orderId = db.insert(
            "INSERT INTO ORDERS (STATUS,TOTAL,CUSTOMER_ID)
              VALUES (
                 ${Order.Status.OPEN.toString()},
                 ${new BigDecimal(0)},${customerId}
              )
            ", ['ORDER_ID']
        );
        newOrder.setOrderId(orderId.intValue());
        db.update(
            "UPDATE CUSTOMER SET OPEN_ORDER = ${newOrder.orderId}"
```

```
        );
    }
    return newOrder;
}
```

addLineItem

The implementation of the addLineItem service operation first checks to see whether the Product exists using the `em.find`. It then queries to check whether a LineItem already exists, and updates the quantity if it does. Listing 9.44 shows the relevant code.

Listing 9.44 addLineItem

```
public LineItem addLineItem(
    int customerId, int productId, long quantity
)
throws CustomerDoesNotExistException,
       OrderNotOpenException,InvalidQuantityException,
       ProductDoesNotExistException {
    if(quantity <= 0 ) throw new InvalidQuantityException();
    LineItem li = null;
    db.inTransaction
    {
        Product product = db.queryFirst(
            "select * from Product where product_id = ${productId}",
            Product.class
        );
        if(product == null) throw new ProductDoesNotExistException();
        AbstractCustomer customer = loadCustomer(customerId);
        Order openOrder = customer.getOpenOrder();
        if (openOrder == null) throw new OrderNotOpenException();
        BigDecimal amount = product.getPrice().multiply(
            new BigDecimal(quantity)
        );
        db.update(
            "UPDATE ORDERS SET
                 TOTAL = ${amount.add(openOrder.getTotal())}"
        );
        LineItem el = db.queryFirst(
            "select * from LINE_ITEM
             where ORDER_ID = ${openOrder.orderId} and
                   PRODUCT_ID = ${productId}
            ", LineItem.class
        );
```

```
        if(el == null)
        {
            LineItem lineItem = new LineItem();
            lineItem.setOrderId(openOrder.getOrderId());
            lineItem.setProductId(product.getProductId());
            lineItem.setAmount(amount);
            lineItem.setProduct(product);
            lineItem.setQuantity(quantity);
            db.update(
                "INSERT INTO LINE_ITEM (
                     ORDER_ID,PRODUCT_ID, amount, quantity)
                 VALUES (
                     ${lineItem.orderId}, ${lineItem.productId},
                     ${lineItem.amount}, ${lineItem.quantity})"
            );
            li =  lineItem;
        }
        else {
            el.setQuantity(el.getQuantity()+ quantity);
            el.setAmount(el.getAmount().add(amount));
            db.update(
               "UPDATE LINE_ITEM SET
                   quantity = ${el.getQuantity()},
                   amount = ${el.getAmount()}"
            );
            li =  el;
        }
    }
    return li;
}
```

removeLineItem

This service implementation simply issues a delete in the context of an `inTransaction`, as shown in Listing 9.45.

Listing 9.45 removeLineItem

```
public void removeLineItem(int customerId,int productId )
throws CustomerDoesNotExistException, OrderNotOpenException,
       ProductDoesNotExistException, NoLineItemsException,
       GeneralPersistenceException {
    db.inTransaction
    {
```

```
        Product product = db.queryFirst(
            "select * from Product
             where product_id = ${productId} ", Product.class
        );
        if(product == null) throw new ProductDoesNotExistException();
        AbstractCustomer customer = loadCustomer(customerId);
        Order openOrder = customer.getOpenOrder();
        if (openOrder == null) throw new OrderNotOpenException();
        db.update(
            "DELETE FROM LINE_ITEM
             WHERE PRODUCT_ID = ${productId} AND
                   ORDER_ID = ${customer.openOrder.orderId}"
        );
    }
}
```

submitOrder

This service method changes the status of the order and removes it from the `openOrder` property of the abstract customer class. Listing 9.46 shows the implementation.

Listing 9.46 submitOrder

```
public void submit(int customerId)
throws CustomerDoesNotExistException,
       OrderNotOpenException, NoLineItemsException {
    db.inTransaction
    {
        AbstractCustomer customer = loadCustomer(customerId);
        Order openOrder = customer.getOpenOrder();
        if (openOrder == null) throw new OrderNotOpenException();
        if (openOrder.getLineitems() == null ||
            openOrder.getLineitems().size() <= 0)
            throw new NoLineItemsException();
        db.update(
            "UPDATE ORDERS
             SET STATUS = ${Order.Status.SUBMITTED.toString()}
             where ORDER_ID = ${openOrder.orderId}"
        );
        db.update("UPDATE CUSTOMER SET OPEN_ORDER = NULL");
    };
}
```

Figure 9.12 shows the common exceptions. You can examine them in code form from the download.

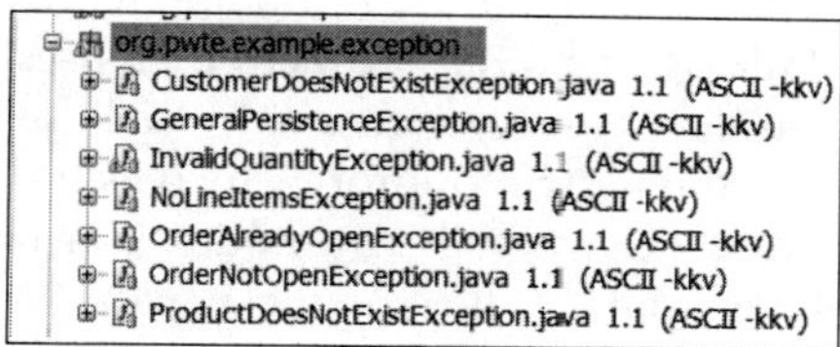

Figure 9.12 Application exceptions.

Packaging the Components

Project Zero applications have a particular layout for their directory structure. This layout provides organization around the parts that make up your application and convention around how your application works. If you follow the conventions and structure defined by Project Zero, your application will be easier to construct and maintain, and you will have less configuration information to provide with the application. Figure 9.13 shows the basic layout of a Project Zero Module and folder structure. The Project Zero Website has a section explaining the complete details [Zero 7].

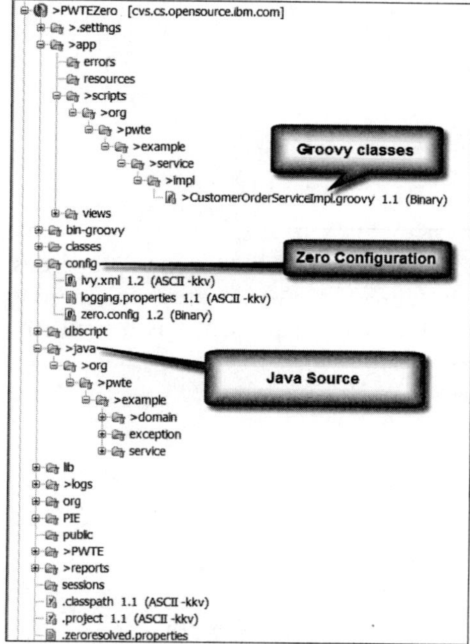

Figure 9.13 Project Zero layout.

In the `config` directory, you will find an `ivy.xml` file. Ivy is a build system from Apache that can ensure your application is using the right versions of the libraries you declare as dependencies in the config file. In Ivy, these libraries are called modules. A module represents an artifact, which is code packaged as either a JAR file or a Zero ZIP file. Zero then uses Ivy to find a module that matches each dependency you declared. Ivy can search the local repository that Zero creates on your system, or it can search remote repositories such as the Project Zero package repository. When a match is found, Ivy downloads the module's artifact into your local repository as necessary and updates your application's classpath to include the dependency. For more information on Ivy, see [Ivy]. Listing 9.47 shows the `ivy.xml` file for our example where we specify Zero packages and database drivers.

Listing 9.47 ivy.xml

```
<?xml version="1.0" encoding="UTF-8" standalone="no"?>
<ivy-module version="1.3">
...    <!--removed package info in text-->
<dependencies>
  <dependency name="zero.core.webtools" org="zero" rev="1.0+"/>
  <dependency name="zero.core" org="zero" rev="1.0+"/>
  <dependency name="commons-dbcp" org="commons-dbcp" rev="1.2.1"/>
  <dependency name="commons-logging" org="commons-logging" rev="1.0.4"/>
  <dependency name="commons-pool" org="commons-pool" rev="1.3"/>
  <dependency name="derbyclient" org="org.apache.derby" rev="10.2.2+"/>
  <dependency name="zero.data" org="zero" rev="1.0+"/>
  <dependency name="junit" org="junit" rev="4.1"/>
  <dependency name="ant" org="ant" rev="1.6.5"/>
 </dependencies>
</ivy-module>
```

The other important configuration file is `zero.config`, which contains runtime properties stored in the Global Context. Listing 9.48 shows the `zero.config` we use to define the DataSource that the Zero Manager will use—it should look familiar to you as it is nearly identical to Listing 9.3.

Listing 9.48 zero.config

```
# HTTP port (default is 8080)
[/app/http]
port=8080
# This config is for Apache Derby databases:

[/app/db/pie/config]
class=org.apache.derby.jdbc.ClientDataSource
serverName=localhost
portNumber=1527
```

```
databaseName=PWTE
connectionAttributes=create=true
```

Unit Testing

We created a separate Project Zero application with specialized unit testing in a Web 2.0 environment. The Unit Test Project includes our application via the `ivy.xml` file. Figure 9.14 shows the layout of the Unit Test Zero application.

The source for our unit test is implemented in Groovy. It is the same common unit test we used to test the other frameworks examined in this book, except we used the Groovy extensions to JUnit instead of Java. Examine the downloadable source for details (see Appendix A, "Setting Up the Common Example").

The Project Zero applications execute in a standalone VM. The goal is to just run the application. For testing, you can right-click on any Zero Project and run it as illustrated in Figure 9.15. In our case, you run the Unit Test Project, which in itself is a Project Zero application. As stated earlier, you can include Zero packages inside of another.

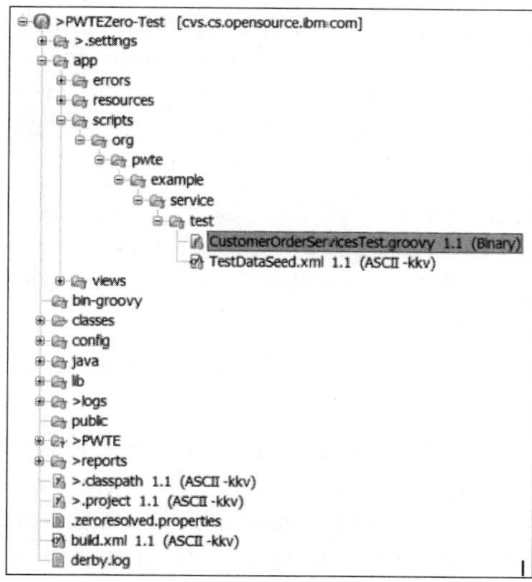

Figure 9.14 Unit Test case.

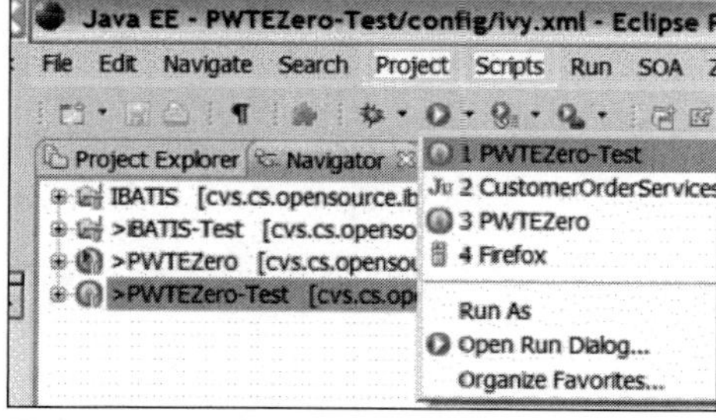

Figure 9.15 Running the test.

Deploying to Production

The persistence layer of a Project Zero application does not have any extra considerations for deployment. The Project Zero architecture allows you to override configurations, so you can provide an override for the Data Source definition as part of your deployment process.

The Project Zero tooling allows you to export applications to be copied for deployment.

You would use the command-line tools for Project Zero to run the application. As a matter of fact, Project Zero allows for pure command-line development of applications as well. The deployment process would just involve running the application using the command-line tools. See the Project Zero developer guide for how to use the command line features [Zero 8].

Summary

This chapter showed how pureQuery technology is optimized for SQL-based development; and how your ability to exploit its tooling may make it well worth choosing pureQuery over straight JDBC or other Table Gateway type frameworks like iBATIS. We also discussed its tight integration with IBM databases so that if you prefer to use an ORM-based framework, especially with an IBM database as the platform of choice, choosing one that is built on top of pureQuery may be your best solution. As concrete examples of this, we showed how the JPA provider could exploit the option to precompile your mapping to generate underlying static SQL. IBM's JPA provider based on OpenJPA is being enhanced to support this feature.

In addition, if you need to move beyond the Enterprise into Web 2.0-based development, using pureQuery in the context of Project Zero may be ideal. We showed you a brief preview of Project Zero using pureQuery to execute the SQL needed to persist objects in the context of applications written in the Groovy scripting language.

We also discussed how pureQuery is in its initial release and the IBM Data Tools continue to evolve to support the full SOA life cycle.

We discussed how Project Zero is evolving, as well. We examined Milestone 1 in detail, and touched on how Milestone 2 and beyond of Project Zero detailed in the website introduces the Zero Resource Model [Zero 9] for mapping database data to RESTful services. As a "sneak peek" of this future state (subject to change, of course), you can define a model as shown in Listing 9.49 in a file named `customer.groovy` within a folder called `/app/models`.

Listing 9.49 Zero Resource Model

```
import zero.resource.fields.*
fields = [
    name: [type: 'CharField', max_length: 30],
    birthDay: [type: 'DateField'],
    is_child: [type: 'BooleanField'],
]
```

```
collections = [
    orders: [member_filters: [is_child: true]],
]
```

A developer would be able to invoke a RESTful service directly through an HTTP request, or invoke it programmatically from applications written in other languages.

This sneak peek illustrates one of the most important aspects of Project Zero that we covered—its pioneering use of Community-Driven Commercial Development (CD^2), where you can follow the progress and provide your input to impact the future direction. The end-goal of developing Project Zero on top of pureQuery is that you can generate fully functional web services around optimized SQL with minimal steps to meet your enterprise requirements now and in the future.

Links to developerWorks

A.9.1 *Overview of pureQuery Tools*
General overview of the pureQuery tools
www.ibm.com/developerworks/db2/library/techarticle/dm-0709surange/

A.9.2 *pureQuery: IBM's New Paradigm for Writing Java Database Applications*
General introduction to pureQuery.
www.ibm.com/developerworks/db2/library/techarticle/dm-0708ahadian/

A.9.3 *Detect and Fix SQL Problems Inside Java Program*
Article showing how to use the pureQuery tools to detect SQL problems with your application
www.ibm.com/developerworks/db2/library/techarticle/dm-0709surange2/

A.9.4 *Building RESTful Services for Your Web Application with Project Zero*
Tutorial on Project Zero showing Data APIs in Action
www.ibm.com/developerworks/ibm/library/i-zero1/

A.9.5 *RESTful applications in an SOA*
Part 2 of tutorial on Project Zero showing Data APIs and ZRM in Action
www.ibm.com/developerworks/ibm/library/i-zero2/

A.9.6 *Use Project Zero's Data Access APIs to Build a Simple Wiki*
An article illustrating the data access API's in Project Zero in the context of building a Wiki.
www.ibm.com/developerworks/web/library/wa-pz-wiki/

References

[Fielding] Fielding, Roy Thomas. *Representational State Transfer (REST).* www.ics.uci.edu/~fielding/pubs/dissertation/rest_arch_style.htm

[Groovy 1] *Groovy: An agile dynamic language for the Java Platform.* groovy.codehaus.org/

[Groovy 2] *Groovy Closures.* groovy.codehaus.org/Closures

[Groovy 3] *Groovy GStrings.* groovy.codehaus.org/Strings

[IBM DS] *IBM Data Studio.* https://www.ibm.com/software/data/studio/

[Ivy] *Apache Ivy Website.* ant.apache.org/ivy/

[Zero 1] *What is Project Zero?.* www.projectzero.org

[Zero 2] *Project Zero: Frequently Asked Questions (FAQ).* www.projectzero.org/wiki/bin/view/Documentation/ZeroFAQ

[Zero 3] *Configuring Data Access in Project Zero (Milestone One).* www.projectzero.org/wiki/bin/view/Documentation/MilestoneOne/DataAccess

[Zero 4] *Project Zero Configuration.* www.projectzero.org/wiki/bin/view/Documentation/CoreDevelopersGuideConfig

[Zero 5] *Project Zero Global Context.* www.projectzero.org/wiki/bin/view/Documentation/CoreDevelopersGuideGlobalContext

[Zero 6] *Project Zero PHP Support.* www.projectzero.org/wiki/bin/view/Documentation/PhpDevelopersGuide

[Zero 7] *Project Zero Application Directory Layout.* www.projectzero.org/wiki/bin/view/Documentation/CoreDevelopersGuideApplicationLayout

[Zero 8] *Project Zero Command Line Reference.* www.projectzero.org/wiki/bin/view/Documentation/CoreDevelopersGuideCliReference

[Zero 9] *Project Zero Resource Model Overview.* www.projectzero.org/wiki/bin/view/Documentation/CoreDevelopersGuideResourceModel

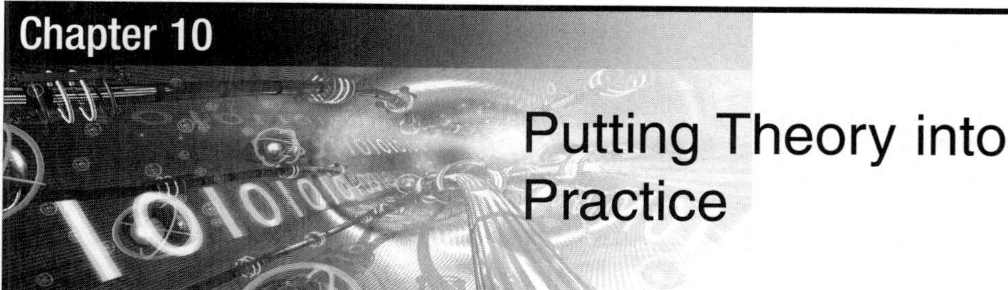

Putting Theory into Practice

It has taken a lot of persistence (in the "perseverance" sense of the term) for you to get to this chapter. Congratulations!

So you should know by now that this book has been all about asking and then answering common questions that you may encounter when deciding which persistence mechanism to use in a given application development project.

Having reached this point, we find that the most common question we are asked is "What do I do now?" In other words, how do you put the theory of the first four chapters and the knowledge contained in the detailed evaluations of the next five chapters into practice?

Answering that question is the purpose of this final chapter.

The Evaluations at a Glance

Now that you have seen each framework in isolation, how do they stack up together? Let us briefly summarize each section of the questionnaire into a table (see Table 10.1 through Table 10.6) for easy reference and, as described in Chapter 4, "Evaluating Your Options," for an apples-to-apples comparison. For details on the meaning of each, see the related evaluations in Chapters 5 through 9.

Background

Table 10.1 Background at a Glance

	JDBC	iBATIS	Hibernate Core	Open JPA	pureQuery
Type of Framework	Direct Access API	Table Gateway	Domain Mapper	Domain Mapper	LINQ and Table Gateway
History	1997	2003	2001	2001 (as Kodo)/ 2005 (as OpenJPA)	2007

Architectural Overview

Table 10.2 Architectural Overview at a Glance

	JDBC	iBATIS	Hibernate Core	Open JPA	pureQuery
Standards Supported	JDBC 1.2, 3.0, 4.0	None	None (Hibernate JPA, JPA 1.0)	JPA 1.0; EJB 3.0	None
Minimum Platform	JSE	JSE	JSE	JSE	JSE
Dependencies	JDBC Driver	JDBC Driver Several Apache Projects shipped with product.	JDBC Driver Several Apache Projects shipped with product.	JDBC Driver Several Apache Projects shipped with product.	JDBC Driver, JCC Driver for enhanced performance
Vendors	Many	Apache	JBoss	BEA, IBM	IBM
Licenses	Many	Apache	LGPL	Apache	IBM

Programming Model

Table 10.3 Programming Model at a Glance

	JDBC	iBATIS	Hibernate Core	Open JPA	pureQuery
Initialization	DriverManager DataSource	SQLMap	Session Factory	Entity Manager Factory Injection inside EJB 3 Container	Data Factory Interface
Connection	Connection	SQLMap Instance	Session	Entity Manager	Data
Transactions	`Connection.setAutoCommit(false)`, JTA, EJB CMT	`SqlMap.begin()`, `SqlMap.commit()`, `SqlMap.rollback`, JTA, EJB CMT	JDBC, JTA API, EJB CMT	Entity Transaction JTA, EJB CMT	Data Interface demarcation, JTA, EJB CMT
Create	SQL insert	SQL insert	HQL insert, getters, Native SQL, Criteria, `Session.save`	getters, `em.persist`	SQL insert
Retrieve	SQL select	SQL select	HQL select, HQL from clause, getters, Native SQL select, Criteria API, `session.load`	EJB-QL select, assessors, Native, `em.find`	SQL select
Update	SQL update	SQL update	HQL Update, setter, Native SQL, Criteria, `session.save`, `session.saveOrUpdate`	EJB-QL UPDATE, getter, Native SQL Update, `em.merge`	SQL update
Delete	SQL delete	SQL delete	HQL, assessors, Native SQL, Criteria	EJB-QL, assessors, Native	SQL delete

continues

Table 10.3 Continued

	JDBC	iBATIS	Hibernate Core	Open JPA	pureQuery
Stored Procedures	SQL Callable Interface	Stored procedure tags	Native SQL	Native SQL	SQL Callable Annotation and API
Batch	Batch statements	Batch statements	Insert, Update, Delete batching	Update, Delete Catching, ISome vendors Tx Batching	Batch Statements
Extension Points	Driver implementations	Cache, types	Cache, types	Cache, types	Scripting, cache, types
Error Handling	Checked SQLException or subclass	Checked SQL Exception or subclass	Unchecked Hibernate Exception	Unchecked Exceptions	Unchecked DataRuntime Exception

ORM Features Supported

Table 10.4 ORM Features Supported at a Glance

	JDBC	iBATIS	Hibernate Core	Open JPA	pureQuery
Objects	Row	POJO to SQL in SQLMap	POJO to Domain in XML (JPA annotations supported)	JPA annotations or XML	Integrated query, annotation, or XML
Inheritance	Simulated via root-leaf and union tables	Custom	Single Table, Concrete subclass, Full inheritance chain	Single Table, Concrete subclass, Full inheritance chain	Custom
Keys	ROW_ID retrieval in JDBC 4.0	Key retrieval through `<selectKey>`	Supported for generated key and automatic retrieval, composite	Supported for generated key and automatic retrieval, composite	Custom, ROW_ID retrieval

	JDBC	iBATIS	Hibernate Core	Open JPA	pureQuery
Attributes	Columns	Setters/ getters	XML or annotation	XML or annotation	XML or annotation
Contained Objects	Limited types, Custom assembled columns	Support for populating graph from SQL	Component (including collections)	Embeddable Objects	Custom
Relationships	Foreign keys, association tables	Support for Join to Object Graph	1-to-1, 1-to-Many, Many-to-Many, uni- and bidirectional, Secondary Table	1-to-1, 1-to-Many, Many-to-Many, uni- and bidirectional, Secondary Table	Partial support for Join to Object Graph
Constraints	Limited, e.g., Null, Not Null, Unique	DB	In ORM and DB	In ORM and DB	DB
Derived Attributes	Limited, e.g., `MAX`, `count`	Custom	Life cycle	Life cycle	Custom

Tuning Options

Table 10.5 Tuning Options at a Glance

	JDBC	iBATIS	Hibernate Core	Open JPA	pureQuery
Query Optimizations	Manual	Manual	Lazy or eager columns	Lazy or eager columns	Manual
Caching	Manual	Support to cache results, plug-in third-party caches	Support to cache objects and results, plug-in third-party caches	Support to cache objects and results, plug-in third-party caches	Support to cache results, plug-in third-party caches
Loading Related Objects	Manual with Join	Manual with Join	Eager or lazy relationships	Eager or lazy relationships	Manual with Join

continues

Table 10.5 Continued

	JDBC	iBATIS	Hibernate Core	Open JPA	pureQuery
Locking	Isolation Levels	Isolation Levels	Isolation Levels, Lock API, Version Number support	Isolation Levels, Lock API, Version Number support	Isolation Levels

Development Process for the Common Example

Table 10.6 Development Process at a Glance

	JDBC	iBATIS	Hibernate Core	Open JPA	pureQuery
Defining the Objects	Create POJO	Create POJO and SQLMap	Create POJO and Hibernate Mapping files	Create POJO with annotations, or POJO with XML	Create POJO with annotations, and execute in SQL
Implementing the Services	Code using APIs	Code using SQLMap	Code using Session	Code using the Entity Manger	Special Service Annotation for SQL generation or use of Data API
Packaging the Components		Bytecode enhance-ment for lazy loading		Bytecode enhancement	Precompile options for static SQL

What Do You Do Now?

As we have done before in this book, let us start with what *not* to do in order to better motivate you for what you *should* do.

Don't Reinvent the Wheel to Avoid Making Trade-offs

Chapters 5 through 9 and the summary tables in the previous sections explore the details of JDBC, iBATIS, Hibernate Core, OpenJPA, and pureQuery within the context of our questionnaire. Within this context, you can see that each mechanism has its strengths and weaknesses. In other words, none is perfect for every situation; so you will likely have to make trade-offs for whichever mechanism you choose. For example:

- **JDBC** is good for applications in which the queries are dynamic and you need programmatic control of various tuning features to maximize performance. However, as the coding examples show, JDBC is relatively complex to use because you have to code the persistence logic yourself.
- **iBATIS** does a great job of insulating your object programmers from the details of JDBC and SQL by providing some ORM functions and keeping the SQL in a separate config file —especially applications that are based heavily on Stored Procedures or well-architected SQL from a DBA. However, if you prefer not to explicitly code SQL or if your domain objects have a complex life cycle, then iBATIS is not likely the best choice for you.
- **Hibernate Core** has a much more advanced ORM layer and has served as the basis for the new JPA standard; however, developers should begin to use the Hibernate JPA APIs if standards are important. Also, if you are using the JBoss Application Server, using Hibernate Core is a natural choice.
- **OpenJPA**, like Hibernate, has an excellent ORM layer that lets your Java programmers think in object terms. It has the additional advantage of being based on an industry standard and the capability to annotate the code and forgo the need for a mapping XML. ISVs may find the Apache license a better option for shipping software solutions based on OpenJPA. In addition, if you are using the WebSphere Application Server or WebLogic Server, using the OpenJPA-based runtime shipped with their container makes the most sense.
- **pureQuery** enables relational queries to be embedded in the Java code itself; however, it is relatively new as of publication and may undergo a number of changes that could impact code you write today. That said, it can have major advantages from a performance and tracing standpoint, especially if using DB2. Furthermore, pureQuery can be used in other types of environments, such as Web 2.0-based environments. Like iBATIS, applications that are based heavily on stored procedures or SQL written by a separate role such as a DBA should consider pureQuery as well. It is also worth noting that another persistence mechanism, such as the Groovy API's in Project Zero, may choose to implement on top of the pureQuery engine to exploit the performance and management features.

Some architects will not be willing to make the trade-offs associated with each of these mechanisms and will instead use this knowledge as an excuse to invent their own persistence framework exactly tailored to their requirements. Although inventing your own persistence layer can be fun, especially for architects with a strong computing science background, we advise against doing so because it puts your programmers in the middleware business instead of developing mission-critical enterprise applications.

Why is this? Because it may seem relatively simple to develop a framework on top of a mechanism such as JDBC, but the runtime aspects of such a framework are only the tip of the iceberg. Very quickly, you will find yourself having to develop a number of tools to support other aspects of the application such as:

- Analysis, design, coding, and unit testing of each component
- Configuration and assembly of an end-to-end functional application
- Functional verification testing and debugging
- Deployment into system test or production environments
- Operations, including admin, monitoring, problem determination, and tuning

Further, if you build your own homegrown framework, you must also write documentation and create training programs for each of these tools geared toward the roles that use them. The reality is that the need to support your framework with tooling, documentation, and training will totally consume the resources of your team, leaving them no time to build any enterprise applications.

Invariably your requirements will change as user expectations and underlying technologies change, leaving you in the same situation you are in now—needing to understand how to make hard choices and real trade-offs among existing mechanisms.

Embrace and Extend Open-Source Projects

If after understanding the challenges you still find yourself tempted to build your own proprietary persistence mechanism, we recommend that you keep in mind the overarching goals of any framework, whether used for providing persistence or another major aspect of the solution architecture:

- Less skill required to build solutions through separating the concerns
- Higher quality solutions through reuse of assets and best practices
- Faster development times through tooling that targets the roles involved

We also recommend that you use the template developed in Chapter 4 as a guide to the questions you must be prepared to answer. In other words, reuse the questionnaire as an outline of your requirements, and fill in the details of each section the way you imagine your framework will be.

Our hope is that this exercise will lead you back to choosing an existing mechanism instead of building one yourself. But with that said, there may come a time when you must do some invention to meet specific project requirements that cannot be met in any other way.

In this case, we strongly recommend that you exploit an open-source community project like iBATIS or OpenJPA and extend it only as much as is needed for your project. This approach will let you piggyback on the skills and supporting tools developed by the community—including vendors who have embraced the project and any associated standards.

Assuming you take our advice to focus on the business applications that support your enterprise, you can submit your extensions back to the open-source community so that you aren't stuck supporting them. You will be surprised at how quickly runtime components and associated tools and documentation you never dreamed of will emerge from the collective wisdom of the open-source community.

Use an Agile Process and Continually Refactor

Exploiting the open-source community is one way to embrace change rather than trying to insulate your team from it. You can design your development processes to embrace change as well. We have found that agile approaches are best because they focus your attention on the practical problems that need to be solved during development of small but essential "increments" of application functions.

Agile incremental approaches fit well with our philosophy to "think before you act—just don't do all of your thinking before acting." That is, you should analyze the requirements before you design a solution, and then code, test, and deploy the application components; however, you should not do all the analysis, then design the entire solution, and then code the entire application before you test it on your users.

Although it is not the intent of this book to be a definitive guide for agile methods, Figure 10.1, a graphic from the Rational Unified Process (RUP), shows how a disciplined software engineering method (thinking before you act) can work together with an agile approach (not doing all of your thinking before acting).

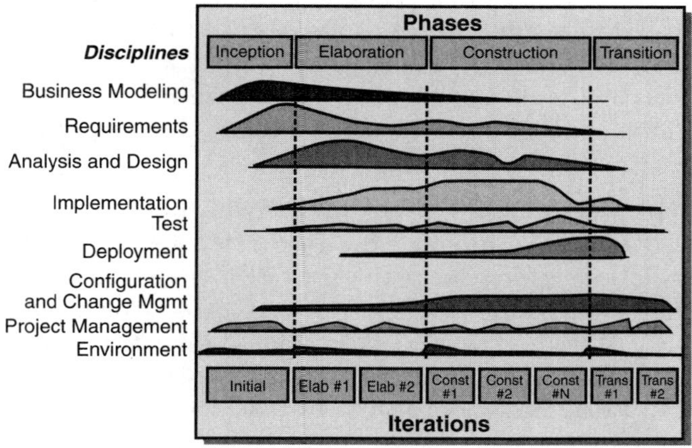

Figure 10.1 The Rational Unified Process.

See the excellent IBM Press book on RUP by Joshua Barnes for more details [RUP]; however, the basic idea is that you use all the disciplines (shown as rows in Figure 10.1) to some extent or another in every phase (shown as columns)—each of which represents a project in its own right. And each phase can have a number of smaller, possibly overlapping increments to further break down the deliverable units. The graphs shown in each row indicate the amount of effort devoted to that discipline within that phase or iteration. So, for example, in the early inception phase, which is all about trying to prove the feasibility of the project, you will see more focus on modeling the business processes being supported and their requirements, but with enough analysis, design, implementation, test, and deployment to understand the end-to-end process.

The benefit of an agile approach like RUP boils down to early and often validation, which leads to refactoring the application components into better and better solutions before inertia sets in to your design and makes it nearly impossible to change.

Here is how we have applied RUP to meeting enterprise persistence requirements:

1. **Establish project constraints.** Scope a release to support some essential business processes. Chapter 2, "High-Level Requirements and Persistence," serves as a good guide to capture the high-level functional and quality-of-service requirements you are intending to meet.

2. **Identify representative use cases.** Pick some use cases out of the complete list that are indicative of the points of variability within the architecture, and then model them in detail. Chapter 3, "Designing Persistent Object Services," will help here. Use these requirements to customize your questionnaire for evaluation; we recommend starting with the one provided in Chapter 4. (See the Download site for an electronic version that you can edit.)

3. **Develop candidate architectures.** Design, implement, and test solutions for those use cases using one or more of the mechanisms that best fit the requirements. For a real project we would go a step beyond the unit tests described in Chapters 5 through 9, and actually "stress" test these candidates in as close to a real production environment as possible. (See the Download site for code you can use as a starting point and Appendix A for instructions on setup and executing the test cases in an Eclipse environment.)

4. **Customize the development process.** Based on the results (which may result in more than one choice of mechanism depending on the use case requirements), create an architecture "cookbook" for each representative use case that your team can use in later phases to develop the remaining use cases of that "type." You should test this cookbook on a "typical" team of developers in order to validate that you can get the same results as you did with the lead architects who designed the solution, possibly with process assist tools developed with the Rational Method Composer [A.10.1].

A.10.1

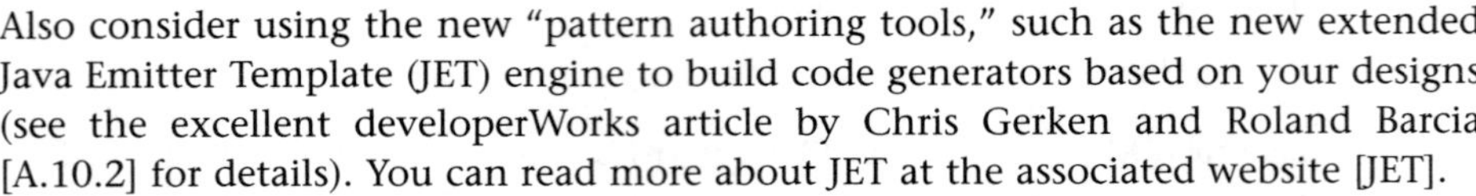

Also consider using the new "pattern authoring tools," such as the new extended Java Emitter Template (JET) engine to build code generators based on your designs (see the excellent developerWorks article by Chris Gerken and Roland Barcia [A.10.2] for details). You can read more about JET at the associated website [JET].

A.10.2

We like to do these steps as early in the process as possible—such as during the inception phase (although they apply to any phase). Figure 10.2 shows these steps graphically.

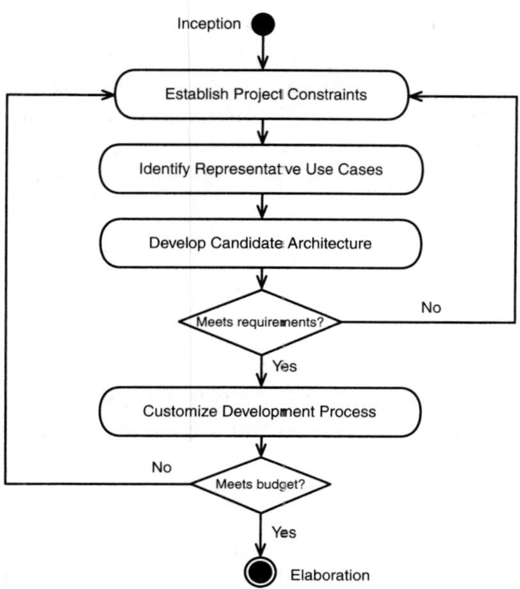

Figure 10.2 Steps we like to follow during the RUP inception phase.

This approach ensures that you meet the IT requirements associated with persistence before you invest too much time in a particular "pattern."

Be Prepared to Revisit Your Decisions

We also recommend that you document your decisions as you make them so that (a) you do not continually have the same discussions over and over again, and (b) you can more easily determine the impact of changing your mind or refactoring the design by understanding the dependencies between decisions. Minimally, we like to capture the following aspects of each decision (again, listed as a set of questions that need to be answered for those who follow you):

- **Issue**—What is the problem you were trying to solve?
- **Context**—Where in the architecture does this issue come up? What were the assumptions?
- **Forces**—What are the functional and nonfunctional requirements that will drive the decision?
- **Alternatives**—What approaches did you consider? How do they solve the issue? What were the pros and cons of each, taking into account the context and forces?
- **Decision**—What was your decision and why?
- **Related issues**—Based on your decision, what other issues come up that are dependent on this one?

Within the context of persistence in the enterprise and this book, Chapter 4 documents the general set of forces we like to consider (with Chapters 1-3 providing the background); and Chapters 5 through 9 give you a good head start on the alternatives to consider, as well as details on how they solve the problem. Your specific project requirements add to the context and forces and will enable you to enumerate the pros and cons and make your decision. Documenting these decisions and dependencies will help you retrace only the steps necessary when and if you change your mind.

Summary

A journey of 1,000 miles begins with the first step. And though it may seem like you have come 1,000 miles already, the journey has really just begun. Our hope is to have given you the right mix of abstract theory and concrete examples so that you can put these principles into practice.

Specifically, this book has done the following:

- Recounted a brief history of object-relational mapping approaches that positioned the leading Java persistence mechanisms with respect to those that have been used to develop successful enterprise solutions in the past.
- Explored the high-level requirements of enterprise applications and how they drive the need for persistence of data and object-relational mapping.
- Explored how domain modeling can be used to capture the detailed design and introduced a hypothetical Order Management application to illustrate the three basic ORM approaches.
- Introduced a method for an "apples to apples" comparison of persistence mechanisms based on a questionnaire derived from these enterprise requirements and a common example.
- Analyzed five popular Java persistence mechanisms in the context of this questionnaire—both to give you a fish for today and to teach you how to fish for tomorrow.

Hopefully, we have asked and answered enough of the typical questions and provided enough "escape valves" for embracing change that you feel confident enough to take the next step on your own.

And finally, we sincerely wish you luck in your adventures in providing persistence within the enterprise—one step at a time.

Links to developerWorks

A.10.1 *Rational Method Composer, Part 1: Key Concepts*

This first of a series by Peter Haumer describes the basics of the Rational Method Composer.

www-128.ibm.com/developerworks/rational/library/dec05/haumer/ index.html

A.10.2 *Get Started with Model Driven Development using the Design Pattern Toolkit*

This excellent two part series on how to use the Design Pattern Toolkit to make Model Driven Development a practical reality was authored by Chris Gerken, the primary inventor of DPTK, and Roland Barcia, one of the authors of this book.

Part 1: www.ibm.com/developerworks/websphere/techjournal/0607_barcia/0607_barcia.html

Part 2: www.ibm.com/developerworks/websphere/techjournal/0610_barcia/0610_barcia.html

References

[JET] *JET Model-to-Text (M2T)*. www.eclipse.org/modeling/m2t/?project=jet

[RUP] Barnes, Joshua. *Implementing the IBM Rational Unified Process and Solutions: A Guide to Improving Your Software Development Capability and Maturity*. IBM Press, 2007

Appendix A

Setting Up the Common Example

This book comes with sample code (available on the book's companion website) that implements the common example used throughout the technology evaluation chapters, 5-9. This appendix will show you how to set up and run the example for each persistent technology. In addition, this appendix documents how to set up Apache Derby with the schema for the common example, how to import each sample into a Java Eclipse Development Environment, and how to run the Unit Test to test our persistence action.

We must begin with a caveat: This appendix and the links necessary to download materials were accurate at the time we went to press. However, there is no guarantee that the links will still be active when you are reading this. If you find that links are broken, try to use a popular search engine from your browser to find the materials.

We also need to mention that we treat some references a bit differently in this appendix than we do in the other chapters. Because this appendix is basically a checklist you need to follow, we include links associated with instruction steps directly in the text—to keep you from getting the "whiplash" that can occur from jumping back and forth. Where we do have references to material that provides extra background or details that may be of interest to some of you, we will treat them in the usual way.

Brief Background of Supporting Technologies

In this section, we give a brief overview of other technologies we used to run the example. Specifically, we discuss the database we used, Apache Derby. We briefly talk about the Eclipse platform as an IDE, and we discuss JUnit and DbUnit.

Apache Derby

Apache Derby is an open-source, standards-based database written purely in Java. Its diminutive footprint makes it especially attractive for development testing. The database system is based on technology donated to the Apache Software Foundation by IBM. The database is released under the Apache Derby project.

Apache Derby traces its roots back to 1996, when Cloudscape, Inc. embarked on the task to build a database server written in the Java language. As history would have it, a year later, Cloudscape, Inc. produced its first database release, called JBMS. Shortly after, that database was named Cloudscape®. In 1999, Cloudscape, Inc. was acquired by Informix® Software Inc. IBM bought Informix in 2001, and the IBM Cloudscape found its way into a number of IBM middleware products as an embedded database engine. IBM donated the Cloudscape database to the Apache Software Foundation in April 2004. That event marked the birth of the Apache Derby project. In July 2005, the Derby project hatched from the Apache incubator and is now a subproject of the "DB" top-level project at Apache. Sun Microsystems joined the Derby project right before Derby graduated from incubation. In December 2006, with the release of Java 6, Sun started packaging Derby in the JDK as Java DB.

Apache Derby is ideal for development and proof of concept efforts. Apache Derby's ease of use and small footprint were some of the key motivators for using it as the testbed of examples in this book.

Eclipse

Eclipse is an extensible open-source IDE (Integrated Development Environment). The Eclipse Project was launched in November 2001, when IBM donated $40 million worth of source code derived from its WebSphere Studio Workbench. The tandem combination of the Eclipse platform combined with the Java Development Tools (JDT) produced by the Eclipse Project yields an IDE that has gained great respect throughout the Java development community. Most of IBM's modern suite of application development tools, including Rational Application Developer, Rational Software Architect, and the WebSphere Application Server Toolkit, are built on top of the Eclipse Platform.

For this book, the familiarity of much of the Java development community with Eclipse was our motivator for choosing it as the IDE for development. Of course, there is nothing binding you to use a particular IDE (or any at all, for that matter). You could opt to be a purist and stick to the command line. Of course, you can also mow your lawn with a pair of scissors. We just don't find it to be very efficient.

JUnit and DbUnit

JUnit [Junit] is a unit-testing framework for the Java programming language that we explained briefly in Chapter 3, "Designing Persistent Object Services." Because JUnit and DbUnit are so important to the setup, we feel the information is worth repeating.

Created by Kent Beck and Erich Gamma, JUnit is one of, and arguably the most successful of, the xUnit family of frameworks that originated with Kent Beck's SUnit. JUnit has spawned its own ecosystem of JUnit extensions. "JUnit" is also a synonym for unit tests in general, as in, "Did you run the junits before you checked in?"

Experience gained with JUnit has been important in the development of test-driven development, and as a result, some knowledge of JUnit is often presumed in discussions of agile test-first approaches—for example, in the book *Test-Driven Development: By Example* [Beck].

One extension of JUnit is DbUnit [DbUnit]. DbUnit is a JUnit extension targeted for database-driven projects that, among other things, puts your database into a known state between test runs. This is an excellent way to avoid the myriad of problems that can occur when one test case corrupts the database and causes subsequent tests to fail or exacerbate the damage. DbUnit is an open-source framework created by Manuel Laflamme.

DbUnit has the capability to export and import your database data to and from XML datasets. Since version 2.0, DbUnit can work with very large datasets when used in streaming mode. DbUnit can also help you verify that your database data matches the expected set of values.

In our common example, we use JUnit and DbUnit to test our Service Interface.

Setting Up the Prerequisites

Download Source Code

Download `PWTE.zip` from the book website,

ibmpressbooks.com/title/9780131587564.

Once unpacked, the zip file includes the directory structure shown in Figure A.1.

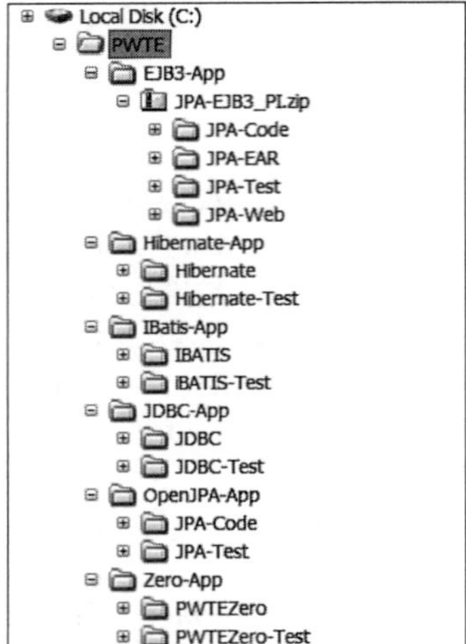

Figure A.1 Download Directory Structure

JDK 5.0

The examples require a Java 5.0 development environment. A Java 5.0 development kit can be acquired from the following online resources:

www.ibm.com/developerworks/java/jdk/
java.sun.com/javase/downloads/index_jdk5.jsp

Eclipse 3.2+

Acquire Eclipse 3.2.2 or later from the following website:

www.eclipse.org/downloads/

Apache Derby Eclipse Plug-in

Acquire and install the Apache Derby Core and UI plug-ins for Derby 10.2 or later from the following website:

db.apache.org/derby/integrate/plugin_howto.html

Project Zero M1 Eclipse Plug-In

The Milestone 1 Project Zero Eclipse Plug-in is required to work with the example. We have not tested in future Milestones. The Eclipse update site and corresponding directions for installation can be found at the following site:

www.projectzero.org/wiki/bin/view/Download/WebHome

Importing and Running the Code for a Particular Persistence Technology

In this section, we give you step-by-step instructions on how to load the source code for each of the technologies and how to run the unit test. We assume that you will read the chapters that accompany each technology for an understanding of the application. We also assume that you have set up the prerequisites in the preceding section.

Importing the Java SE Applications

This section walks you through importing the code for the various technologies that run in a Java SE application. From your Eclipse workspace you will import the JDBC Project into your Eclipse workspace. You can right-click from the Project or Package Explorer and select Import, as shown in Figure A.2.

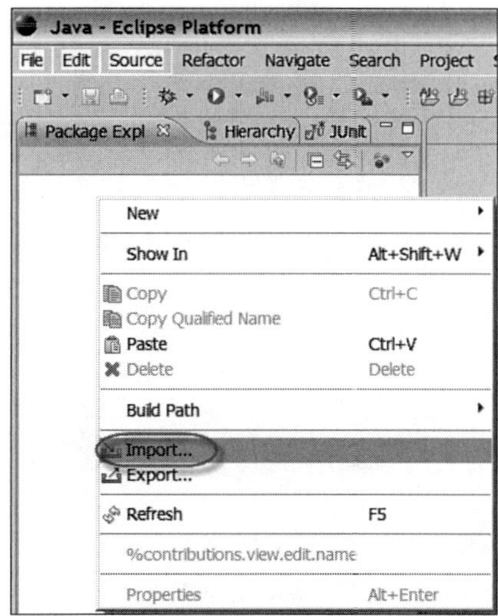

Figure A.2 Import menu option.

Select `Existing Projects into Workspace`, as shown in Figure A.3, and then click Next.

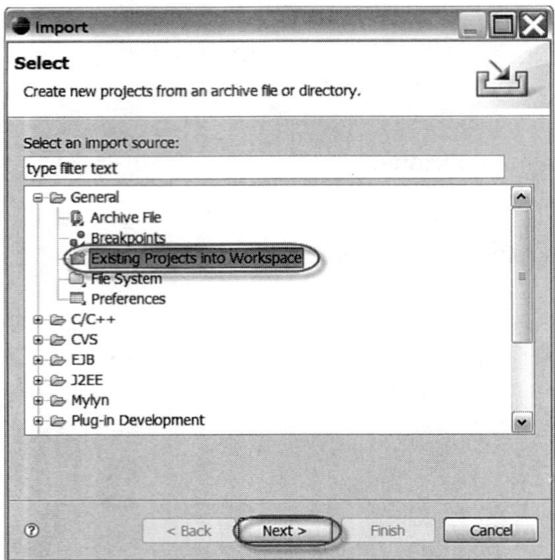

Figure A.3 `Existing Projects into Workspace` folder.

Inside the Import Projects screen, the root directory should be *<Location to where you extracted the Zip>*`/PWTE`, as shown in Figure A.4. Select all the projects under Projects. Ensure that the Copy Projects into Workspace option is selected. Click Finish.

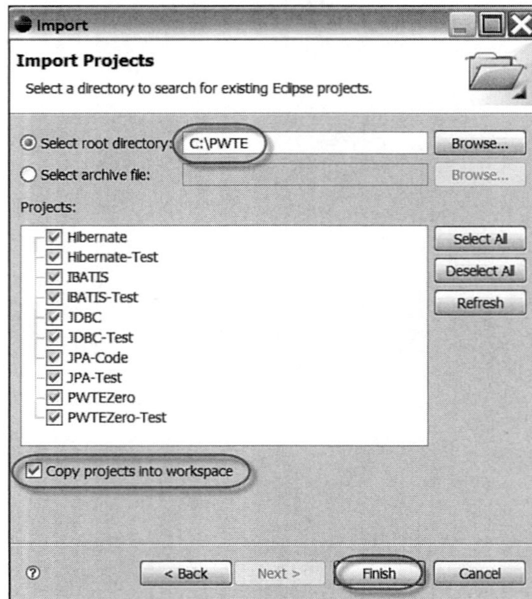

Figure A.4 Import Projects screen.

Resolving DbUnit for the Projects

The Test Projects depend on DbUnit. All Test Projects except for Project Zero (we will configure that one later) have an Eclipse User Library configured for DbUnit. Right-click on the `DbUnit` folder and select Configure, as shown in Figure A.5, for the JDBC-Test, iBatis-Test, Hibernate-Test, and JPA-Test.

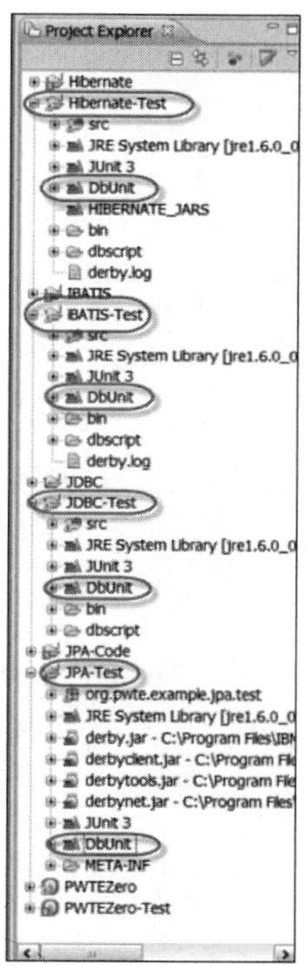

Figure A.5 Configure the DbUnit Library.

Click the User Libraries button. Then select DbUnit and click Add Library, as shown in Figure A.6. There you can add the `dbunit-2.2.jar` file that you downloaded from the DbUnit site discussed in the section "Setting Up the Prerequisites."

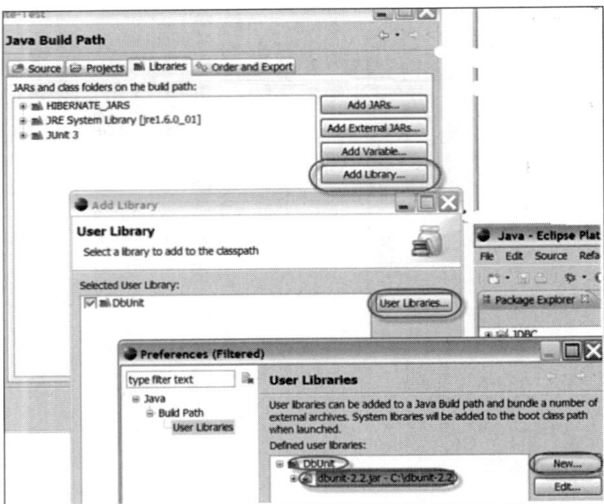

Figure A.6 Add dbunit-2.2jar to the Library.

Add Apache Derby Nature

Next, right-click on JDBC-Test (or any Test Project) project and select Apache Derby, Add Apache Derby Nature, as shown in Figure A.7.

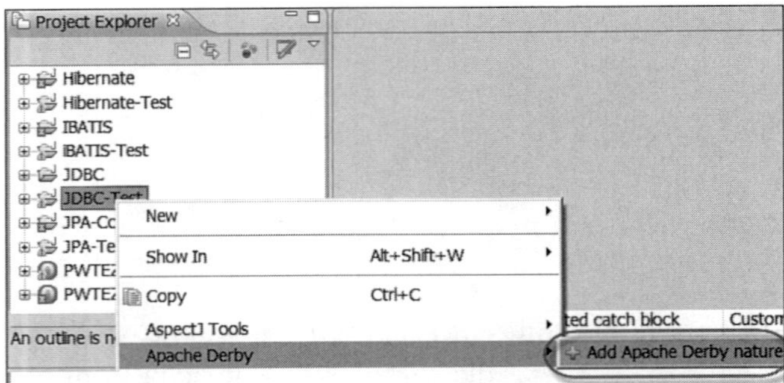

Figure A.7 Add Apache Derby Nature.

Start the Apache Network Server

Right-click the project again and select Apache Derby, Start Derby Network Server, as shown in Figure A.8.

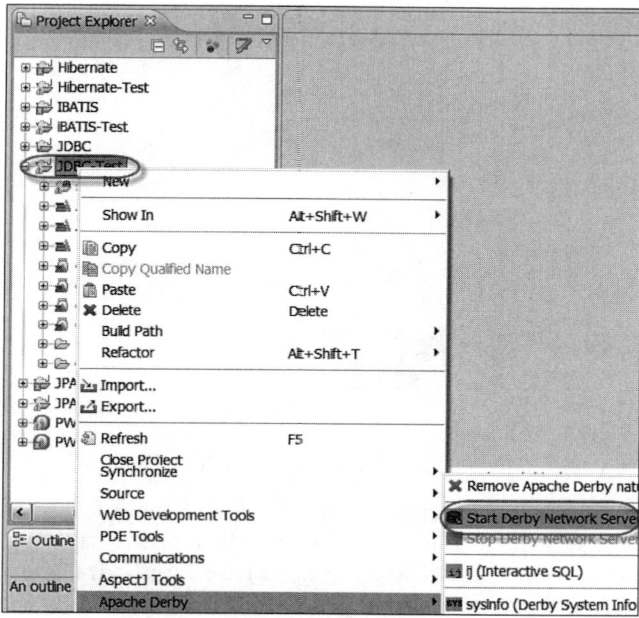

Figure A.8 Start the Network Server.

The Console should display the Apache Derby Network Server with a status showing it as started.

Running the Database Script

Under the JDBC-Test Project, expand the `dbscript` folder and right-click on `schema-1.4.sql`. Select Apache Derby, Run SQL Script Using "ij". As a brief explanation, ij is the command-line tool for Derby that runs the SQL scripts. The step shown in Figure A.9 will create the necessary tables for the common example applications.

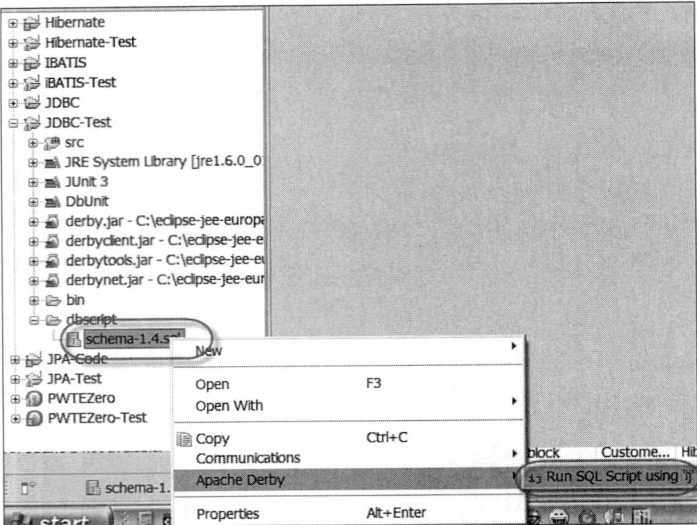

Figure A.9 Run the SQL Script using ij.

The console should display the result of the table it creates. There will likely be some errors the first time you run a script because the script will attempt to delete the tables in case they existed already. Do not worry too much about any delete errors you see. This extra delete step makes the script more robust so that it can be run in any state to initialize the database tables.

Running the JDBC Unit Test

From the Package Explorer, in the Java Perspective, expand the `src` folder. Expand the Java package `com.pwte.example.jdbc.test`. Right-click on `CustomerOrderServicesTest.java` and select Run As, then JUnit Test, as shown in Figure A.10.

The JUnit View should open and display six successful JUnit results, as shown in Figure A.11.

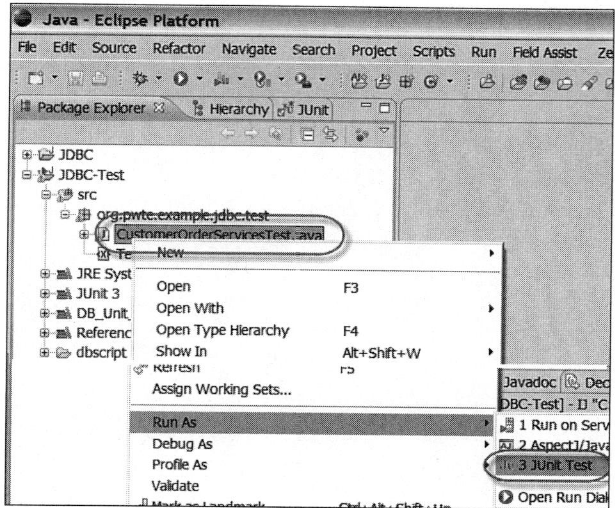

Figure A.10 Run the JUnit test.

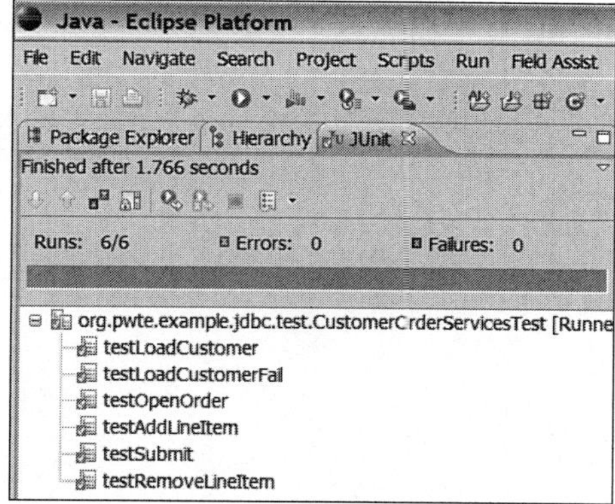

Figure A.11 JDBC Unit test results.

Resolve iBATIS Dependencies

This section walks you through running the application for the iBATIS application shown in Chapter 6, "Apache iBATIS." ***You need to download version 2.3 of iBATIS from here:*** ibatis.apache.org/javadownloads.cgi.

You need to add your dependency to iBATIS. Expand the iBATIS Project. From the Project Explorer, right-click `IBATIS_LIBRARY` and select Configure, as shown in Figure A.12.

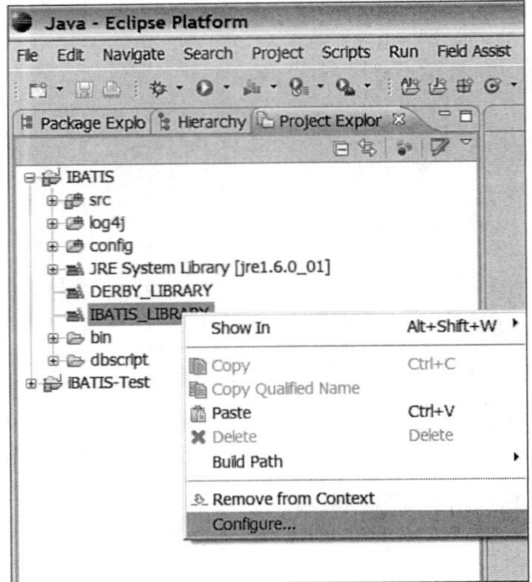

Figure A.12 Configure the iBATIS library.

Click the User Libraries button. Then select the DbUnit and click Add JARs, as shown in Figure A.13. There you can add the `ibatis-2.3.0.xxx.jar` and `log4j-1.2.15.jar` files that you downloaded from the ibatis site shown in the beginning of this section.

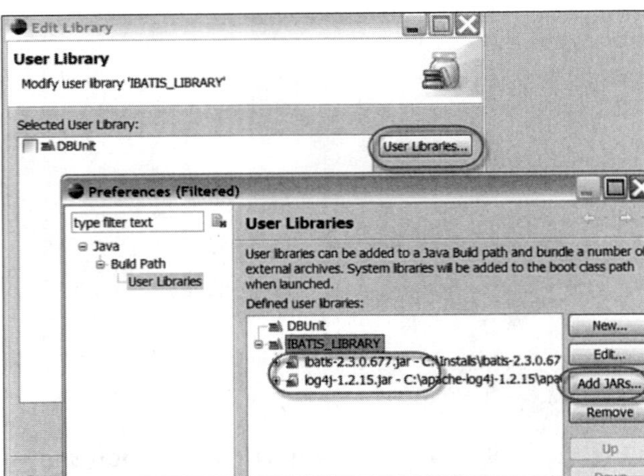

Figure A.13 iBATIS user libraries.

Running the iBATIS JUnit

From the Package Explorer, in the Java Perspective, expand the `src` folder. Expand the Java package `com.pwte.example.ibatisc.test`. Right-click on `CustomerOrderServicesTest.java` and select Run As, then JUnit Test, as shown in Figure A.14.

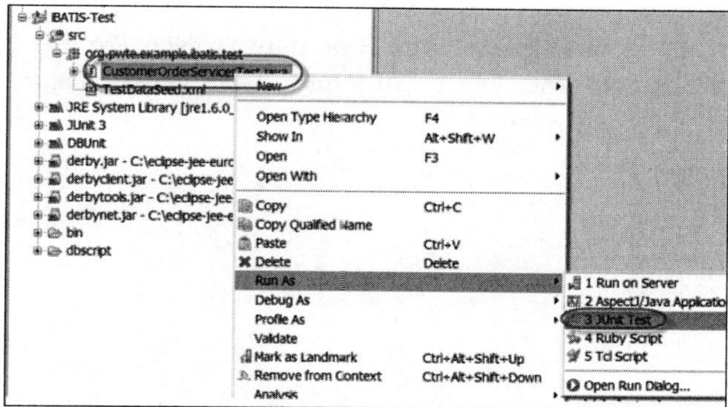

Figure A.14 Run iBATIS.

The JUnit View should open and display six successful JUnit results, as shown in Figure A.15.

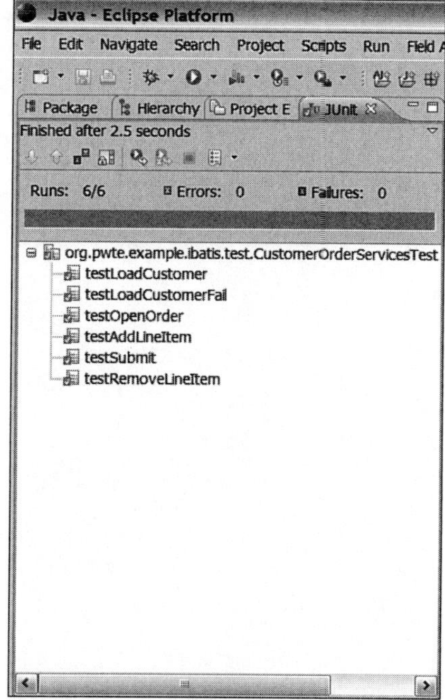

Figure A.15 iBATIS JUnit result.

Resolve Your Hibernate Dependencies

This section walks you through setting up the code and application for the JDBC application shown in Chapter 7, "Hibernate Core." ***You need to download Hibernate 3.2 from here:*** sourceforge.net/project/showfiles.php?group_id=40712&package_ id=127784&release _id=529023.

You need to add your dependency to Hibernate. Expand the Hibernate Project. From the Project Explorer, right-click `HIBERNATE_JARS` and select Configure, as shown in Figure A.16.

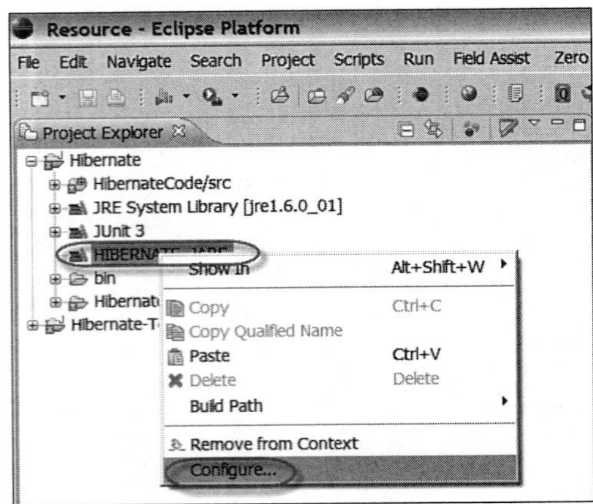

Figure A.16 Hibernate Library.

Click the User Libraries button. Then select `HIBERNATE_JARS` and click Add JARs, as shown in Figure A.17. Add the following JARs (available as part of the Hibernate distribution):

- `hibernate3.jar`
- `xml-apis.jar`
- `dom4j-1.6.1.jar`
- `common-collections-2.1.1.jar`
- `commons-logging-1.0.4.jar`
- `cglib-2.1.3.jar`
- `asm.jar`
- `jta.jar`

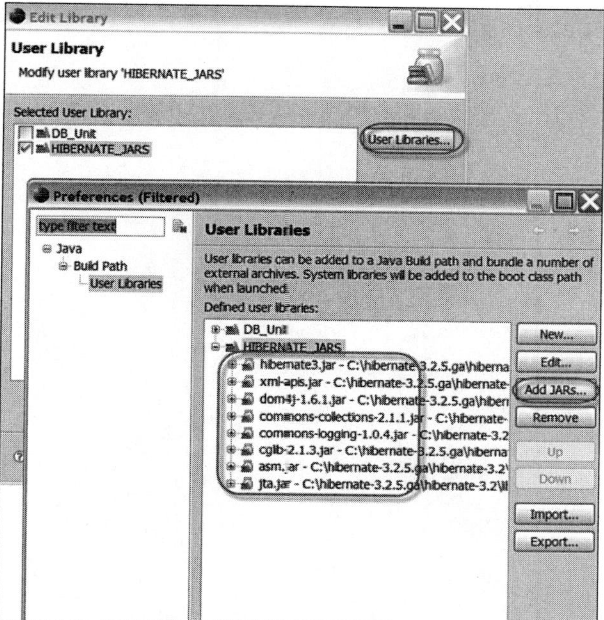

Figure A.17 Hibernate dependencies.

Running the Hibernate Application

From the Package Explorer, in the Java Perspective, expand the `src` folder. Expand the Java package `com.pwte.example.hibernate.test`. Right-click on `CustomerOrderServicesTest.java` and select Run As, then JUnit Test, as shown in Figure A.18.

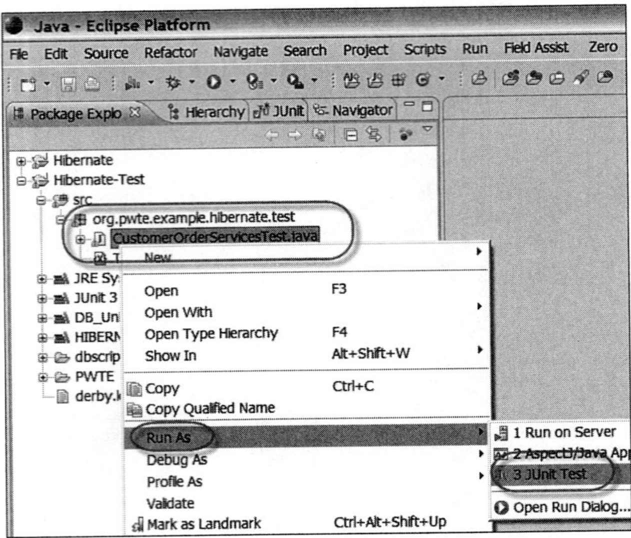

Figure A.18 Run the JUnit test.

The JUnit View should open and display six successful JUnit results, as shown in Figure A.19.

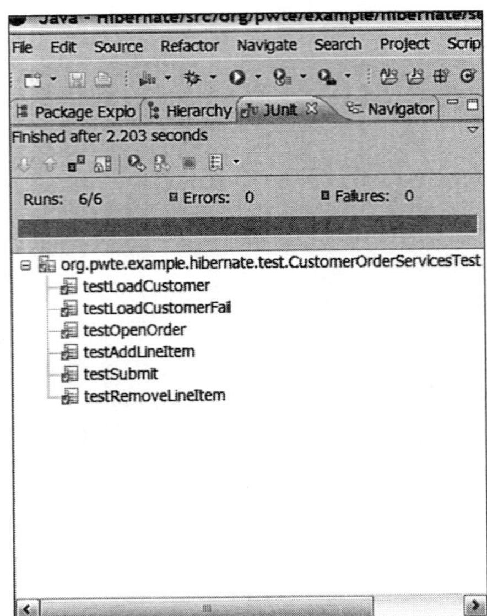

Figure A.19 Hibernate JUnit result.

Resolving OpenJPA Dependencies

This section walks you through setting up the code and running the application for the OpenJPA application in Chapter 8, "Apache OpenJPA." This is the Java SE version. The next section shows you how to run the Java EE version. To do this, ***you first need to download version 1.0.1 of OpenJPA from here***:

openjpa.apache.org/downloads.html.

You need to add your dependencies to OPEN_JPA. Expand the OpenJPA Project. From the Project Explorer, right-click `OPEN_JPA` and select Configure, as shown in Figure A.20.

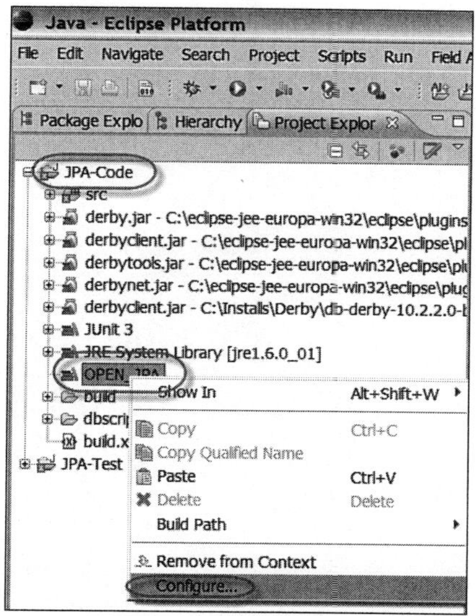

Figure A.20 Configure the OPEN_JPA Library.

Click the User Libraries button. Then select `OPEN_JPA` and click Add JARs, as shown in Figure A.21. Add the following JARs (available as part of the Open distribution):

- `openjpa-1.0.1.jar`
- `geronimo-jta_1.1_spec-1.1.jar`
- `serp-1.13.1.jar`
- `commons-collections-3.2.jar`
- `commons-lang-2.1.jar`
- `commons-logging-1.0.4.jar`
- `commons-pool-1.3.jar`
- `geronimo-jpa_3.0_spec_1.0.jar`

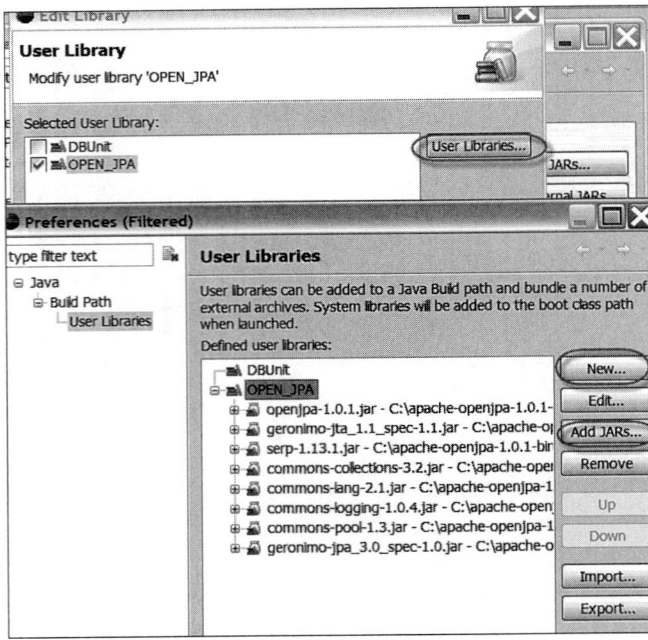

Figure A.21 Add OPEN_JPA JARs.

Run Byte Code Enhancement for OpenJPA

OpenJPA needs bytecode enhancement of the persistent classes, as described in Chapter 8, to the persistent classes. We provided a build script that runs the enhancer. Right-click the `build.xml` file, as shown in Figure A.22, and select Run As, then Ant Build (the second option with the 3).

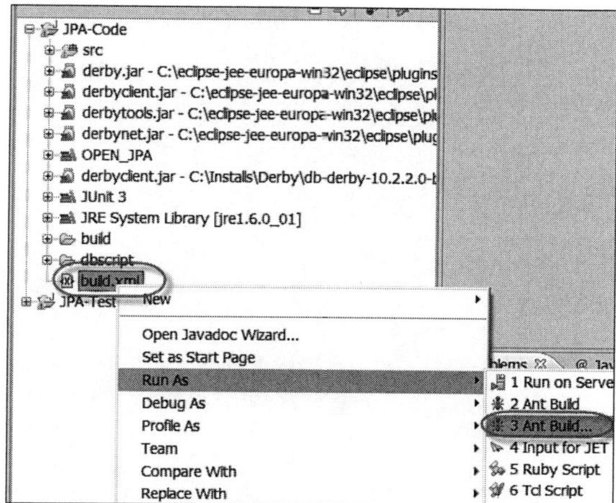

Figure A.22 Open Ant Build.

Click on the Classpath tab and add the OpenJPA JARs included in the distribution, as shown in Figure A.23.

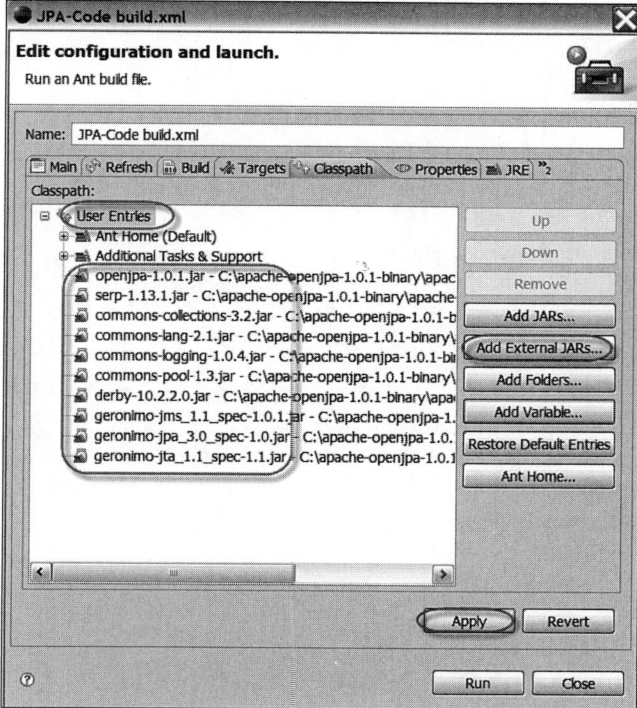

Figure A.23 Ant dependencies.

Under the Targets tab, select Enhance. Then click Run, as shown in Figure A.24.

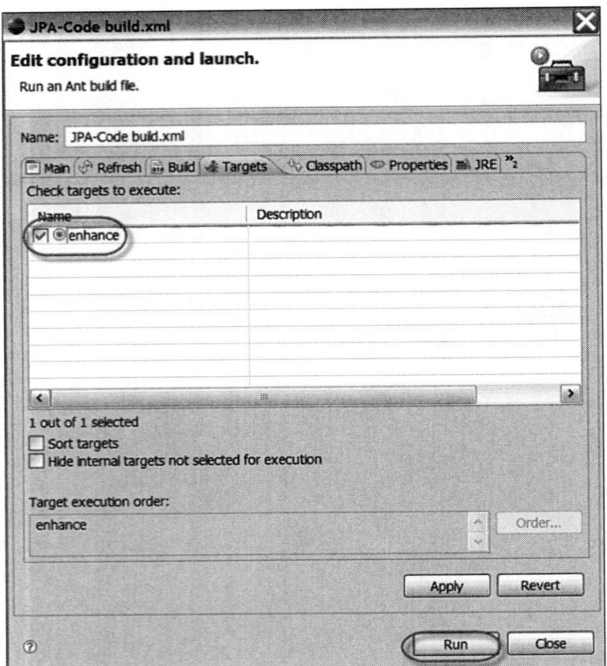

Figure A.24 Run Enhance.

The console should display the results, as shown in Figure A.25.

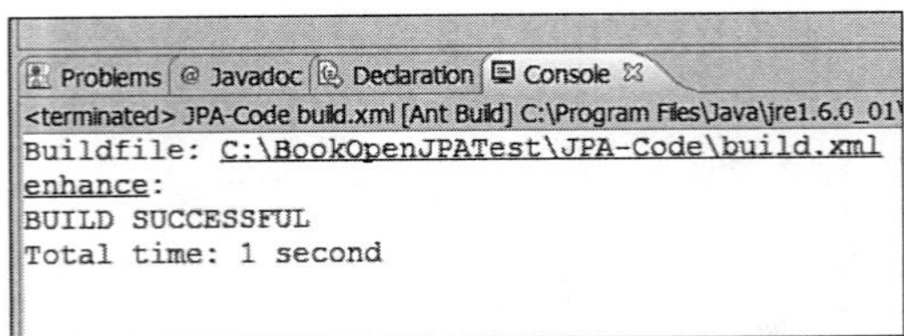

Figure A.25 Open JPA Bytecode Enhancement Results screen.

Running the OpenJPA Application

From the Package Explorer, in the Java Perspective, expand the `src` folder. Expand the Java package `com.pwte.example.jdbc.test`. Right-click on `CustomerOrderServicesTest.java` and select Run As, then JUnit Test, as shown in Figure A.26.

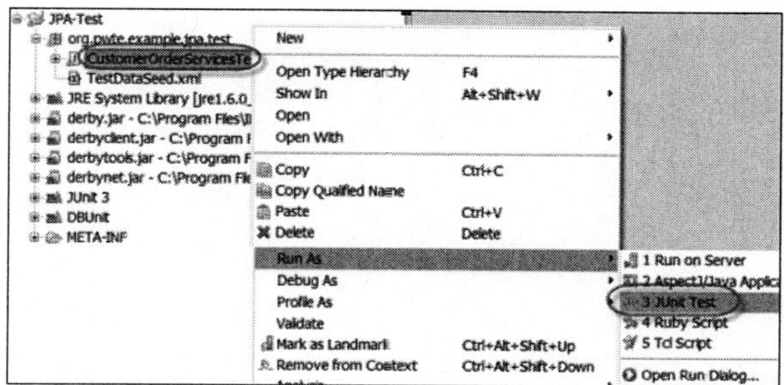

Figure A.26 Run SQL Script.

The JUnit View should open and display six successful JUnit results, as shown in Figure A.27.

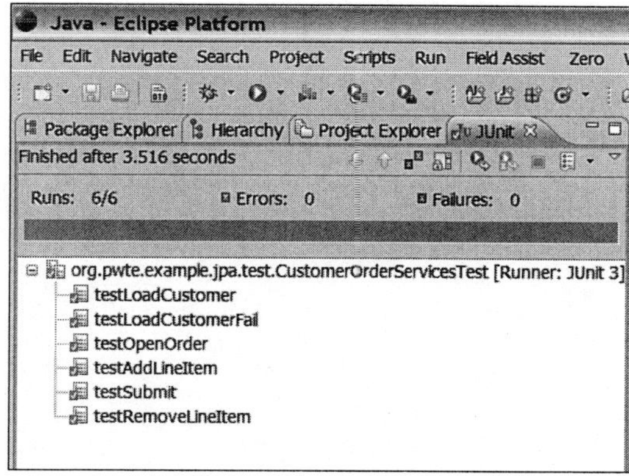

Figure A.27 JUnit result.

Running Project Zero Application

This section walks you through setting up the code and running the application for the Project Zero application shown in Chapter 9, "pureQuery and Project Zero," utilizing the pureQuery technology.

Install the M1 release to work with the sample, right-click the `PWTEZero-Test` application, and select Run As, then Project Zero Application, as shown in Figure A.28.

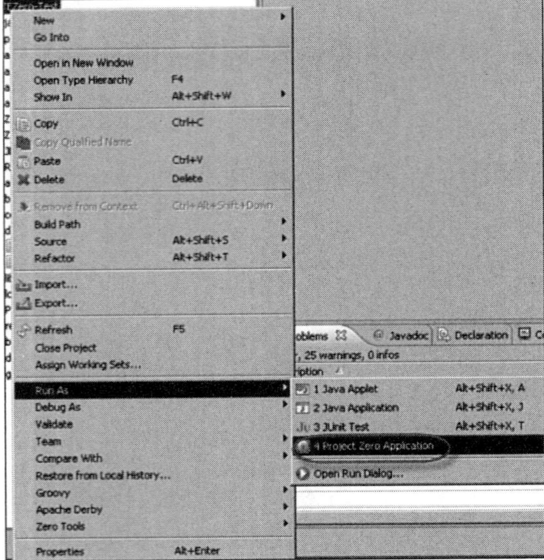

Figure A.28 Run the Project Zero application.

Enter the following address into a browser:

localhost:8080/resources/ZeroTestRunner?format=html

The result should be a page that successfully runs the unit tests, as shown in Figure A.29.

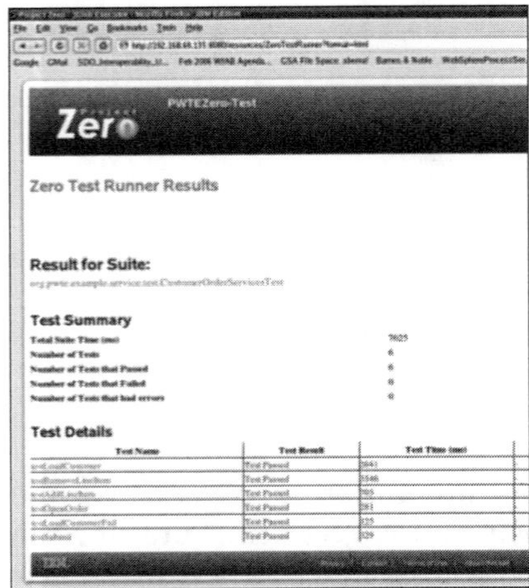

Figure A.29 Run Project Zero tests.

Stop the database.

Running EJB3 Application with IBM EJB 3 Feature Pack

This section walks you through setting up the code and running the application for the OpenJPA application, shown in Chapter 8, inside a Java EE. Unlike in the preceding section, we will use Rational Application Developer version 7.5, which is in beta. You can download the Open Beta for Rational Application Developer here:

www14.software.ibm.com/iwm/web/cc/earlyprograms/rational/RAD75OpenBeta/?S_TACT=105AGX23&S_CMP=RHP.

Rational Application Developer comes with WebSphere Application Server 6.1 with the EJB 3 Feature Pack preconfigured. (The installation instructions are available on the site.) After you have it installed, follow the directions that follow.

You can right-click from the Project or Package Explorer and select Import.

Select Project Interchange under the `Other` folder, as shown in Figure A.30.

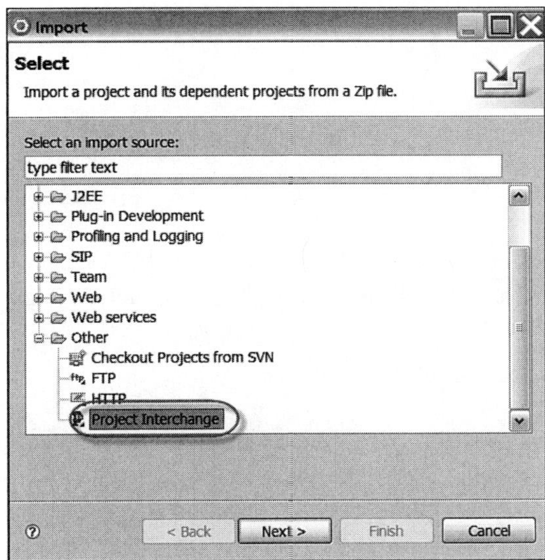

Figure A.30 Project Interchange.

Enter `<place where you unzipped download>/PWTE/EJB3-App/JPA-EJB3_PI.zip` and select the four projects, as shown in Figure A.31.

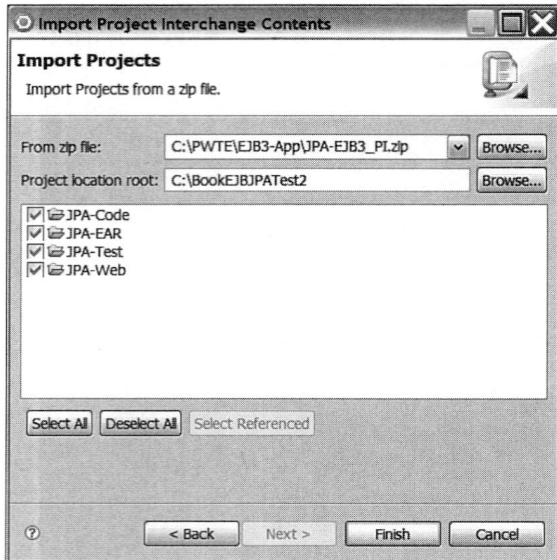

Figure A.31 Project Interchange.

Next, right-click on the `JPA-Code` project and select Apache Derby, Add Apache Derby Nature, as shown in Figure A.32.

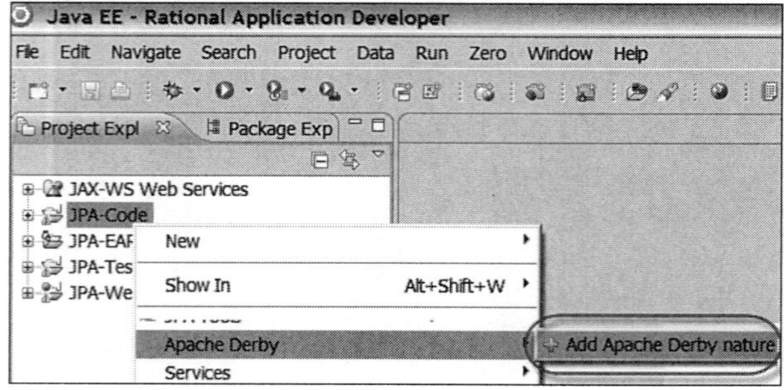

Figure A.32 Apache Nature.

Right-click the Project again and select Apache Derby, then Start Derby Network Server, as shown in Figure A.33.

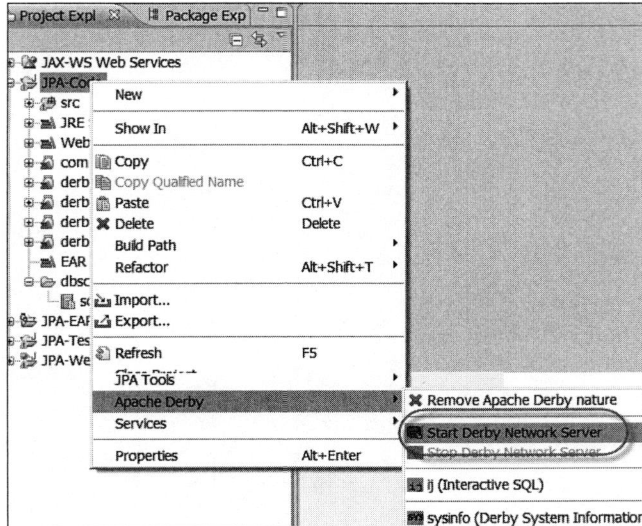

Figure A.33 Start Derby Server.

Under the JPA-Code Project, expand the `dbscript` folder and right-click on `schema-1.4.sql`. Select Apache Derby, then Run SQL Script Using "ij". (As noted previously, ij is the command-line tool for Derby that runs the SQL scripts. This will create the necessary tables for creating the example.) Figure A.34 shows the example.

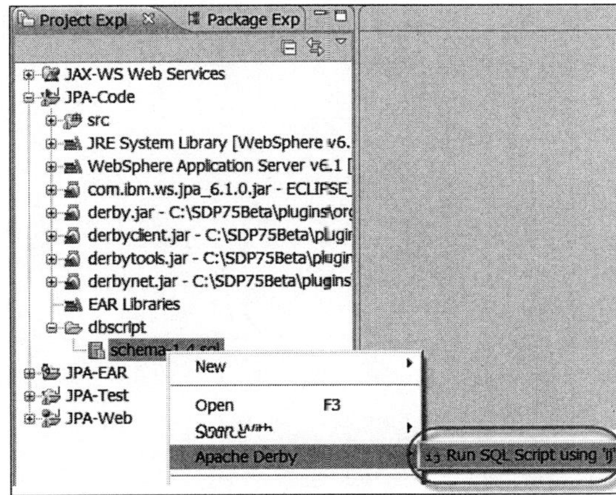

Figure A.34 Run dbscript.

The unit tests run inside of a Java EE Container. To run the tests, copy the dependencies shown in Figure A.35 into the directories shown (JUnit 3.8, JUnit EE, Derby client and tools, and DbUnit).

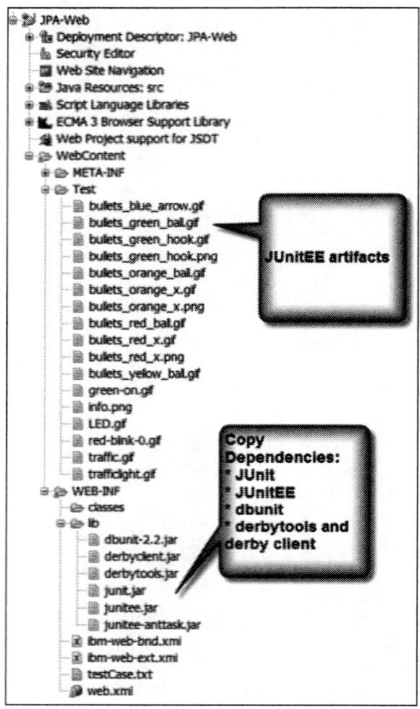

Figure A.35 Dependencies.

Next, you will run the application in the Server. You can do this by expanding the JPA-Web project from the Project Explorer as shown in Figure A.36. Right-click on the JUnitEEServlet and select Run As, then Run on Server.

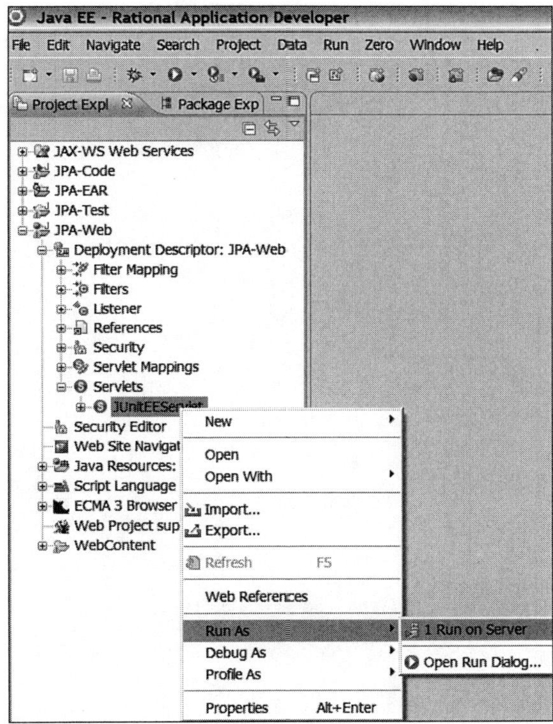

Figure A.36 Run on Server.

From within the Run on Server Wizard, shown in Figure A.37, check the Always Use This Server When Running This Project option (this will keep you from repeating this test on subsequent runs).

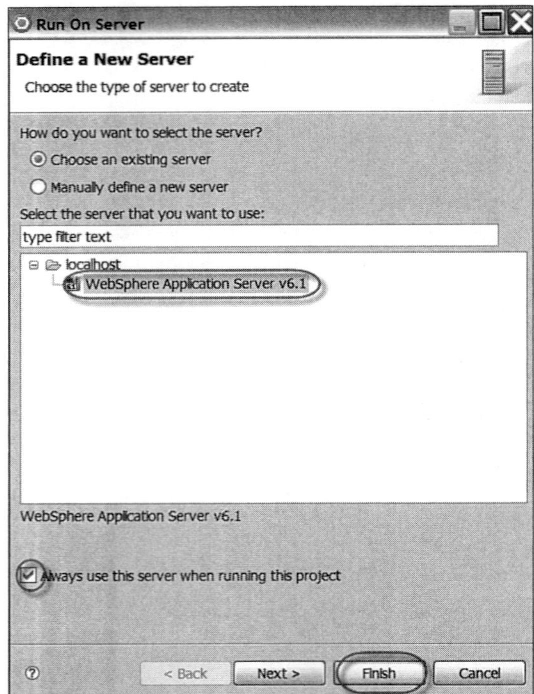

Figure A.37 Run on Server Wizard.

The Servers View should show a State of Starting, as shown in Figure A.38.

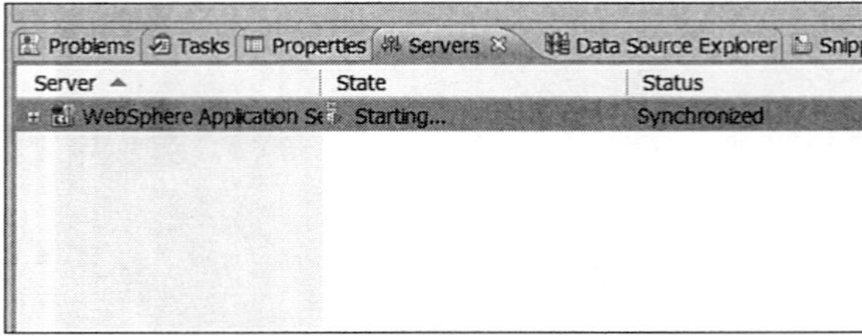

Figure A.38 Server starting.

Examine the console to ensure that the Server starts and the application is started, as shown in Figure A.39.

```
57I: The server is binding the Cust
57I: EJB jar started: JPA-Code.jar
59I: Loading Web Module: JPA-Web.
50I: Web Module JPA-Web has been bo
21I: Application started: JPA-EAR
10I: Document cells/IBMROLY50Node0:
10I: Document cells/IBMROLY50Node0:
```

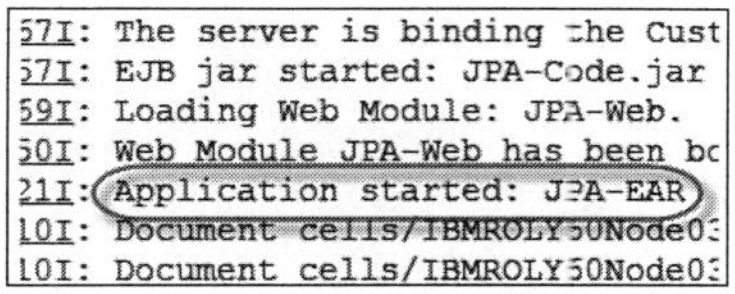

Figure A.39 Application started.

RAD 7.5 should load a browser with the JUnit EE Servlet to run the test case from within the container. Enter the test class (`org.pwte.example.jpa.test.CustomerOrderServicesTest`) in the Test Suite section, as shown in Figure A.40.

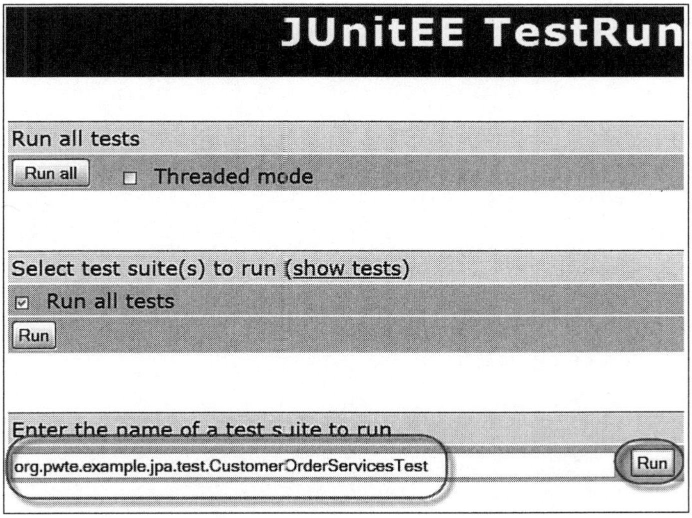

Figure A.40 Run the test case.

The test cases should run and the results displayed as shown in Figure A.41.

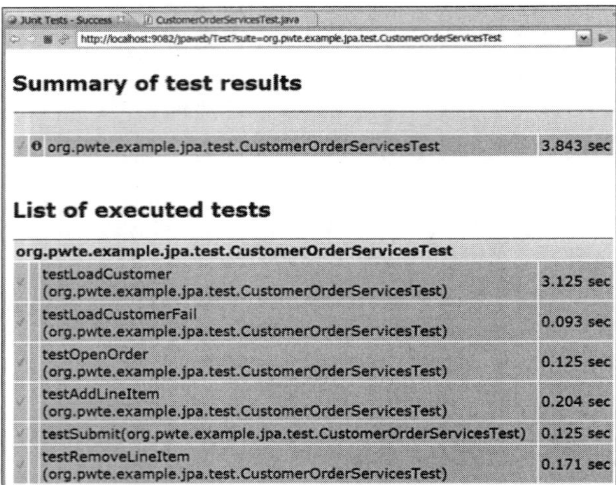

Figure A.41 Test case result.

Troubleshooting

If the unit test cases fail due to a violation, it is most likely because of a previous failure in running the test cases causing the data to be in an inconsistent state. If you rerun the database script to drop and re-create the tables, it should remove this issue and bring you back to a consistent state. Figure A.42 shows an example.

Figure A.42 Example of a common error you may get when running these steps.

References

[Beck] Beck, Kent. *Test Driven Development: By Example.* Addison Wesley 2002

[DbUnit] *DbUnitFramework.* www.dbunit.org/

[JUnit] *JUnit.org: Resources for Test Driven Development.* www.junit.org/

Index

Symbols

A

B

C

E

K

L

P

S

T

U

V

W-X-Y-Z

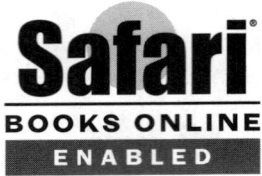